More Than Altruism

More Than Altruism

THE POLITICS OF PRIVATE FOREIGN AID

Brian H. Smith

PRINCETON UNIVERSITY PRESS

PRINCETON, NEW JERSEY

A12 1846- 7/2

Copyright © 1990 by Princeton Univesity Press
Published by Princeton University Press, 41 William Street,
Princeton, New Jersey 08540
In the United Kingdom: Princeton University Press, Oxford

Library of Congress Cataloging-in-Publication Data

Smith, Brian H., 1940–
More than altruism : the politics of private foreign aid / Brian H. Smith.
Includes bibliographical references.
1. Economic assistance, American—Developing countries—Moral and
ethical aspects. 2. Economic assistance, Canadian—Developing
countries—Moral and ethical aspects. 3. Economic assistance,
European—Developing countries—Moral and ethical aspects.
4. United States—Foreign relations. 5. Canada—Foreign relations.
6. Europe—Foreign relations. 7. Non-governmental organizations—
Developing countries. I. Title.
HC60.S548   1990   338.9′17301724   89-38399

ISBN 0-691-07845-9 (alk. paper)

This book has been composed in Linotron Times Roman

Princeton University Press books are printed
on acid-free paper, and meet the guidelines for
permanence and durability of the Committee on
Production Guidelines for Book Longevity of
the Council on Library Resources

Printed in the United States of America by Princeton University Press,
Princeton, New Jersey
10 9 8 7 6 5 4 3 2 1

TO MARY KAYE, SEAN, AND KATIE

Who gave so much that this book be written

Contents

Tables

Preface

To some, this will be a disappointing book. Those who want a description of all the good humanitarian work by international charities will not find this the central focus, though the book contains information of this nature (especially the long analysis on nonprofits in contemporary Colombia in chapter 8).

To others, the very association of the words *politics* and *charities* will seem to give this book the objective of muckraking—or even worse, the exposé of some very delicate political work on behalf of vulnerable groups abroad. These persons feel that such activities would be better left in relative secrecy for fear that some governments will use the information to discredit or thwart this important work.

I have written the book neither to repeat the acclaim international charities have already received nor to discredit their invaluable contributions. The book is meant to describe and analyze an important positive dimension of international charities, already well-known to governments and political activists in many parts of the world (including repressive states) but relatively unknown to the average citizens—including many contributors to international nonprofit organizations. This is the political dimension—namely, how some charities and some who subsidize them (including governments) attempt to influence through their activities at home and abroad the distribution of resources and power and the decisions of policymakers regarding them. This influence is not self-serving nor does it result in any lucrative gain for the charities themselves. Nor does it involve gross misuse on their part of donor money given to alleviate global suffering and poverty. It is, however, a controversial aspect of the work of many international charities (especially those based in Europe and Canada), since a definition of what is a just and fair distribution of resources and power is not shared by all who support such charities and since not all donors know this is a goal of many of the nonprofits to which they contribute.

Moreover, the book focuses on those charities with a leftist political agenda—namely, those that espouse a significant shift in resources and power from rich to poor nations and from rich to poor within developing countries. I have not singled out these organizations while overlooking others. These are the organizations that have been in the forefront of international charitable work over the past generation and that also allow themselves to be studied.

Rightist political groups, active in recent years in channeling money to Central America as manifested in the Iran-Contra affair in the United States, have recently begun to create nonprofit organizations to pursue their overseas agendas. They clearly need more attention by scholars and the public alike. These newer conservative organizations, however, are far more surreptitious about their operations (since many of them are illegal), and many are not deserving of the term *charities* since their objectives normally are to harm the poor or in the very least perserve the power of those who oppress them.

This book, for better and for worse, therefore, is about the latent agendas currently being pursued by various partners in the reputable international charities network. To those disappointed or angry with this book, my only response is that better information about the actions of basically good people attempting to alleviate human suffering in the long run cannot help but to make their admirable work more effective.

Finally, to those who want a brief overview of the major findings of this book, I would *not* suggest reading the last chapter ("Conclusions") first. I would recommend, instead, looking at chapter 1, especially the section entitled "Methodology and Argument." Then, read the "Conclusions" section at the end of *each* chapter, and finally, the last chapter (chapter 9), which casts the findings in a larger theoretical framework about the role of nonprofits as system-maintenance organizations.

Acknowledgments

I wish to thank the Program on Nonprofit Organizations (PONPO) of the Institution for Social and Policy Studies at Yale University for its financial support and constructive criticism for the research and writing related to this project. Without such assistance, and the continual confidence in me, offered by those affiliated with PONPO—especially John Simon and Paul Dimaggio—I would not have been able to complete this manuscript.

Although not formally part of PONPO, Juan Linz of Yale—through PONPO and on his own—several times during the writing process provided me with extremely helpful suggestions on how to place the study of nonprofit organizations in a wider theoretical and political framework. To him now, as in the past while preparing my first book (*The Church and Politics in Chile*), I am deeply grateful.

While in Colombia in mid-1984, Senator Eduardo del Hierro Santacruz was most generous and helpful in introducing me to several officials in the Colombian government. They, plus the senator himself, provided me with invaluable perspectives from the public sector on the role of the nonprofit organizations in the socioeconomic development of that country.

The persons I interviewed in the nonprofit organizations and in governmental agencies in Europe, Canada, Colombia, and the United States all were the most cooperative. I could not have gathered the necessary data for this book without their assistance. Hans Hoyer, of Lutheran World Relief, was particularly helpful in giving me extended comments on the first draft of this manuscript, and the Colombian Jesuits at CINEP, where I had an institutional affiliation during 1984, were most cordial and helpful.

I am also most grateful for grants received to carry out portions of this research from the Inter-American Foundation (fall 1982–spring 1983), the National Endowment for the Humanities (fall 1983), the Social Science Research Council (fall 1983), the Fulbright Scholars Research Program (summer 1984), and the Institute for the Study of World Politics (spring 1985). All of these grants enabled me to carry out field research in Europe, Canada, the United States, and Colombia, and to prepare the first draft of the manuscript.

The stimulating comments received on this first draft by several of my former colleagues in the political science department at the Massachusetts Institute of Technology (M.I.T.) in the fall of 1985, along with those in PONPO at Yale, enabled me to sharpen the focus of the first draft and highlight what is now the central theme in the final version—namely, the political story underlying private foreign aid. To them—especially Peter Smith, Lucian Pye,

Willard Johnson, Hayward Alker, Lincoln Bloomfield, Michael Lipsky, and Donald Blackmer—I am most appreciative.

The manuscript never would have been readable had it not been for the high degree of competence (and patience) of Eva Nagy at M.I.T., who deciphered my inscrutable handwriting and translated it into readable form on a word processor between 1985 and 1987. She is also the most professional secretary I have ever had the privilege of working with, and to her I shall always be grateful.

At other stages of the writing, both Alex Merton and Bonnie Wolf were a great help in the preparation of the text. To them also I owe great appreciation.

Finally, the personal price paid by my wife Mary Kaye and my two children, Sean and Katie, to provide me with the time, space, and love necessary to carry out this project was very high. They have my eternal love, and I hope in the years ahead to give back in some part what they have given me during this research and writing.

Abbreviations

ACP	African, Caribbean, and Pacific Countries (forty-five European colonial territories aided by the EEC)
ACVAFS	American Council of Voluntary Agencies for Foreign Service (1943–1984)
ADRA	Adventist Development and Relief Agency (Washington, D.C.)
ADS	Alternative Development Strategy
AFSC	American Friends Service Committee (Philadelphia)
AID (USAID)	U.S. Agency for International Development (Washington, D.C.)
AIFLD	American Institute for Free Labor Development (Washington, D.C.)
AITEC	International Action for Appropriate Technology (Boston)
American ORT	American Organization of Rehabilitation through Training (New York)
ANUC	National Association of Peasant Beneficiaries of Government Services (Bogotá)
ARA	American Relief Administration (1919–ca. 1924)
ARK	American Relief for Korea (1950–1953)
BHN	Basic Human Needs
BMZ	German Ministry for Economic Cooperation (Bonn)
CA	Christian Aid (London)
CAFOD	Catholic Fund for Overseas Development (London)
CANSAVE	Canadian Save the Children (Ottawa)
CARE Canada	Canadian Cooperative Assistance for Relief Everywhere (Ottawa)
CARE France	French Cooperative Assistance for Relief Everywhere (Paris)
CARE USA	U.S. Cooperative Assistance for Relief Everywhere (New York)

CARITAS	Catholic Charities (Catholic social service organizations at national and diocesan levels in Europe and Latin America)
CCF	Christian Children's Fund (Richmond, Va.)
CCFD	Catholic Committee against Hunger and for Development (Paris)
CCIC	Canadian Council for International Cooperation (Ottawa)
CCODP	Canadian Catholic Organization for Development and Peace (Montreal)
CCTV	Colombian Coordination Agency for Voluntary Work (Bogotá)
CDU	Christian Democratic Union (Federal Republic of Germany)
CEBs	Base ecclesial communities (in Latin American Catholic Church)
CEBEMO	Central Agency for Joint Financing and Development (Oegstgeest, the Netherlands)
CEBRAP	Brazilian Center for Analysis and Planning (São Paolo)
CEC	Commission of the European Community (Brussels)
CEDES	Center for Studies on the State and Society (Buenos Aires)
CENPRODES	Center for the Promotion of Development (Secretariat of the Catholic Episcopal Conference of Colombia, Bogotá)
CFOs	Cofinancing Organizations
CIA	U.S. Central Intelligence Agency (Langley, Va.)
CICARWS	Commission on Interchurch Aid, Refugees, and World Service of the World Council of Churches (Geneva)
CIDA	Canadian International Development Agency (Ottawa)
CIDSE	International Cooperation for Socioeconomic Development (Brussels)
CIMADE	Ecumenical Aid Service (Paris)
CINEP	National Center for Research and Popular Education (Bogotá)
CLUSA	Cooperative League USA (Washington, D.C.—renamed National Cooperative Business Association [NCBA] in 1986)
CODEL	Coordination in Development (New York)

CODESARROLLO	Corporation for Development (Medellín)
COMINTERN	Communist International (1919–1943)
COOPCENTRAL	Central Cooperative for Social Promotion (Santander, Colombia)
CRB	Committee for the Relief in Belgium (1914–1918)
CRS	Catholic Relief Services (New York)
CSU	Christian Social Union (Federal Republic of Germany)
CUNA	Credit Union National Association (Madison, Wis.)
CUSO	Canadian Universities Service Overseas (Ottawa)
CWDE	Center for World Development Education (London)
CWS	Church World Service (New York)
DAC	Development Assistance Committee, OECD (Paris)
DANCHURCHAID	Danish Church Aid (Copenhagen)
DCV	German CARITAS Association (Freiburg im Breisgau, Federal Republic of Germany)
DECs	Development Education Centers (Great Britain)
DESCO	Center for the Study and Promotion of Development (Lima)
DEVELOPMENT GAP	Development Group for Alternative Policies (Washington, D.C.)
DPG	Development Program Grant
DRI	Integrated Rural Development Program (Colombia)
ECAD	European Consortium for Agricultural Development (Milan)
ECOSOC	United Nations Economic and Social Council
EDF	European Development Loan Fund (Brussels)
EEC	European Economic Community
EZE	Protestant Association for Cooperation in Development (Bonn)
FAO	United Nations Food and Agricultural Organization (Rome)
FDP	Free Democratic Party (Federal Republic of Germany)
FEDESARROLLO	Foundation for Higher Education and Development (Bogotá)
FES	Friedrich Ebert Foundation (Bonn)
FESCOL	Friedrich Ebert Foundation of Colombia (Bogotá)

FFHC	Freedom from Hunger Campaign of the UN Food and Agricultural Organization
FINACIACOOP	Financial Cooperative of the Government of Colombia (Bogotá)
FINSOCIAL	Financing Agency for Social Development (Medellín)
FMME	Fund for Multinational Management Education (New York)
FPP Canada	Foster Parents Plan, Canada (Toronto)
FPP Netherlands	Foster Parents Plan, the Netherlands (Amsterdam)
FPP USA	Foster Parents Plan, United States of America (Warwick, R. I.)
FRG	Federal Republic of Germany (West Germany)
FUNDAEC	Foundation for the Application and Teaching of Science (Cali, Colombia)
GDR	German Democratic Republic (East Germany)
Grupo PROJECTOS	Projects Group (Bogotá)
GVN	Government of South Vietnam (Saigon)
HAVA	Haitian Association of Voluntary Agencies (Port au Prince)
HIVOS	Humanistic Institute for Cooperation with Developing Countries (The Hague)
IAF	Inter-American Foundation (Rosslyn, Va.)
IBRD	International Bank for Reconstruction and Development (Washington, D.C.)
ICA	U.S. International Cooperation Agency (1954–1961)
ICCO	Interchurch Coordination Committee for Development Projects (Zeist, the Netherlands)
ICVA	International Council of Voluntary Agencies (Geneva)
IDB	Inter-American Development Bank (Washington, D.C.)
ILO	International Labour Organization (Geneva)
IMCA	Major Institute for Peasants (Buga, Colombia)
INTER PARES	Among Equals (Ottawa)
INTERACTION	American Council for Voluntary International Action (New York and Washington, D.C.)
ISDI	Inter-American Social Development Institute (renamed Inter-America Foundation [IAF] in 1972)
ISS	Institute of Social Studies (the Hague)
IVS	International Voluntary Services (Washington, D.C.)

JDC	American Jewish Joint Distribution Committee (New York)
JUSOS	Young Socialists (Federal Republic of Germany)
KAS	Konrad Adenauer Foundation (Sankt Augustin, FRG)
LORCS	League of Red Cross Societies (Geneva)
LWF	Lutheran World Federation (Geneva)
LWR	Lutheran World Relief (New York)
MISEREOR	Campaign against Hunger and Disease in the World (Aachen, Federal Republic of Germany)
MNCs	Multinational Corporations
MSF	Doctors Without Frontiers (Paris)
NAPA	National Association of Partners of the Alliance (Washington, D.C.)
NCC	National Council of Churches (New York)
NCO	National Committee for Information on Development (the Hague)
NGOs	Nongovernmental Organizations
NIEO	New International Economic Order
NOVIB	Netherlands Organization for International Development (the Hague)
NTF	New Transcentury Foundation (Washington, D.C.)
OAS	Organization of American States (Washington, D.C.)
OCIT	Office of Interinstitutional Cooperation (1978–1982)
ODA	British Overseas Development Administration (London)
ODC	Overseas Development Council (Washington, D.C.)
ODI	Overseas Development Institute (London)
OECD	Organization for Economic Cooperation and Development (Paris)
OFRRO	U.S. Office of Foreign Relief and Rehabilitation Operations (1942–1943)
OMB	Office of Management and the Budget (Washington, D.C.)
ONGs	*Organizaciones Nogubernamentales* (Nongovernmental Organizations)
OPG	Operational Program Grant
Oxfam	Oxford Committee Against Hunger

Oxfam America	Oxford Committee Against Hunger of America (Boston)
Oxfam Belgique	Oxford Committee Against Hunger of Belgium (Brussels)
Oxfam Canada	Oxford Committee Against Hunger of Canada (Ottawa)
Oxfam UK	Oxford Committee Against Hunger of the United Kingdom (Oxford)
PACT	Private Agencies Collaborating Together (New York)
PADF	Pan American Development Foundation (Washington, D.C.)
PAID	Private Agencies in International Development (1980–1984)
PAN	National Nutritional Program (Colombia)
PEM	Minimum Employment Program (Chile)
PIN	National Integration Plan (Colombia)
PL 480	U.S. Public Law 480—Agricultural Trade, Development, and Assistance Act (1954)
PONPO	Program on Nonprofit Organizations, Institution for Social and Policy Studies, Yale University
PRI	Institutionalized Revolutionary Party (Mexico)
PS	Socialist Party (France)
Pvd A	Labour Party (the Netherlands)
PVOs	Private Voluntary Organizations
RIO	Reshaping the International Order (A study report of the Club of Rome in 1976)
SCF	Save the Children Federation (Westport, Conn.)
SCI	International Civil Service (ca. 1925–ca. 1955)
SEPAS	Evangelical Service for Social Action (Diocesan social service agencies of Catholic Church in Colombia)
SIDA	Swedish International Development Authority (Stockholm)
SILONG	Information and Liason Service with NGOs (Paris)
SPD	Social Democratic Party (Federal Republic of Germany)
SUCO	Service Universitaire Canadien Outre-mer (Montreal)
TAICH	Technical Assistance Information Clearing House, American Council of Voluntary Agencies for Foreign Service

TCA	U.S. Technical Cooperation Administration (1950–1954)
UNDRO	United Nations Disaster Relief Office (Geneva)
UNHCR	United Nations High Commission of Refugees (Geneva)
UNICEF	United Nations International Children's Emergency Fund (New York)
UNRRA	United Nations Relief and Rehabilitation Administration (1943–1947)
UNRWA	United Nations Relief and Works Agency (Geneva)
USAID (AID)	U.S. Agency for International Development (Washington, D.C.)
USITRAS	Federated Syndicate of Workers in Santander (Santander, Colombia)
UUSC	Unitarian Universalist Service Committee (Boston)
VSO	Voluntary Service Overseas (London)
WCC	World Council of Churches (Geneva)
YMCA	Young Men's Christian Association (Chicago)
YWCA	Young Women's Christian Association (New York)

More Than Altruism

CHAPTER ONE

Introduction

SINCE the 1960s there has been a steady increase in private foreign aid. In 1964 North Atlantic private voluntary organizations (PVOs) or nongovernmental organizations (NGOs) sent overseas approximately $2.8 billion (in 1986 dollars), and by 1980 their annual resource transfers to Asia, the Middle East, Africa, and Latin American totaled $4.7 billion—a 68 percent increase in real value in just sixteen years. By the 1980s there were over forty-six hundred PVOs/NGOs (including church-related missionary and service agencies, secular nonprofit organizations, credit and cooperative associations, foundations, and educational and labor groups) that received donations and grants in North Atlantic countries and transmitted them to counterpart private nonprofit institutions in the Third World. Up to twenty thousand organizations in developing countries now receive this assistance and pass it on in one form or another to the poor.[1]

One reason for this increase of private involvement in foreign aid has been the growing reputation of nonprofit institutions in the United States, Canada, and Europe for being efficient and cost-effective channels of help in disasters. During famines, floods, earthquakes, and refugee crises, PVOs/NGOs are now seen as having the capacity to react more quickly and impartially than government institutions in bringing aid to the victims of such occurrences overseas.[2]

After publicity about the severe famine in Ethiopia began in October 1984, for example, the three hundred U.S. PVOs engaged in assistance to Africa increased their aid to that continent by almost two-thirds by the end of 1986 (from $485.6 million to nearly $800 million). This was largely the result of an outpouring of generosity from U.S. citizens exposed to concentrated media

---

[1] Organization for Economic Cooperation and Development (OECD), *Directory of Non-governmental Organizations*, 2d ed., rev.; Van der Heijden, "Development Impact and Effectiveness of Nongovernmental Organisations," p. 2; Van der Heijden, "Reconciliation of NGO Autonomy," pp. 104–5. In the United States nonprofits engaged in foreign aid are normally called private voluntary organizations, or PVOs. In Europe and Canada, however, the more common name of such institutions is nongovernmental organizations, or NGOs. Throughout this book, I shall use the term "PVOs" when referring to the U.S. groups; the term "NGOs" when describing the European and Canadian agencies; and "PVOs/NGOs" when referring to both together. The term "North Atlantic" will refer to institutions based in Europe, Canada, and/or the United States. Throughout this book, all dollar figures will be given in constant 1986 values.

[2] Cuny, *Disasters and Development*.

attention on the famine in 1984 and 1985. The PVOs in the United States that are active in overseas work (numbering over five hundred) have an estimated 10 to 20 million constituents in the general public (volunteers, donor members). They maintain regular communications with several million more through the church affiliations that many have. These support groups are readily mobilized during disasters abroad, especially now that such events receive quick and widespread attention in the mass media.[3]

The most important factor, however, in explaining the growing resources available to nonprofit organizations for overseas work has been the dramatic increase in governmental subsidies to PVOs/NGOs. In 1973 governmental members of the Organization for Economic Cooperation and Development (OECD)—which includes the United States, Canada, nineteen Western European nations, Australia, New Zealand, and Japan—gave to PVOs/NGOs based in their respective societies a total of $778.2 million in subsidies over and above the $3.4 billion these nonprofits received from private sources. By 1980 public grants had grown over 90 percent in real value to $1.5 billion. Hence, by 1980, in addition to the $3.2 billion in private resources sent overseas by all North Atlantic nonprofits, $1.5 billion in more aid was channeled through these agencies from home-government sources. This government assistance in 1980 accounted for almost one-third of the organizations' total assets (31.9 percent).[4]

In 1976, the European Economic Community (EEC) began multilateral cofinancing of European-based NGOs at the rate of $4.8 million annually, but by 1982 this increased to $22.7 million a year. These subsidies had supported a total of 856 overseas projects through the end of 1981. Between 1975 and 1982 the World Bank (IBRD) involved 650 PVOs/NGOs in one hundred different Bank-financed projects in developing countries, and at the end of 1983 set up a joint committee with PVOs/NGOs to give them greater access to the various policy-making divisions of the Bank. This has led to an ongoing dialogue between the Bank and PVOs/NGOs on mutual development policies, on possibilities of joint education among the general public in North Atlantic countries, and on mechanisms for possible direct Bank funding of PVO/NGO projects.[5]

Multinational corporations (MNCs) have also begun testing ways in which

[3] American Council for Voluntary International Action (INTERACTION), *Diversity in Development*, pp. 2, 8, 43.

[4] Lissner, *Politics of Altruism*, p. 41; Van der Heijden, "Reconilication of NGO Autonomy," pp. 104–5; OECD, "Government Subsidies to Voluntary Agencies."

[5] Brusasco, "Cooperation between NGO's and the EEC"; "Cooperation between the World Bank and Nongovernmental Organizations," both in OECD, *Role of Nongovernmental Organisations*, pp. 56–57, 62–65; "World Bank/NGO Committee"; "World Bank/NGO Cooperation"; International Bank for Reconstruction and Development (IBRD), *Cooperation between the World Bank and Nongovernmental Organizations (NGOs)*.

they can cooperate with PVOs/NGOs and their local counterparts in developing countries. Through a process called intermediation, some PVOs/NGOs in recent years have been helping MNCs relate better to local and smaller investment opportunities overseas—especially in agriculture.[6]

There is increasing governmental interest in the international nonprofit sector because there are unique comparative advantages PVOs/NGOs claim to have in reaching precisely those lower-income groups in developing countries that government or corporation aid often does not touch. In 1973 the U.S. Congress mandated a "new directions" approach for U.S. bilateral aid that would focus more directly on the needs of the poorest majority in the Third World. It also urged that U.S. bilateral assistance "be carried out to the maximum extent possible through the private sector, particularly those institutions which already have ties in the developing areas, such as educational institutions, cooperatives, credit unions, and voluntary agencies." The reasons given were that PVOs through their network of private counterparts in developing societies are able to get to the grassroots level better than foreign governmental agencies (who work from the top down through host-government institutions) and were not so tied to official foreign policy objectives of the U.S. government. The feeling of the Congress was that PVOs could reach the rural poor through means not available to the U.S. Agency for International Development (AID) and thus could help fulfill the spirit of the "new directions" mandate.[7]

In the late 1970s the Office of Management and the Budget (OMB) issued a report on U.S. PVOs in foreign aid. It gave as additional reasons for U.S. government subsidies to PVOs that they were very active in fostering small-scale, self-help and self-sustaining initiatives among the Third World poor; were more innovative than government-managed projects; had much lower overhead costs than government aid programs; and represented a "lower level of U.S. Government visibility than direct bilateral assistance." The Congress has continued to be confident about PVOs, and in the early 1980s required that from 12 to 16 percent of AID's annual budget be channeled through PVOs working overseas.[8]

Canadian and European bilateral and multilateral government agencies have voiced similar and additional reasons for expanding their own subsidies to NGOs. The Canadian International Development Agency (CIDA), which began matching grants to Canadian NGOs in 1968, attempts "to tap, for development purposes, the wide range of expertise, experience and services" of the Canadian nonprofit sector; "to offer more flexible and innovative means of

---

[6] Truitt, ed., *Multinationals.*

[7] AID, *A Look to the Future,* pp. 100–103.

[8] Schwartz, "Private and Voluntary Organizations in Foreign Aid," p. 16; AID, *AID Partnership in International Development,* p. 8. In 1983 the U.S. Senate required that this minimum be at least 15 percent for FY 1984.

development assistance'' than is normally possible in official aid programs; to encourage more ''Canadians to participate in international development''; and to forge ''relationships as equals and partners with people and institutions in developing countries.''

The Ministry of Economic Cooperation (BMZ) of the Federal Republic of Germany (FRG), which began cooperating with FRG NGOs in 1962, reasons that NGO programs ''are planned and implemented'' by partner groups in the Third World, ''often benefit the neediest people in the developing countries, and help them cater to their basic needs,'' and ''reach groups which would be barely accessible to the official cooperation agencies.'' The EEC justifies its increased subsidies to NGOs on the grounds that their host of small projects has a ''considerable multiplier effect'' in development dynamics from the bottom up. It also believes that NGOs manifest great ''efficiency, speed and flexibility'' in both planning and execution of projects, and that they are able to ''adopt their approach, virtually day-by-day, to changing economic, political and technical circumstances.'' Thus, they can act ''as the exact opposite of bureaucratic, in the pejorative sense of the word.''[9]

The MNCs find that environments overseas change rapidly in some countries, and they are looking to other North Atlantic private groups with partners in such societies to explain what is happening. They also find that PVOs/ NGOs in some cases have developed low-cost and efficient methods of educating and training personnel, which corporations might adopt. The MNCs find that nonprofits sometimes give good advice through their own experience at the local level on how to invest in areas hitherto inaccessible to corporations, especially in the small business sector.[10]

Hence, the importance of PVO/NGO overseas assistance is not reflected in the relatively small amount of resource transfers to developing countries they make in comparison with governmental and profit-making institutions—$4.7 billion in 1980, as compared to $37.8 billion by public agencies, and $13.3 billion by corporations. In fact these other two sectors are looking to nonprofits to improve their own access to and impact on that informal sector of the economy in developing countries most directly involving low-income groups. The PVOs/NGOs are believed to possess those necessary qualities for addressing the needs of low-income sectors that governmental and business organizations normally do not possess—smallness, good contacts at the local level, freedom from political manipulation, a labor- rather than a capital-intensive orientation, innovativeness, and flexibility in administration.

---

[9] ''The Canadian International Development Agency NGO Program''; ''Economic Cooperation between NGOs and the German Federal Ministry for Economic Cooperation''; Brusasco, ''Cooperation between NGOs and the EEC,'' all in OECD, *Role of Nongovernmental Organisations*, pp. 50, 54–55.

[10] Avrin Mclean, *U.S. Philanthropy*, pp. 66–67.

PARADOXES IN PRIVATE FOREIGN AID

The agendas of many North Atlantic nonprofits do not always coincide exactly with those of their private and governmental donors. In some cases, in fact, they appear to be at odds with donor intentions. Many now are defining themselves more as developmental (focused on long-term structural change) rather than relief (committed to immediate alleviation of suffering) institutions. Although their funds from private donors in the United States, Canada, and Europe expand the most during times of overseas disasters (and therefore are given primarily for relief purposes), the official positions of these institutions are now articulated more in terms of attacking the deeper underlying causes of poverty abroad (a developmental objective). A 1985 survey of seventy-seven U.S. PVOs engaged in assistance to Africa (whose income has risen dramatically since the Ethiopian crisis was first publicized) indicated that seventy-five aspire mainly to promote long-term structural change rather than to immediately alleviate suffering.[11] Although the primary motive of many private sponsors still is relief-oriented and most responsive to addressing short-term crises (hunger, sickness, homelessness), the goals of PVO staffs are somewhat different and geared to developmental objectives such as income generation, training, education, public health, and community development.

Moreover, despite the image that nonprofits enjoy for having certain comparative advantages over public institutions as conduits of foreign aid, little systematic evaluation has been done to measure the validity of these claims. These include innovativeness, the capacity to reach the poorest sectors through partnerships with Third World private groups, and the generation of a multiplier effect on development dynamics through sponsorship of replicable grass-roots programs. Information feedback and accountability mechanisms to donors regarding project effectiveness, poverty reduction, and impact on wider socioeconomic processes in Third World societies are largely underdeveloped among PVOs/NGOs.

Judith Tendler's secondary analysis in 1981 of seventy-five evaluations of PVO projects done in the late 1970s led her to conclude that claims by U.S. nonprofits could not be proven with the methods used by PVO evaluators. Frequently these evaluations stressed quantifiable data while overlooking the qualitative issues. They also tended to be insular in their focus since they relied predominantly on evidence supplied by PVO staffs or those directly involved in the leadership of the overseas projects. There was little interviewing of nonleader beneficiaries, community members not participating in or benefiting from projects, other community organizations, or those working for

---

[11] INTERACTION, *Diversity in Development*, p. 12. As will be seen in chapter 3, I found this same discrepancy between staff development-oriented values and private donor preferences for charitable activities in my own survey of nonprofits, especially for those based in the United States.

government agencies in the same area. Nor was the experience of learning from development efforts in public sector organizations in the same services taken into account for comparative purposes. Tendler concluded:

> Literature and knowledge is by and about PVO organizations, not about the world and the problems in which the project is taking place, or about the general class of problems being dealt with and the experience in dealing with them. Given the kinds of persons not interviewed, and the kinds of literature not cited, it is understandable that PVO evaluations do not give much of a feeling for the areas in which PVOs are innovative, the extent to which the decisionmaking processes they promote are participatory, and the extent to which their projects reach the poor.[12]

She found that the extant evaluations she examined, as uneven in quality as they were, suggested that sometimes PVO projects abroad do not work with the poorest of the poor but with those with some resources and skills who are able to benefit easily from credit or training. The studies also showed that rather than always being innovative, at times PVOs replicate known techniques in service delivery and that they can also be in competition with, or surrogates for, governmental services in Third World countries rather than pioneering catalysts for better public policies.[13] Hence, at times there can be a gap between performance and expectation regarding private foreign aid.

Moreover, many North Atlantic nonprofits are coming to define their development objectives in political rather than economic terms. A growing number believe that the causes of poverty in developing countries include imbalances of power and resources between affluent minorities and poor majorities, between urban and rural sectors, between men and women, or between ethnic groups controlling government and other ethnic groups within these countries. Some also blame what they consider unjust international structures as the cause for Third World poverty, such as unequal trade relations between North Atlantic and developing countries, selective investment policies of MNCs, and arms sales and aid from their own nations to Africa, the Middle East, Asia, and Latin America.[14]

As a result, many North Atlantic nonprofits (predominantly in Canada and Western Europe) claim to fund private groups overseas who are attempting to work for significant redistribution of power in favor of the poor—i.e., who help grassroots groups become more aware of the injustices they suffer at the hands of indigenous political and economic elites or who assist local communities to organize themselves to oppose exploitative economic or political

---

[12] Tendler, *Turning Private Voluntary Organizations into Development Agencies*, pp. 127, 131–32.

[13] Ibid., pp. 11–14, 25–28, 48–50, 84–93, 105–9.

[14] INTERACTION, *Diversity in Development*, p. 13; Lissner, *Politics of Altruism*, pp. 257–61; Brian H. Smith, "U.S. and Canadian PVOs as Transnational Development Institutions," p. 130.

structures. Many Canadian and European NGOs (and a few U.S. PVOs) also carry out aggressive education and lobbying activities in their respective countries. These challenge home-government foreign policies toward developing countries in trade and aid, overseas investment priorities and labor practices of MNCs, and consumption patterns and life styles of citizens in their own societies that the nonprofits consider to be harmful to Third World needs.[15]

Even some nonprofits that do not openly espouse political change as a major part of their overseas objectives (the vast majority of U.S. PVOs) do aim to widen social participation overseas through strengthening the autonomy and effectiveness of grass-roots community organizations managed by the poor themselves. Such strategies at least potentially can have a political impact due to the absence, or narrow scope, of democratic institutions in many Third World countries.[16]

Host governments in developing countries have allowed nonprofit organizations in their own societies (now numbering up to twenty thousand in Asia, the Middle East, Africa, and Latin America) to receive this private aid from abroad for activities that are not part of their own public programs. This has been true in both authoritarian and democratic societies alike. Yet in both types of regimes projects supported by the international nonprofit sector and administered by private groups within the targeted societies have, in fact, not only economic but at times political consequences.

In authoritarian contexts local or indigenous nonprofits with foreign support sometimes provide opportunities for those who are opponents of government to carry out a variety of socioeconomic programs on behalf of the urban and rural poor, or to conduct research programs with results that are often critical of regime policies. This has been the case in several Latin American countries over the past decade, such as Brazil, Chile, Bolivia, El Salvador, prerevolutionary Nicaragua, Peru, and Paraguay.[17] In Brazil and Peru, both of which adopted democratic rule in the early 1980s, many new leaders in local political and labor organizations that have emerged since the military left power came from this network of community organizations supported by the nonprofit sector during the previous era.[18]

In societies that have enjoyed continuous democratic rule throughout the 1960s and 1970s, such as Colombia, the nonprofit sector has also supported a whole series of developmental projects aimed at the very poor who do not ordinarily benefit from the import substitution, capital intensive model of development promoted by the governments. This sector is also creating autono-

[15] Brian H. Smith, "U.S. and Canadian PVOs," p. 130; Minear, "Reflections on Development Policy."
[16] INTERACTION, *Diversity in Development*, p. 14.
[17] Fernandes, "Las ONGs", Frühling, "Nonprofit Organizations as Opposition to Authoritarian Rule"; Berryman, *Religious Roots of Rebellion*.
[18] Moreira Alves, "Grassroots Organizations, Trade Unions, and the Church."

mous social organizations among the rural and urban poor opposed to the paternalistic form of party politics that has long characterized the regimes.[19]

In other formal democracies of the Third World, such as India, indigenous nonprofits (with considerable international support) also are pursuing alternate economic and political agendas among those not enjoying many benefits from the prevalent model of development. In India, in fact, some are called "nonparty political formations" (NPPFs), since they are publicly attempting to set a new, more equitable and participatory agenda for traditional political parties.[20]

It is clear, therefore, that a considerable part of the North Atlantic nonprofit sector that engages in overseas aid is clearly promoting more than charitable goals abroad that are often uppermost in the minds of its private donors. It is also supporting groups in the Third World and advocacy programs at home that are different from and sometimes opposed to strategies of development endorsed by government policymakers both in their home societies and abroad. Ironically, however, North Atlantic nonprofits are coming to depend more and more on public grants authorized by home-government parliaments precisely at the time when they seem to be at odds with many objectives of their home governments overseas. Moreover, many local Third World nonprofits supported by this private transnational aid network often seem to be opposed to the policies of their own governments, thereby potentially creating not only problems for themselves but diplomatic tensions in government-to-government relations as well. The ultimate recipients of such aid—the poor at the grass-roots level in developing countries—are also participating in programs that seem to go far beyond meeting their immediate basic needs. This could precipitate serious problems for recipients with local government authorities since the objective is reordering power balances in society from the bottom up.

QUESTIONS UNDERLYING THE PARADOXES

The paradoxical cooperation among the various participants in the private transnational aid network—North Atlantic governments, North Atlantic private donors, North Atlantic nonprofits, host governments in developing nations, Third World nonprofits, Third World poor—raises a serious of questions about the interests of each, and what the partners gain from mutual collaboration when their agendas often seem quite divergent.

1. North Atlantic Private Donors: Why would private philanthropy continue to be given to organizations that increasingly are being subsidized by the state with tax

---

[19] Brian H. Smith, "Nonprofit Organizations and Socioeconomic Development in Colombia."
[20] Sheth, "Grassroots Initiatives in India"; Sethi, "Groups in a New Politics of Transformation"; Sethi and Kothari, eds., Non-Party Political Process.

revenues? Why do citizens make contributions to organizations for charitable purposes that increasingly are turning away from such activities towards long-term structural objectives? Why do private citizens support nonprofits if many such organizations challenge government and corporation policies abroad as well as their own lifestyles and attitudes?

2. North Atlantic Donor Governments: Why would North Atlantic governments in the 1950s and 1960s offer subsidies to nonprofits and thus surrender some control over significant amounts of their own scarce resources in foreign aid precisely at a time when they began to make major official efforts in influencing Third World development? Why have they continued such grants throughout the 1970s and early 1980s when the impact of nonprofits on economic development has not yet been substantiated? Why have public subsidies in Europe and Canada increased precisely at a time when many NGO agendas have become overtly political overseas and at home and often in opposition to their respective governments' official foreign policies? Do North Atlantic governments, in fact, exercise controls over controversial activities of nonprofits, and, if so, what are they?

3. North Atlantic Nonprofits: Why would North Atlantic nonprofits that have historically played critical roles in overseas relief aid want to shift their focus during the 1950s and 1960s to longer-term developmental assistance when they had no proven track record in this area? Why would some, and not others, also begin to include a political agenda in their mission definition? Why would North Atlantic nonprofits (especially in Europe and Canada) risk a loss of autonomy, and possible sanctions, by becoming increasingly dependent on home governments when their agendas abroad and at home could be embarrassing to public officials? What leverage do nonprofits have with home governments that allow them some freedom to pursue their own agendas with public funds? Are there limits beyond which they cannot go in pursuing such agendas, and, if so, what are the boundaries?

4. Governments in Developing Countries: Why do host governments in the Third World allow indigenous private organizations to bring in outside resources (some of which originate from foreign governments) over which their own public officials exercise no direct control? Why do Third World governments allow domestic groups to use such funds when the projects and groups involved sometimes have objectives contrary to prevailing government policies? Do host governments exercise controls over indigenous nonprofits, and when are they invoked?

5. Indigenous Third World Nonprofits: Do, in fact, Third World nonprofits that receive foreign subsidies act as "trojan horses" for foreign interests within their own societies? What are the boundary lines for indigenous nonprofit action permitted by host government authorities? What is the impact that these indigenous private organizations have on economic and political structures of their own societies, and is the new development rhetoric of North Atlantic PVOs/NGOs matched by the actual project results overseas? If not, why do foreign PVOs/NGOs continue to fund Third World counterparts?

6. Grass-Roots Beneficiaries of Indigenous Nonprofit Services: Do the ultimate recipients of private foreign aid in developing countries have as their goal challenging the political and economic elites of their respective locales through such
programs, or do they have other agendas? What strategies do these recipients
employ to prevent such projects from bringing them into direct and constant confrontation with dominant power elites in their societies, and under what circumstances do they enjoy effective protections?

THEORETICAL CHALLENGES UNDERLYING THE PARADOXES

The paradoxes of private foreign aid present important challenges both to traditional theories of nonprofit organizations in Western democratic society as
well as to concepts of national sovereignty in international relations. In neither
realm do existing theoretical frameworks of analysis seem to explain adequately the complex role of nonprofits in foreign aid.

Historical Rationale for Nonprofits

Historically, theological explanations justified the creation and maintenance
of nonprofit service organizations in Western societies. In both Jewish and
Christian traditions, the poor have always represented God in a special way.
In Jewish teaching, concern for the widow, the orphan, the homeless, and
strangers in need was a central religious obligation (Exod. 22:20–24). By
feeding and clothing the poor, the Christian believes he or she is performing
the service to Jesus himself (Matt. 25:31–46). Moreover, not only is personal
religious salvation enhanced for both the Jew and Christian who are just and
compassionate, but the strength and health of the religious community is
served as well as that of the wider society.[21]

Private service organizations in Western society, in fact, emerged under
religious sponsorship. In the Middle Ages, churches, monasteries, and syna-
gogues (normally free of tax responsibilities) cared for the poor as a way of
helping individual citizens fulfill their religious responsibilities and as a means
for doing what government could not, or would not, do adequately.

Later, when secular charitable associations emerged in the seventeenth and
eighteenth centuries, these often were granted tax immunity, since, like religious institutions, they were seen by government to be performing important
personal and social services that the state otherwise would have to perform at
citizen expense. Secular theories about nonprofit service organizations also
began to emerge at this time, building upon both the personal and the com-
munal explanations of the Judeo-Christian tradition.

According to Adam Smith, the secular exercise of charity was an expression

---

[21] Douglas, *Why Charity?*, pp. 79–83; Neusner, "Righteousness—Not Charity."

of humanitarian sympathy, involving both a feeling for other individuals and an ability to picture oneself in their place. Responding to others in distress fulfilled deep personal humanitarian aspirations. It also came to be understood, according to George Simmel, as a way of promoting the good of the whole of society. By taking care of those who could not help themselves, charitable orgnizations might possibly rehabilitate them into economically productive citizens. At the very least, such aid would prevent "their impulses from leading to the use of violent means to enrich themselves."[22]

Hence, nonprofit service institutions in the early modern period came to be seen as expressions of humanitarian concern as well a means to maintain the social system. They headed off or relieved social tensions in society so as to basically preserve a differentiation among economic groups and thus maintain the status quo. Nonprofit service organizations enhanced societal stability by serving as instruments of social control.

Recent Theories

By the nineteenth century charitable organizations in some parts of Europe and in the United States—both religious and secular—expanded their functions to include care for the aged, handicapped, mentally ill, and preschool children of working parents. Not only in caring for the poor, but in these other areas as well, they acted as vanguards for state welfare programs. Gradually, as public awareness and pressure grew, universal and more comprehensive services began to be provided by government agencies to these previously overlooked groups. This clearly was the pattern in England in the nineteenth century, in the United States until the 1940s, and in the Netherlands until the mid-1950s. Moreover, even as governments in Western industrialized societies became involved in comprehensive welfare service delivery, nonprofits continued to work in the same fields. They now often act as complements of public agencies, experimenters in service improvements, and as advocates of better quality performance.[23]

Moreover, in the Netherlands beginning in the mid-1950s and in Canada and the United States in the mid-1960s, private voluntary service organizations began to receive substantial public subsidies to extend service coverage into areas national and local governmental agencies had not reached. These grants were designed to upgrade the administrative and professional capacities of nonprofit organizations that continued as primary providers in many welfare services (the Netherlands and Canada), or to offer more choices to recipients served by inefficient public bureaucracies (the United States). In the United States by the late 1970s, for example, well over half of all annual federal

[22] Adam Smith, *Theory of Moral Sentiments*, pp. 9–10; Simmel, "The Poor"; Commission on Private Philanthropy and Public Needs, *Giving in America*, pp. 60–63.
[23] Kramer, *Voluntary Agencies*, pp. 173–92, 212–32.

grants to the states for welfare activities ($2.5 billion to $4.1 billion) were spent on contract agreements between state agencies and nonprofit service institutions.[24]

Recent theories about the function of nonprofit service institutions in Western democracies have continued to stress, therefore, the important system maintenance function they perform. These theories (elaborated primarily by economists and political scientists) argue that nonprofits fill gaps left by the commercial and governmental sectors in meeting important public needs in heterogenous democratic capitalist societies.

Henry Hansmann, an economist, has argued that the core purpose of the nonprofit sector is to operate in those areas where consumers (buyers of goods or services, and contributors to charity) have no way to police commercial producers by ordinary contractual devices—e.g., if the possibility of cheating to increase profits is great due to the absence of effective marketing competition for a certain commodity, or if the service is to be delivered to a far-off place so that donors do not see the beneficiaries. The nonprofit organization, which has a legal commitment is to devote its entire resources to the provision of a promised service or good, becomes a more attractive intermediary between giver and recipient than profit-making institutions in such situations.[25] In such work, public trust is guaranteed by the performance of certain tasks by the nonprofit sector rather than leaving them to forces in the marketplace.

Others have stressed the comparative advantage of nonprofit organizations vis-à-vis government in performing certain needed public functions. Burton Weisbrod, also an economist, believes that nonprofits support collective consumption goods (items that benefit more than one person simultaneously) for which there is not yet a demand from the majority of citizens or for which a majority of citizens are prepared to pay in taxation only in amounts that a minority considers inadequate.[26]

James Douglas—a political scientist and author of *Why Charity?*—sees democratic governmental institutions categorically restrained from discriminating in their public policies in favor of one group of citizens against another due to the necessity of the guaranteeing equality for all before law. When societies are heterogeneous with differing needs for public goods, however, this restraint often keeps democratic governments from meeting the demands of all persons or groups adequately. Representative governments also are working under a majoritarian constraint as well, Douglas claims. They must constantly avoid an overactive policy that collides with strongly held views

---

[24] Ibid., pp. 19–36; Steven Rathgeb Smith, "Regulating the Welfare State," telephone interview with Dr. Michael Krashinsky, University of Toronto.

[25] Hansmann, "Role of Nonprofit Enterprise."

[26] Weisbrod, "Towards a Theory of the Nonprofit Sector," p. 172; see also Weisbrod, *Voluntary Nonprofit Sector*, pp. 51–76.

and interests of groups (whether a majority or minority) and, at the same time, avoid deadlock and stagnation on important public issues.[27]

Nonprofit organizations, according to Douglas, are free of both constraints. They can innovate and develop particular policies targeted to the needs of specific groups since they are private. Moreover, when a minority has strong views that society needs some particular social service (and government by a weak opposition from a majority of citizens is prevented from carrying it out), nonprofit institutions can act to provide such a service. They can do so particularly if the opposition of the majority springs from a reluctance to pay the cost through taxation rather than opposition to the service itself.[28]

The only two limitations, according to Douglas, are that (1) the minority's view of the needed public good should not collide with an equally intense view that it is bad or something forbidden by law—e.g., giving free drugs to teenagers and (2) society must be satisfied that the view is reasonable, whether or not a majority actually holds it—e.g., a religious or ethical system, a different concept of education, an innovative approach to health or social service.[29]

Douglas also recognizes that tax exemption for such nonprofit service organizations makes sense theoretically since they provide a benefit the state does not adequately perform, and hence they lessen the burden on the public purse. Such tax exemptions also allow governments to encourage certain activities of a public nature without actually accepting responsibility for them—especially when there is not a public consensus that the state should take on these functions (e.g., support for religious education). Moreover, when there is a consensus that these functions should be supported with public resources but the state does not have the full administrative capacity (the poverty program in the United States in the 1960s) or personalized skills to perform them well (e.g., care for handicapped preschool children), public subsidies to or purchases of service contracts from nonprofits become a way for government to fulfill this mandate.[30]

In all of these circumstances, according to Douglas, the diversity of society is preserved, the legitimacy of government is enhanced, public bureaucracies are saved from expense, and representative governments are able to depoliticize some controversial public services. In return for tax exemption in the performance of such services to society, nonprofit organizations (especially in Anglo-American societies) are restricted by law from devoting a "substantial part of their activities to influence legislation" and from participating in political campaigns. A trust for the attainment of a political objective is not considered to be a charity nor to be worthy of tax exemption. Attempts by nonprofits to change laws or public policies go beyond their charitable mandate, and, in

---

[27] Douglas, *Why Charity?*, pp. 116–28.

[28] Ibid., p. 128.

[29] Ibid., pp. 130–32.

[30] Ibid., pp. 132–34, 140–41.

all likelihood, will cost taxpayers more, not less, if these attempts are successful.[31]

In fact, when nonprofit service organizations have entered into partisan politics in the United States—especially with the use of public subsidies—government has acted decisively to thwart their purpose or to invoke tax law sanctions. When local nonprofit organizations using U.S. government funds to carry out social services among the urban poor in the late 1960s began to mobilize the poor in community action programs and pressure local government agencies for more and better public services and for greater input into local government decision making by the poor, city officials around the country complained strongly to federal authorities. Federal funds were subsequently redirected to less controversial programs over which local governments had more control.[32] When U.S. nonprofit organizations carrying out domestic social services with public funds began to lobby extensively against federal cutbacks in their subsidies in the early 1980s, explicit regulations were issued by the Office of Management and Budget (OMB) forbidding the use of public funds for any political advocacy work whatsoever.[33]

Hence, recent theoretical explanations from economics and political theory about the nonprofit sector in democratic society continue to build upon older religious and ethical arguments. Nonprofit service agencies continue to be justified on the basis that they perform a useful public function for the community as a whole, which neither business nor government can carry out adequately. They act in a more personal way than government or business, and thus mediate personal humanitarian concerns in the public forum. They also strengthen the stability of the social, economic, and political system in heterogeneous democratic societies by relieving certain real or potential tensions. Moreover, if they step beyond their allotted boundaries and enter partisan politics, they risk losing their tax-exempt privileges or governmental support, since political officials then view them not as performing a system-maintenance function but as subverting established public authority.

Current Challenges to the Theories by International Charities

None of these theoretical explanations from theology, sociology, economics, or political science about the purpose of nonprofit service organizations in democratic Western society seem to explain how they are functioning today in foreign aid. Religious and humanitarian motives may well be uppermost in the minds of private donors, but the goals of many organizations go well beyond

[31] Ibid., pp. 68–70; see also Commission on Private Philanthropy and Public Needs, *Giving in America*, pp. 25–26.

[32] Marris and Rein, *Dilemmas of Social Reform*, pp. 208–23; Cloward and Fox Piven, *Politics of Turmoil*, pp. 284–351.

[33] *Federal Register* 49, 83 (April 27, 1984): 18276.

the alleviation of immediate suffering. Many do not appear to be performing a system-maintenance function by filling gaps left by profit-making or governmental institutions in foreign aid. Instead they are challenging existing social structures. They are not trying to save money for citizens in their home societies but are advocating changes in official aid and trade policies of their home countries that will cost taxpayers and consumers more, not less, in prices and revenues. Many are also receiving public subsidies but attempting to achieve ends (political change at home and abroad) that a majority of citizens may very well not consider a public good, or at least a reasonable goal, for both tax-exempt and publicly subsidized organizations.

Moreover, these paradoxes, or apparent gaps between image and reality, in international charities raise critical questions for national sovereignty. International law recognizes the territorial integrity of each nation. The United Nations Charter forbids any foreign intervention into the domestic affairs of countries. The charter of the Organization of American States (OAS) interprets this not only to include armed interference but also "any other intervention which threatens the personality of the state and the political, economic and cultural elements which constitute it."[34]

National governments exercise jurisdiction, therefore, over all foreigners who enter their territories and can regulate such activities to protect national interests. Private associations are not guaranteed any legal immunities since they are not subjects of international law—only representatives of nation states and intergovernmental organizations (e.g., ambassadors) have some immunities. In recent years, in fact, there has been a growth of laws in developing countries restricting foreign private organizations—e.g., establishing terms for MNC investments to maximize benefits for the host country.[35]

Moreover, international private organizations traditionally have been regulated by nation states when they manifest a clear ideological or political orientation. Religious movements in the post-Reformation and Napoleonic eras were brought under national control to enhance national stability and unity. In the early twentieth century Western governments used police powers against some of their own domestic private organizations that received aid from abroad out of concern that they were falling under control of the Communist International (COMINTERN). Free and socialist-dominated trade unions were, in fact, manipulated by the now defunct COMINTERN during the interwar period, and Moscow continues to exert influence in the domestic affairs of many nations today through front organizations. The Nazis similarly infiltrated private organizations in various European nations during the 1930s.[36]

Hence, at various times in modern Western history, international private

[34] Organization of American States (OAS), *Charter of the Organization of American States* (Washington, D.C.: General Secretariat, OAS, 1972).

[35] Sigmund, *Multinationals in Latin America*; Stepan, *State and Society*, pp. 230–89.

[36] Lador-Lederer, *International Non-Governmental Organizations*, pp. 239–40.

organizations have been considered by host governments as instruments of foreign ideological or political influence and therefore harmful to national sovereignty. These included religious organizations, scientific associations, labor groups, sports and youth clubs, and women's institutions. Such organizations have from time to time served as means for foreign governments or political movements to exert influence in the internal affairs of other countries. When their political purpose has been discovered, host governments have not hesitated to take protective measures against them—forbidding representatives access to their territory, monitoring communications and transfers of funds, or eliminating the tax-exempt status of affiliates in their own countries.[37]

Conversely, when foreign political objectives have been pursued through private means by nation states, they often have been kept as secretive as possible, and careful controls are normally exercised by the subsidizing government to prevent diplomatic embarrassments as well as negative political fallout at home. The strong reaction by Latin American governments to the U.S. Defense Department's Project Camelot in Chile when it became public in the mid-1960s is a case in point. Congressional limitations on the CIA's use of private organizations resulted from disclosures in the 1960s and 1970s that it was acting through, or using, various U.S. and foreign private organizations to gain information about sensitive issues abroad or to subvert foreign governments.[38]

The current freedom of North Atlantic charities to operate abroad and support local counterparts in Third World countries would seem to challenge the theory and practice of sovereignty in international relations. The current use of PVOs/NGOs to transmit openly significant amounts of home-government resources abroad not only involves private sector institutions in public sector activities but also allows them considerable discretion of operation—even to the extent of their apparently opposing public sector objectives in both North Atlantic and developing countries. Theoretically, one would *not* expect governments at either end of the private foreign aid network to allow the transnational nonprofit network to carry out such agendas openly, with public subsidies, and without strict public controls.

Many nonprofits based in North Atlantic countries, however, are collaborating with their counterparts overseas in carrying out activities usually considered to be public sector responsibilities (foreign aid). They are doing so with public sector funds, but are left with considerable freedom to pursue their goals, even when in apparent contradiction to both donor-government intentions and host-government interests. The private has become public, and yet

[37] Ibid., pp. 238–39.

[38] Horowitz, ed., *Rise and Fall of Project Camelot*; U.S. Congress, Senate, Select Committee to Study Governmental Operations with Respect to Intelligence Activities, *Hearings*.

accountability to normal political authority has been left quite vague and underdeveloped even when public interests are at stake.

EXTANT LITERATURE ON PVOs/NGOs

The two genres of literature that have dealt specifically with nonprofit organizations in international development do not adequately address the paradoxes underlying cooperation between governments, private citizens, and nonprofits in North Atlantic countries and in the Third World. Those writing from a basic human needs (BHN) or alternative development strategy (ADS) perspective (Sommer, Lissner, Bolling, and Gorman) have stressed the important role PVOs/NGOs can play in creating cost-effective, flexible, and popular alternatives to official government strategies in foreign aid—which they do. Such works, however, have focused almost exclusively on North Atlantic sending agencies and do not incorporate much data or analysis on the economic or political impact of indigenous nonprofits who use the aid in developing countries.[39]

These more general works also do not sufficiently account for significant variations in style and political orientation that exist among aid-sending nonprofits based in the United States, Canada, and Europe. Nor do they adequately assess the controversial agendas many North Atlantic PVOs/NGOs today espouse at home and abroad, nor explain what trade-offs take place among the various actors cooperating in or allowing such strategies at both ends of the transnational aid spectrum.[40]

The other body of literature that deals with PVOs/NGOs in international development is the work of the new transnationalists (Galtung, Alger, Mansbach, and Vasquez). Building on Ernst Haas's functionalist approach to international relations, their basic premise is that nonstate actors in current international relations can and should begin to solve aspects of some of the difficult problems that nation states are unable to address adequately on their own— e.g., poverty, peace, ecology. They believe that people-to-people programs that bridge national borders and link civil societies directly (bypassing governments caught in a morass of bureaucracy and self-serving considerations based on narrow definitions of national interest) can deal more effectively with pieces of such issues. Their argument is that private nonprofit organizations

---

[39] Sommer, *Beyond Charity*; Lissner, *Politics of Altruism*; Bolling, *Private Foreign Aid*; Gorman, ed., *Private Voluntary Organizations*.

[40] Lissner's work, as the title indicates (*The Politics of Altruism*), does treat the political agenda of some North Atlantic nonprofits, but more in a descriptive and hortatory style than in analytical fashion. He does not explain why North Atlantic governments (especially in Canada and Europe) subsidize private organizations that would seem to have political goals quite different from their own or why Third World governments let North Atlantic nonprofits support indigenous groups with a political agenda in their own societies.

can overcome the limits of ideology and patriotism, and thus help construct an international constituency for global humanistic concerns and offer a nonpartisan pragmatic strategy to fulfill them.[41]

Although this body of literature is providing an important framework for understanding how some nonstate actors offer important technical and pragmatic solutions to pressing global problems, it does not analyze sufficiently private actors in international development that are becoming more, not less, ideological in their transnational objectives, even while receiving nation-state subsidies. Such PVOs/NGOs cannot be considered as purely technical institutions, politically nonpartisan, or completely nonstate actors. This literature also does not adequately address the threat to host country sovereignty that the political agenda of such PVOs/NGOs appear to present, nor the strategies governments in developing countries employ to counter them.

Neither of these two schools, therefore, sufficiently explains the reasons why the public and nonprofit sectors in international development collaborate, even when groups on both sides have seemingly contradictory agendas. Neither the tradeoffs nor the ongoing tensions are adequately analyzed. Nor is adequate attention given to the larger theoretical issues—namely the shifting purpose of nonprofit organizations in Western democracies, and the implications of having private sector institutions engage in public sector activities abroad with minimal control by political authorities responsible for national sovereignty.

METHODOLOGY AND ARGUMENT

In the light of the paradoxes involved in private foreign aid, the challenge they present to traditional theories about the nonprofit sector and about national sovereignty, and the inability of the current literature on PVOs/NGOs to explain these apparent contradictions, this book is an attempt to address such issues in both a comparative and cross-national framework. At one level, it examines the role of North Atlantic aid-sending PVOs/NGOs in their home countries—their historical evolution in foreign aid, their diversity in style across various North Atlantic societies, and their relationships with private and governmental donors.

At another level, the study analyzes the role of recipient counterpart nonprofits in Latin America—their interaction with foreign donors and home governments, their local clientele, and the social and political implications of their activities. Special emphasis is given to Colombia—a country that has a wide variety of indigenous nonprofit service organizations and a relatively optimum context for analyzing their activities (formal democracy, and government en-

---

[41] Galtung, "Nonterritorial Actors and the Problem of Peace"; Galtung, *True Worlds*; Alger, "Bridging the Micro and the Macro"; Mansbach and Vasquez, *In Search of Theory*; Haas, *Beyond the Nation State*, pp. 3–126.

couragement for private economic initiatives). Brief examples will also be given of indigenous nonprofit activities in other Latin American countries where the political and economic situation places different opportunities and limitations on their activities—particularly Brazil, Chile, Peru, and Bolivia.

The methods I have used in generating empirical data include the following:

1. In-depth structured interviews (conducted between August 1981 and May 1986) with seventy-five persons in forty-five aid-sending PVOs/NGOs based in the United States, Canada, England, France, Belgium, the Netherlands, the Federal Republic of Germany, and Switzerland.
2. Examination of official documents and publications collected from visits to the headquarters of these PVOs/NGOs, such as annual reports, budgets, public education, and fund raising materials.
3. Analysis of public opinion polls in various North Atlantic countries on the views of the general public about foreign assistance and the role of PVOs/NGOs.
4. Interviews with over a dozen officials in governmental and intergovernmental agencies in North Atlantic countries that have regular dealings with PVOs/NGOs—the House Foreign Affairs Committee, the Senate Appropriations Committee, and AID in the United States; the Canadian International Development Agency (CIDA); the Ministry of Economic Cooperation of the Federal Republic of Germany (BMZ); the Ministry of Foreign Affairs of the government of the Netherlands; the Directorate General for Development of the Commission of the European Community (CEC); and the Development Cooperation Directorate of the OECD.
5. In-depth structured interviews conducted between June and August 1984 with executives in thirty-six indigenous nonprofits in Colombia active in supporting grass-roots development projects among the urban or rural poor (most of whom are receiving grants from one or more of the forty-five PVOs/NGOs I interviewed in North Atlantic countries).
6. On-site project visits to and conversations with participants in grass-roots projects supported by seven of these thirty-six Colombian nonprofits in my survey.
7. Interviews with forty-five others in government, business, academia, and the nonprofit sector, who are either experts in Colombian economic and political development or knowledgeable of the role that indigenous nonprofits play in Colombia and in other Latin American countries.

A more detailed description of the research methodology is included in appendix A.

The argument of this book is that, despite the agenda differences among the major parties involved in the private foreign aid network, there are also shared interests that make collaboration possible. None of the parties are unitary actors themselves. They are made up of clusters of groups, with different perspectives and objectives but with enough overlap to allow mutual cooperation with other actors under certain conditions. Trade-offs occur, with the result that some objectives of each actor or subgroup of actors are often achieved, while others are adjusted or postponed.

Moreover, historically PVOs/NGOs engaged in transnational aid have often been involved in more than humanitarian activities abroad. Frequently they have been active collaborators with North Atlantic government agencies in promoting foreign policy objectives of their home societies, or at least have been tacit supporters by pursuing goals complementary to official policies. Foreign governments have also historically found the international charities network useful in filling gaps in domestic services, which their own public sector agencies have not been able to meet.

In more recent years, more diverse agendas have emerged between some PVOs/NGOs and governments at both ends of the aid spectrum owing to wider political debates both in North Atlantic nations (especially in much of Europe and Canada) and in many Third World countries about the nature and purpose of development. In fact, many PVOs/NGOs have often been directly linked into domestic political subgroups in their home societies who are active in this debate. Many nonprofits in Europe and Canada as well as in developing countries have, in fact, become surrogates for groups (especially those on the left) who disagree with official government development policies at both ends of the official aid spectrum and who seek alternate channels to pursue their vision of a more just global order.

Nevertheless, despite these differences, sufficient pluralism, internal diversity, and mutually accommodating strategies exist that allow for the continuation of historical patterns of cooperation and complementarity between the public sector and nonprofits in both North Atlantic and developing countries. Many PVOs/NGOs have come to rely heavily on public sector subsidies in North Atlantic societies that originated under past close collaboration with home government agencies, and now they do not want to risk serious institutional shrinkage that reliance only on private funds would entail. Moreover, these nonprofits normally represent, or attempt for financial reasons to cultivate, a variety of interests (even if staff preferences are oriented in a political direction), and from time to time submerge or adjust controversial political agendas so as to avoid serious tensions with private or governmental donors. Many charities, for example, still carry out some form of relief work during overseas emergencies, thus satisfying many private donors at home who prefer to give to nonprofits primarily during well-publicized foreign disasters.

Subsidizing governments in North Atlantic countries are themselves internally diverse and also desirous of building the widest possible domestic support for overall foreign aid commitments. By subsidizing some politically controversial agendas at home or abroad of PVOs/NGOs, these North Atlantic government policymakers can also achieve important objectives not ordinarily possible through public sector channels—harnessing and moderating the energies of dissident domestic political groups, gaining their support for expanded official aid budgets, satisfying demands of important constituencies within their own ruling coalitions or the loyal opposition, and establishing contact with dissident political movements abroad that normal state-to-state exchanges cannot achieve.

Overseas the actual projects supported by indigenous nonprofits in Third World countries are far less threatening to the established order than their image or the rhetoric of North Atlantic donor PVOs/NGOs would indicate. They too represent diverse interests, normally including quite politically and economically conservative grass-roots groups that they aid. Although they provide havens for some dissident intellectual, religious, and political groups in their own societies, the actual projects they support tend to concentrate primarily on specific material gains for low-income groups whose needs are not met adequately by domestic government or business institutions. In most instances, they channel the energies of middle-class dissidents into reformist activities not radically challenging established political and economic structures, at least in the short term.

Finally, whenever nonprofits at either end of the international aid spectrum do become a source of serious political embarrassment to public sector policymakers, nation states can and do use a variety of cooptative and restrictive measures to modify and control their activities. Such means include threats or actual curtailments of subsidies, placing conditions on the use of such aid, applying legal procedures restricting political action by tax-exempt organizations, invoking privileges of state sovereignty to control foreign nationals, meeting piecemeal PVO/NGO demands, and using direct repressive measures against the staff or constituents of nonprofits.

Hence, the international nonprofit sector does not present a serious threat to nation-state stability at present, but actually enhances it. In so doing, however, it is acting in pursuit of agendas that extend well beyond charity and altruism, at times with the appearance (albeit not in actuality) of being a serious foe of nation state interests.

Chapter 2 analyzes the major functions of North Atlantic PVOs/NGOs in foreign aid from the sixteenth to the mid-twentieth centuries. It describes how the predecessors of today's development-oriented nonprofits—missionary organizations, cultural and humanitarian groups, and war-relief agencies—normally worked very closely with their respective home-government agencies, and often were formally integrated into official foreign policy objectives of such governments. Some of the largest PVOs/NGOs engaged in overseas activities today, in fact, were founded in this early era, and have had a long tradition of pursuing overlapping, although not identical, objectives abroad with their respective home-government ministries of foreign affairs.

Chapters 3 and 4 deal with the evolution of North Atlantic PVOs/NGOs in the post–World War II era and the differences in their relationships with home governments and private donors in the United States (chapter 3) as compared to Europe and Canada (chapter 4). In the United States, exporting the American belief (shared by Washington and citizens alike) that self-help initiatives and private networks of social participation were effective ingredients of democratic development became a major objective of PVOs in foreign aid in the 1950s and 1960s.

In the smaller countries of Europe, NGOs acted as vanguards for as yet underdeveloped public aid agencies, and in larger nations as more acceptable and less paternalistic channels for aid to groups in newly independent nations sensitive about past colonial domination. Moreover, NGOs in Europe and Canada provided useful surrogates for public aid in meeting basic needs in the Third World once the political rhetoric of left-of-center governments outran their capacity to deliver on previous promises after the post-1973 oil shock.

Chapter 5 examines the largest North Atlantic PVOs/NGOs according to current resource allocations, finding that three major tendencies differentiate these organizations today—relief work (alleviating immediate suffering with food, clothing, and medicine); technical aid (supporting training, education, credit, population control, and basic physical infrastructure); and institution-building (support for multipurpose development programs that, in addition to service provision, strengthen local private community organizations attempting to make the poor more aware of the deeper underlying causes of poverty). This chapter shows that there is a great difference among North Atlantic non-profits in these emphases according to region of origin—with U.S. PVO resources far more skewed to relief work (despite a development-oriented rhetoric) than those of the Canadians and Europeans, who tend to place proportionately more emphasis on technical aid and institution-building and who also include more explicit political objectives in their goal definitions abroad and at home. Three factors account for this divergence: (1) the type of public subsidies available to nonprofits, with food aid constituting the major part in the United States and cash grants the overwhelming proportion in Europe and Canada; (2) greater public awareness in Europe and Canada about the nature of development issues, as well as the wider spectrum of debate among domestic political elites in these nations about Third World needs; and (3) the linkages many European and Canadian nonprofits have with other domestic organizations attempting to influence public policy issues.

Chapters 6 and 7 analyze the trade-offs of interest among private citizens, governments, and international nonprofits in North Atlantic societies. Although perception gaps exist between private donors and PVO/NGO staffs, as well as tensions with government officials because of public advocacy and lobbying activities of some nonprofits in their home societies (especially in Europe and Canada), these normally are not severe enough to precipitate a breakdown in cooperative arrangements since all three groups (private donors, public officials, PVO/NGO staffs) pursue multiple interests. Governments, as well as private donors, also take steps to curb PVO/NGO activities when these become politically unacceptable, and nonprofits themselves tacitly put boundaries on some of their own activities. Moreover, a wider domestic political spectrum in Canada and Western Europe than in the United States accounts for greater government tolerance for, and even tacit approval of, nonprofit political activities. The NGOs in fact can carry out surrogate foreign policies that home governments in these other North Atlantic countries cannot afford to endorse officially but which are important for critical political subgroups whom public policymakers wish to placate in their own societies.

Chapter 8 assesses the trade-offs in relationships among Colombian nonprofits, foreign donors, the public sector and private groups in Colombia itself. It shows that, as in the North Atlantic context, gaps do exist among stated objectives of donors (foreigners) and the actual practice of indigenous nonprofits. This gap is due to the far more modest and limited objectives of projects and their participants than foreign donors (especially Canadian and European NGOs) expect. Colombian nonprofits use foreign assistance primarily to promote technical and production-oriented projects at the grass-roots level, which neither local government nor profit-making institutions can or are willing to provide. Political mobilization of the poor by Colombian nonprofits is not a prime objective (nor in most other Latin American countries where evidence exists), and when it occurs government uses a combination of cooptive and coercive measures to blunt its effect. A brief survey of several other Latin American countries confirms the system-maintenance function of nonprofits in the short run.

Chapter 9 reassesses traditional and recent theories about nonprofit organizations in Western democracy, as well as concepts of national sovereignty in international relations in light of the current practice of nonprofits in foreign aid. It concludes that certain modifications in these theories are in order. Many international charities, for example, have political dimensions, sometimes even partisan ones. Despite this orientation, however, most still serve to stabilize the international system and do not radically threaten nation-state interests at home or abroad. Hence, theories of national sovereignty need no modification in light of the functions that international charities perform.

In the long run they could become destabilizing if some of their latent goals are realized (e.g., strengthening the political power of the poor in developing countries). If such occurs, or if these latent functions become more manifest and overt, the charities are liable to lose some of their privileges. Under such circumstances, governments at both ends of the international aid spectrum are likely to impose stricter controls or deprive them of their tax-exempt status (a confirmation of the thrust of traditional theories about nonprofits).

The most serious challenge to the theory of nonprofits that transnational PVOs/NGOs present is in the area of public trust. A major rationale for the existence and tax-exempt privilege of nonprofits is that they enjoy more credibility than government or profit-making institutions in carrying out needed, but difficult, public tasks. The current perception differences between donor expectations and staff objectives in many transnational nonprofits indicates, however, a credibility gap between image and reality. Ironically, maintaining present arrangements requires such gaps, indicating that a certain amount of duplicity or at least creative packaging of information has come to characterize the transnational nonprofit sector. How much can be tolerated before the theory or the practice changes remains to be seen.

CHAPTER TWO

Historical Role of Private Foreign Aid as an Extension of North Atlantic Nation-State Interests Abroad

CHARITABLE ORGANIZATIONS have a four-century history of international activity. Their past includes a variety of activities ranging from religious evangelization, cultural promotion, and relief aid—all of which long predate their more recent focus on development and continue to characterize part of their overseas work today. One purpose of the next three chapters is to highlight some of the most salient events and turning points in this history and to show how from the beginning governments and nonprofits collaborated in the pursuit of common goals abroad. Another purpose of these chapters is to show some of the historical differences among international charities in relationship with governments in their countries of origin, particularly between those based in the United States and those in other North Atlantic countries. By so doing, we will be better able to understand the diversity of functions that today characterizes PVOs/NGOs in North Atlantic countries and the different purposes various governments have in subsidizing them.

In this chapter we shall examine the evolution of PVOs/NGOs in Western Europe and North America from the sixteenth century until the end of World War II. During this four hundred-year period they played a crucial role in supporting home-government policies in overseas colonial territories (Europe from the sixteenth to early twentieth centuries), or in complementing foreign policy efforts of their home governments during wartime (particularly the United States in the first half of this century). The following two chapters will analyze PVO/NGO relations with home governments since 1945, and how both in North America and Western Europe (in each region for different reasons) they became increasingly useful allies of governments in the promotion of home-country national interests in developing countries.

EARLY INTERNATIONAL CHARITIES

Missionary Organizations

The oldest of the international aid-sending groups in Western societies were church-related. Beginning in the early sixteenth century, religious orders and congregations sent personnel and resources to the Americas, East Africa, Southern Asia, and the Far East to convert native peoples to Christianity.

These missionaries, however, also performed a variety of social and humanitarian tasks (in education, health, and social welfare) in addition to their proselytizing work.

These earliest missionary organizations emerged in the Iberian Peninsula, and from the beginning they were subsidized by the Spanish and Portuguese crowns for both their religious and social work. In return, the respective monarchs were given the privilege of nominating and vetoing papal appointments to the bishoprics in these territories (*patronato real*). Missionary organizations, although private, were considered an arm of the crown in the Spanish and Portuguese empires since church and state were united. They were supported by kings because they helped spread and maintain Iberian culture and control in the New World. They operated schools and universities, took care of many of the social needs of native peoples, and encouraged obedience to the agents of the king as a part of one's responsibilities to God.

In the Americas most Catholic missionaries (Bartolomé de las Casas in the Caribbean and Antonio Valdivieso in Central America being among the notable exceptions) did not openly and repeatedly criticize harsh treatment of Indians and blacks by Spanish and Portuguese *conquistadores*. Although some of the local born creole lower clergy did support political independence movements that spread throughout the Spanish Americas in the early nineteenth century, the vast majority of bishops and Spanish clergy opposed such efforts and openly sided with the Crown.[1]

In the late eighteenth and nineteenth centuries—during the rapid expansion of colonization by Great Britain, France, Germany, Belgium, and the Netherlands throughout Africa and Asia—new Christian missionary societies were created by both Catholics and Protestants. These missionaries pioneered in modern education, medicine, and surgery in China, Africa, and much of India and the Middle East. (They were also joined in their efforts by American and Canadian religious groups by the late nineteenth century).

There can be no doubt, however, that missionary groups also served the interests of colonial administrations by promoting Western (and often European) culture and values. As was the case earlier with religious orders and congregations in Latin America, direct financial grants were made to both Protestant and Catholic overseas mission organizations by home governments in Great Britain, the Netherlands, Germany, France, and Belgium for the schools, clinics, orphanages, and other charitable works that they administered throughout Africa and Asia in the nineteenth and early twentieth centuries.

Even in France, where republican governments fought to reduce Catholic

[1] Mecham, *Church and State In Latin America*; Dussel, *History and the Theology of Liberation*.

Church power and privilege at home in the late nineteenth and early twentieth centuries, public officials maintained cordial relations with French Catholic missionary societies and continued to provide them with subsidies for their educational activities in French African territories. Domestic anticlerical tendencies were overridden by foreign policy concerns, and private religious organizations were cultivated as instruments in spreading and maintaining French culture abroad. In Great Britain, despite the fact that the Anglican Church was officially part of the Crown and the only religious group to receive government support at home, all English Christian churches and personnel abroad were offered subsidies for the schools and hospitals they administered in British colonies.[2]

In turn, as in the case of the earlier Catholic missionaries in the Americas, Protestant and Catholic missionary societies in Africa and Asia in the nineteenth and early twentieth centuries by and large did not question or openly criticize the policies of their respective home governments. They accepted what they considered to be benevolent colonialism, and welcomed steadily increasing government subsidies for their respective charitable works. Moreover, as in the case of Latin America, foreign-born clergy and nuns were not in the vanguard of independence movements in Africa and Asia when these emerged in the early and the mid-twentieth century. Rather, they supported the legitimacy and desirability of colonial rule almost to the end.[3]

Today many of these same missionary organizations founded between the late eighteenth and early twentieth centuries continue to carry out both religious and social activities overseas. In fact, of the 205 largest North Atlantic PVOs/NGOs engaged in various forms of socioeconomic assistance in Latin America, Africa, the Middle East, or Asia in 1980 and 1981 (listed in appendix C of this book), twenty-one—or 10.2 percent—originated as missionary societies or affiliates or religious denominations between 1798 and 1912. Although religious evangelization continues to be the major objective of most, they continue to carry out a whole range of educational, medical, and charitable activities that enhance the material quality of life of the people in developing countries. Moreover, governments in Western Europe (which do not have such strict legal separation of church and state requirements as exist in the United States) continue to provide them with subsidies, although considerably reduced since the end of the colonial era in Africa, Asia, and the Middle East. (See the percentages of public subsidies to these religious organizations in 1980 in appendix C).

[2] The most comprehensive chronicling of the religious, humanitarian, and cultural activities of Christian missionary societies in this period has been done by Latourette, *Christianity in a Revolutionary Age*. See especially vol. 3, *The Nineteenth Century Outside Europe* (1961), and vol. 5, *The Twentieth Century Outside Europe* (1962).

[3] Hastings, *History of African Christianity*, pp. 5–34, 86–107.

Red Cross Societies

Another precursor to current nonprofit activity in socioeconomic development that emerged in the mid and late nineteenth century was the international Red Cross movement. The International Committee of the Red Cross was founded in Switzerland to help the wounded in the War of Italian Succession in the late 1850s. It was followed by the establishment of various national Red Cross societies in Europe and the United States to aid victims of other wars (e.g., the Franco-Prussian War of 1870–1871, and the Spanish-American War in 1898).[4]

As in the case of missionary organizations, these national Red Cross societies also soon came to be partially subsidized by governments since they were valuable instruments in caring for each nation's wounded during wartime. Several were officially endorsed by North Atlantic governments. The American Red Cross, for example, originally founded in 1887 under private auspices, at the turn of the century underwent administrative reorganization. Having provided important service to the American wounded in Cuba during the Spanish-American War, it was granted an official charter by the U.S. Congress in 1905, giving it the status of a semiofficial government agency. Although still technically a private organization, it has received substantial government subsidies ever since, with 54 percent of its overseas resources in 1981 originating from the U.S. government (see table 1 in appendix C).

Almost from their beginnings, most other national Red Cross societies in the North Atlantic region have been closely associated with home governments and also have been substantially subsidized with public funds for their overseas work during wartime or natural disasters. The Swiss Red Cross, for example, founded in 1866, received 60 percent of its funds for overseas work from the Swiss government in 1980, the Canadian Red Cross 63 percent, and the British Red Cross 22 percent. These three, along with the American Red Cross, remain among the largest international charities today that are based in North Atlantic countries (see Tables 1, 4, and 7 in appendix C).

Cultural Associations

Finally, various educational, labor, and professional associations; temperance societies; and women's emancipation groups emerged in Europe and the United States in the nineteenth century. They began to support overseas activities in education, community organization, and service in various parts of the world. In some instances they were projections abroad of new activist groups agitating for change in their native societies (e.g., labor groups, temperance

---

[4] Forsythe, *Humanitarian Politics*, pp. 6–7, 16, 27.

unions, women's organizations) that wanted to gain allies abroad and thus see their ideas influence the policies of other nations. In such instances they were privately funded.

In other cases, however, North Atlantic governments actively sought their assistance. European governments, for example, by the late nineteenth century began to subsidize scholarships and vocational training abroad offered by various home-country universities and foundations. Such strategies provided training for cadres of economically productive personnel in their colonial territories loyal to home-country interests.[5]

In fact, British missionaries from Africa in the years just prior to World War I visited the United States to study the network of vocational training for blacks developed by the Tuskegee Institute and supported by the Phelps-Stokes Fund. These missionaries helped convince the British Colonial Office, searching for a uniform educational strategy to support its policy of indirect rule in Africa, that the Tuskegee philosophy of restricted education for blacks was well suited for strengthening its control in various African territories. The Phelps-Stokes Fund—and later in more substantial terms, the Carnegie Foundation in the 1920s and 1930s—in turn contributed to British-sponsored vocational educational in various territories in Africa.[6]

There was, therefore, a burgeoning of international activity by religious denominations, humanitarian societies, labor and cultural associations, and foundations throughout the nineteenth and early twentieth centuries that coincided with the expansion of colonialism and the spread of North Atlantic economic and political influence in Latin America, Africa, the Middle East, and Asia. In 1800 there were only twelve private, nonprofit institutions based in Europe, Canada, and the United States that engaged in some form of overseas activity. By 1850 there were sixty-six. In 1910, however, on the eve of World War I, there were 344—an increase of more than 400 percent in just sixty years.[7]

Moreover, the vast majority of these early private transnational organizations cooperated closely with and in some cases were significantly subsidized by their respective home governments in the variety of humanitarian, cultural, and economic services they performed abroad—often in colonial territories of these same subsidizing governments. They clearly were, in Simmel's terms, system maintenance institutions, but now transposed from the domestic arena (where many had long been performing needed tasks governments could not, or would not) to the international realm where they began to complement foreign policy interests of their respective home governments.

[5] Lissner, *Politics of Altruism*, pp. 58, 60.
[6] Berman, "Educational Colonialism in Africa."
[7] Lissner, *Politics of Altruism*, p. 59.

WORLD WAR I PERIOD

Wartime Relief Agencies

World War I and its aftermath provided a stimulus for another surge of growth for international charities. In the early years of the war, relief efforts were organized by private citizens in the United States, Canada, Great Britain, Australia, and New Zealand to assist victims in Belgium and France. These received considerable co-funding from their respective governments. The U.S. government (a noncombatant until early 1917) found such organizations that were created by U.S. citizens particularly useful as a way of aiding those in allied countries without violating international conventions restricting the activities of neutral nations.

The American Red Cross, for example, between the outbreak of war in 1914 and the United States' entry in 1917, made 341 shipments of supplies to Europe valued at over $14.9 million (much of it from the U.S. government), all but $2.9 million of which went to allied countries. Many European immigrant groups living in the United States also contributed to relief efforts through several ad hoc groups created at the beginning of the war, a way of helping their relatives in various warring nations (including those in Eastern Europe and Germany up until 1917). Many new relief organizations thus came into being in the United States during the early years of the war, which served well the allied cause abroad.[8]

Perhaps the most famous of these ad hoc nonprofit groups organized to assist European countries friendly to the allies was the Committee for the Relief in Belgium (CRB) under the direction of a successful U.S. businessman, Herbert Hoover, In its four and one half-years of existence, this organization distributed over $7.4 billion in funds and resources in Belgium, $6.5 billion of which originated from the U.S., British, and French governments. The CRB, in fact, acted as a quasigovernmental organization negotiating agreements with various nations and gaining diplomatic privileges and immunities for its ships and personnel. Even the German government respected its agreements with the CRB in the hopes of winning sympathy in U.S. public opinion while the United States remained neutral. The great success of this organization in helping to save over 10 million lives won international acclaim for Herbert Hoover as "the savior of Belgium," and was a major boost to his rising political career.[9]

---

[8] Curti, *American Philanthropy Abroad*, pp. 224–37, 248–58; Bolling, *Private Foreign Aid*, pp. 10–11. In 1917 dollars, the value of the American Red Cross shipments between 1914 and 1917 was $1.75 million. One 1986 dollar (the unit used throughout this book) equals 0.12 1917 dollars, 0.15 1930 dollars, or 0.14 1940 dollars.

[9] Weissman, *Herbert Hoover and Famine Relief*, pp. 24–27.

Postwar Relief to the Soviet Union

In the years immediately following World War I, some of the new U.S. relief agencies, such as the American Jewish Joint Distribution Committee (JDC) and the American Friend's Service Committee (AFSC),[10] joined several others, including the American Red Cross, YMCA, YWCA, and various religious groups and trade union organizations to alleviate famine in the Soviet Union. The U.S. government had no diplomatic relations with the new Bolshevik leaders in Moscow and had angered them as the war was ending with direct support for the White Army. This included some American aid to an unsuccessful allied expeditionary force that landed in northern Russia in 1917 in an attempt to overthrow the Bolsheviks.

By 1921, when hunger was rampant in the Soviet Union, the U.S. government encouraged various PVOs to raise money, collect clothing and blankets, and send volunteers to supervise massive relief programs to aid starving Russians. Twenty four and one-half million dollars worth of army surplus goods were channeled through the American Red Cross, and a total of $490.2 million worth of U.S. private assistance flowed into the Soviet Union during the early 1920s through U.S. relief agencies that worked in partnership both with the U.S. and Soviet governments (despite the strained relations between the two regimes themselves).[11]

One of the most visible and active American private relief agencies in the Soviet Union was Herbert Hoover's American Relief Administration (ARA). Originally set up in early 1919 as a U.S. government agency to administer relief efforts in Europe in the postwar era, it became a private organization after U.S. negotiators concluded their work at the Paris Peace Conference. It continued to channel U.S. government resources to Europe for several years, and in 1921 (when Hoover was U.S. secretary of commerce) received a $122.5 million appropriation from Congress to purchase, allot, and distribute American food in the Soviet Union.

The ARA bought and delivered 540,000 tons of American grain and dairy products to the Soviet Union between 1921 and 1923. This helped bolster agricultural prices in the United States (suffering a severe decline amidst a

[10] Some of these new PVOs existed only for the duration of the hostilities, such as the CRB and the Smith College Relief Unit. Others have remained in operation and today continue to send assistance overseas—the American Jewish Joint Distribution Committee (JDC, 1914), CARITAS Netherlands (1914), the Luxembourg Red Cross (1914), and the American Friends Service Committee (AFSC, 1917). All four of these organizations are today among the 205 largest North Atlantic PVOs/NGOs currently engaged in international work (see appendix C, tables 1, 3, and 7), but now their primary attention is no longer focused on Europe but on the needs of the poor and of refugees in Latin America, Africa, the Middle East, and Asia. Curti, *American Philanthropy Abroad*, pp. 232–37, 249, 253–54.

[11] Bolling, *Private Foreign Aid*, pp. 12–13.

growing surplus of products in the postwar era) and also assisted over 10 million Soviets facing immediate starvation admist severe famine conditions.[12]

The ARA itself had channeled U.S. government resources to the counter-revolutionary White army in 1919 and had as its avowed goals weakening the new Soviet regime and opposing Bolshevik movements in Europe through food distribution (especially in Austria and Hungary). Lenin, however, was convinced that the relief work of the ARA and other American PVOs during the famine (much of it subsidized by the U.S. government) would help avoid potential insurrection among starving Soviets, save scarce resources of his new government, and possibly win recognition and trade agreements from Washington. American resources, moreover, were allowed to go to petty-cap-italist groups that were not priorities of Soviet government aid—peasants, pro-fessional classes, and tradesmen.

The American government through subsidies and encouragement for U.S. PVO activities in the Soviet Union was hoping to strengthen capitalist forces and thereby induce changes in the Soviet system toward a more liberal econ-omy under the recently inaugurated New Economic Program (NEP) an-nounced in 1921. At the very least, it wanted to create a positive impression among Soviet citizens about the United States.[13]

While the first U.S. government objective failed to materialize (since the Bolsheviks consolidated their political and economic control as the famine subsided), the second was accomplished. The ARA and other U.S. PVOs ac-tive in the Soviet Union came to enjoy widespread popularity there as a result of the two years of humanitarian work they carried out. Conversely, Lenin's first objective of heading off expanding domestic discontent was achieved, but he did not gain his second—subsequent diplomatic recognition and renewed trade agreements from the United States.

This episode was an early example of how PVO donor and staff intentions in sending societies can be somewhat different from those of host governments abroad and from the final results of the aid in the receiving countries. It also illustrates how additional agendas beyond the immediate alleviation of human suffering can underly international charity, especially when the political con-text is quite different, or even antithetical, in sending and receiving nations. In such situations, groups at both ends of the spectrum may attempt to use transnational charities to achieve objectives they themselves are unable to re-alize through ordinary state-owned mechanisms.

These have been recurring themes in transnational nonprofit activities over the past 60 years. Private and governmental contributors in North Atlantic countries often have one set of objectives for their philanthropy and indige-nous counterpart PVOs and host governments often have others. Despite these

---

[12] Weissman, *Herbert Hoover and Famine Relief*, pp. 27–29, 34–35, 96–101.
[13] Ibid., pp. 36–37, 198–202.

differences, however, there is often enough overlap of interests among the multiple partners to permit the system to function in a way not threatening to the basic nation-state interests of either rich or poor countries.

INTERWAR YEARS: PIONEERING IN TECHNICAL AID

Prior to the 1920s, almost all North Atlantic nonprofit aid went for disaster relief or refugee aid. The two exceptions were the work of mission societies that, throughout the nineteenth and early twentieth centuries, began to devote a significant part of their resources for technical assistance in education and health and the Carnegie Philanthropy, which built a series of libraries throughout the United Kingdom between 1890 and 1917 and supported scientific research and various studies on behalf of peace during the same era.[14]

The Middle East

In the 1920s several voluntary organizations began to deal with some of the longer-term problems underlying poverty uncovered during relief efforts carried out during the war and its immediate aftermath. The Committee for Relief in the Near East—founded in 1915 to assist Greek, Syrian, Arab, and Armenian refugees and war victims during the disintegration of the Ottoman Empire—continued its relief work up until the mid-1920s. It received contributions from Protestant churches throughout the United States as well as strong encouragement from the U.S. government since it attempted to head off the spread of Russian influence in the Middle East in the post–World War I era.

When the pressing problems requiring relief had subsided, the committee commissioned a study by an outside fact-finding group to assess the needs of the region and to recommend whether American philanthropy should continue in the context of modernization already under way in the countries of the Near East. The subsequent report surveyed needs in education, health, welfare, agriculture, and industry. It recommended the continuance of American philanthropy, but suggested more coordination among American groups (Near East Relief itself, the YMCA, and various missionary schools and colleges). It also stressed the importance of working with indigenous public and private organizations in these countries to promote longer-term technical solutions to poverty through programs designed to enhance self-reliance (and thus help offset growing Russian influence in the region). This study gave a new direction for overseas aid programs that later was to become known as technical assistance.[15]

[14] Lissner, *Politics of Altruism*, p. 55; Curti, *American Philanthropy Abroad*, pp. 188–98, 227–28, 245–47, 249.

[15] Ross, Fry, and Sibley, *Near East and American Philanthropy*, pp. vii–xii, 289–98 (cited in Curti, *American Philanthropy Abroad*, p. 268).

Between 1915 and 1930, Near East Relief sent over $617.4 million in cash collected in U.S. Protestant congregations to the region, along with $169.6 million in food aid supplies donated by the U.S. government, railroad companies, and foreign governmetns. In addition to assisting refugees and orphans in the post war years, however, it also began new industries and disseminated advanced agricultural methods including better seeds and improved strains of cattle. In 1930 Near East Relief became the Near East Foundation, which continues to operate today, sending nearly half a million dollars in aid annually to rural populations of the Middle East and Africa through technical training programs and demonstration projects in agriculture and disease control.[16]

Various American Jewish organizations became increasingly active after World War I in the Middle East as well, supporting Zionist settlers in Palestine—promised, but later denied, a homeland by the British Balfour Declaration. The American Organization of Rehabilitation through Training (American ORT) was founded in this period (1922), and along with other Jewish organizations it began to emphasize self-help projects among settlers in Palestine enhancing long-term economic and social development, especially in agriculture.[17]

The Far East

Parallel shifts away from an exclusive focus on relief to more emphasis on technical aid began to occur during the 1920s in the Far East as well, especially among American missionary societies, relief agencies, and foundations active in China. Rising feelings of nationalism in China in the 1920s precipitated criticisms (in China itself, as well as in Europe and the United States) of paternalistic and religiously dogmatic methods of Chinese mission schools. A reevaluation of missionary activities carried out in the 1920s produced a new approach that emphasized the promotion of social welfare, no longer as a means for religious conversion but as a value in itself in testimony to Christian beliefs. Hospitals, clinics, and the training of doctors received increasing support in mission budgets thereafter, and more responsibilities were given to native Chinese in administering Christian institutions. Efforts were also made to avoid waste resulting from duplication of energies among various mission societies and to reduce competition in fund-raising.[18]

Several serious famines and floods in China in the late 1920s also stimulated more coordinated action by secular U.S. PVOs active in relief work in that country. Six U.S. and fourteen Chinese groups formed the International Fam-

[16] Latourette, *Christianity in a Revolutionary Age*, vol. 5, p. 295; AID, *Voluntary Foreign Aid Programs*, 1982–83, pp. 15, 31.

[17] Bolling, *Private Foreign Aid*, p. 14.

[18] Commission of Appraisal, *Rethinking Missions*; Lamberton, *St. John's University of Shanghai*, pp. 110–11 (both cited in Curti, *American Philanthropy Abroad*, pp. 329, 331).

ine Relief Committee in 1920. Throughout the decade some of its members, under the inspiration of the American Red Cross, gave attention to longer-term solutions to disasters by including work-relief projects in their programs, such as well digging, tree planting, road construction, and dam building.[19]

China was also the focus of much of the innovative work in medical education funded by the Rockefeller Foundation. It spent nearly $302.2 million for this purpose between the end of World War I and 1949, when the Communists came to power. In the 1930s in China it also began experiments in agricultural demonstration and rural reconstruction. The foundation contributed to the building or improvement of medical training institutions in other parts of the world—Brazil, Lebanon, Singapore, Thailand, and the South Pacific area. Its International Health Division organized in 1929 was a pioneer in the area of public health through support for the training of medical professionals and paraprofessionals abroad and through its experiments in bringing major diseases under control in tropical countries. In the early 1940s the foundation also began experiments in Mexico to improve food crop production (especially corn, wheat, and beans) as a solution to world hunger.[20]

While these efforts by U.S. PVOs were on a modest scale with resources nowhere near able to meet global needs, much of what was going on during the interwar period was breaking new ground for all future overseas aid, private as well as public. Relief was gradually giving way to a focus on longer-term technical solutions, and it was the private nonprofit sector, not governments, which was taking the lead in this new direction of overseas aid.

In fact, when President Truman established the U.S. Technical Cooperation Administration (TCA) in 1950, as will be described later, it drew to a considerable extent upon the expertise of those involved in the early PVO technical programs in the 1920s, 1930s, and 1940s. Moreover, the innovative experiments in health and agriculture supported by some groups in the interwar period (e.g., the Rockefeller Foundation) led to scientific breakthroughs that had permanent and widespread beneficial results. They produced the Green Revolution in the 1960s and 1970s, and made possible the worldwide availability of vaccines against various tropical diseases in the post–World War II era.[21]

Growth of Nonprofit Aid

Between 1919 and 1939, the total American contribution to voluntary organizations for overseas work was over $8.3 billion. Seventy percent of these resources ($5.8 billion) were channeled through religiously affiliated organizations. Protestant groups sent $4.2 billion mainly to India, China, and Japan, with substantial grants to Latin America and Africa. Catholic organizations

[19] Curti, *American Philanthropy Abroad*, pp. 348–58.
[20] Ibid., p. 337; Bolling, *Private Foreign Aid*, pp. 49–57.
[21] Lissner, *Politics of Altruism*, p. 56; Bolling, *Private Foreign Aid*, pp. 47–49.

collection $617.1 million, primarily for Europe and China. The American Jewish community contributed $1 billion, almost all of which went to suffering Jews in Poland, Germany, and Palestine. Nonsectarian PVOs gave the other 30 percent ($2.5 billion) for educational, scientific, and humanitarian purposes, mainly in China and countries bordering the eastern Mediterranean.[22]

This interwar period was also a period of rapid growth in the overall number of U.S. PVOs. Fifteen (18.8 percent) of the 80 largest U.S. PVOs in 1980 began between 1918 and 1938 (see tables 1–3, appendix C). Some of these were created primarily to engage in overseas relief, as conflicts and natural disasters ocurred again in the 1930s in various parts of the world. Others, however, from the start included more of a technical or educational orientation to their work influenced by the new trends among PVOs begun in the 1920s.[23]

Some new overseas aid-sending NGOs emerged in Europe and Canada as well during the interwar period, which were created primarily to do relief work. Today they are among the largest still in operation, and several include a significant (or exclusive) focus on development-type work.[24]

Nonprofits as Complements to Government Interests

All of the contributions by missionaries, PVOs, and foundations to technical training and institution building in the Middle East, Africa, and China during the interwar years undoubtedly improved the quality of life of the respective recipient populations. Nevertheless, more than altruism was involved.

U.S. business and government interests were growing in these areas of the world after World War I, and missionary, PVO, and foundation activities in the technical field were a means of establishing more long-term U.S. influence in these regions. Improving human capital through education and medicine expanded worker productivity, promoted modern agricultural and industrial culture, and created trained cadres of indigenous leaders favorable to Western trade and investment. Just as the British Colonial Office by the 1920s was adapting and promoting the Tuskegee/Phelps-Stokes philosophy of vocational

[22] Curti, *American Philanthropy Abroad*, pp. 410–11.

[23] The new American PVOs created between the two world wars that at the beginning emphasized relief (most of which now include an emphasis on development) were Save the Children Federation (1932), the International Rescue Committee (1933), Foster Parents Plan USA (1937), and Christian Children's Fund (CCF, 1938). Those founded in this era that from the beginning had a significant development thrust included Institute of International Education (1919), Mennonite Central Committee (1920), American ORT (1922), Planned Parenthood Federation (1922), Catholic Medical Mission Board (1924), Experiment in International Living (1932), the Ford Foundation (1936), and the Association for Voluntary Sterilization (1937).

[24] These European private organizations included Swedish Save the Children (1919), World University Service in Switzerland (1919), Danish Church Aid (DANCHURCHAID, 1922), Canadian Save the Children (CANSAVE, 1923), and Canadian Foster Parents Plan (1937).

training to solidify its control in Africa (with the help of the Carnegie Foundation), U.S. corporately sponsored foundations and missionary organizations were trying in the same era to promote economic or cultural change in the Middle and Far East that would favor long-term U.S. interests.[25]

WORLD WAR II PERIOD

U.S. Government Use of PVOs

The World War II period and its aftermath produced a further stimulus for the growth in the number and scope of transnational nonprofit organizations. Again, as in the early years of World War I, nonprofit groups became the vehicle to provide rapid assistance to victims of war and also the means whereby the U.S. government could circumvent neutrality restrictions and help European countries fighting Nazism. During the first year of the conflict (1939–1940), 362 new relief agencies registered under the terms of the Neutrality Act of 1939 (which required government monitoring of all U.S. voluntary agencies collecting money for relief purposes in belligerent nations). Throughout the entire period of neutrality (1939–1941), 545 PVOs registered with the U.S. government to carry out relief work in Great Britain, France, the Netherlands, Norway, Poland, Greece, Italy, or Palestine.[26]

Between 1939 and 1941 the total value of foreign war relief sent overseas by U.S. PVOs was $284.7 million. Approximately 80 percent of these funds were donated by those in the United States with family or ethnic ties to people residing in the European or Near Eastern countries aided. The total amount of U.S. PVO aid from private sources to all foreign nations during the same two-year period reached $1.3 billion, including assistance to China, Latin America, Africa, or other areas of the world outside the conflict. As part of this, the U.S. government allocated $385.8 million for the American Red Cross in 1940 and 1941 to aid war victims in Europe, the Middle East, Asia, and Africa—but not in Nazi-controlled or occupied countries after June 1940.[27]

Hence, well over one-fourth (29.7 percent—$385.8 million of $1.3 billion) of U.S. PVO aid sent to all foreign countries during the first two years of the war, when the United States was officially neutral, came from the U.S. government. This was channeled through the American Red Cross to assist civil-

---

[25] Brown, "Rockefeller Medicine in China."

[26] Curti, *American Philanthropy Abroad*, p. 414; Bolling, *Private Foreign Aid*, p. 16; Ringland, "Organization of Voluntary Foreign Aid," pp. 384, 390. Several of those founded during World War II continue to be active today and are among the largest U.S. aid-sending nonprofits. These include the Unitarian Universalist Service Committee (UUSC, 1939), the Board of Global Ministries of the United Methodist Church (1941), Catholic Relief Services (CRS, 1943), and World Relief Corporation (1944).

[27] Curti, *American Philanthropy Abroad*, pp. 427–28, 438–40; Ringland, "Organization of Voluntary Foreign Aid," p. 391.

ians in countries fighting the Nazis (particularly Great Britain after June 1940). Moreover, the U.S. government revoked the licenses of more than three hundred U.S. PVOs engaged in overseas assistance by the end of the neutrality period in order to reduce competition and duplication, or in some cases for purportedly cooperating too closely with governments in Axis-dominated countries.[28]

Once the United States formally entered the war in late 1941, private overseas U.S. philanthropy was brought under even tighter control by the U.S. government and made an integral part of the U.S. war effort (as it had been during U.S. engagement in World War I). The War Relief Control Board set up by President Roosevelt in 1942 (modeled on Canadian procedures set up by their War Charities Act) was given the responsibility to exercise continuous oversight of U.S. nonprofit organizations active in overseas aid for the remainder of the war. It was to register PVOs and coordinate PVO fund-raising activities, define ethical standards of solicitation, regulate the timing of fund drives, require accurate PVO accounting, and further eliminate or merge agencies in the interest of efficiency. Moreover, the board exerted pressure on many U.S. PVOs to get the word *American* incorporated into their names so that the origin of the aid would be clearly known abroad.[29]

The board reduced the number of PVOs in operation to eliminate duplication. It limited the duration of PVO fund-raising campaigns and forbade other nonprofit agencies to solicit when the American Red Cross was conducting drives or when U.S. War Bond sales were going on. Administrative costs of PVOs were thus reduced from 10.6 percent of total expenditures in 1942 to 4.8 percent in 1944, and the overall number of PVOs sending aid abroad declined from 223 in late 1941 to sixty-one in 1945. U.S. private philanthropy abroad thus became an integral and more efficient part of the U.S. war effort.[30]

In addition to monitoring and weeding out U.S. PVOs, the War Relief Control Board also stimulated the creation of a new private agency with close ties to the U.S. government—the National War Fund—to provide coordination and reduce competition for private funds among the agencies it certified. Private contributions to U.S. PVOs engaged in overseas aid did, in fact, increase dramatically after 1941. In 1941 the combined total of aid sent overseas by all U.S. voluntary agencies was $615 million (almost 60 percent by nonsectarian groups). By 1945 the annual total had reached $1.4 billion (two-thirds by non-

---

[28] Curti, *American Philanthropy Abroad*, pp. 429–33; Ringland, "Organization of Voluntary Foreign Aid," p. 390.

[29] Curti, *American Philanthropy Abroad*, p. 453. Several agencies altered their titles accordingly—such as the American Relief for France (formerly the French Relief Fund), the American Relief for Holland (previously the Queen Wilhelmina Fund), and the American Society for Russian Relief) (originally Russian War Relief).

[30] Ibid., p. 454; Ringland, "Organization of Voluntary Foreign Aid," p. 390; Bolling, *Private Foreign Aid*, p. 16.

sectarian organizations), and in the last year of the war over three-fifths of this aid was in the form of gifts in kind (food, medicine, clothing, blankets).[31]

In 1942 the U.S. government also created the Office of Foreign Relief and Rehabilitation Operations (OFRRO) to aid over the long term the needy survivors of the war, particularly with U.S. grain reserves that it began to buy and store during that year. It was absorbed a year later into the United Nations Relief and Rehabilitation Administration (UNRRA), which distributed over $15 billion in resources to war victims and refugees between 1943 and 1947 (when it was terminated)—70 percent of which was donated by the U.S. government and much of it in food.[32]

Amidst growing concerns among voluntary agencies that they might not be involved in rehabilitation efforts after the war (especially if private contributions declined when the conflict ended), PVO administrators and supporters in 1943 began to speak out on the necessity of continued private aid even after the hostilities ceased. In the same year the first federation of U.S. PVOs—the American Council of Voluntary Agencies for Foreign Service, ACVAFS (with 19 members)—was created at the urging of the War Relief Control Baord to work in a coordinated way with the U.S. War Department and UNRRA. Both of these public agencies were to exercise jurisdiction over American relief agencies in U.S.-occupied countries after the war. The ACVAFS was not an operational agency. Rather, it served as a coordinating body to promote greater consensus and cooperation among its members on matters of common concern through its functional, country, regional, and ad hoc committees. These subgroups, made up of representatives of member agencies with considerable overseas experience, were of continuous service for the remainder of the war to various agencies of the U.S. government, especially in resettling European war refugees in the United States.[33]

Hence, during World War II American PVOs became even more closely identified with U.S. government war objectives than they had been in World War I. Almost all of their resources were raised from private sources for humanitarian purposes abroad, but most of this charity was sent only to allied countries (even when the United States was officially neutral). Moreover, once the United States entered the war, it imposed strict limits and monetary procedures on PVOs to insure their maximum support for U.S. war policies.

PVOs in Canada and Europe: Some Dissent from the War Effort

In Canada and Europe during the late 1930s and early 1940s, several new nonprofits were created in response to the destruction and suffering caused by

---

[31] Curti, *American Philanthropy Abroad*, pp. 452, 455–456, 462.

[32] Curti, *American Philanthropy Abroad*, pp. 456–57, 483–84.

[33] Ibid., pp. 457–59; Ringland, "Organization of Voluntary Foreign Aid," p. 385. Telephone interview with the late Bernard Confers, LWR.

World War II.[34] Unlike the situation in the United States, these European non-profits (or NGOs) were not always in agreement with the policies being pursued by their home governments. In fact, at times they openly opposed them.

Ecumenical Aid Service (CIMADE) was established by French Protestant churches in 1939 to assist refugees fleeing the advance of Nazism in Europe. Even after the surrender of France in 1940, CIMADE continued operations, and throughout the remainder of the war ministered to the needs of political prisoners in detention centers in France. On several occasions it protested to the Vichy government regarding the treatment of captives and also used its own church networks (as well as contacts with the French underground) to assist Jews in France seeking to avoid deportation to Germany.[35]

The Oxford Famine Relief Committee in Great Britain was founded by a group of faculty and students at Oxford University in 1942. Many of them were members of the Society of Friends (Quakers) who were concerned about the effects on innocent civilians of the policy of unconditional surrender of Germany agreed upon by allied leaders at a summit meeting in Casablanca that same year. This decision required a total blockade of countries under Nazi domination and also forbade all aid to noncombatants in these nations.

By this time there was a dissident mood growing among a number of prominent British citizens—led by Dr. George Bell, the Anglican Bishop of Chichester—who were arguing publicly against the policy of total war. They protested the condemnation of the whole German people and opposed the allied demand for unconditional surrender of the Axis Powers on grounds that it would merely unite the Germans behind Hitler and prolong the war. They also criticized the indiscriminate bombing of German cities as both immoral and futile and protested the economic blockade of the continent, which they argued hurt not the Germans but innocent people in the occupied countries sympathetic to the allies.[36]

The Oxford Famine Relief Committee (later called Oxfam) was formed in the midst of this public dissent. It organized a delegation to the British Ministry of Economic Warfare, followed by a written petition with eight thousand signatures demanding a lifting of the blockade so that relief supplies could be shipped into Belgium and Greece. The petition was refused on the grounds that such aid might benefit the German occupying forces in those countries.

[34] In Canada these included the World University Service of Canada (1939) and the Canadian Organization for Rehabilitation Through Training (Canadian ORT, 1940). In Europe, which bore the brunt of the war's' destruction, several new organizations emerged to assist refugees or to aid starving victims during the conflict. These included the French Ecumenical Aid Service (CIMADE, 1939), in Great Britain both the Oxford Famine Relief Committee (1942, later named Oxfam), and Christian Reconstruction in Europe (1942, renamed in 1952 Christian Aid), and the Danish Association for International Cooperation (1944).
[35] Ecumenical Aid Service (CIMADE), "La CIMADE a 40 ans."
[36] Whitaker, *Bridge of People*, pp. 14–15.

The committee, however, mounted a modest aid effort of its own by sending aid to the Greek Red Cross for noncombatant famine victims.[37]

Thus, although the vast majority of North Atlantic nonprofits acted as complements to and extenders of nation-state interests during World War II, there were some that took a public stance (totally supported by private funds) in opposition to the policies of their home governments. Such occurred only in Europe and were associated with Protestant religious communities in France and Great Britain.[38]

CONCLUSIONS

Since the sixteenth century many charitable organizations in North Atlantic countries have been important transnational actors. They have performed a variety of tasks beyond their own borders ranging from religious evangelization, education, cultural exchange and promotion, and disaster relief. All of these functions long predate more recent activities of the transnational nonprofit sector in the realm of socioeconomic development.

During this long period, North Atlantic governments have valued the role charitable agencies played as complements of, and sometimes as surrogates for, their own foreign policies. In fact, the earliest international charities— European Christian missionary societies created between the sixteenth and eighteenth centuries—from the beginning received significant financial aid from their respective home governments for their promotion of Western cultural values in colonial societies. The majority of international charities that have emerged in the last one hundred years, although not subsidized at their creation by home governments, also clearly served their governments' interests abroad through the various cultural and relief activities they performed.

The United States government in particular, beginning in the World War I era, came to see the value of PVOs when it could not act officially to promote its interests abroad. The PVOs were surrogates for U.S. government interests in neutrality periods during the two world wars and in the Soviet Union in the early 1920s. They also helped extend Western values and interests into areas where U.S. government influence was tenuous (the Middle East and China during the interwar period).

Unlike Europe, where missionary societies existed from the beginning, the U.S. government in the early twentieth century seldom provided financial subsidies to PVOs (with the exception of food subsidies to the ARA for the Soviet

---

[37] Ibid. See also Stamp, "Oxfam and Development," p. 85.

[38] In the United States, opposition to the policies of total war during the 1940s was much weaker and scattered than in Great Britain. Toward the end of the war, a few religious leaders and other individuals did criticize indiscriminate bombing of German cities, but there was no active movement against such policies in this country, such as occurred in Great Britain. See Ford, "Morality of Obliteration Bombing," 261–309, and Brittain, "Massacre by Bombing."

Union in the early 1920s and financial aid to the American Red Cross during World War II). It relied instead on legal regulations to integrate PVOs into its foreign policy objectives during World War II. Moreover, administrators of PVOs voluntarily endorsed U.S. government policies abroad (tacitly or explicitly). In no way did they consider themselves at odds with official government objectives.

It was during World War II—and only in Europe, where the brutality of the conflict was experienced first hand—when some distancing of international charities began to occur from the policies pursued by their home governments. The totalitarian and genocidal policies of the Third Reich and the severe consequences for innocent noncombatants on the continent of the unconditional surrender strategy of the allies precipitated this opposition. Groups in France and Great Britain expressed open dissent to positions of their home governments and worked through newly created NGOs to achieve their objectives.

In both instances—CIMADE in France, the Oxford Famine Relief Committee in Great Britain—their resistance failed to alter significantly the policies in question (deportation of Jews from Vichy France and the allied blockade of the continent). Both NGOs, however, took some action in opposition to the governments in power in their respective societies to assist those suffering the brutality of war. In each case, these nonprofits were not isoalted actors but were parts of larger groups (albeit small minorities) in these two countries resisting or beginning to question some of the war strategies pursued by their governments.

Both of these examples were forerunners of trends that have emerged in several European countries and in Canada in more recent years. There a significant number of international charities have come to oppose what they consider to be morally questionable policies of their respective governments towards developing countries. As will be described in chapter 5, these organizations are also integrated into and are expressions of wider domestic political movements dissenting from several official government policies toward the Third World.

CHAPTER THREE

U.S. Private Foreign Aid since World War II: Exporting the American Dreams of Self-Reliance and Democracy

WORLD WAR II AFTERMATH (1945–1950)

In the immediate postwar years, U.S. PVOs continued to play a critical role in overseas relief. Their activities expanded considerably as liberated European countries faced after May 1945 the immense task of recovery. Although the U.S. government in 1948 inaugurated the five-year Marshall Plan (valued at $59.2 billion) for the reconstruction of Europe, 500 million people—almost one-third of the world's population—were suffering from food shortages. As a result, private contributions to PVOs for relief and reconstruction (especially in Europe) increased dramatically in the late 1940s.

American citizens with ethnic, family, and religious ties to Europe wanted to assist in the alleviation of hunger, sickness, and homelessness. PVOs, due to their excellent reputation of relief during the war, continued to receive significant private philanthropy for the reconstruction of Europe. Between 1946 and 1949, U.S. charities sent abroad $5.4 billion, over 40 percent more in constant dollars than the amount they gave between 1942 and 1945 ($3.8 billion).[1]

Beginning of Public Subsidies to PVOs

The U.S. government recognized the importance of voluntary agencies in complementing its own new commitments in foreign assistance in the postwar period. It took a number of steps—with the cooperation, agreement, and sometimes urging from the U.S. PVOs themselves—to continue the close collaborative relationships established during World War II between its own agencies and the nonprofit sector in overseas aid.

In 1946 President Truman dissolved the War Relief Control Board. However, "to tie together the government and private programs in the field of

---

[1] Curti, *American Philanthropy Abroad*, p. 507. Several new U.S. charities also came into being when the war ended to assist in the rehabilitation of Europe—Lutheran World Relief (1945), Cooperative for American Remittances to Europe (CARE, 1945, later renamed Cooperative for American Relief Everywhere), Church World Service (1946), Meals for Millions (1946), and Direct Relief International (1948).

foreign relief,'' in the same year he appointed an Advisory Committee on Voluntary Foreign Aid attached to the Department of State and composed of representatives from PVOs and the government. Although federal licensing of PVOs was no longer required, other forms of regulation continued. These affected export licenses, allocations of government food, and public relations activities.

The new advisory committee also invited PVOs to continue on a voluntary basis what they had been obligated to do by law during the war—namely, to record with the government for public inspection quarterly financial statements, monthly reports of foreign money and commodity transfers, periodic budgets and public audits, and current reports on domestic and overseas operations. All 61 of the U.S. PVOs licensed by the War Relief Control Board and still active in overseas assistance at the end of World War II responded positively to this request.[2] In return for such cooperation, these charities became eligible for the first time to receive assistance in cash and goods from the U.S. government, a privilege only the American Red Cross had previously enjoyed.

In 1947 the Congress appropriated $24.5 million to pay the overseas transportation costs of voluntary agency supplies determined to be "essential supplements"—food, clothing, and expendable medical and hospital supplies—to the government's own foreign relief. The U.S. government also sold at cost to a new cooperative venture created by twenty-two U.S. PVOs in 1946 over 7.5 million army surplus Ten-in-One Rations. This new PVO was called CARE (Cooperative for American Remittances to Europe, later renamed Cooperative for American Relief Everywhere). These supplies were then transported and sold in Europe by CARE at $25 and $50 each to friends and relatives of U.S. citizens. By the end of 1948, CARE had distributed nearly $236.3 million worth of relief supplies in Europe, Japan, and Korea, much of it food bought at subsidized prices from the U.S. government.[3]

One year later, the legislation that authorized the Marshall Plan—the Economic Cooperation Act of 1948—also provided for public subsidies to cover transportation costs for all relief shipments to Europe by U.S. PVOs registered with the Advisory Committee on Voluntary Foreign Aid. It also authorized the secretary of state to negotiate arrangements with European countries participating in the Marshall Plan for the duty-free entry of PVO relief supplies and defrayment of inland transport costs from European counterpart funds. The Mutual Security Act of 1951 extended these reimbursements for transportation of PVO supplies to include shipments to other countries eligible for U.S. government aid, especially those that were a major focus of U.S. security and

[2] Ringland, "Organization of Voluntary Foreign Aid," pp. 386, 390.
[3] Curti, *American Philanthropy Abroad*, pp. 491–502.

economic interests—the Arab states, Israel, India, Pakistan, South Korea, and the American republics.[4]

Reasons for New Government Interest in PVOs

Although these new public subsidies for PVOs were due in part to lobbying efforts by the newly created PVO federation ACVAFS (which wanted to expand the institutional apparatus its PVO members had created during the war years), a major impetus came from the Congress. The United States for security reasons had to contribute to the recovery of Western Europe (to check further Soviet expansion) and also begin aid to other parts of the world where new U.S. security and economic interests were growing in the wake of the demise of European colonialism (especially Asia and the Middle East). The consensus in Congress in the late 1940s was that it would be easier for Americans to support new U.S. government aid programs abroad if they observed and supported the success of private agencies in overseas relief and reconstruction efforts. By providing subsidies to PVOs, the Congress would enhance the relief work of PVOs, give PVOs more visibility in the eyes of Americans, and thereby hopefully build a wider base of public support for all foreign assistance programs, governmental and private.[5]

An added reason that Congress in the late 1940s decided to channel some public resources through charities was the fact that it wanted to maximize the possibility that such aid would reach those most in need abroad. New official bilateral economic aid programs had to be channeled through host governments, some of which were plagued by corruption or poor administration.[6] Multilateral aid programs such as the UNRRA faced the same difficulties and could not bypass corrupt or inept governments in attempts to aid the poor in host countries. The Soviets also had a role in the administration of resources by these intergovernmental organizations, and this made the U.S. government reluctant to channel significant amounts of its resources through such institutions.

After 1947, in fact, U.S. government contributions for the relief work of the UNRRA (which constituted the vast majority of that agency's funds) ceased because the U.S. government could not control the final destination of such aid. U.S. private voluntary agencies, however, were free to bypass foreign governments and thus could serve as a guarantee that at least some U.S. government assistance would reach the poorest, not be wasted or spent on host government programs not directly benefiting low-income people or be subjected to Soviet pressure to get as much UNRRA funds as possible into Eastern Europe.

[4] Ringland, "Organization of Voluntary Foreign Aid," p. 387.
[5] Telephone interview with the late Bernard Confers, LWR.
[6] Ibid.

A final stimulus to U.S. government interest in PVOs in the post–World War II era was their usefulness as channels for disposing of surplus agricultural commodities. During World War II the U.S. government had guaranteed high food prices to farmers to stimulate agricultural production for the war effort. It maintained price supports in the immediate postwar period to prevent the severe decline in the U.S. agricultural sector as had happened in the years immediately following World War I. In the post–World War I era, as discussed in chapter 2, the Congress had authorized subsidies to Herbert Hoover's ARA to buy up U.S. surplus food products for the starving in the USSR.

Building on this precedent, the Agricultural Act of 1949 authorized the U.S. Department of Agriculture to donate surplus farm products (butter, cheese, and rice) in U.S. government reserves to U.S. PVOs registered with the Advisory Committee on Voluntary Foreign Aid. Through such a strategy additional assistance would reach Europe and more U.S. food surpluses would be disposed of in a way that did not detract from farm prices at home. Moreover, by enhancing the relief efforts of U.S. PVOs for individual Europeans, U.S. government personnel could devote more of their own time and energies to administering larger programs (authorized by the Economic Cooperation Act of 1948) aimed at rebuilding Europe's physical infrastructure—roads, communications, energy, and industry.[7]

Thus a convergence of interests among private donors, PVO administrators, and U.S. public officials in the immediate postwar period led to the expansion of U.S. PVO activities overseas (especially in Europe) and to a strengthening of PVO-government ties. Private citizens in the United States wanted to contribute to the relief of immediate suffering caused by the war (especially among relatives and friends in Europe), and PVO executives wanted to continue service networks created during the war. Moreover, groups in the U.S. Congress, the Department of State, and the Department of Agriculture all saw PVOs as useful instruments to accomplish various government objectives (1) to mobilize public opinion in favor of new U.S. commitments abroad, (2) to dispose of surplus agricultural commodities, (3) to bypass corrupt or inept foriegn governments, and (4) to circumvent multilateral organizations in which the Soviets exercised a voice but whose costs were shouldered primarily by the United States.

U.S. PVOs DURING THE COLD WAR (1950–1960)

Expanding Technical and Social Service Aid by Church-related PVOs

In the 1950s many U.S. missionary societies expanded projects that built up technical infrastructure, such as schools, hospitals, and training programs.

---

[7] Sullivan, "Politics of Altruism: Introduction to the Food-for-Peace Partnership," pp. 763–64.

These trends, begun by some missionary societies in the 1920s in China and the Near East as described in chapter 2, came to constitute a more sizeable part of the activities of many missionaries in other parts of Asia, Africa, and Latin America by the 1950s. Newly independent countries received greater attention from U.S. Protestant and Catholic religious groups, especially after the 1949 victory of Chinese Communist forces in 1949 made ex-China missionaries available for work elsewhere. Emphasis was placed on local self-reliance in Asia, Africa, and Latin America by training leaders in technical fields and by supporting programs aimed at eliminating illiteracy, disease, and inefficient agriculture. In such a way, missionaries hoped to demonstrate their secular usefulness to host country populations amidst rising feelings of nationalism in the postcolonial era and to check the attraction of communism among the chronically poor in such societies.

In 1950 the combined expenditures by major U.S. Protestant denominations for overseas technical assistance was estimated at $168.6 million. By 1956 $262.2 million was directly linked with social welfare and education, especially in Asia, Africa, and Latin America. This accounted for about 50 percent of the overseas budgets of Protestant missionary societies that supported 23,532 personnel abroad. In 1956 U.S. Catholics provided $201.7 million to support 5,000 missionaries overseas. They were sponsoring over 65,000 projects in technical assistance in developing countries by 1958, reaching as many as 100,000 people.[8]

Several of the new church-supported relief agencies set up during or just after World War II—Catholic Relief Services (CRS), Church World Service (CWS), Lutheran World Relief (LWR)—were not controlled by church boards as were the old missionary societies established in the late eighteenth and nineteenth centuries. Like the American Friends Service Committee (AFSC) and the Unitarian Universalist Service Committee (UUSC), they were created to provide overseas assistance by their respective denominations but not to engage in proselytizing. They were service agencies ready to help meet the basic material needs of all groups regardless of creed and did not have the sectarian image that characterized some of the older missionary groups.[9]

As these new church-supported PVOs shifted their focus away from Europe after the late 1940s and devoted more attention to Asia, Africa, and Latin America, they received increasing U.S. government subsidies in food and ocean freight reimbursements. They also began to receive small government grants for their technical assistance projects. Church-related agencies came to dominate the field of voluntary foreign aid once again, since many of the ad hoc ethnically oriented secular groups set up during World War II to aid Eu-

[8] Curti, *American Philanthropy Abroad*, pp. 576–77; Bock, *Fifty Years of Technical Assistance*, p. vii; Considine, *Technical Assistance Activities*, p. 17.

[9] Bolling, *Private Foreign Aid*, p. 36.

rope dissolved. Between 1946 and 1953, 64 percent ($3.2 billion of $5 billion) of all U.S. PVO overseas assistance was administered by church-affiliated organizations, reestablishing the pattern set during the interwar period (1919–1939).[10]

PVOs Assist U.S. Government in Technical Aid

After the recovery of Europe, when the United States government began to commit itself to longer-term foreign aid to the newly emerging nations, it turned to PVOs for advice on how to set up effective technical assistance programs. Organizations such as the Near East Foundation and several church-affiliated institutions were consulted by the U.S. Technical Cooperation Administration (TCA)—set up in 1950 to carry out President Truman's Point Four program of technical aid. The TCA asked PVOs for advice in effective techniques of service delivery to developing countries, particularly in the Middle East and Asia. Some nonprofits were also given contracts by the TCA (the Near East Foundation, AFSC, UUSC, CRS) to enlarge their own training and agricultural programs in those regions (Near East Foundation in Iran) or begin programs in new regions (AFSC in India, UUSC in Cambodia, CRS in Vietnam). Between 1951 and 1956 the TCA allocated $916.6 million in contracts for technical aid abroad through U.S. private institutions, and over one-half (approximately $411 million) was awarded to American nonprofit service agencies.[11]

U.S. government grants to PVOs were given according to U.S. foreign policy objectives, since they were made available primarily for projects in countries the United States had targeted as security priorities amidst its growing preoccupation with communism in the 1950s. In awarding contracts to PVOs, the TCA set down clear guidelines in 1951 and 1952 to guarantee that PVO activities would be closely coordinated with U.S. bilateral aid programs and according to the priorities of the host governments. In addition to demanding that all PVO programs supported by the U.S. government be nonsectarian, involve no proselytizing, and be carried out by those with sound administrative experience, the guidelines also required that host governments first request the services of voluntary agencies before PVOs entered their territories and that PVOs coordinate with U.S. bilateral programs of technical aid when under U.S. government contract.[12]

One of the most innovative areas in technical assistance, carried out by church-affiliated PVOs in the 1950s in close cooperation with and with finan-

[10] Ringland, "Organization of Voluntary Foreign Aid," p. 391.

[11] "Doing Good Abroad," 141.

[12] Curti, *American Philanthropy Abroad*, pp. 608–15; telephone interview with Bruce Nichols, Carnegie Council on Ethics and International Affairs; Hoskins, "Voluntary Agencies and Foundations," p. 65.

cial support from the U.S. government, was International Voluntary Services (IVS). Set up in 1953 with U.S. government aid by Protestant and Catholic overseas missionary and service agencies, IVS helped coordinate the assignment of young volunteers to developing countries for technical assistance in education, agriculture, housing, health, and sanitation. It drew upon the experience of other church organizations overseas (many of which relied on expatriate volunteers for short-term commitments), and in some ways paralleled an earlier European private counterpart—International Civil Service (SCI)—to be described in chapter 4. The IVS was established in the United States to align closely church-related sending agencies to the new technical programs sponsored by the U.S. government overseas and thus to enhance the impact of overall U.S. efforts in foreign technical training.[13]

The board of directors of IVS was soon expanded to include representatives of secular institutions (land-grant colleges and the World Federation of Country Women). Substantial grants and donations were subsequently received from government, foundations, and businesses. By 1960 projects had been completed in Egypt, Jordan, Iraq, and Nepal, and in the same year 60 young American volunteers were working at the local level of Ghana, Vietnam, and Laos. The IVS received commendation from several foreign governments and the U.S. Congress, and it served as a forerunner and model for the U.S. Peace Corps created in the Department of State during the early months of the Kennedy administration in 1961.[14]

PVOs at War Again

During the Korean War years (1950–1953), U.S. PVOs also proved to be useful instruments in the accomplishment of U.S. government policies abroad. At the urging of the departments of State and Defense and representatives of the United Nations, several PVOs—including AFSC, CWS, LWR, CRS, and the YMCA set up a cooperative to collect clothing for Korea—the American Relief for Korea (ARK). All voluntary cash contributions were channeled through the Advisory Committee on Voluntary Foreign Aid in the Department of State. The U.S. Army shipped and distributed free of charge all PVO cash and clothing contributions (which by 1954 exceeded $44.5 million) through the facilities of the United Nations Command and the South Korean government.[15]

In such a way, PVOs once again became closely integrated into the overall war objectives of the U.S. government. In doing so, they took some of the burden off government officials in carrying out relief projects in areas where

[13] Curti, *American Philantropy Abroad*, p. 615.
[14] Ibid., p. 616.
[15] Ibid., pp. 561–62; Ringland, "Organization of Voluntary Foreign Aid," p. 388.

vital interests of the United States were at stake and its armed forces engaged in combat.

PVOs as Expanding Conduits for Surplus Food Distribution

In the aftermath of the Korean War, U.S. government food surplus reserves rose dramatically. Farm bloc interests in Congress pressed for an expansion of overseas distribution of U.S. government surplus food commodities so that prices in the U.S. domestic market would not plummet. The Agricultural Trade, Development, and Assistance Act of 1954 (PL 480) was passed to accomplish this, and PVOs received broader authorization to distribute government surplus food abroad. They were also given access to a larger variety of commodities than before, and the U.S. government absorbed transportation costs for shipments from Midwest storage bins to seaports. By 1956 these commodities included not only dairy products, but also wheat and wheat products, corn, and cornmeal. The Congress also agreed to pay the full cost of all ocean shipments of surplus goods by PVOs overseas. In 1953 the total tonnage of food shipped by PVOs was 140,000, but by 1956 this had jumped to 610,000 and was valued at $754.3 million.[16]

In the United States, therefore, in the post–World War II years, the arguments were made in the executive branch (persons in State and Defense), in the Congress (farm bloc representatives), and in PVOs themselves for official aid to nonprofits during peacetime. These converging pressures resulted in significant public grants in cash and commodities to many PVOs engaged in overseas work. Of the $5 billion of monetary and material aid sent overseas by PVOs (excluding the Red Cross) between 1946 and 1953, $525.9 million (10.5 percent) came either directly from the U.S. government ($347.9 million) or from various United Nations agencies ($178 million) with budgets supported primarily from the U.S. government.[17]

Overlapping Interests of Government and PVOs

Commenting in 1954 on these new cooperative arrangements between the PVOs and the U.S. government, Arthur Ringland, former consultant to the War Relief Control Board and executive director of its successor, the Advisory Committee on Voluntary Foreign Aid, emphasized how important the post–World War II period was in beginning a new era in government-PVO relations for peacetime. He also stressed that he believed that for PVO aid to be most productive it should be closely tied to government efforts abroad:

[16] Sullivan, "Politics of Altruism: Introduction to the Food-for-Peace Partnership," p. 764; Roberts, "Meals for Millions," p. 191; AID, *Look to the Future*, p. 56.
[17] Ringland, "Organization of Voluntary Foreign Aid," p. 391.

The President, when he enjoined the Advisory Committee upon its establishment [1946] to "tie together the governmental and private programs in the field of foreign relief," set up a benchmark that has been the point of reference in the relations of the Government and the voluntary agencies throughout the postwar years. This tying together has marked the most productive relief and rehabilitation operations of the registered voluntary agencies; for voluntary foreign aid is most productive when it complements public aid and that of all the local agencies in participating countries. . . .

. . . A pattern of organization has been developed adequate for participation in services of relief, rehabilitation, technical assistance, and self-help. To this end cooperation has been established by the agencies, shared by their constituencies, our Government, and the governments of the participating countries and their local social services. Such integration of operations assures the productive use abroad of the contributions of the public at home. The task of the Advisory Committee on Voluntary Foreign Aid, of the American Council of Voluntary Agencies for Foreign Service, and of the registered agencies, has been to assure this integration.[18]

A corresponding sentiment about the desirability of close integration of public and private U.S. aid efforts was voiced from the nonprofit side a few years later by ACVAFS. In a 1959 letter sent to the overseas field staffs of its member PVOs dealing with government surplus commodities (and accompanying a manual of distribution procedures), the Council concluded that

it is in the best interest of all responsible people that the voluntary agency be registered with government. This is a protection for the legitimate agency and tends to eliminate those which are not qualified to serve according to their declared intent. The voluntary agency has a special kind of function in rendering services which government and other private sources are not able to provide. The ideal is a partnership concept in which the work of the voluntary agency and other private sources complement the work of government in the service of mankind.[19]

Thus, as the U.S. government turned its attention from Europe to the developing world—where 80 new countries received independence in the 1950s and 1960s—PVOs did the same. When U.S. bilateral and multilateral aid was increasing in Asia, Africa, and Latin America after 1950, PVOs began shifting more of their attention to these same areas and in so doing also received increased government aid. In 1946, 85 percent of all PVO overseas assistance was sent to Europe. By 1960, however, 69 percent was either going to Asia (52 percent), Latin America (11 percent), or Africa (6 percent), with Europe receiving less than one-third (31 percent).[20]

[18] Ibid., pp. 386, 392.
[19] ACVAFS, "Letter to a Colleague," New York, March 1959 (cited in Hoskins, "Voluntary Agencies and Foundations," p. 65).
[20] AID, *Voluntary Foreign Aid Programs*, 1975, p. 19.

By the end of the 1950s, the fifty-five U.S. PVOs registered with the U.S. government were raising over $940.6 million a year on the average (from private and public sources) and involved millions of Americans as supporters or members. Abroad they contributed to projects in 103 countries, affecting the lives of several hundred million people.[21]

Just as PVOs had proved to be useful partners in furthering U.S. interests abroad in the massive reconstruction efforts in Europe during the immediate postwar period, they continued to act in close cooperation with the U.S. government in joint efforts for relief and technical aid in developing countries throughout the 1950s. During the Cold War period, when security concerns dominated U.S. government objectives in foreign aid, government policymakers considered PVOs to be effective organs in checking the spread of communism since they worked at the grass-roots level among poor sectors of developing countries and strengthened the network of private organizations in these nations. The PVOs also enhanced the image of American values among the recipients of their aid by softening suspicions that food and technical assistance were merely government-to-government instruments of power politics.[22]

A Small Minority of PVOs Distance Themselves from the U.S. Government

Some PVOs during the 1950s worried about the close association that was developing between nonprofits and the government as part of a strategy to stop communism. The AFSC in 1956 terminated its contractual arrangements with the ICA to provide technical assistance to community development projects in India when the U.S. government insisted that AFSC personnel be subject to a security check before being hired. Heifer Project International complained about the heavy emphasis being placed on all U.S. aid to fight communism and win military allies. The UUSC withdrew from U.S. government contracts because of delays, red tape, and indirect limits on its freedom.[23]

By and large, however, not many complaints were raised about the close integration of public and private overseas aid efforts. The overwhelming majority of nonprofit organizations felt that public subsidies enabled them to ac-

---

[21] Hoskins, "Voluntary Agencies and Foundations," pp. 58, 61–62. Several new U.S. PVOs were created in the 1950s to engage in technical assistance abroad. One was the Asia Foundation (1951), whose purpose was to provide support for educational, cultural exchange, and community development projects that strengthened private institutions in Southern Asia and the Far East. Others included the Population Council (1952) and the Pathfinder Fund (1957)—both of which focused on assisting in the dissemination of birth control information and techniques in developing countries. All three of these new secular nonprofit organizations received from the start significant contracts from the International Cooperation Agency (ICA), the successor to the TCA and the public agency responsible for implementing U.S. bilateral economic assistance abroad after 1953.

[22] Curti, *American Philanthropy Abroad*, p. 617.

[23] Ibid., pp. 612–13; Hoskins, "Voluntary Agencies and Foundations," pp. 65, 67.

complish far more abroad than they could by relying on private donation
alone.

Foundations Also Actively Support U.S. Policies Abroad

Even the major foundations—which relied exclusively on private financial
sources—viewed themselves as an important part of the overall U.S. government effort to check the attraction of communism in developing countries. In
the 1950s the large U.S. foundations—Rockefeller, Ford, and Carnegie—all
expanded their overseas aid to strengthen institutions of higher learning and to
provide scholarships for indigenous youth to study in the United States. The
goal was to prepare cadres of leaders well trained in public administration,
agricultural economics, and in the natural and social sciences. In such a way,
it was hoped that these men and women would be capable of managing economic growth and political stability in their respective societies within a capitalist framework and thereby would remain sympathetic to Western values
and interests.[24]

What the foundations undertook overseas in the 1950s was seldom initiated
without U.S. government approval and support. Student recruitment for foundation scholarships, for example, was often done with the help of U.S. government representatives. In 1956 the president of the Ford Foundation—which
sent abroad over $320.5 million between 1951 and 1959 (especially to Asia
and the Middle East where the attractions of communism and the feelings of
nationalism were strongest)—boasted that it was of "special significance that
no statesman or official of government, either our own or of the United
Nations or of the countries where we have worked, have ever differed with
our major premises."[25]

Host Country Governments Endorse PVO Aid

From the perspective of host-country government officials in societies where
U.S. voluntary agencies and foundations were at work in technical assistance
during the 1950s, activities sponsored by U.S. nonprofits were seen as a positive factor enhancing, not threatening, their own objectives. Not only did
PVOs under contract with the U.S. government have to be invited in by host
country officials, but it was the common practice of major U.S. foundations
supported exclusively with private funds also to follow this same practice.

Many foreign government personnel accepted advice more readily on sen-

[24] Berman, "Foundations' Role in American Foreign Policy"; Berman, *Influence of the Carnegie, Ford and Rockefeller Foundations*.

[25] H. Rowan Gaither, Jr., "The Ford Foundation and Foreign Affairs: An Address Delivered
. . . at the Twenty-fifth Year Service Dinner of Dunwoody Industrial Institute," Minneapolis,
May 3, 1956 (cited in Curti, *American Philanthropy Abroad*, p. 617).

sitive issues (e.g., population control) from persons working for private agencies than from U.S. government representatives. In addition, in newly emerging nations where the institutions of local government were weak and mechanisms to articulate people's needs to central government authorities underdeveloped, PVOs began to serve as channels of communication between local people and their respective government agencies. They also assisted groups at the grass-roots level to bring their problems and needs to the attention of the authorities in effective and coordinated ways. Far from being seen as a threat to the objectives of host country officials, PVOs engaged in relief and technical assistance were seen as facilitators assisting them in carrying out needed tasks they were not yet equipped to perform on their own.[26]

U.S. Private Donors Accept New PVO Orientation

Finally, from the viewpoint of American private donors, the fact that U.S. PVOs expanded their technical assistance abroad in the 1950s had a special appeal since they were exporting the "American dream"—namely, the ability to solve socioeconomic problems through private self-help initiatives rather than through government handouts. A series of articles written by British correspondents for the *Economist* in London in the late 1950s on the role of U.S. voluntary agencies in overseas technical assistance underscored this additional reason for their popularity with American private donors:

> Roughly speaking, the things aimed at are those which, to an American eye, appear most needed—health and clean water, plentiful crops, houses with tights roofs, the right and indeed the duty to learn, the ambition and the opportunity to get ahead without stepping too hard on the next man. These are the things which to an American are essential and ought to be acceptable everywhere. The programmes as they emerge are expressions of American experience, American dreams, American shrewdness and American biases, against the background of a pervasive memory that it is not so very long since Americans worked their own way out of primitive conditions, and of an insistent belief that the techniques which they found useful then may now also be useful elsewhere.[27]

PVOs DURING THE 1960s

During the 1960s this growing close cooperation between PVOs and the U.S. government was even further expanded. In contrast to the Eisenhower administration, which had used U.S. bilateral aid primarily as a means to further U.S. strategic interests during the Cold War, the Kennedy administration emphasized socioeconomic development and political democracy as important

---

[26] "Doing Good Abroad," 1158; Hoskins, "Voluntary Agencies and Foundations," p. 66.
[27] "Doing Good Abroad," 1159.

goals of U.S. foreign assistance. Concern with communism in U.S. government decision-making about foreign assistance did not subside. Rather, the Kennedy administration viewed self-sustaining economic growth within pluralist democratic structures as the best guarantee against communism in Asia, Africa, the Middle East, and Latin America.

The Alliance for Progress, announced in March 1961, became the showcase for this new U.S. approach to development, and it promised $36.7 billion of economic aid to Latin America by 1970 if recipient governments would promote land and tax reforms and commit more of their own resources to social services for the poor in their respective societies. The assumptions underlying the Alliance (articulated by President Kennedy and the Charter of Punta del Este in August 1961) also included the expectation that the people of Latin America would participate to the maximum degree in shaping economic and social policies through political participation and a variety of self-help programs.[28]

New and Expanded Uses of Food by PVOs

One major area where the U.S. government increased its reliance on PVOs in the 1960s was in the distribution of surplus agricultural commodities. The PVOs that were supporting feeding programs in developing countries with U.S. government surpluses found that these were absorbing more surplus food than the older relief projects in Europe. The PVOs were also beginning to experiment with new uses of food aid such as school lunch programs and food-for-work projects—e.g., wages-in-kind in exchange for participation in road building, tree planting, well digging.

Therefore, ACVAFS in the 1950s began to press Congress not only for greater amounts of food subsidies but also for more flexibility in their use. This coincided with interests among some members of Congress (led by Senator Hubert Humphrey) to join U.S. food surplus disposals abroad more closely to economic development efforts. The Kennedy administration strongly supported this concept, and even before taking office President-elect Kennedy created a Food-for-Peace Office in December 1960 (headed by George McGovern) to coordinate overseas food distribution with development priorities.[29] By so doing, U.S. government food surpluses could continue to be distributed overseas (thus assisting American farmers), but now under the rubric of development (a prime concern in the Kennedy foreign aid program) rather than relief.

In 1961 the Congress consequently amended Title 2 of PL 480 to provide surplus commodities to PVOs for development purposes. It also allowed de-

[28] Levinson and de Onis, *Alliance that Lost Its Way*, pp. 65, 186; Bolling, *Private Foreign Aid*, p. 22.
[29] Cited in AID, *Look to the Future*, p. 29.

fraying costs of PVO food-for-work projects from local currency accounts accruing from the sale of U.S. surplus commodities by Third World governments (authorized under Title 1 of PL 480). These amendments paved the way for a substantial increase in PVO participation in the distribution of U.S. government food surpluses abroad. By the end of the 1960s over 30 billion pounds of agricultural commodities—valued at close to $14.4 billion—had been distributed abroad by PVOs since PL 480 took effect in 1954 (two-thirds after 1960).[30]

Congressional Interest in Promoting Popular Participation Abroad

In the mid-1960s in the United States there was a growing emphasis on grassroots mobilization to push for needed changes in public policies and to make local government agencies more accountable to citizen demands. The civil rights movement and the Economic Opportunity Act of 1964, which required maximum feasible participation of citizens in carrying out federally subsidized local poverty programs, were manifestations of this trend. At the same time, the president and the Congress became more interested in including popular participation abroad as part of U.S. foreign aid objectives.

There was uneasiness in the Congress in the mid-1960s that U.S. foreign aid had not promoted effective political participation in Third World countries. Criticisms had been raised in Congress even before the end of the Eisenhower years (by Senators Wayne Morse and Frank Church, among others) that too heavy an emphasis in U.S. foreign aid on security objectives in the 1950s (out of fears of communism) had led to the strengthening of authoritarian governments of the right in the Third World. There was a sense among a small but influential group in the Congress that insufficient attention in U.S. aid programs had been given to support nongovernmental institutions such as trade unions, cooperatives, and local community organizations that would strengthen the vitality of civil society in developing countries.

Manifestations of this congressional concern with political development in contrast to security objectives in foreign assistance were reflected in a number of legislative initiatives in the early and mid-1960s. Senator Hubert Humphrey (D-Minn.) contributed an amendment to the Foreign Assistance Act of 1961 stating that it was part of U.S. policy "to encourage the development and use of cooperatives, credit unions, and savings and loan associations" through the

[30] Sullivan, "Politics of Altruism: Introduction to the Food-for-Peace Partnership," p. 766; Linden, *Alms Race*, p. 32; Roberts, "Meals for Millions," p. 42. In the late 1960s over a dozen PVOs were participating in the Food-for-Peace program. The five largest however, were handling over 95 percent of the total—CARE, JDC, CRS, CWS, and LWR—of which all but JDC had come into existence during or just after World War II. AID, *Look to the Future*, p. 54; Sullivan, "Politics of Altruism: Introduction to the Food-for-Peace Partnership," p. 765.

use of U.S. economic aid to developing countries.[31] The amendment received strong endorsement by his colleagues in the Senate since many viewed this both as a means to strengthen private organizations separate from central government bureaucracies in developing countries and also as another extension (as was technical assistance) abroad of a successful strategy used to alleviate poverty in the United States. Senator John Sherman Cooper (R-Ky.), in seconding this amendment, argued that "these institutions here are good in themselves. They have been good in this country. I think they would be good in other countries."[32]

Representative Clement J. Zablocki (D-Wis.) introduced another amendment a year later making the strengthening of local community development a goal in U.S. foreign economic assistance. It required that in recipient countries, especially those with agrarian economies where local rural structures for citizen input into government were weak or nonexistent, "emphasis shall be placed upon programs of community development which will promote stable and responsible governmental institutions at the local level."[33]

Legislative initiative to strengthen local democratic processes abroad through U.S. economic assistance culminated in new additions to foreign aid legislation in 1966 and 1967. It occurred just at the time when the U.S. military involvement in Vietnam was beginning to escalate. It was partly a reaction in Congress to presidential reemphasis on Cold War issues in foreign policy.

In the wake of the introduction of American troops in Vietnam (and the Dominican Republic) in 1965 and a renewed emphasis on security issues after President Johnson came to power, the Congress moved to insure that this would not lead to a return of strong support for authoritarian governments in U.S. foreign assistance programs. A new section (Title 9) was added to the Foreign Assistance Act of 1961 entitled "Utilization of Democratic Institutions in Development." It required that in implementing foreign aid, emphasis be placed on "assuring maximum participation in the task of economic development on the part of the people of the developing countries, through the encouragement of democratic, private and local governmental institutions."[34]

The House Committee of Foreign Affairs (where the amendment originated as a result of bipartisan initiatives by Representatives Douglas Fraser [D.-Minn.], Clement J. Zablocki [D-Wis.], and F. Bradford Morse [R-Mass.]) issued a report on the legislation wherein the amendment was interpreted. The Committee argued that "there is a close relationship between popular partici-

[31] *Foreign Assistance Act of 1961*, Public Law 87-195 (75 stat. 424), part 3, chap. 1, sec. 601.

[32] *Congressional Record* (Senate), 87th Cong. 1st sess., August 18, 1961, p. 16392.

[33] *Foreign Assistance Act of 1962*, Public Law 87-565 (76 Stat. 225), Part I, Chap. 6, Sec. 461.

[34] *Foreign Assistance Act of 1966*, Public Law 89-583 (80 stat. 795), part 1, chap. 2, title 9, sec. 281.

pation in the process of development and the effectiveness of that process." Therefore, it urged AID (since 1961, the administering arm of U.S. foreign economic assistance) to promote "a larger measure of popular participation in development" especially

> through the fostering of cooperatives, labor unions, trade and related associations, community action groups, and other organizations which provide the training ground for leadership and democratic processes; . . . through broader and more effective utilization of the experience and resources of existing private and voluntary organizations; and, generally, through the building of democratic private and public institutions at all levels—local, state and national.[35]

In 1967 Congress made further clarifications as to the meaning of Title 9. The Foreign Assistance Act of 1967 underlined that a major purpose of U.S. development policy should be "maximum participation in the task of economic development by the people of less developed countries through the encouragement of strong economic, political and social institutions needed for a progressive democratic society." One criterion for giving economic assistance to a foreign government henceforward was to be "the extent to which the government of the country is including the role of the people in the developmental process."[36]

PVOs Endorsed as Instruments of U.S. Political Objectives Abroad

The Congress in this 1967 legislation also authorized funds for inservice training of AID personnel to familiarize them with the purpose of Title 9 and "to increase their knowledge of the political and social aspects of development."[37] One such in-service training program was held at the Massachusetts Institute of Technology (M.I.T.) in mid-1968 for AID personnel with social scientists who were experts on political development. The report issued at the end of the six-week seminar on how to implement Title 9 concluded that AID should consult more with U.S. private foundations and voluntary agencies supporting overseas development activities. It indicated that those groups could be of great help to AID in carrying out the democratic thrust of Title 9, since many of them (especially church-affiliated PVOs) were in "daily and significant touch with precisely those elements of host-country populations with which U.S. mission personnel least frequently come in contact: the urban poor, the peasants, the forgotten of the earth."[38]

The conference also recommended that where methods could be developed

---

[35] U.S. Congress, House, *Report of the Committee of Foreign Affairs.*

[36] *Foreign Assistance Act of 1967*, Public Law 90-137 (81 stat. 445), part 1, chap. 2, sec. 207(a) and 208 (c).

[37] Ibid., part 1, chap. 2, title 9, sec. 281(e).

[38] Hapgood, ed., *Role of Popular Participation in Development*, p. 168.

to assure compatibility of purpose, coordination, and performance between AID and PVO-sponsored projects overseas, the U.S. government should give more direct financial grants and technical support to these nonprofits. The rationale was that these organizations were working closely with private grassroots groups in developing countries and therefore would help fulfill the purpose of Title 9 for U.S. foreign assistance.[39]

The conference recommended that nongovernmental organizations could at times serve as surrogates for the U.S. government in those Third World countries where U.S. bilateral assistance was limited or nonexistent:

> In countries ripe for pluralistic development but where political animosities block greater U.S. participation (e.g., Arab states), the U.S. might make available to NGOs information on opportunities for their activities. . . . In countries where the U.S. presence is limited due to the lack of economic potential or the minimum nature of U.S. interests (e.g., most of Africa) the U.S. could benefit from NGO operations, and could in turn assist the NGOs by working with the host-government to ease their entry, providing information on local opportunities and in general using its good offices. In this way the NGO could become an American-sponsored and locally recognized substitute for a U.S. public foreign aid program and could help directly in advancing Title IX goals.[40]

In situations where U.S. official aid might be curtailed due to growing authoritarian policies, the conference concluded that U.S. nonprofit groups might also serve U.S. objectives. They could do so by remaining in the country to strengthen indigenous private groups, and thus pave the way for a more open society at some time in the future:

> The U.S. might . . . choose to dissociate itself from the regime by withdrawing or sharply curtailing its presence, including aid, but might seek to maintain NGO activities as a connection with the national Title IX allies who some day might change the country's direction.[41]

What was clear throughout the 1960s was the fact that both policymakers and scholars in the United States began to recognize the potential of nonprofit organizations in promoting new U.S. political objectives in Third World countries other than helping to check communism. The PVOs could establish a U.S. presence in any type of regime where the U.S. government influence was restricted. They could also, in conjunction with private counterparts in Third World societies, help articulate and mobilize popular demands, thus making governments more accountable to citizens and thwarting tendencies to authoritarianism either on the left or on the right.

[39] Ibid., pp. 166–71.
[40] Ibid., p. 172.
[41] Ibid., p. 176.

These legislative initiatives were not endorsements for radical change or revolution abroad. They did reflect, however, a growing consensus in the Congress by the late 1960s that the promotion of internal political and social change along democratic lines in developing countries should play a greater role in U.S. foreign economic assistance. They also indicated that U.S. policymakers began to see the international nonprofit network as one important means whereby the U.S. government could exercise influence in political development abroad without incurring the costs that direct government initiatives sometimes precipitate.[42]

New thinking in government circles about the desirability of having AID use American nonprofit organizations as channels to promote U.S. political objectives in the Third World countries occurred at the same time that criticisms emerged of direct U.S. government efforts (through the CIA and the Department of Defense) to influence political outcomes in these same societies. Project Camelot was a Department of Defense–funded research project in Chile in the mid-1960s to determine the causes of political instability and to assess the strength of that country's democratic institutions in the face of rising political power of leftist movements and parties. When it was publicized, it was severely criticized both by political leaders and government officials throughout Latin America as well as by U.S. academics and policymakers. As the Vietnam War expanded, strong public criticism began to appear in U.S. journals denouncing all secretive activities by the CIA to thwart leftist tendencies in developing countries (sometimes through laundered subsidies to private U.S. and foreign organizations such as universities and student organizations).[43]

It was becoming clear to several in Congress, therefore, that U.S. foundations and development-oriented voluntary agencies were sometimes in a better position to promote private institutions abroad whose democratic thrust coincided with U.S. interests than U.S. government agencies through direct (albeit

[42] Both Louis Hartz and Robert Packenham have described this democratic theme running through American foreign policy preferences and objectives over time. Hartz traces it back to the beginning of the republic and argues that it resulted from the absence of a feudal tradition in the United States. Packenham sees it as integral to the liberal ideology dominant in domestic politics, which characterizes much of our view of foreign policy. He does, however, indicate that promotion of democratic political development abroad since World War II has been only one—and often only a minor—objective of U.S. foreign policy. Fighting communism and furthering economic growth in developing countries have frequently overshadowed this democratic thrust. He states that this goal was a major consideration of both the Kennedy administration and the Congress during the 1960s when Title 9 was passed. Neither Hartz nor Packenham, however, address the role of PVOs in promoting democratic ideals abroad in the post–World War II period. See Hartz, *Liberal Tradition in America*, and Packenham, *Liberal America and the Third World*.

[43] Irving Louis Horowitz, ed., *Rise and Fall of Project Camelot*; David Horowitz, "Billion Dollar Brains"; Nelson, *Aid, Influence and Foreign Policy*, pp. 145–46.

sometimes secretive) aid. The PVOs had credibility abroad for being effective relief and technical organizations that stayed clear of political controversy. They were well received in many developing countries due to the intermediary functions they performed between underdeveloped governmental institutions and marginalized groups in society.

Government Stimulates New PVO Initiatives Abroad

As a result of these new legislative initiatives in the 1960s, AID provided additional grants and contracts to PVOs to help accomplish its new mandate. After the Humphrey amendment to the Foreign Assistance Act of 1961, urging more support for cooperatives, credit unions and savings and loan associations abroad, domestic PVOs with good track records in these areas in the United States began to assist in the operation or creation of overseas counterpart groups in developing countries with grants or contracts from AID.[44]

New PVOs were also created and from the start received U.S. government contracts or grants. Some promoted overseas agricultural cooperatives, credit institutions, or foundations.[45] Others concentrated their efforts on leadership training for labor organizations,[46] on strengthening indigenous private enterprise abroad through the engagement of U.S. business expertise,[47] or on technical assistance for local private development organizations in the Third World.[48] In all cases, these new PVOs received significant AID encouragement and financial assistance. In some cases, these new nonprofit organizations were even created in direct response to AID appeals that the U.S. private sector assist it in carrying out its new mandate to promote political development abroad.[49]

PVOs in Vietnam Complement U.S. Objectives

During the mid-1960s, the U.S. government established close cooperative arrangements with PVOs working in South Vietnam, but more in the area of relief than development. A delegation of PVO representatives of ACVAFS visited Saigon in 1965, just when U.S. involvement was accelerating, and

[44] These included the Cooperative League USA (CLUSA), founded in 1916, and the Credit Union National Association (CUNA), created in 1934.

[45] The Pan American Development Foundation (PADF), started in 1962, and Agricultural Cooperative Development International, begun in 1963, were two such PVOs.

[46] These included the American Institute for Free Labor Development (AIFLD, 1961), the African-American Labor Center (1964), and the Asian American Free Labor Institute (1968).

[47] The National Association of Partners of the Alliance (NAPA, 1964), and the International Executive Service Corps (1964).

[48] New Transcentury Foundation (NTF, 1968), and Technoserve (1968).

[49] For example, NAPA and the International Executive Service Corps.

observed: "The role of the voluntary agencies, whose programs vary considerably from one to another, is supplemental to that of the government. . . . There should be no slackening of support for both types of activity, governmental and private, especially since they are working in increasingly close and effective collaboration."[50]

In fact, during the period of intense U.S. involvement in the war, CARE, CRS, World Vision, IVS, the American Red Cross, and Vietnam Christian Services (an ad hoc consortium founded by CWS, LWR, and the Mennonite Central Committee) all were active in Vietnam. They helped care for refugees and contributed relief assistance to strategic hamlet programs with considerable aid from the U.S. government.[51]

In 1972, as an extreme example, 94 percent of CRS's budget of $10.2 million for South Vietnam was material and cash subsidies from U.S. government agencies. The CRS thus could distribute large amounts of food and clothing to South Vietnamese military personnel and dependents. In Cambodia, the activities of CRS on behalf of refugees enabled the U.S. embassy to accomplish some of its own objectives while staying within tight personnel restrictions set by the U.S. Congress for the region.[52]

Dramatic Increase in PVO Reliance on Government Aid

As a result of the increased public subsidies in cash and materials to PVOs during the 1960s, by the early 1970s the percentage of total PVO resources constituted by government aid rose dramatically. It had almost tripled since the 1940s.

Government aid had averaged 10.5 percent of total PVO income ($525.9 million of $5 billion) between 1946 and 1953, but by the mid-1960s had risen to a 20.2 percent annual average ($282.8 million of $1.4 billion in 1964). By 1973 the annual proportion from the federal government had jumped to 27.5 percent ($643.5 million of $2.3 billion). About two-thirds (65.1 percent) of this government aid ($418.9 million) was in the form of donated food and excess property or overseas freight reimbursements to ship it. The other one-third ($224.6 million) consisted of government grants or contracts for technical and development assistance.[53]

---

[50] David Marr, "The Politics of Charity," *Indochinese Chronicle* (October–November 1974), p. 3 (cited in Sommer, *Beyond Charity*, p. 97).

[51] Sommer, *Beyond Charity*, p. 97. See also Lissner, *Politics of Altruism*, pp. 99–100.

[52] Sommer, *Beyond Charity*, p. 97. See also, Rashke, "GVN/CRS/USAID"; "Catholic Charity Allegedly Aided U.S. War Effort," *Washington Post*, December 13, 1976, p. 1; "Priest Denies Mishandling Viet Aid," *Washington Post*, December 14, 1976, pp. 3, 6.

[53] AID, *Voluntary Foreign Aid Programs*, 1974, p. 12; Bolling; *Private Foreign Aid*, p. 185; Lappé, Collins, and Kinley, *Aid as Obstacle*, p. 170.

PVOs DURING THE 1970s

PVOs Lobby for Additional Government Aid

During the late 1960s and early 1970s there was growing disappointment in the PVO community that new government assistance was not even greater, especially grants for development projects. Support for PVOs from private sources in the United States leveled off since philanthropy began to focus more on domestic problems of poverty and civil rights as urban unrest and violence flared up in the United States in the mid and late 1960s.

Many PVOs were also dissatisfied with the amount of funding given them by AID as a result of Title 9 of the Foreign Assistance Act of 1966. They had expected that a significant percentage of AID's annual allotment from Congress would be channeled through them after the passage of this legislation, thus helping to offset a declining rate of increase in contributions from the private sector. By 1972, however, the PVO share of AID's budget was only 1.5 percent. The vast bulk of AID funds continued to focus on government-to-government transfers for large scale, capital-intensive projects.

Some PVOs also began to complain about AID's desire to have them use its grants only in countries selected on the basis of U.S. foreign policy interests. In addition, they were uncomfortable with what they considered burdensome reporting requirements and delayed payment schedules.[54]

Amidst such dissatisfaction, some nonprofits began to pressure Congress in the late 1960s to allocate more funds for their oversea activities. These PVOs took the lead in pressuring Congress to create a separate government agency to channel funds directly to U.S. nonprofits for private development projects.[55]

Renewed Congressional Interest in the Grass Roots Abroad

Pressures from PVOs coincided with rising interest among some in the Congress to channel more foreign economic assistance into grass-roots development. Despite the Alliance for Progress (begun in 1961) and Title 9 of the Foreign Assistance Act of 1966, a few Congressmen—led by Dante Fascell (D-Fla.) and F. Bradford Morse (R-Mass.), both on the House Subcommittee on Inter-American Affairs—felt that the $27.4 billion of economic assistance sent to Latin America during the 1960s had not achieved the results Congress intended. The aid did contribute to industrial development and overall eco-

---

[54] Mashek, *Inter-American Foundation*, p. 18.

[55] Ibid. The leaders in this campaign included AIFLD, PADF, and NAPA—all of which had been founded in the 1960s with AID funds and which expected even more government aid as time went on. Also involved were CLUSA and CUNA, which had begun overseas aid also at the behest of AID in the 1960s.

nomic growth, but had not significantly improved the quality of life of the majority of the Latin American people who still were poor.[56] As a result, the Congress authorized in Part 4 of the Foreign Assistance Act of 1969 the creation of a separate government corporation to channel funds for local development projects in Latin America administered by private organizations—the Inter-American Social Development Institute (ISDI), renamed the Inter-American Foundation (IAF) in 1972.[57]

Although Congress did not rule out the possibility of ISDI working through PVOs, an early decision by its board of directors forbade this. Within the first two months of its existence (March–May 1971), the ISDI received about $162.4 million of project funding requests from PVOs, many of which had actively supported its creation in the hope of getting more congressional subsidies for their own activities overseas. Since ISDI only had about $135 million at its disposal, meeting PVO requests would more than have depleted its budget. The board (the majority of its members were from the private sector and all were appointed by the president), in order not to deplete its own scarce resources too rapidly, decided instead to work directly with private grass-roots organizations in Latin America. The decision was a disappointment to many PVOs who had so strongly supported, both through publicity and congressional testimony, the legislation creating ISDI.[58]

Growing Criticisms by Scholars of U.S. Foreign Aid

The establishment of ISDI did not terminate criticisms about the ineffectiveness of U.S. foreign aid. Several studies by U.S. academics and journalists appeared in the early 1970s highlighting the ineffectiveness of government assistance (both bilateral and multilateral) in significantly alleviating poverty in developing countries. Some (Goulet and Hudson; Adelman and Taft Morris; Paddock and Paddock) argued that although U.S. official aid stimulated economic growth, it had not substantially helped the one billion people who lived in chronic poverty in the Third World and who constituted 40 percent or more of the population in those countries. It had focused instead, these authors claimed, on capital-intensive industrial and infrastructural projects that tended to benefit primarily those who already had some resources or skills. The benefits simply had not "trickled down" to the poor.[59]

[56] This was the judgment of the House Subcommittee on Inter-American Affairs. Their conclusions about the ineffectiveness of U.S. economic aid in helping alleviate the chronic poverty of the majority poor in Latin America during the 1960s were incorporated into the "Report of the House Committee on Foreign Affairs," *Foreign Assistance Act of 1969*, part 4, sec. 6.

[57] Ibid.

[58] Mashek, *Inter-American Foundation*, pp. 42, 48; Meehan, *In Partnership With People*, p. 16.

[59] Goulet and Hudson, *Myth of Aid*; Adelman and Taft Morris, *Economic Growth and Social Equity*; Paddock and Paddock, *We Don't Know How*.

Others (Levinson and de Onis; Wall) highlighted the fact that most U.S. government aid was in the form of loans rather than grants, exacerbating balance of payments problems for developing countries. Increased exports did not help offset this gap, they argued, due to the chronic asymmetrical trade relations between developed and developing countries.[60]

Some (Asher; Paddock and Paddock; Wall) emphasized the political constraints of public aid (especially bilateral assistance). They claimed that the U.S. government imposed many strings on its use (e.g., requiring recipients to buy American products), which were obstacles to alleviating poverty abroad. They also pointed out that governments in many developing countries (through which all U.S. bilateral and multilateral aid was channeled) often chose not to use the assistance to help the neediest, since elites were in control of the power structures and made sure the bulk of foreign resources primarily served their own economic interests.[61]

None of this critical literature argued that the U.S. government should substantially increase its subsidies to nonprofit organizations as a solution to problems with governmental programs. The literature did, however, further stimulate congressional interest to discover ways to improve overall U.S. aid performance. By the early 1970s this interest led several in the Congress to look once again to PVOs as part of the solution.

The "New Directions" Mandate for U.S. Foreign Aid

At the same time that these criticims of foreign aid were being articulated, there were mounting political obstacles to getting foreign assistance legislation approved in Congress. In both 1971 and 1972, foreign aid bills were rejected in Congress due to the growing opposition in both chambers to the prolongation of the Vietnam War by the Nixon administration and the heavy emphasis on military assistance in the administration's foreign aid proposals. It was clear that Congress would approve no new foreign assistance legislation in the latter years of the Vietnam War that did not reassert economic and humanitarian objectives as its prime goals.

As a result, several members of Congress—led again by Donald Fraser (D-Minn.) and Clement Zablocki (D-Wis.), both of whom were influential in getting citizen participation amendments written into U.S. foreign aid legislation in the mid-1960s—began drafting legislation in early 1973 to overhaul U.S. foreign economic assistance. With the help of the Overseas Development Council (ODC)—a private research institute in Washington founded in 1969 to sponsor studies, publications, and conferences on development needs of the Third World—these members prepared new amendments to foreign aid legis-

[60] Levinson and de Onis, *Alliance that Lost Its Way*; Wall, *Charity of Nations*.

[61] Asher, *Development Assistance*; Paddock and Paddock, *We Don't Know How*; Wall, *Charity of Nations*.

lation that required AID to shift its emphasis to programs aimed at benefiting the majority of people who were living in poverty.[62]

These amendments—known as the "new directions" mandate—required that U.S. development assistance place less emphasis on capital-intensive projects or large infrastructural programs and more on projects directly aimed at meeting the basic needs of the poor—food production, nutrition, health, education, and rural development. It reiterated the thrust of Title 9 of the Foreign Assistance Act of 1966—namely, popular participation—and stressed that to be effective in meeting the basic needs of the poor AID-sponsored programs be "carried out to the maximum extent possible through the private sector, including those institutions which already have ties in developing areas, such as educational institutions, cooperatives, credit unions, and voluntary agencies."[63]

The New Mandate and PVOs

In the 1973 amendments the Congress explicitly identified U.S. nonprofit organizations as effective channels for reaching grass-roots private groups abroad. The amendments also urged increased AID subsidies to PVOs:

> Private and voluntary organizations and cooperatives . . . embodying the American spirit of self-help and assistance to others to improve their lives and incomes, constitute an important means of mobilizing private American financial and human resources to benefit poor people in developing countries. The Congress declares that it is in the interest of the United States that such organizations and cooperatives expand their overseas development efforts without compromising their private and development nature. The Congress further declares that the financial resources of such organizations and cooperatives should be supplemented by the contribution of public funds for the purpose of undertaking development activities in accordance with the principles set forth in the [Foreign Assistance Act].[64]

Representatives of ACVAFS testified in support of these amendments during congressional hearings, and so did several of its larger member PVOs—CARE, CRS, and CWS. They all argued for a greater emphasis on meeting the needs of the poorest sectors abroad. They claimed that traditional "trickle down" approaches to development had not done this.

A common theme running through PVO testimonies was that nonprofits were developing unique expertise in alleviating poverty and meeting basic

---

[62] A description of the origins of the 1973 amendments to the foreign assistance legislation and the key persons involved in drafting them, can be found in the excellent study by Ziskind Berg, "1973 Legislative Reorientation."

[63] *Foreign Assistance Act of 1973*, Public Law 93-189 (87 stat. 714), part I, chap. 1, sec. 102(b)(3).

[64] Ibid., sec. 123.

needs. Beginning in the 1950s, and more so in the 1960s, they argued, PVOs shifted their focus from relief to attacking structural causes of poverty. They no longer dealt only with symptoms. Due to their new development emphasis and the network of contacts they had developed in Third World countries, they argued that they were in an excellent position to meet the objectives of the "new directions" mandate. Therefore, they concluded, PVOs should be given increasing amounts of cash assistance for grass-roots development projects overseas.[65] The Congress concurred.

The Foreign Assistance Act of 1973 was passed in December with little resistance in either chamber. President Nixon signed it enthusiastically. He was eager to set a renewed humanitarian tone for U.S. foreign aid and thus make U.S. assistance more acceptable to Third World countries in the post–Vietnam War era.

Humanitarian Thrust of the "New Directions" Mandate

Ellen Ziskind Berg's research on the motives of those congressional and AID personnel responsible for drafting the 1973 legislation and guiding it through the legislative process indicates that pragmatic rather than ideological concerns were responsible for the new emphasis. Votes simply were not there for the old program because of its close association with security objectives during an unpopular war in Southeast Asia. Something new was needed to rekindle support for foreign assistance among members of Congress and U.S. citizens alike. Focusing more assistance on the direct alleviation of poverty—some of which was to be channeled through nonprofit organizations which high credibility as humanitarian agents both in Congress and with American citizens—was chosen as a means to accomplish this.[66]

Berg found, moreover, that there was no intention among the congressional and AID staff whom she interviewed that the "new directions" focus on the poorest sectors in developing countries should be a destabilizing political force within these societies, even in authoritarian regimes. The new basic needs thrust was not meant to promote either socialist tendencies or stimulate significant political pressure by the poor in developing countries for a major redistribution of existing wealth. Rather, the thinking of U.S. policymakers was that the popular participation thrust of the 1966 legislation should be explicitly joined to economic progress. Charles Paolillo, an AID official on leave at ODC who actually drafted the amendments, acknowledged that it was impossible for AID after Title 9 was passed in 1966 to convince government officials

[65] U.S. Congress, *Mutual Development and Cooperation Act of 1973.*

[66] In the preparation of her master's thesis, Ziskind Berg conducted interviews with thirteen persons from Congress, congressional staffs, AID, and the ODC, all of whom played active roles in the drafting and guidance of the amendments through the legislative process. See Ziskind Berg, "1973 Legislative Reorganization," chap. 5.

in foreign countries to go along with a popular participation strategy unless it could be demonstrated that these would foster economic growth. All those Berg interviewed believed that the Title 9 legislation of 1966 placed too much emphasis on political development without linking it to economic objectives. Paolillo stated that it was the feeling in Congress and AID by 1973 that both participation and economic development should go hand in hand and that participation assured more equitable development: "Thus far the best most countries have been able to achieve has been broad based development with a politically repressive government, or narrow based development with a relatively freer government. What this legislation contemplates is the kind of broad based development that can take place in the framework of political systems which enable people to participate in the decisions which affect their lives."[67]

U.S. private voluntary organizations, whose track records in relief and technical assistance had remained consistently high among host country officials since the 1950s, became in 1973 a logical conduit for increased U.S. public assistance for three reasons. Congress wanted to ensure that greater amounts of foreign aid reach the poorest abroad. It also wanted to regain the confidence of the American people in foreign aid after the Vietnam War. Finally, it was eager to convince third world governments that U.S. foreign policy henceforth was to emphasize alleviation of poverty and equitable development, not popular revolutions nor U.S. intervention in the internal political affairs of foreign countries.

This search to ground U.S. foreign policy objectives on humanitarian principles was begun by the Congress in 1973 and continued for the remainder of the 1970s. Congress in 1975 further amended foreign assistance legislation, requiring that U.S. aid be terminated to regimes that consistently violated the basic human rights of their citizens, unless serious security interests of the United States were at stake. President Carter made the promotion of human rights and the fulfillment of basic socioecnomic needs of the poorest citizens in developing countries cornerstones of his foreign policy objectives between 1977 and 1981. During these years many in Congress favored PVOs as instruments in achieving these goals, looking to them as important sources of information about human rights conditions abroad and increasing subsidies to them for their work among the poor overseas.

New Government Measures to Assist PVOs

After the passage of the "new directions" legislation in late 1973, several new steps were taken by AID to provide increased support for PVOs working abroad. In 1974 AID established a new office to facilitate working agreements with PVOs, the Office for Private and Voluntary Cooperation. AID designed

[67] Ibid., pp. 179, 184.

several new types of assistance during the rest of the decade for PVOs, which included (1) operational program grants (OPGs), covering up to 75 percent of costs for specific projects carried out overseas by PVOs over a two- or three-year period; (2) matching grants, covering up to 50 percent of costs for a broad range of PVO-sponsored activities in a particular area of development or for program expansion into new areas; (3) development program grants (DPGs), supporting the upgrading of the professional administrative capacities of PVOs; (4) institutional support grants, assisting PVOs unable to raise sufficient resources from the private sector to carry out important development projects for several years with government support; (5) consortium grants, strengthening emerging networks or federations of PVOs to cooperate more effectively and exchange more information, or as consortia to sponsor development projects overseas; and (6) management services grants, awarded to some technically oriented PVOs to provide management or program support services to other PVOs in the areas of accounting assistance, fund-raising advice, and evaluation techniques.[68]

The amount of U.S. government aid to PVOs in the 1970s rose steadily in real terms. Total government contributions to PVOs registered with the Advisory Committee on Voluntary Foreign Aid increased from $643.5 million in 1973, to $757.5 million in 1978, to $830.4 million in 1982. As a result, overall government assistance as a percentage of PVO resources expanded again, rising from 27.6 percent in 1973 to 38.9 percent in 1982. Moreover, the proportion of the overall AID budget channeled through PVOs rose from 1.5 percent in 1972 to 14.3 percent by 1982. The PVOs were getting what they wanted.[69]

CONCLUSIONS

In the post–World War II era PVO cooperation with the U.S. government significantly expanded. In some cases this built upon previous close patterns of wartime collaboration established during the two world wars and included nonprofit administration of public subsidized humanitarian and relief in Europe in the late 1940s, in Korea in the 1950s, and in Vietnam and Cambodia in the 1960s and early 1970s.

New motives emerged in the late 1940s and early 1950s, however, which stimulated added government interest in assisting PVOs for other than wartime purposes. These included government interest in building a strong domestic constituency for overall foreign aid, the increasing need to find cost-effective outlets to export expanding government surplus food commodities, the neces-

---

[68] Bolling, *Private Foreign Aid*, pp. 187–88.

[69] AID, *Voluntary Foreign Aid Programs*, 1974, p. 12; AID, *Voluntary Foreign Aid Programs*, 1979, p. 18; AID, *Voluntary Foreign Aid Programs*, 1983, p. 21; Bolling, *Private Foreign Aid*, p. 186.

sity to bypass multilateral relief agencies, which included Soviet participation, and the desire to strengthen private institutions (as a bulwark against communism) and train cadres of leaders favorable to the West in emerging nations.

For their part, many PVO administrators were eager to receive government assistance in money or food. They had built up organizations and constituencies during World War II and in the reconstruction of Europe that they did not want to dismantle or lose. Government subsidies helped them accomplish this. Shifting their geographical focus in the 1950s to newly emerging and developing countries and expanding their functional specialization to include technical aid as well as relief gave PVOs a new raison d'être. This made them even more attractive to the U.S. government and to private citizens alike who were interested in exporting the "American dream" of solving socioeconomic problems through private means.

Many new and strongly nationalistic countries in the 1950s found PVOs a more politically palatable way of accepting U.S. economic assistance since the aid was indirect. They also saw PVOs as useful instruments in building bridges to marginal sectors of their own populations during an era when their administrative outreach and service skills were yet underdeveloped.

During the 1960s and 1970s other forms of collaboration between the U.S. government and PVOs were forged out of new common interests. Some in Congress and the administration in the 1960s wanted to sever the close relationship of U.S. economic aid with security objectives that had emerged during the Cold War and had promoted, in their opinion, a pattern abroad equally dangerous to U.S. interests as communism—namely, right-wing authoritarianism. Congress came to view popular participation in foreign aid projects as an important strategy for countering such authoritarianism, and thus endorsed PVOs as one way to stimulate more grass-roots involvement of citizens in Third World societies. Later, during the Vietnam era when Congress was seeking support for U.S. foreign aid both at home and abroad by reemphasizing its humanitarian focus, PVOs became attractive conduits for additional aid due to their nonpolitical image and excellent reputation for helping the poor abroad.

The PVOs thus expanded both in number and scope of activity in the 1960s in response to development needs in the Third World and as a reaction to new subsidies offered to the U.S. government. Several new technically oriented PVOs were created, and older domestic ones established overseas programs for the first time. This was due primarily to specific AID requests that the nonprofit sector assist in expanding its activities into areas where PVOs had expertise—credit unions, labor organizations, cooperatives, and local community development.

Private contributions to PVOs leveled off precisely when older and younger nonprofits were taking on such new commitments abroad. Foundations, corporations, and individual donors during the 1960s all began to focus more of their philanthropy on pressing domestic problems such as racial discrimination and urban poverty than on the more remote needs of developing countries. The PVOs began, therefore, to look more aggressively in government circles by the late 1960s for resources to support their expanding commitments in the Third World.

Several began to lobby for new government mechanisms that would facilitate greater and more flexible public subsidies to nonprofits. The PVO community failed in its first major lobbying effort (namely, to obtain subsidies from the new government-created ISDI in 1971). They were more successful in 1973 as the Vietnam War was ending because they found several responsive allies in Congress searching for mechanisms to restore a humanitarian tone to U.S. foreign economic assistance.

There was no proof that PVOs made a substantial impact on alleviating longer-term causes of poverty. Many, however, were targeting their resources on groups in developing countries that the Congress in its "new directions" legislation of 1973 defined as priorities for U.S. foreign economic assistance and which were not benefiting significantly from traditional forms of government-to-government aid.

The PVOs also enjoyed high credibility as apolitical humanitarian organizations in the eyes of both the U.S. public and many Third World government leaders. Since the 1950s these foreign officials had welcomed PVO assistance as complements to their own underdeveloped service mechanisms for reaching marginal sectors of their societies. This reputation of usefulness to host governments made PVOs particularly attractive channels of U.S. government aid after subversive activities by the CIA inside developing countries in the late 1960s and early 1970s drew strong criticism at home and abroad. Hence, when the Congress in 1973 was searching for ways to convince the American people not to become isolationist and to prove to Third World governments that the political-development thrust of Title 9 of the 1966 foreign assistance legislation had no destabilizing or interventionist purpose, it found U.S. PVOs helpful and willing partners for channeling more U.S. government aid to the neediest in developing countries.

Different but complementary concerns of the U.S. government and PVOs in the 1960s and 1970s coupled with the inadequacy of private philanthropy to meet expanding PVO commitments abroad, accounted for the steady increase of public subsidies to PVOs after 1973. Pressing pragmatic interests on both the public and nonprofit side accounted for this new partnership in foreign aid established in the "new directions" legislation of 1973.

The promotion of democratic processes abroad, although since 1966 part of the legal rationale for public subsidies to PVOs, was downplayed in the 1973 legislation due to congressional fears of its interventionist political overtones in the post–Vietnam War era. As we shall see in chapter 5, this objective of promoting popular participation to strengthen democracy and thwart authoritarianism is still part of the PVO agenda. It is often submerged or unarticulated in their public statements precisely, however, because PVOs wish—as did the Congress when it expanded subsidies to them in 1973—to preserve an apolitical image overseas and among American private donors.

CHAPTER FOUR

European and Canadian Private Foreign Aid since World War II: Creating New Modes of Political and Economic Influence Abroad in the Post-Colonial Era

- RELIEF WORK OF NGOS IN THE LATE 1940S AND 1950S

Immediately after World War II several new international charities emerged in Western Europe and Canada to assist the victims of war and aid in the reconstruction of Europe, and many received subsidies from their home governments. Some European governments that had remained neutral during the conflict (e.g., Sweden, Denmark, and Switzerland) engaged in substantial efforts during the immediate postwar period to assist neighboring nations plagued with famine and homelessness. Sweden sent 2 percent of its GNP to war-torn Europe in the late 1940s in a "Marshall Plan" of its own, and much of this through nonprofit organizations since it did not yet have a public agency to administer foreign assistance.[1]

As economic recovery accelerated in the late 1940s, NGOs based in larger European nations (especially Great Britain and France) expanded their relief efforts to other parts of the world suffering from the ravages of war or famine—particularly where their own colonial interests were strong. Conflict on the borders of Pakistan and India in 1947, refugees from the Arab-Israeli War in 1947 and in Hong Kong from mainland China after 1949, and famine in India in 1951 all attracted the attention of British NGOs such as Oxfam and Christian Reconstruction in Europe (in 1952 renamed Christian Aid, CA), and CIMADE in France.

UN Stimuli for Increased NGO Activities

Various United Nations agencies in the postwar years also made special appeals to nonprofit organizations to assist in rehabilitation and reconstruction. This was due to both the massive need and the excellent record already established by NGOs in relief work. Such appeals stimulated a good response from

[1] Michanek, *Role of Swedish NGOs*. These new NGOs included Swiss Protestant Aid (1945), Canadian Unitarian Service Committee (1945), Canadian Lutheran World Relief (1946), CARE Canada (1946), the Swiss Village of Children/Pestalozzi Program (1946), Norwegian Save the Children (1947), Norwegian Church Aid (1947), and the Cooperative Development Foundation of Canada (1947).

European NGOs since much of the U.N. relief focused not only on Europe itself but also on the Middle East and North Africa, where strong cultural and economic ties to Europe still prevailed. A close working relationship emerged between many European voluntary agencies and the UNRRA until its demise in 1947 (when U.S. assistance was withdrawn for political reasons).

When the UNRWA was established in 1948 to meet the needs of Palestinian refugees, it sought the help of nonprofit agencies, and both British and French NGOs responded very positively. The United Nations Appeal for Children was also launched in 1948 to support the newly created United Nations International Children's Emergency Fund (UNICEF), and many European and Canadian (as well as U.S.) nonprofits supported this effort in their home societies. In return for collecting funds in their respective countries to aid needy children abroad through UNICEF, PVOs/NGOs were allowed to keep a share of the proceeds. This was particularly appealing and helpful to European charities that wanted to replenish funds depleted by wartime relief and postwar reconstruction efforts and also to find new challenges abroad once European recovery was completed.[2]

Other UN initiatives in the late 1950s also spurred the expansion of European NGO relief efforts. By the late 1950s there were 15 million homeless persons throughout the world. Some were European casualties of World War II, but the majority were victims of political upheavals that had occurred during the 1950s in other parts of the world—Hungary after the aborted 1956 revolt, Algeria during the war of independence against France beginning in 1954, and the Tibet during its uprising in 1959. Many who had fled mainland China after Mao's victory in 1949 still were not settled into new permanent homes by the late 1950s. As a result, in 1959 the United Nations initiated World Refugee Year to solicit financial contributions for displaced persons in Europe, North Africa, and Asia and to seek the liberalization of North Atlantic immigration criteria on behalf of these refugees.

Voluntary agencies throughout North Atlantic countries participated in fund-raising campaigns to support resettlement efforts during World Refugee Year. The NGO efforts in Europe were particularly vigorous both because of traditional European interests in all of the countries where turmoil was occurring and because economic recovery in Western Europe by the late 1950s had been accomplished, thus providing a wider resource base for philanthropy. Contributions to NGOs during 1959 were especially generous in both Great Britain and the Netherlands, where donations far exceeded expectations.

Many of the European NGOs that participated in this UN initiative also inaugurated information campaigns to educate their respective donors and home publics about the refugee problem and its causes, many of which were political. Some also participated in lobbying efforts in their own countries to

---

[2] Lissner, *Politics of Altruism*, p. 63.

raise immigration quotas so that displaced persons from several of these global trouble spots could migrate to Europe.[3]

Private Funding for Expanding NGO Activities

Unlike the situation in the United States, where public subsidies to PVOs in money and kind were well under way by the end of the 1950s, European governments were not giving significant financial assistance to international charities before the mid-1960s. In the 1950s none of the European governments had established specialized agencies for foreign assistance to developing countries (such as the TCA in the United States, created in 1950). Nor did any have surplus food in storage, as was the case with the U.S. government both after World War II and the Korean War. Countries such as Great Britain, France, Belgium, and Portugal by the 1950s did send more technical assistance to colonial territories as pressures for independence mounted. This assistance, however, was administered by expatriate experts working for their respective home governments, which wanted to maintain direct control over the preparations for independence. European NGOs did not act as conduits for this aid.

In Sweden—where no colonial ties existed and where the government wanted to begin expanding its overseas influence for economic, political, and humanitarian reasons in the early 1950s—the Ministry of Foreign Affairs invited forty-four NGOs in 1952 to set up the Central Committee for Swedish Technical Assistance to Less Developed Countries. For ten years this committee—made up of representatives from domestic trade unions, consumer cooperatives, adult education associations, and NGOs already at work in overseas relief work—functioned as Sweden's semiofficial development cooperation organization. It received some funds from the government to cover administrative costs, but the majority of its assets came from private donations raised during massive fund-raising campaigns that the committee carried out among Swedish citizens throughout the 1950s.[4] Hence, the overseas activities of European NGOs for the first two decades after World War II— albeit clearly complementary to or surrogates for home government foreign policy objectives and encouraged by intergovernmental organizations of the United Nations—were financed almost entirely by private resources.

GROWING PRIVATE INTEREST IN NGOS DURING THE 1960S

In 1960 the UN Food and Agricultural Organization (FAO) initiated the Freedom From Hunger Campaign (FFHC). This UN initiative stimulated further action in the European nonprofit community. The campaign led to the creation

---

[3] Ibid.; Curti, *American Philanthropy Abroad*, pp. 572–73; Jones, *In Famine's Shadow*, pp. 36–37.

[4] Michanek, *Role of Swedish NGOs*.

of FFHC committees in several European countries, which included representatives of voluntary agencies, political parties, church groups, governments, professional associations, and trade union organizations. These coalition committees raised funds from private donors for FAO-sponsored programs aimed at alleviating hunger in developing countries. The emphasis, however, moved quickly away from feeding to attacking the causes of famine. The maxim of the fund-raising drive led by NGOs and others in Europe became: "Give a man a fish, and you feed him for a day; teach him to fish, and you feed him for a lifetime."[5] A predominantly relief focus among NGOs, preeminent during the postwar years and other crises in the 1950s, was giving way to a concentration on longer-term solutions.

Political Linkages of NGOs

The foundation of these broad-based committees in Europe brought NGOs into closer cooperation with other organizations in their home societies, several of which (governments, trade unions, political parties) saw the causes of world hunger to be political. In some instances, new NGOs grew out of FFHC committees and as a result had in their ranks from the start significant trade union or political party activists. Many of these activists were arguing publicly for more just home-country policies towards overseas territories and newly emerging nations by the late 1950s.[6]

Older groups in Great Britain, such as Oxfam and War on Want, also worked closely with trade unions, parties and government representatives on the FFHC campaign. War on Want itself was created in 1951 by several prominent members of the Labour Party and those with pacifist movement affiliations. It not only supported overseas projects but from the beginning acted as a pressure group at home to get Conservative Party governments (in power throughout the 1950s) to grant independence to British colonies in Africa and Asia and to commit greater resources to their socioeconomic development. In 1967 Oxfam and other British NGOs lobbied Parliament to pressure the government in Lagos to allow safe passage of international food aid to Biafra during the Nigerian civil war.[7]

Hence, in the late 1950s and increasingly so in the 1960s, some European NGOs began to act as part of wider political coalitions in their home countries

[5] Lissner, *Politics of Altruism*, p. 65; D'Orfeuil, *Cooperer autrement*, p. 37; Jones, *In Famine's Shadow*, p. 40; Whitaker, *Bridge of People*, p. 21.

[6] The Catholic Committee/Freedom from Hunger (Joint Hands) in Spain (1959), the Committee for the Freedom from Hunger Campaign (1960) and the Catholic Committee Against Hunger (1961)—both in France, Freedom from Hunger (later renamed German Agro Action) in the FRG (1962), and the Catholic Fund for Overseas Development (CAFOD) in Great Britain (1962)—all were examples of this new type of NGO that emerged out of the FAO campaign with close affinity to other organizations in their societies with political agendas.

[7] Nightingale, *Charities*, p. 242.

working to influence immigration policies, to support independence for colonies, and to bring about increased foreign public aid to alleviate world hunger. They also started education campaigns at home to heighten public awareness about each of these issues. As in the case of CIMADE in Vichy France and the Oxford Famine Relief Committee in wartime England (the forerunner to Oxfam), these NGOs were not acting alone. They were part of a movement cutting across several levels of society, including labor, professional, religious, and political groups that were beginning to act at the time as a political lobby on behalf of those in need abroad, especially in those societies of Africa, the Middle East, and Asia where European colonial ties were strong.

Public debate was particularly sharp in those European countries facing the challenge of decolonization. In Great Britain the Labour Party, out of power from 1951 to 1964, took the lead in the 1950s, arguing for political independence of the Crown's African and Asian colonies—a policy resisted by the governing Conservative Party until the early 1960s. In France in the mid-1950s, several party leaders of the center and left led by Pierre Mendes France, began to argue against the policy of French Union, devised immediately after World War II to keep colonies as integral parts of France. The Algerian War (1954–1962) intensified this debate, precipitated the rise and fall of several governments, and eventually led to a schism among Socialists in 1961.[8]

Even in smaller nations that had no colonial past (Sweden and Canada) or had divested themselves of colonies immediately after World War II (the Netherlands), there was a growing public interest by the late 1950s in the affairs of developing and newly emerging nations. For Sweden and the Netherlands this resulted from a desire to expand trade relations and gain more ready access to needed raw materials to sustain strong welfare-state economies enjoying a postwar boom. For both of these nations, Asia, Africa, and Latin America also represented a new humanitarian frontier where they wanted to play roles different from those of the superpowers by advocating justice and peace.

Canada by the mid-1950s was beginning to play an active and independent role in world affairs as a mediating force. It was a leading participant in UN peacekeeping missions in Indochina in 1954 and in the Suez in 1956. It also began to look more to developing countries as an area of the globe in which it might effectively use its limited but important influence as a "middle power."[9]

Therefore, many European and Canadian NGOs by the late 1950s and early 1960s were acting in a domestic political milieu not dominated by preoccupations with communism, as in the United States. In their home context, Eu-

---

[8] Emerson, *From Empire to Nation*, pp. 37–85; Hanrieder and Auton, *Foreign Policies*, pp. 135–46, 244–58.

[9] Michanek, *Role of Swedish NGOs*; Arnold, *Implementing Development Assistance*, pp. 69, 99, 105–8; Nossal, *Politics of Canadian Foreign Policy*, pp. 9–13, 53–58.

ropean elites were searching for ways to maintain or expand their economic and moral influence in the newly emerging nations. The NGOs were expressions of this search through private means. As in the U.S. case, however, nonprofits in Europe and Canada were extensions of their civil societies abroad—not in the sense of exporting ideas of self-reliance and democracy but as a means to continue their countries' influence in new nations recently severed from colonial control.

From Relief to Development

In such a context, even older European nonprofit organizations that previously focused on relief activities also began to devote more of their attention to development projects in Africa and Asia by the 1960s. They too were influenced by the longer-term structural emphasis for aid articulated by FAO and were coming to the conclusion that their own future usefulness in developing countries would depend upon how they addressed alleviation of the causes of poverty. They began to see that, although short-term relief efforts were necessary in times of disaster (severe famine, earthquakes, floods, refugees fleeing war or oppression), the solutions to the deeper causes of human suffering required support for programs that would increase the skills and self-reliance capacities of the poor.

For example, Oxfam in Great Britain prior to the 1960s had concentrated on providing immediate relief to the hungry, sick, or homeless overseas. By the end of the decade, however, it was spending 90 percent of its budget to improve medical and social welfare facilities or to support agricultural development and training.[10]

Several new private volunteer sending organizations were also established in Europe in the late 1950s and early 1960s, modeled on International Civil Service (SCI) but now oriented toward developing countries. The SCI had been established in Europe during the 1920s, building on the experience of volunteer work camps that aided in the reconstruction of villages in France and Germany after World War I. During the interwar years, SCI had spread across Europe (and had even reached India), engaging youth in short-term volunteer commitments for peacetime construction projects. It was active again the post–World War II era in European reconstruction. Once this task was completed, the idealism of SCI turned to other areas of the world—especially to the territories in Africa, the Middle East, and Asia that were preparing for political independence but that were still in great need of qualified personnel in education, health, engineering, agronomy, and public administration.

---

[10] Jones, *In Famine's Shadow*, pp. 42–43; Whitaker, *Bridge of People*, pp. 21–22. Oxfam in Great Britain was also renamed Oxfam UK in the 1960s when other independent Oxfam groups began to emerge in other countries—Belgium (1964), in Canada (1966), and in the United States (1970).

The SCI experience thus gave rise to the creation of a new generation of voluntary service organizations in Europe (counterparts of IVS founded by church groups in the United States in 1953, mentioned in chapter 3).[11]

New Church Initiatives in Development

The other major force in the expansion of overseas activities by the European nonprofit sector in the late 1950s and early 1960s was the churches. As indicated in chapter 2, from the sixteenth to the early twentieth centuries, Catholic and Protestant churches in Europe established overseas mission societies to provide important educational, social, and cultural resources for the legitimation and solidification of home-country colonial interests in Latin America, Africa, the Middle East, and Asia. By the late 1950s, however, as movements for independence in many remaining colonial territories gained momentum, European churches began to commit more resources to the long-term development of these territories to insure their own continued presence after decolonization.

They felt the need to distance themselves from the close association they had with colonial policies as independence approached. The credibility of their missionary activities in the postcolonial era would greatly depend upon their usefulness in serving both the spiritual and socioeconomic needs of these societies—and also in respecting the national autonomy of such countries.

As independence approached, indigenous church leaders in these colonial societies began to exercise pressure on European Christians through international organizations such as the World Council of Churches (WCC) in Geneva (which they were joining in greater numbers by the 1950s) and the Vatican in Rome. Out of a growing awareness of the needs of these new churches and their people in developing countries, both the WCC and Pope John XXIII urged North Atlantic Christians to dedicate more of their resources not just to evangelization efforts in such territories but also to meeting the socioeconomic needs of the people.

In 1958 the WCC, in response to calls from new member churches in Africa and Asia, adopted and circulated to all UN delegations a resolution introducing the concept of a 1 percent aid target for North Atlantic countries. The WCC became the first international organization to espouse what the UN General Assembly adopted as a goal for its member nations three years later—

---

[11] These new NGOs included the British Volunteer Service Overseas (VSO, 1958), the German Association for Development Aid (AGEH, 1959), Canadian Universities' Service Overseas (CUSO, 1961), Service Universitaire Canadien Outre-mer (SUCO, 1961), the French Association of Volunteers for Progress (AFVP, 1963), the Danish Volunteer Service (DVS, 1963), and the Organization of Netherlands' Volunteers (SNV, 1965). Morris, *Overseas Volunteer Programs*, pp. 2–5.

namely, that the flow of resources to developing countries should equal at least 1 percent of annual national income of rich nations.[12]

Pope John XXIII in 1960 issued a call to North American and West European Catholics to commit 10 percent of their clerical and religious personnel to Latin America by the end of the decade. These new personnel were to serve not only the spiritual but also the material needs of the poorest sectors in Latin American countries. Traditionally such groups had very weak formal ties to the institutional church and now were feeling the attraction of Marxist movements, especially in the wake of Fidel Castro's successful revolution in Cuba in 1959. The pope also strongly endorsed the FAO's Freedom from Hunger Campaign (FFHC) begun in 1960, and called upon the entire Catholic population in Western Europe and North America to become actively involved in the effort to eradicate global starvation.[13]

The Second Vatican Council in Rome (1962–1965), where over two thousand bishops from all over the world gathered to update the message of the Catholic Church for the mid-twentieth century, was a critical meeting place for religious leaders from rich and poor nations to discuss global needs. It was an important learning experience for North Atlantic church leaders, especially for those in Europe who, throughout the long colonial period, had been accustomed to think of and treat African and Asian clerics as subordinates.

At the council bishops from former colonial territories and other developing countries spoke out strongly about the need for the Catholic Church to commit itself to social justice and the alleviation of global poverty if it was to make its voice credible in a late twentieth-century world. Their frankness to North Atlantic bishops in face-to-face encounters over a three-year period was a critical factor in producing several of the pronouncements at the council, which committed the Catholic Church to work for greater global justice and more social action on behalf of the poor in developing countries.[14]

These pressures on European churches to distance themselves from their past paternalistic relationships with counterparts in colonial territories led to the creation in the late 1950s and 1960s of new religiously sponsored development organizations in Europe, separate from older mission societies. Their purpose was to respond exclusively to the socioeconomic needs of developing societies. Unlike the pattern established during the colonial era, all the funding from the beginning came from private (not governmental) sources, largely the result of special church collections at Christmas or during Lent. The funds also bypassed local governmental structures in developing countries and went directly to private groups serving the needs of the poor. Although local coun-

---

[12] Lissner, *Politics of Altruism*, p. 65.

[13] Mutuale-Balume, *Workers for Development*, p. 13.

[14] The document, "Pastoral Constitution on the Church in the Modern World (*Gaudium et spes*)," issued in the last year of the Second Vatican Council, reflected several of these concerns of bishops from developing countries. See Abbott, *Documents of Vatican II*, pp. 199–308.

terpart church organizations were the primary recipients of such aid, the projects they supported had to be nonsectarian in scope and open to all in need regardless of creed.

Some of these new church-sponsored development organizations grew out of efforts initiated in response to the FFHC.[15] Others were in direct response to feedback from missionaries pressing home-country churches to help solve the socioeconomic problems of underdevelopment closely associated with a long colonial past.[16]

The nonconfessional Dutch development agency, the Netherlands Organization for International Assistance (later renamed the Netherlands Organization for International Development, NOVIB) was founded in 1956, also partly under the inspiration and assistance of returning Dutch mission personnel from Indonesia. Its purpose was not only to collect funds for socioeconomic projects in developing nations but also to stimulate a critical awareness of the moral obligations the Netherlands had to promote social justice abroad after a long colonial past, culminating in a bitter war of independence in Indonesia in the late 1940s.

Although the Federal Republic of Germany did not have bitter or guilt-ridden memories of a recent colonial past, a widespread desire to distance itself from the tragic Nazi experience amidst rapid national economic recovery after the war stimulated German churches in the 1950s to focus on developing-country needs. Part of the motive was a desire by church leaders to reestablish moral credibility at home and abroad after the tacit acceptance by many Christian leaders (especially Catholic bishops) of the Hitler regime. Part was to repay to others in need for the generosity Germans had received in the immediate postwar years from other Western countries. Part was to provide a new moral challenge to German Christians in the midst of emerging national prosperity and the decline of poverty at home.

Consequently, in 1958 the German Catholic bishops established Campaign Against Hunger and Disease in the World (MISEREOR), and a year later the Protestant churches created Bread for the World (*Brot für die Welt*). Both charities were financed by annual appeals to German Christians to support socioeconomic projects administered by local church organizations in Africa, Asia, and Latin America, but not oriented to religious conversions. From the start both NGOs also included, as part of their mission, campaigns to educate German Christians at home about the needs and realities of the poor in developing countries.

[15] Such were CAFOD in Great Britain (1962) and the French Catholic Committee Against Hunger and For Development (CCFD) in France (1967).

[16] These involved Entraide et Fraternité and Broederlijk Delen in Belgium (both founded in 1961, a year after the Belgian Congo gained independence and where bloody civil war was occurring) and the Interchurch Coordination Committee for Development Projects (ICCO), created in 1964 in the Netherlands by returning Dutch missionaries from Indonesia.

Hence, for some Europeans enjoying the fruits of successful postwar economic recovery, contributing to NGOs in the 1960s was a way of soothing uneasy consciences (stimulated by new messages of religious leaders) in the face of chronic poverty in developing nations. For others, especially those with bitter memories from a recent colonial or domestic political past, NGOs were attractive since they helped create a different and more human face of Europe to the world—being what one Belgian commentator termed *temoins de bonne moralité* (witnessess of a good morality).[17]

GOVERNMENTS AND NGOS DURING THE 1960s

Pressures on European Governments to Initiate Aid Programs

In the early 1960s, all European governments were feeling significant pressures to initiate, or to increase substantially, official assistance to developing countries. By the mid-1950s the United States Congress had begun to ask publicly (as stated in the Mutual Security Act of 1956) that Europe give more to help developing nations to keep them free of communist domination, thus taking some of the burden off the shoulders of the United States. In 1960, when the Organization for Economic Cooperation and Development (OECD) was founded to promote greater economic collaboration among North Atlantic countries, a Development Advisory Group within it (renamed the Development Assistance Committee [DAC] in 1961) was set up in large part due to United States demands that European nations—enjoying an economic boom after full postwar recovery—become more involved in aiding developing countries.[18]

In 1961, the United Nations General Assembly, primarily because of the urging of newly independent nations that began to constitute a significant block of member countries by 1960, designated the 1960s as the United Nations Development Decade. The resolution set as a target minimum annual growth rate of aggregate national income of 5 percent in developing countries by the end of the 1960s. To achieve this, the General Assembly adopted the WCC goal by asking rich nations to contribute 1 percent of their respective annual national incomes to developing countries by 1970. The General Assembly resolution also emphasized the importance of mobilizing not just capital but also human resources in developing countries so as to achieve sustained growth rates. It suggested that the total number of technically trained personnel (in education, health, agronomy, engineering and public administration) be increased at least 10 percent a year by 1970.[19]

Although the United States had created in the Department of State mecha-

[17] Piret and Galand, *L'Aide de la Belgique*, pp. 200, 221.

[18] *U.S. Statutes at Large*, vol. 70, part I, p. 555; Interview with Hendrik van der Heijden, OECD.

[19] United Nations, *United Nations Development Decade*, pp. vi–vii, 116–118.

nisms to administer foreign economic assistance beginning in 1950, by the early 1960s most European nations were only taking the first steps to do so. Traditional colonial administration offices were winding down their operations in Great Britain, France, and Belgium, but new ministries of economic cooperation were only beginning to emerge—France, 1961; Belgium, 1962; Great Britain, 1964.

In noncolonial and smaller European nations as well as in Canada, such offices were created only during the year of the 1961 U.N. resolution or later—Germany and Switzerland, 1961; Denmark and Sweden, 1962; the Netherlands, 1963; Canada, 1968. There simply were no mechanisms in place in most of these other North Atlantic nations to respond quickly to the mounting pressures on them by the United States and the United Nations to inaugurate or increase substantially foreign economic assistance to all needy nations in the developing world.

Governments in Europe and Canada during the 1960s also realized that it was necessary to mobilize public opinion in their respective societies—enjoying the fruits of hard-earned, postwar recovery—to pay higher taxes so as to support substantially increased official foreign aid. This was particularly necessary if aid was to extend beyond the ex-colonial group of nations to others that had never been linked culturally or economically to their own societies.

The UN General Assembly resolution of 1961 also emphasized the development of human resources beyond capital investment and physical infrastructure. Although the ex-colonial powers of Great Britain, France, and Belgium had expatriates who had worked in colonial territories prior to independence, these were not numerous enough to expand training programs to all developing countries. Nor were all such personnel skilled in areas such as education and vocational training. The smaller and noncolonial European powers, as well as Canada, did not even have such cadres available.

The newly emerging nations (especially in Africa where the weight of colonial administration and cultural dominance had been the heaviest) were very sensitive about protecting their newly won independence. Feelings of nationalism were running high in the 1960s throughout former French, British, and Belgian colonies in Africa. Although practically all wanted to continue close commercial ties with their former colonial patrons, many wanted to diversify their aid sources to protect political autonomy. They preferred to attract the assistance of smaller European nations (especially the Netherlands and the Scandinavian countries) that had no traditional involvement in Africa and enjoyed a more neutral political image. African and Asian countries also were coming to appreciate the work of newly emerging European NGOs that were supported by private funds and that consequently were independent of government financial control (even if based in the countries that had been former colonial powers).[20]

[20] Interview with Rev. Henri Madelin, S.J., Society of Jesus in France.

Public Sector Interest in NGOs

For all of these reasons, governments throughout Europe and in Canada in the early and mid-1960s took greater notice of international charities based in their own societies. Some European government representatives along with some from developing countries spoke out in the United Nations encouraging an expanding role for NGOs during the remainder of the Development Decade.

Several European governments began to offer subsidies to volunteeer-sending NGOs and to draw upon their expertise and personnel in setting up their own volunteer agencies (at the urging of the United States after the establishment of the U.S. Peace Corps by President Kennedy in 1961). Others inaugurated cofinancing or matching-grant arrangements to support up to one-half the cost of NGO projects abroad. They hoped to broaden the impact of their own public resources by stimulating a growth of private donations to NGOs for foreign assistance, thereby moving closer to the 1 percent target of overall national income given for development abroad by 1970.

UN Support for NGOs

In 1963 Great Britain introduced in the UN General Assembly a resolution, cosponsored by four other North Atlantic nations (the Netherlands, Ireland, Canada, and Austria) and by nine developing countries in Latin America (four), Africa (two), and Asia (three). It appealed to North Atlantic nongovernmental organizations "to put their increased enthusiasm, energy and other resources into a world campaign in the basic human fields of food, health and education (including training) to start in 1965 [when the FAO's FFHC was scheduled to terminate] and to continue for the remainder of the United Nations Decade."[21]

The resolution, passed unanimously, also called upon member nations "to facilitate in all appropriate ways the efforts of their non-governmental organizations taking part in such a campaign." It further urged continual support by UN specialized agencies for NGO work, especially as a way "to improve understanding" and establish "closer contact between peoples . . . in the developed and developing countries."[22]

Keith Unwin, the British Minister at the United Nations for Economic and Social Affairs, when first introducing the resolution in the Economic and Social Council (ECOSOC), expanded upon the educational role that European NGOs were beginning to play in their home societies on this front during the FFHC:

It is most important that the objectives of the Development Decade should be known in the developed countries. The United Kingdom Committee of the Freedom from

[21] Overseas Development Institute (ODI), *Not By Government Alone*, p. 41.
[22] Ibid., pp. 41–42.

Hunger Campaign has expended very nearly as much effort in educating the British public about the problems of the developing countries as it has in supporting projects in the developing countries themselves. This educational role is important, not only for the particular purposes of this Resolution, but also to improve the general climate for the provision of aid, whether private or public. When a government wishes to respond to initiatives taken in this Committee or in any other forum, it can do little without the support of its people; and the people will only give this support if they know why government action is needed. . . . This second objective, therefore, the spread of knowledge, has a very wide scope, and we hope that voluntary organizations in all countries will have it constantly in mind.[23]

This 1963 UN initiative, led by Great Britain, had important political implications. It not only strongly endorsed the work of NGOs in overseas development but also legitimized their role in conducting advocacy campaigns in Europe to raise awareness about needs abroad. This was something that many European NGOs were beginning to do, but which had political implications since such advocacy often involved challenging home-government policies in trade, immigration, and aid.

The resolution also was a diplomatic achievement, especially for its European government sponsors. It took some of the pressure off them to provide all the requested increases in foreign assistance from tax resources since it implicitly urged more private philanthropy for foreign aid. By including several smaller, noncolonial European sponsors as well as Canada in the resolution, it also helped satisfy strong feelings of nationalism in newly independent states desirous of access to alternate channels of public and private aid beyond that offered by former colonial governments. Hence, European governments, NGOs, and developing-country governments all gained important political objectives by this resolution.

Initiation of Public Subsidies to NGOs

One response to the resolution was the inauguration of subsidy programs by several governments in Europe and in Canada for NGOs based in their own societies. Volunteer-sending nonprofits began to receive public grants for their work in developing countries.[24] The parliaments in some European countries and in Canada during the 1960s also authorized matching grants for NGOs that supported overseas development projects with private funds. These were nations either with distant colonial pasts, or none at all, and hence no public aid-delivery mechanisms in place in developing countries (e.g., Sweden and the Federal Republic of Germany). They needed NGO outreach as complements to their own official efforts so as to meet the aid target designated by

---

[23] Ibid., pp. 45–46.
[24] Morris, *Overseas Volunteer Programs*, pp. 6–7; OECD, *Development Assistance Efforts*, pp. 47–52.

the United Nations and to pave the way for greater commercial ties between themselves and developing countries.

SWEDEN

After ten years of delegating NGOs (supported mostly by private resources) as the semiofficial Swedish presence in overseas development, the Swedish parliament in 1962 embarked on an ambitious plan to extend its commercial and diplomatic relations with newly emerging nations. As a part of this effort it established the Agency for International Assistance in the Ministry of Foreign Affairs to initiate an official bilateral aid program. The ministry consulted NGOs and even integrated some directly into its new bilateral aid program. Other Swedish NGOs were given subsidies for administrative costs (as in the past) and matching grants for the support of their overseas programs.

In 1965, when an expanded public aid program was put under the direction of the semiautonomous Swedish International Development Authority (SIDA) in the Ministry of Foreign Affairs, NGOs were given representation on its board of directors. In such a way, the expertise as well as the extensive network built up by Swedish NGOs overseas between 1952 and 1962 were made available to the government. This saved SIDA much time and effort in creating its own bilateral program.[25]

FEDERAL REPUBLIC OF GERMANY (FRG)

In the same year that Sweden inaugurated its bilateral aid program (1962), the FRG *Bundestag* created a Ministry for Economic Cooperation (BMZ) as the primary coordinating body for its bilateral aid programs (separate from the Ministry of Foreign Affairs). At the time, the new Christian Democratic (CDU) government of Konrad Adenauer was feeling particular pressure from the Kennedy administration to expand substantially its foreign assistance programs due to the remarkable economic prosperity the Federal Republic of Germany (FRG) was enjoying (including a 7.5 percent rate of growth throughout the 1950s, better than all other industrial nations). Moreover, for its healthy economy to continue to grow, the FRG in the early 1960s needed to expand aid and trade relations with developing countries where an increasing amount of its raw materials originated.[26]

Although some FRG bilateral economic assistance had begun in the mid-1950s, it consisted largely of export credits and small amounts of technical assistance concentrated on a few countries of primary concern to Germany foreign policymakers—India, Israel, Turkey, and Greece. Many of the personnel in the new BMZ also lacked practical experience in developing coun-

[25] Arnold, *Implementing Development Assistance*, p. 115. See also Michanek, *Role of Swedish NGOs.*

[26] Arnold, *Implementing Development Assistance*, pp. 31–34, 45; Knusel, *West German Aid*, pp. 1–14.

tries. As in the Swedish case, the FRG needed a more visible national presence in Latin America, Africa, and Asia.[27]

Moreover, the *Bundestag*'s own Holstein Doctrine (in effect throughout most of the 1960s) forbade German assistance to any nation recognizing the German Democratic Republic (GDR). This limited the possibilities for the FRG to initiate bilateral aid programs in the 1960s, since many newly emerging nations (especially in Africa and Asia) wanted to remain politically nonaligned in the East-West struggle and thus were establishing diplomatic relations and economic ties with countries in both power blocs.

Finally, due to the recent past of the Third Reich, the FRG had to act delicately in attempting to reestablish itself as a world power in the 1960s. If it only relied on direct governmental efforts (especially in the aid field), these might have conjured up images of its aggressive imperial past. It needed to find a variety of ways to assert itself as a significant international actor. One means was a reliance on indirect initiatives through the private sector. This was particularly appealing to the new CDU government of Adenauer, which had a strong ideological commitment to the principle of subsidiarity in policy implementation.[28]

For all of these reasons, the CDU-controlled *Bundestag* in 1962 authorized the BMZ to begin a matching-grant program for NGOs. This aid in the beginning was given primarily to German church-sponsored NGOs, due to the wide international reach religious organizations enjoyed in developing countries, and to the FRG FFHC organization both for its overseas work and because of its active education efforts at home.

The *Bundestag* also authorized the four political party foundations in the FRG, almost entirely supported by government funds and active in labor leadership training in the FRG and Europe, to begin an aid program to developing countries. These foundations received subsidies for strengthening cooperatives, trade unions, political party organizations, and grass-roots self-help projects among the poor. They included the Friedrich Ebert Foundation (Social Democratic Party), the Konrad Adenauer Foundation (Christian Democratic Union), the Friedrich Naumann Foundation (Free Democratic Party), and the Hanns-Seidel Foundation (Christian Social Union).

The NGO matching-grant program in the FRG from the beginning thus had not only humanitarian but also political objectives. Public aid through religious and FFHC-related NGOs provided the government some of the expertise and international reach it lacked in developing nations. Using such conduits also helped the government finesse the Holstein Doctrine, which forbade bilateral aid, but not indirect assistance, to nations recognizing the GDR.

Since such aid was channeled through private groups, it would also hope-

[27] Arnold, *Implementing Development Assistance*, p. 33.
[28] Interview with Dr. Lilli Feldman, Tufts University.

fully avoid an imperialistic image for the FRG government. In such a way, a beneficient FRG presence would be established in newly emerging nations that might also enhance possibilities for FRG ties in other areas—e.g., private investment and trade relations. Moreover, aid to NGOs would enable them to become more visible on the home front where their educational efforts were helping mobilize FRG public opinion in favor of expanded national commitments in foreign aid.

Finally, by providing assistance to the political foundations to launch overseas aid programs, the *Bundestag* hoped to recruit the constituencies of these organizations in the FRG (cooperatives, trade unions, adult education centers, and political party cadres) to support of an expanded foreign aid program. The work of these political foundations overseas in strengthening private constituencies and institutions would also fit well with one of the major FRG foreign policy concerns in the 1960s (flowing from the Holstein Doctrine)—namely, thwarting communism and promoting democratic processes.

THE NETHERLANDS

In two other cases in the 1960s—the Netherlands in 1965 and Canada in 1968—parliaments also began cofinancing arrangements with aid-sending NGOs in their countries. In both cases, the primary motive was to complement and extend newly inaugurated official bilateral assistance programs and to gain an apolitical "easy entry" into many new nations that they hoped would later lead to the establishment or expansion of trade, investment, and bilateral aid arrangements.

Like Sweden, the Netherlands in the mid-1960s wanted to find a ready source of outreach and expertise to extend its economic assistance to new areas of the developing world (Indonesia and Surinam, its two ex-colonies, were receiving all of its small bilateral program in the early 1960s). As in the Swedish case, not only humanitarian concern (emphasized in the 1961 UN Development Decade resolution) but also the economic need to increase the number of its trading partners and gain greater access to raw materials for its expanding economy in the 1960s stimulated an interest in NGOs among Dutch policymakers.

The Dutch government had cosponsored the 1963 UN resolution endorsing the work of NGOs in development and calling for greater nation-state support for their work. This resonated with a long tradition of subsidiarity in Dutch society (parallel to Sweden) whereby various private organizations carried out public functions—schools, hospitals, and social welfare agencies, 90 percent of which are private in the Netherlands but since World War II heavily dependent on government aid. The Dutch government relied significantly on this private social network to deliver services in the postwar period rather than establishing its own public sector in these areas. Each of the four major "pillars" (*zuilen*) in Dutch society—Catholic, Neo-Calvinist, Liberal Protestant, and humanist—had its own array of private associations, many of which received public aid proportionate to its own constituency's share of the national population.[29]

For these reasons, coupled with the fact that new Dutch church-sponsored NGOs were beginning to become active in both foreign aid and development education at home by the mid-1960s, the Dutch Parliament inaugurated a cofinancing aid program for Dutch nonprofits in 1965. This was one year after it created a Directorate General for International Cooperation in its Ministry of Foreign Affairs, headed by a new secretary of state for development.

The three Dutch Christian parties (the Catholic People's Party and the two Protestant parties, Christian Historical Union and the Anti-Revolutionary Party) were the major proponents of this initiative in parliament. A major reason was the available international network that church-sponsored organizations could use in administering the subsidies.

The socialist-oriented Labour Party (Pvd A), however, was uneasy about the cofinancing proposal at first. Although a strong supporter of development aid, it also wanted a maximum of governmental control in the administration and also a nonsectarian character to it. It believed subsidies would provide church-affiliated NGOs, already well connected abroad, with a strong advantage over nonsectarian NGOs, such as NOVIB, just beginning to establish overseas contacts. The Pvd A went along with the arrangement, however, with the understanding that no confessional work would be supported, that the Directorate General for International Cooperation scrutinize each project proposal for cofinancing by NGOs, and that secular NGOs (such as NOVIB) would be encouraged to present development projects to the government as well.[30]

In a press interview soon after the parliament's approval of 5 million Dutch Florins for the NGO matching-grant program, the secretary of state for development in the Netherlands highlighted the advantages for the government that would result from such an arrangement. He stressed the values of experience, trust, and efficiency that these new subsidies would provide for the overall Dutch foreign aid program in developing countries:

> The decision of the government finds its basis in the thinking that certain NGOs have a much longer experience in developing countries than we (the Dutch government) have. Moreover, those NGOs do enjoy . . . the trust of the people, something that we still have to try to obtain. We are also of the opinion that given a certain sum of money we can get better results if we cooperate with persons who have the knowledge, the experience and the insight to carry out successfully certain plans in aid-requesting countries.[31]

[29] Kramer, *Voluntary Agencies*, pp. 19–20.
[30] Kierstens, *Are NGOs In?*, pp. 9–12.
[31] Cited in ibid., p. 13.

CANADA

Several of the same reasons behind the initiation in 1965 of public subsidies to Dutch NGOs motivated similar action by the Canadian parliament in 1968. Canada began to stake out for itself a role as an international middle power in the 1950s through participation in a number of UN peacekeeping operations. To further establish Canada as a significant independent actor in global politics, the parliament created an External Aid Office in 1960, which in 1968 was expanded into an autonomous government department and renamed the Canadian International Development Agency (CIDA). Even after eight years of bilateral assistance, however, the government still lacked in 1968 aid ties with many developing nations. The government also found the administrative costs of its government-to-government assistance higher than expected, partly due to the lack of sufficient numbers of experienced personnel administering bilateral programs.[32]

When Canadian local governments began in the 1960s to expand domestic social service coverage in health and education, in so doing they provided subsidies to private hospitals and universities rather than create parallel state structures. A system of subsidiarity—prevalent in several European countries as well (notably, the Netherlands, Germany and Sweden)—was attractive to the Conservatives who were in power in many of these local governments. They considered nonprofits a better alternative to the expansion of the public bureaucracy. As a result, Canadian charitable organizations began to receive substantial local government revenues for their operations in the mid-1960s. They willingly became surrogates for and complements to the public sector.[33]

Building upon this successful domestic arrangement and needing to find mechanisms to extend the scope of its aid abroad, the Canadian Parliament in 1968 initiatied a matching-grant program for Canadian NGOs engaged in international development. Not only were overhead costs substantially lower in the NGO network than in government-to-government programs, but the countries in which the nonprofits were supporting projects far surpassed in number those in which Canadian bilateral aid ties were operative (only three in 1961—India, Pakistan, and Sri Lanka).[34]

Pragmatic Agenda of Governments in Assisting NGOs

The U.S. Congress in the mid-1960s, as described in the previous chapter, began to look more to the transnational nonprofit sector as an additional way to export liberal ideology to developing countries. European and Canadian

---

[32] Bruneau, Jorgensen, and Ramsay, "CIDA," p. 14.

[33] Telephone interview with Dr. Michael Krashinsky, University of Toronto.

[34] Canadian Council for International Cooperation (CCIC), *Report on the Task Force on Government Funding*, p. 4.

parliaments, however, had primarily pragmatic agendas in mind when they inaugurated matching grants to their NGOs working overseas.

Mounting pressures from former colonies for substantial increases in economic aid in exchange for continuing commercial ties, lack of experts and extensive public-sector conduits through which to meet such requests quickly, a desire to present a better image of their national purpose abroad after previous imperialistic policies, and domestic precedents of private-public partnerships in social service delivery all were factors in accounting for the initiation of governmental aid to transnational NGOs in several European nations and Canada in the mid and late 1960s. Ideology was not the prime motive for an emerging government interest in NGOs. This was to become a factor, however, in the 1970s.

GOVERNMENT STRATEGIES AND NGOS IN THE 1970s

Increasing domestic political debate in Europe and Canada over issues of equity in international relations emerged in the late 1960s and early 1970s as a result of several converging factors. These included student protest movements, a series of international development study commissions in which Europeans and Third World representatives played a prominent role, the electoral successes of left-of-center political parties in several countries, and the tarnished image of the United States (even among the political right) as a result of the Vietnam War.

Pragmatic reasons, however, continued to play a role in legitimizing public support for NGOs, especially as surrogates for what governments themselves could not, or would not, undertake to alleviate global poverty. This was especially true after the first oil shock of 1973 and growing Third World demands for a new international economic order. Although left-of-center governments in Europe and Canada were ideologically sympathetic to such pressures, they were unable to meet this agenda due to their own economic difficulties in the latter half of the 1970s, precipitated by rises in oil prices.

Increasing Commitment to Third World Interests by the European Left

By the late 1960s and early 1970s, Third World countries became more central in foreign policy debates in Europe and Canada, due in large part to the increased political participation of youth. Student movements that erupted in 1968 in France, West Germany, and the Netherlands not only focused on issues of equity in domestic politics, such as university reforms and worker-participation in management, but also on what they considered to be imperialism, especially American imperialism, in developing countries. The Vietnam War was at its height, and these youth groups saw American involvement in Southeast Asia as a manifestation of growing capitalist imperialism in developing countries.

They also bitterly denounced their own governments for not vigorously opposing U.S. policies in Vietnam, for their failure to meet adequately the needs of developing countries through more generous aid and trade policies, and for failing to put more controls on home-country private firms investing abroad. Many student groups also established solidarity committees with armed liberation movements in Latin America, Africa, and Asia as part of a global struggle against capitalism.[35]

Unlike American youth movements of the 1960s—which focused on discreet grievances (discrimination against blacks, urban and rural poverty, conscription during the Vietnam War)—corresponding movements in Europe at the time perceived issues in more ideological (and specifically Marxist) terms and as symptoms of major weakness in the global capitalist system. They went well beyond Vietnam in their international concern. They placed pressure on governments, and leftist political parties, to address the economic and social needs of all developing countries by effecting major changes in Third World domestic as well as international economic structures.

Also unlike the case in the United States, some of these movements had an important impact on the party system of their countries. In Germany the Young Socialists (JUSOS) was established during this period inside the Social Democratic Party (SPD), numbering 80,000 by 1977. They exerted pressure throughout the 1970s on the SPD to take more critical positions against the United States in Vietnam and against German private investment in authoritarian regimes in Latin America. They also urged party leaders to support liberation movements in Third World countries.[36]

In France in the late 1960s many Catholic Action youth and labor leaders from the French Democratic Labor Confederation cut their official ties to the Catholic Church. They subsequently moved further to the left politically amidst a milieu of growing political unrest among university and working-class groups at the time. Some joined the Socialist Party (PS), and formed alliances with those in the PS arguing for more decentralization in government and worker self-management in industry. These Catholic youth were beginning to play a significant role inside the PS by the early 1970s, pressing for stronger party endorsement of trade reforms and greater French economic assistance beyond its overseas territories and former colonies. They strengthened the position of others within the PS arguing for similar strategies. The party program of 1972, in fact, officially endorsed price guarantees for Third World goods sold in France, the suspension of French arms sales to developing countries, and the termination of many privileges for French overseas territories and ex-colonies.[37]

Moreover, from the late 1960s to the late 1970s center-left parties kept or

---

[35] Bourges, *French Student Revolt*, p. 28.

[36] Braunthal, *West German Social Democrats*, pp. 85–86, 283.

[37] Berger, "Religious Transformation and the Future of Politics"; Hunzinger, "La politique étrangère du parti socialiste."

gained power in several European countries and in Canada. Socialist, Social Democratic, labour, or coalition governments with Social Democratic participation ruled in Belgium (1969–1974), the Netherlands (1972–1978), the FRG (1969–1982), Austria (1970–1986), Sweden (1932–1976), Denmark (1971–1973, 1975–), Great Britain (1974–1979), Portugal (1974–1976), and Canada (1968–1979, 1979–1984). All of those governments were ideologically sympathetic to Third World needs. In several cases they made increased aid to developing countries one of their official goals.

Moreover, leaders of these center-left parties—Willy Brandt in the FRG, Olof Palme in Sweden, Joop den Uyl in the Netherlands, Mario Soares in Portugal, Bruno Kreisky in Austria, Harold Wilson in Great Britain, and Pierre Trudeau in Canada—from the late 1960s to the mid-1970s publicly, and repeatedly, argued for more development aid as matter of justice owed to Third World countries. Several also appointed to administer their respective aid ministries in the 1970s party idealists who had very strong commitments to the alleviation of Third World poverty—Erhard Eppler of the SPD in the FRG, Jan Pronk of the Pvd A in the Netherlands, and Dame Judith Hart of the Labour Party in Great Britain.[38]

The Socialist International in the 1970s also served as an important exchange point for development ideas and strategies among these leaders and ministers of center-left European parties. At that moment it was trying to play a more active role in counterbalancing U.S. hegemony. It thus reached out to include new participants from the Third World—particularly from Latin America, where many intellectuals and young political activists were strongly influenced by neo-Marxist dependency theory analysis of international economic relations. It hosted several conferences in Europe and sent political missions to developing countries during the 1970s. These provided opportunities for leftist Third World political leaders and intellectuals to present their views on needed global changes to European Socialist, Social Democratic, and Labour Party representatives (including to those out of power in France and Spain).[39]

Symbolic Actions by the Right in Europe and Canada

By the early 1970s, center and center-right parties—especially Christian-inspired parties in countries such as the FRG, the Netherlands, and Belgium—shared the left's view that more should be done for developing countries. Like center-left parties in Europe, they supported in their respective parliaments increased appropriations for official aid. Several rightist parties in Canada and Europe (particularly in France and Great Britain) were far more sympathetic to Third World aspirations than the Republican Party in the United States.

[38] Arnold, *Implementing Development Assistance*, pp. 35, 71.
[39] Interview with Hendrik van der Heijden, OECD. See also Evers, "European Social Democracy in Latin America."

Charles de Gaulle, for example—after setbacks to French foreign policy objectives in Indochina in 1954, the Suez in 1956, and Algeria in 1962—attempted to reestablish French prestige in international affairs by setting a course for France independent of U.S. hegemony. Part of his strategy was to espouse several of the items on the agenda of developing countries after the mid-1960s, including increased economic assistance by both superpowers, nonintervention in the domestic affairs of developing nations by outside powers, and international price stabilization for agricultural commodities. De Gaulle also increased French economic and technical assistance and entered into some preferential trade agreements with developing countries.[40]

Even though much of this aid and trade under de Gaulle went to French overseas territories, departments, and ex-colonies in Africa (and resulted in material benefits for France), the impact of such measures was not lost on developing countries, even those without close cultural and economic ties to France. Although de Gaulle could not deliver all that he espoused or convince other North Atlantic countries to agree to tariff and commodity price changes, the fact that he publicly identified with developing countries' interests and heralded them on trips through Asia, Africa, and Latin America in his last years in office was an important symbolic action that enhanced French prestige in these countries. Such a strategy created a positive and independent image for France vis-à-vis the United States during the escalation of the Vietnam War. De Gaulle's symbolic successes were also not lost on others in the French right. They were continued by President Valéry Giscard d'Estaing during his term in the late 1970s.

In both Great Britain and Canada, although lacking the flare of a de Gaulle, rightist parties from the early 1960s on were officially supportive of increased aid to the Third World. After the process of decolonization was completed, British power in developing countries increasingly depended on diplomatic and moral influence (as in the case of France), since the 1967 sterling crisis limited the amount of resources available for British overseas aid. The right in Great Britain recognized the importance of at least rhetorically supporting Third World needs. The Conservative Party, under the leadership of Edward Heath between 1965 and 1975 (who was prime minister from 1970 to 1974), agreed in principle with many of the policies espoused by the Labour Party (in power from 1964 to 1970 and from 1974 to 1979)—namely, that the level of British aid should be higher and that economic assistance be given with few strings attached. The fact that neither party could deliver on such promises in the 1970s did not detract from the symbolic importance of bipartisan British endorsement of Third World interests.[41]

In Canada the Progressive Conservative Party, traditionally more pragmatic

---

[40] Hanrieder and Auton, *Foreign Policies of West Germany, France and Britain*, p. 148.

[41] Telephone interview with Alonso Roberts, CA.

than many of its European counterparts, went along with Laborite Pierre Trudeau's new foreign policy initiatives of the late 1960s and the early 1970s. There was growing criticism in Canada beginning in the mid-1960s that the country was fast becoming a vassal of the United States as levels of U.S. ownership of Canadian companies increased and as U.S. immigration into Canada accelerated during the Vietnam War. Foreign policy debates in the late 1960s and early 1970s centered around the nature of Canada's relationship to the United States and whether the country was merely a "junior partner" or "satellite" in an American empire.[42]

In such a context the Progressive Conservative Party felt it necessary to distance itself somewhat from its traditional position as staunch defender of U.S. interests. Consequently it tacitly supported Trudeau's policies of diplomatic recognition of the People's Republic of China, reduced Canadian troop commitments to NATO, and encouraged attempts to expand Canadian influence and presence in the Third World through increased foreign aid.[43]

Mounting Third World Pressures on Europe and Canada after 1973

Despite the left's increased commitments to Third World needs in the late 1960s and early 1970s (largely due to ideology) and symbolic or rhetorical gestures by the right (largely due to pragmatism), aid from most European nations and Canada (albeit enjoying increasing economic prosperity) did not significantly increase. The growth of official aid from OECD countries did rise slightly from $21.7 billion in 1967 to $23.2 billion in 1973, but this failed to keep pace with their GNP growth rates. In fact, overall OECD aid as a percentage of GNP in constant terms substantially declined, from 0.42 percent in 1967 to 0.29 percent in 1973—further receding from the readjusted level of 0.7 percent set by the UN General Assembly in 1971 as an aid target for the Second Development Decade (1970–1980).

In the 1960s, despite some gains in health and literacy during an era of economic growth in much of the developing world, more people there were living in serious poverty by 1970 than had been a decade earlier. This was due both to accelerated population growth and economic policies that concentrated resources on urban rather than rural areas and on capital rather than labor-intensive programs—neither of which directly benefited the vast majority of unskilled laborers and peasants constituting 40 to 50 percent of the Third World populations.[44]

This widening gap between strong rhetorical support by many political lead-

[42] Gordon, *A Choice for Canada*; Clarkson, ed., *Independent Foreign Policy*; Warnock, *Partner to Behemoth*.

[43] Nossal, *Politics of Canadian Foreign Policy*, pp. 13–14; Landes, *Canadian Polity*, pp. 260–63.

[44] OECD, *Twenty-five Years of Development Cooperation*, 49, 52.

ers in Europe and Canada and the actual aid performance of OECD nations amidst growing poverty overseas was sharply challenged by Third World leaders after the October 1973 oil shock. In a special session of the UN General Assembly in early 1974, principles for a new international economic order (NIEO) were strongly endorsed at the urging of developing country representatives, who by then constituted an overwhelming majority of delegates.

Those who were oil-importing countries (the vast majority) suffered severe trade imbalances and mounting debt problems in the wake of oil price increases in late 1973. The principles they thus articulated for an NIEO called for changes in the international economic system based on "equity, equality, sovereignty, interdependence, common interests and cooperation among all regardless of their economic and social systems." The purpose of a new order was to "correct inequalities and rectify current injustices, eliminate the growing gap between the developed and developing countries, and thus guarantee peace and justice for future generations."[45]

The "Plan of Action" recommended by the General Assembly to implement these principles included the following recommendations, all aimed at effecting significant policy changes by governments or corporations of industrial nations:

1. Market arrangements assuring stable, remunerative, and equitable prices for export commodities of developing countries.
2. Processing in developing countries of raw materials extracted by foreign firms.
3. Reduction or removal in developed countries of tariff barriers affecting export products of developing countries.
4. Substantial increases in financial aid to developing countries on softened terms and in predictable, continuous, and increasingly assured flows.
5. Reconfirmation of developed country commitments to reach annual concessional aid transfers amounting to 0.7 percent of GNP no later than 1980.
6. Convening of a major international conference under UN auspices to devise ways of mitigating the debt burden of developing nations.
7. The establishment of an international code of conduct for the transfer of technology to developing countries corresponding to their special needs.
8. The implementation of national and international policies to counter the "brain drain" of qualified personnel from developing to developed countries.
9. Encouragement by home governments to their respective transnational enterprises that they participate in investment projects within the development plans of developing countries.[46]

[45] UN General Assembly, Resolution 3201, April 1, 1974.
[46] These are among the significant recommendations of the UN Sixth and Seventh Special Sessions of 1974 and 1975, as summarized in Tinbergen, *Reshaping the International Order*, pp. 48–49.

In addition to this escalating pressure by developing nations for major re-structuring of global economic relations, a series of international conferences and commissions subsequently issued reports calling for similar drastic re-forms both among and inside nations to alleviate global poverty. The 1976 World Employment Conference, sponsored by the UN International Labour Organization (ILO), criticized traditional forms of aid as ineffectual for as-sisting the poor due to its primary concentration on large, capital-intensive infrastructural projects. The conference argued instead for a basic-human-needs (BHN) approach, which targeted aid on improving food, shelter, pota-ble water, clothing, health, employment, and education for the bottom 40 per-cent of income groups who constituted the hard-core poor in developing coun-tries. Such a strategy, argued the conference, required not only more effective aid policies by rich nations but also structural reforms within developing coun-tries such as a major focus on rural development by governments, significant agrarian reform, and "mass participation of the rural population in the internal political process so as to safeguard their interests."[47]

As a follow-up to the resolutions adopted by the Sixth Special Session of the UN General Assembly in 1974, the Club of Rome commissioned a blue-ribbon committee of experts to suggest in more detail what was needed to implement the NIEO. Its report—known as the RIO (Reshaping the Interna-tional Order) study and issued in 1976, the year of the ILO World Employment Conference—espoused an ideology for global development of "humanistic socialism" based on equity, freedom, democracy and participation, solidarity, cultural diversity, and environmental integrity. It called for industrial coun-tries to substantially increase economic assistance (by $23 billion annually for ten years) to meet the most basic needs of the poor in developing countries. It urged them to limit their own domestic consumption of scarce world re-sources, curb spending on armaments, and monitor the social costs of new technologies being developed in and exported from their own societies. The report also called for more "consciousness raising" among citizens in the in-dustrialized countries to convince them of the necessity for such an agenda. Finally, it urged major structural changes inside developing countries, such as land reform, the expansion of labor-intensive employment opportunities, and redistribution of resources from rich minorities to the poorest 40 to 50 percent of the population.[48]

Both the ILO World Employment Conference and the RIO study were shaped by development experts around the globe, but those from Europe and developing countries dominated. The RIO study group was headed by a lead-

[47] International Labour Organization (ILO), *Employment, Growth, and Basic Needs*, pp. 189–214.
[48] Tinbergen, *Reshaping the International Order*, pp. 61–68, 74–77, 111, 129, 133.

ing Dutch development economist Jan Tinbergen and was given major financial support by the Dutch government at the urging of Jan Pronk, minister for development cooperation in the Labour government. Both of these reports were given far more attention among European policymakers and European media than in the United States. The U.S. delegate to the ILO World Employment Conference, in fact, expressed serious reservations about the final report's endorsement of an NIEO.

In 1978, as a follow-up to these two ILO-sponsored initiatives, Willy Brandt, outgoing chancellor of the Federal Republic of Germany, convened an Independent Commission on International Development Issues (later known as the Brandt Commission) with the participation of several leading European and Canadian political figures from the right and left, such as Edward Heath of Great Britain, Olof Palme of Sweden, Jan Pronk of the Netherlands, Edgard Pisani of France, and Joe Morris of Canada. The commission's report (issued in 1980) confirmed the major recommendations of the UN special session in 1974, as well as those of the ILO Conference and RIO study. These called for major structural transformations in the international economic system and inside developing countries favoring the poorest sectors.[49]

As was the case with the ILO World Employment Conference and the RIO study, European and Third World representatives dominated membership on the Brandt Commission, with only two U.S. participants among its twenty members. Neither of the U.S. participants—Katharine Graham, publisher of *The Washington Post*, and Peter Peterson, chairman of the board of Lehman Brothers—were top political figures. Like the two ILO-sponsored events, the Brandt Commission report had much less impact on political discourse in the United States than in Europe and Canada because there was little public debate on Third World issues at the time, other than over how to end the Vietnam War.

It was evident that the thrust of these proposals required far more profound political and economic transformations, both internationally and within developing countries, than those envisioned in the "new directions" approach for foreign aid begun in the United States in 1973. The basic-needs strategy endorsed that year by the U.S. Congress (analyzed in the previous chapter) did not require significant alterations of international trade and investment policies. Nor did it endorse significant power changes inside developing countries. It aimed at widening the participation of the poorest sectors in the benefits of expanding economic growth spurred by increased aid, not at shifting radically the balance of existing economic and political power among nations or in favor

---

[49] Independent Commission on International Development Issues (Brandt Commission), *North-South*, pp. 380–92.

of the poor inside developing nations—the approach explicitly endorsed in the more controversial NIEO agenda.

New Diplomatic and Aid Strategies in Europe and Canada after 1973

Given the serious gap between rhetoric and performance in European and Canadian aid policies by the early 1970s and the mounting pressure for more serious commitments to developing countries' needs, policymakers in Europe and Canada after 1973 had to find more effective measures. Their own societies, however, were also experiencing serious negative economic effects from the 1973 oil price increases and the second price shock of 1978. Economic downturn, followed by recession, began to plague their domestic economies from the mid-1970s on, making substantial increases in overseas aid very difficult to sell to their respective publics.

Moreover, many of the points on the agenda of the NIEO clearly required very significant changes in private lifestyles and policies in their home societies. A very strong and widespread domestic political base would be needed to undertake such transformations, something which political leaders could not generate during a period of declining economic prosperity after 1974. Members of the OECD Development Assistance Committee (DAC), in fact, met in 1975 to address the NIEO agenda, but the meeting produced no agreement for a strategy on how to begin to implement such proposals.

Both President Giscard d'Estaing of France and Prime Minister Trudeau of Canada personally undertook diplomatic efforts in the late 1970s and early 1980s to promote greater North-South understanding and cooperation. Following de Gaulle's symbolic gestures of identifying with Third World issues, Giscard convened the Conference on International Economic Cooperation in Paris, where delegates from twenty-seven developed and developing nations met over an eighteen-month period (from December 1975 until June 1977) to discuss several of the items on the NIEO agenda, including trade, commodity prices, and debt. No substantial agreements, however, were reached between rich and poor nation representatives at the conference.

France subsequently took the leadership in the United Nations on behalf of an Integrated Program for Commodities and lobbied other North Atlantic countries to support price stabilization for Third World exports (including oil and other sources of energy badly needed by European industries in the wake of the 1973 oil shock). Again, these diplomatic overtures by Giscard's government failed to produce significant breakthroughs on the NIEO agenda.[50]

Pierre Trudeau of Canada, following a return to power after a brief absence in 1979, undertook in 1980 and 1981 another major diplomatic initiative to generate agreement among the major powers for new steps on a North-South

[50] Hessel, "France and the Third World."

dialogue. A special focus of his attention was attempting (to no avail) to get the Reagan administration to hold global negotiations on the growing gap between industrialized and developing countries.[51]

No substantive agreements between rich and poor nations resulted from these diplomatic initiatives. Issues of primary concern to Third World countries in the NIEO agenda—e.g., sweeping tariff reforms by North Atlantic countries, limitations on MNCs, curbs on armament spending, guarantees for price stabilization of Third World commodities—all were far too difficult politically and economically for North Atlantic countries to implement.

Individually as well as collectively, however, some European governments beginning in 1975 did try to improve their overseas aid performance so as to make a greater impact on Third World poverty. Following the example of the 1973 "new directions" approach of the U.S. Congress (and the World Bank's support in the same year for a "global impact" to eradicate poverty), several nations committed themselves to focusing greater portions of their aid on the poorest people in the Third World.

A white paper on new directions for aid policy in Great Britain (issued in 1975, one year after the Labour Party came to power again) indicated that British aid would henceforth be concentrated on the poorest countries and poorest sectors within them, and that aid to such nations would be exclusively in grant form. The FRG in a statement the same year redefined its development aid policy along similar lines, promising that rural development and agriculture within the poorest nations would receive the concentration of its official aid.[52]

The nine member nations of the EEC signed a five-year collective agreement in late 1975 with forty-five former European colonial countries in Africa, the Caribbean and the Pacific (ACP countries). This first Lomé Convention, as it was called, provided for the stabilization of export earnings from primary products for these ACP countries, removed tariff and quota barriers on ACP industrial exports to EEC nations, and set up a multilateral European Development Loan Fund (EDF) for both ACP and nonassociated developing nations.[53]

In 1977 the members of DAC, two years after having been unable to address in comprehensive fashion the NIEO agenda, adopted a statement on "Development Cooperation for Economic Growth and Basic Human Needs." This

---

[51] Nossal, *Politics of Canadian Foreign Policy*, p. 96. See also Nossal, "Personal Diplomacy and National Behavior."

[52] Ministry of Overseas Development, *Changing Emphasis in British Aid Policies*; Federal Ministry for Economic Cooperation (BMZ), *Development Policy Concept of the Federal Republic of Germany*.

[53] "Statement by DAC members on Development Cooperation for Economic Growth and Meeting Basic Human Needs," October 27, 1977 (cited in Arnold, *Implementing Development Assistance*, p. 177).

position paper recommended that all OECD member nations make a primary focus of their official aid programs meeting the most basic survival needs of the poor in developing countries, a policy already officially endorsed by the United States in 1973, and by Great Britain and Germany in 1975.[54]

A Second Look at NGOs by European Governments

As part of the new commitment to focus more aid on the basic survival needs of the poorest people overseas, governments in Europe and Canada began to look more to NGOs for assistance. After the mid-1970s, several governments and intergovernmental organizations that were giving very minimal or no assistance to NGOs initiated substantial matching grants to NGOs for their overseas projects—Great Britain and Finland in 1975, the CEC, Belgium, and Switzerland in 1976, France and Ireland in 1977. After the mid-1970s, others who had inaugurated NGO cofinancing programs in the 1960s—the FRG, the Netherlands, Sweden, and Canada—all significantly increased their public subsidies to nonprofits supporting overseas projects.

Although their own overall official aid flows jumped about 15 percent in real terms in nine years (from $14.8 billion in 1973 to $17 billion in 1982), public aid channeled through NGOs from Europe and Canada increased 425 percent in constant value from 1973 to 1983—from $160 million to $680 million. As a result, the percentage of European and Canadian NGO overall resources provided by government grants increased from 16 percent in 1973 to 36 percent in 1983 (see table 7.1).[55]

The Labour government in the Netherlands, for example, despite reservations voiced by some members when cofinancing of NGOs began in 1965, found after ten years of experience that such an arrangement had been eminently successful from an administrative vantage point. By having the major NGO organizations prescreen and administer many projects to be financed whole or in part by the government, much time was saved for the government's own Directorate General for International Cooperation—especially during a period of expanding official aid commitments after 1965.[56]

In 1975, therefore, more flexibility was introduced into the Dutch NGO cofinancing program, waiving the requirement the NGOs must always pay at least 25 percent of project costs and increasing allowances for administrative expenses. Moreover, in 1980 the parliament approved block grants to the four NGOs involved in the arrangement (CEBEMO, Catholic; ICCO, Protestant; NOVIB, nondenominational; HIVOS, humanist), thus eliminating completely

[54] Gruhn, "Lomé Convention."

[55] CCIC, *Report of the Task Force on Government Funding*, p. 8; Van der Heijden, "Development Impact and Effectiveness of Nongovermental Organisations," tables 2 and 3; AID, *Voluntary Foreign Aid Programs*, 1974, p. 12.

[56] Arnold, *Implementing Development Assistance*, pp. 95–96.

the necessity of prior government approval of projects to be cofinanced and requiring instead subsequent periodic reports done jointly by government and NGO staffs. As a result of these changes, Dutch government grants to NGOs increased from $91.7 million in 1976 to $122.2 million in 1983.[57]

One reason for this increased interest in NGOs in Europe was their contacts overseas with grass-roots organizations in both urban and rural areas, and thus their ability to reach quickly the poorest sectors—the ones targeted as a priority in the NIEO agenda. Moreover, since the 1960s, almost all the major European NGOs claimed to be focusing much of their development aid precisely on the type of projects emphasized by the blue ribbon study commissions—health, labor-intensive employment, low-income housing, and training—although no substantial evidence as yet existed to estimate their impact on eradicating poverty.

Little official bilateral aid from Europe, however, reached the hard-core poor overseas since it was channeled through host-country governments that mostly emphasized large infrastructural projects and capital-intensive industrial programs. The NIEO agenda strongly urged developing-country governments to place less emphasis on such priorities and to focus more of their attention on providing basic services for the poorest 40 to 50 percent in their respective societies. It was not evident, however, that many were either politically willing or administratively able to make the structural and redistributional changes such exhortations required.

Under such conditions, NGOs became attractive alternatives for European parliaments and aid agencies to finesse administrative and political difficulties overseas. The NGOs were more cost-effective than bilateral mechanisms due to their lower overhead expenses and smaller projects. Cofinancing agreements thus enhanced efficient use of scarce aid resources for European governments during economic difficulties of the mid and late-1970s.

For example, although it had officially committed itself in 1975 to focus more of its official aid on rural development, the SPD government in the FRG found that supporting labor-intensive technology and health and nutrition projects in the poorest nations was quite difficult. A three-year assessment of its aid program, published in 1978 by the BMZ, indicated that recipient governments continued to request the FRG to support (with its highly developed technology) their own emerging modern industrial sectors rather than focusing on BHN programs. The report emphasized the administrative problems involved in trying to reach the poorest sectors overseas, particularly when host governments refused to readjust their own development plans. It also underscored the high investment costs and difficulties in achieving spread effects in small projects targeted to meet basic necessities of the poorest sectors. As a

---

[57] OECD, *Collaboration Between Official Development Cooperation Agencies*, pp. 48–49; OECD, *Twenty-five Years of Development Cooperation*, p. 152.

result, the report concluded that BHN projects were perhaps best left to non-governmental organizations, which purportedly had the needed skills and local contacts to implement them more efficiently than large official aid organizations.[58]

It was also true, however, that as this three-year BMZ study concluded, the *Bundestag* was placing more conditions on its own bilateral aid programs so as to link official development assistance more closely to the generation of employment in FRG industries (such as shipbuilding and railway equipment production) that were experiencing particular economic difficulties after the second global oil shock of 1978. The SPD had to take care of domestic business interests if it was to remain in power. After 1978, therefore, 10 to 15 percent of the BMZ's budget was earmarked for developing country purchase of equipment from these two key industries.[59]

Hence, increased subsidies to NGOs became attractive to the SPD regime, given both the foreign political and the domestic economic constraints on FRG official aid policies by the late 1970s. The BMZ grants jumped from $84.2 million in 1976 to $194.8 million in 1983—a real increase of 131 percent in just seven years.[60] Through such a strategy the SPD government could target some of its resources directly on BHN projects abroad as demanded in the NIEO agenda. By working through NGOs it could also save the bulk of its resources for bilaterally supported projects producing substantial positive feedback on the FRG economy.

Active NGO Lobbying for Public Subsidies

An additional reason for government interest in nonprofits was the fact that by the mid-1970s NGOs themselves were engaging in active lobbying campaigns to get their respective parliaments to initiate or substantially increase public subsidies for their overseas activities. Many made the argument to their governments that they had a comparative advantage over public agencies both in reaching the poor and in meeting directly basic needs. Some also pointed to successful and popular cofinancing arrangements already in existence for several years in Sweden, Germany, the Netherlands, and Canada. The NGOs in Great Britain, France, Belgium, Switzerland, Finland, and Ireland all pointed to these examples in neighboring countries to help convince their own parliaments that such arrangements should be created in their own countries, thereby reducing public-sector costs in attempting to implement part of the NIEO agenda.

[58] *Development and Cooperation*, (Bonn), March 1978 and May 1978 (cited in Arnold *Implementing Development Assistance*, pp. 37, 38, 66).

[59] Arnold, *Implementing Development Assistance*, p. 37. See also Cziempiel, "Germany and the Third World."

[60] OECD, *Collaboration between Official Development Cooperation Agencies*, p. 152.

The fact that European and Canadian NGOs were sharing information and strategies on a more regular basis by the mid-1970s—through participation in regional federations of NGOs such as the International Council of Voluntary Agencies (ICVA) in Geneva and the International Cooperation for Socioeconomic Development (CIDSE), headquartered in Brussels—increased their knowledge and expertise as an effective lobbying force. For example, at the urging of various European NGO leaders (who had close personal friendships with CEC officials), the CEC established an NGO-Liaison Committee in 1976. This not only further enhanced collective interaction among European NGOs but also gave them more visibility and legitimacy in the public aid sector. In the same year, the CEC also began a multilateral cofinancing program for NGOs. It recognized that this arrangement would allow its own development resources to reach well beyond the ACP nations covered by the 1975 Lomé Convention.

The "piggyback" effect was an additional argument used by NGOs with their home governments for beginning or substantially increasing cofinancing arrangements. Although governments in Europe and Canada had committed themselves to a BHN approach as part of their response to the NIEO, many—especially some of the smaller nations—simply did not have extensive aid missions throughout the developing world. Even large countries such as Great Britain, France, and Germany had bilateral aid agreements with twenty-five or fewer countries in 1980. As a group, European and Canadian NGOs were active in over one hundred countries by the late 1970s, and their respective home governments and intergovernmental organizations could extend their own resources far more quickly and economically over a much wider geographical area through matching grants to NGOs rather than by attempting to expand costly official aid delivery systems.

By channeling more public resources through NGOs, European governments could keep their own costs down at a time of economic entrenchment, fill gaps in their own techniques or geographical scope of overseas aid, finesse domestic economic constraints on their own overseas aid programs, and bypass intransigent Third World governments that theoretically supported a full NIEO agenda in international forums but at home were reluctant to carry out a substantial redistribution of economic and political power within their own societies. Other factors besides documentation of successful development impact, therefore, stimulated increased government interest in and support for NGOs in Europe and Canada after 1975.

From the NGO side, there was also growing interest in new or increased government financing after the mid-1970s. European and Canadian NGOs, in the wake of the oil shock of 1973 and the subsequent domestic economic decline in their respective societies, began to experience problems in generating private funds. Philanthropy for overseas activities declined in the mid-1970s as Europeans and Canadians became more concerned about domestic economic problems. Private donations to NGOs fell from $842.6 million in 1973 to $738.7 million in 1975. By the 1980s they had recovered, reaching $1.11 billion in 1980 and $1.21 billion in 1983. However, the real rate of growth in private donations from 1973 to 1983 (44 percent) was much less than the increases home governments were willing to give them during the same ten-year period. Public subsidies, as mentioned earlier, between 1973 and 1983 jumped 425 percent in real terms, from $160 million to $680 million (see table 7.1).[61]

Need for Greater Public Support of Foreign Aid

A final reason for the increase in public subsidies to NGOs in Europe and Canada from the mid-1970s on was the need for governments to reaffirm citizen support for foreign aid. In the 1960s one of the reasons NGO subsidies were begun by governments in Sweden, the FRG, the Netherlands, and Canada was to stimulate indirectly a public mandate for new official aid commitments. By the mid-1970s, however, a prime concern of governments in Europe and Canada was to keep the public interested in aid at a time when (1) the governments themselves recently had made strong ideological commitments to increase their support for Third World countries, and (2) their own economies were suffering significant setbacks in growth rates and balance of payments ratios.

Many of the NGOs had begun educational programs for their donors and the wider public in their home societies in the 1950s or early 1960s. These were not merely publicity efforts centered around fund-raising campaigns. By the 1970s many NGOs were distributing books, pamphlets, and film strips to make contributors and the society at large more aware of developmental needs abroad—especially the plight of the poorest sectors in Third World nations. During the FFHC in the early 1960s, many of these NGOs had begun working closely with trade unions, professional associations, adult education centers, and cooperatives at home societies to stimulate greater awareness of developing nations' needs. By the 1970s they had also built an extensive domestic educational network through schools, churches, and civic associations.

Part of the increase in government subsidies to NGOs in the 1970s, therefore, was earmarked specifically for development education. Unlike the situation in the United States after 1973, where AID substantially increased its grants to PVOs for overseas projects or for upgrading their own administrative structures, in several other North Atlantic countries public subsidies were given specifically for NGOs to expand their existing domestic programs of consciousness raising.

Canada took the lead in giving educational subsidies to NGOs in 1971

[61] Van der Heijden, "Development Impact and Effectiveness of Nongovernmental Organisations," table 2; CCIC, *Report of the Task Force on Government Funding*, p. 8; AID, *Voluntary Foreign Aid Programs*, 1974, p. 12.

through its Public Participation Program. By the late 1970s CIDA was providing nearly $3 million annually for Canadian NGOs to prepare and distribute development materials at home. By the late 1970s nine European nations had also initiated aid for NGO educational programs, reaching a combined total of over $19.9 million in 1977—with the Netherlands ($5.1 million), Sweden ($4.5 million), and the FRG ($3.9 million) accounting for the bulk of these grants.[62]

By providing matching grants in the late 1970s for NGO domestic education, European and Canadian governments wanted to achieve two goals: (1) stimulate increased philanthropy for international assistance by helping NGOs expand their visibility among actual and potential donors at home and (2) solidify citizen support for larger governmental aid commitments abroad during hard economic times. Although not addressing the more difficult items on the NIEO agenda, political officials were hoping to close the gap somewhat between their expanded rhetorical commitments to the South in the 1970s and the actual performance of their aid and trade programs constrained by domestic economic and political factors.

Although some of these NGO programs (as mentioned earlier) included criticisms of home-country policies in aid, trade, and overseas investment, European parliaments and official aid agencies believed the trade-off of costs and benefits was in their favor. They also realized they had several means at their disposal to prevent NGO pressures at home from becoming politically embarrassing (which will be described in chapter 7).

CONCLUSIONS

European and Canadian NGOs shared some similarities with PVOs in the post–World War II era: (1) early concentration on relief in the immediate postwar years, (2) a shift of interest to longer-term socioeconomic development programs in the 1950s and 1960s, and (3) lobbying activities in parliaments for increased public subsidies in the wake of declining private support in the 1970s.

However, throughout the thirty-five-year period from 1945 to 1980, there were several factors that made the evolution of European and Canadian NGOs different from that of their counterparts in the United States. These relate to the timing and type of government subsidies received, the different motivations of both private and governmental donors to NGOs, and the particular relationships that most of these other North Atlantic nations had with developing countries.

Unlike the situation in the United States in the postwar years, European and Canadian governments did not own surplus domestic food commodities that

[62] OECD, *Collaboration Between Official Development Cooperation Agencies*, pp. 18–71.

they needed to dispose of abroad to protect domestic agricultural prices. The NGOs in these societies were thus not induced to prolong relief-type work overseas beyond the late 1940s and early 1950s because they simply had no access to massive material assistance from their home governments as did PVOs.

Nor did European governments, in the wake of the devastating domestic impact of World War II, have the resources to initiate grants to nonprofits as early as in the United States. Many European governments also had a strong interest in maintaining control for as long as possible over colonial territories. They wanted to use their scarce aid resources to influence directly the evolution of these societies moving towards independence in the late 1940s and 1950s. Thus, they had no interest in initiating subsidies to NGOs until well into the 1960s, when full economic recovery was secured and the process of decolonization well under way (ten years after government grants to PVOs began in the United States).

European and Canadian NGOs thus more quickly distanced themselves from relief-type work than several of their large U.S. counterparts, who by the 1950s increasingly came to rely on government food subsidies. Unlike PVOs, NGOs were also forced by the economic and political constraints on their governments to go longer without public cash subsidies for overseas development work. They had to rely exclusively on private donations to undertake expanding overseas development commitments in the 1950s. All of these differences—no food subsidies, a quicker end to an exclusive focus on relief, and only private support for the initiation of Third World development efforts—were major factors that distinguished NGOs from PVOs in the post–World War II period.

Most Europeans (with the exception of citizens of the FRG) were also less preoccupied than were Americans with stopping communism, promoting democracy, and strengthening free enterprise abroad. Other motives for supporting nonprofits were more pressing among Europeans and Canadians. They included (1) creating a humanitarian image for themselves in ex-colonial territories, (2) getting a "foot in the door" economically in the developing world through private surrogates where no colonial heritage existed, and (3) stimulating a greater domestic interest in international commitments in the wake of the collapse of the old colonial order. All of these concerns of both private donors and public policymakers in much of Europe and Canada accounted for expanding contributions to NGOs in the late 1950s and 1960s.

Hence, predominantly pragmatic reasons accounted for increased private and public sector interest in NGOs in both Europe and Canada by the 1960s. In contrast, both U.S. government leaders and citizens at first had more ideological reasons for contributing to PVOs—fighting communism, indirectly subverting right-wing authoritarian regimes, or exporting the American success dream.

Ironically, however, by the 1970s ideological reasons were the major causes for new or expanded contributions to NGOs in Europe and Canada, particularly on the part of government leaders. Unlike the United States, the political spectrum traditionally has had a significant competitive left in electoral politics. The late 1960s and early 1970s was a time, in fact, when center-left parties in several of these countries simultaneously came to exercise or share executive power. They did so with significant support of younger citizens fresh from radical political experiences of student activism in the 1960s. These new governments all felt ideologically compelled, therefore, to show renewed interest in and make expanded promises to Third World nations.

This came at a time when the prestige of the United States in the Third World was tarnished by the Vietnam War. The political left in both Europe and Canada believed it could exploit American weakness by building new lines of influence of their own into developing countries. The center and right in Europe and Canada went along with some of these new initiatives—even making some symbolic gestures of their own toward the Third World—to distance themselves from too close an association with declining U.S. influence internationally.

These political leaders, however, were soon "hoisted on their own petards." In the wake of the oil price shocks in the mid and late-1970s, Third World countries began to call in political IOUs more aggressively, just at a time when several governments in Europe and Canada were least able to convert their new promises into improved aid performance.

In this context, and as a partial response to the NIEO agenda, European and Canadian policymakers adopted the concept of a BHN approach to development—something current in the thinking of their own development economists and already endorsed by both the U.S. government and the World Bank in 1973. However, to begin to shift even some of their limited public aid resources in this new direction quickly and cheaply, they needed delivery systems that could bypass reluctant or incompetent host governments and penetrate to the local level in Third World countries. The NGOs provided important mechanisms to accomplish these objectives due to their contacts with local private counterparts abroad. The NGOs thus enabled European and Canadian governments to make good, at least partially, on ideologically motivated promises when both their financial and administrative capacities to do so were lacking.

The NGOs also became an attractive way for governments to rebuild domestic support bases for overall foreign aid commitments, or at least to keep it from evaporating further. From the early 1960s NGOs had created educational networks at home that were closely linked with those elite groups critical for moulding a stronger constituency for foreign assistance—labor unions, professional associations, cooperatives, adult education centers, schools, and religious institutions.

In contrast, in the United States there was declining interest both in Congress and among citizens in "making the world safe for democracy" in the wake of the Vietnam War and amidst increasing media exposés of CIA covert activities in Third World countries. To justify continued aid to developing countries in the early 1970s, Congress had to articulate reasons other than stopping communism or promoting democratic political development abroad. Neither the majority of American citizens nor most Third World leaders—both critical of U.S. military and covert actions abroad in the name of freedom—would accept the traditional liberal rationale of the 1950s and 1960s for U.S. foreign assistance.

Amidst such a crisis in liberal ideology, humanitarian reasons emerged as the official rationale for U.S. foreign aid programs after 1973—of which a BHN approach to development was a part. As with Europe and Canada, the U.S. government also needed alternate delivery mechanisms to guarantee that some of its aid resources would reach the poorest sector overseas. The PVOs offered such conduits to the economically marginalized abroad.

In expanding public grants to American nonprofits for overseas aid in 1973, the U.S. Congress thus down played the ideological purposes of such aid. It had endorsed in Title 9 of the Foreign Assistance Act of 1966 the usefulness of local nonprofit organizations as carriers of democratic values in developing countries. In 1973 it backed away somewhat from this position for fear of conjuring renewed images abroad of U.S. imperialism as the Vietnam War was winding down and the CIA was coming under heavy criticism. Instead, the Congress, in the "new directions" legislation of 1973, emphasized the critical role of both U.S. and indigenous Third World nonprofits for reaching and alleviating the economic plight of the poor—not for expanding their political power. The United States was turning to a BHN agenda (and therefore to PVOs) just when it was submerging explicit political emphases in its foreign aid rhetoric. Such a strategy was clearly not a means of making good on ideological commitments to the Third World as was the case in Europe and Canada. It was a way of finessing a difficult political problem after an unpopular war.

As we shall see in chapter 5, differences in domestic political culture in the United States from that in much of Europe and Canada—the lack of a salient domestic political left, less sharply defined ideological attitudes about foreign aid in government and society, and a transnational nonprofit sector unconnected to a network of politically active institutions domestically—all continue to shape the character of PVOs, especially their penchant to avoid anything that appears to be political. Differences in each of these dynamics in Europe and Canada also help answer some of the questions raised in chapter 1 as to why many NGOs in these other countries today espouse overt political objectives both at home and abroad.

CHAPTER FIVE

Current Diversity in Private Foreign Aid Objectives: American Pragmatism versus European Utopianism

GIVEN SOME important differences between the evolution of PVOs and NGOs, one would expect that the current priorities among these voluntary agencies might also be diverse. In the interviews I conducted in the early 1980s in Europe, Canada, and the United States, I found this to be the case.

The PVO community as a whole is still more oriented to relief of immediate suffering abroad than is its European and Canadian counterpart, which tends to place more of its resources on longer-term developmental programs. Proportionately, far more nonprofits in Europe and Canada also espouse significant political change abroad and attempt to influence public policies at home on behalf of Third World needs.

These critical differences are directly linked to the resource base of PVO aid, as compared to European and Canadian NGO aid. They are also due to the different relationships nonprofits maintain with other private institutions in their respective home societies across the North Atlantic region and to diverse political cultures in their home societies.

PRIORITIES AND MISSION DEFINITION OF PVOS

Relief Agencies

In the official language of all fifteen PVOs I interviewed in 1982 and 1983 (see appendix B for the list), there was great emphasis placed on promoting long-term socioeconomic change, as opposed to providing relief to alleviate immediate suffering. This is true even among the older organizations that originally had been established in the 1930s and 1940s to assist war refugees or disaster victims—CARE USA, CRS, CWS, LWR, ADRA, SCF, and FPP USA.

Now, all of these nonprofits in their official documents emphasize that they address structural causes of poverty by enhancing technical skills and access to resources or by supporting local organizations that can promote greater self-reliance among the poor. One or more of these themes are highlighted in the literature describing the goals of these agencies and are ingredients of what they consider to be their new thrust in promoting development.

For example, CARE USA, set up at the end of World War II to transport food, clothing, and medicines to war-torn Europe, now stresses that it exists both to "assist the poor in the developing world to achieve sustained improvements in their lives and to offer relief in times of crises when there is acute suffering and life is threatened."[1]

The CRS is the official aid agency of the American Catholic Church, established during World War II to carry out overseas relief. Its charter states that in addition to providing assistance "to impoverished people to alleviate their immediate needs," CRS aims to "support creatively self-determined community activities of people struggling to eradicate the root causes of their poverty [and] to collaborate with groups of good will in programs contributing to a just society in which all may freely participate."[2]

The CWS, founded by the National Council of Churches just after World War II for humanitarian work abroad, today makes this official policy statement: "An effective battle against disease, hunger, poverty and disaster calls not only for relief assistance but development aid that enables people to conquer their problems themselves. Church World Service provides many resources that allow development to germinate—tools, skilled people, money. . . ."[3]

The FPP USA, which began in the 1930s as an orphan-support agency, now defines its goals in much wider terms:

Our programs are designed to help families and communities become more self-reliant. We help families develop the means, abilities and ideas necessary to meet their own needs.

Our programs emphasize individual self-help, widespread participation and project sustainability.[4]

In my interviews with executive and staff persons in all fifteen PVOs, it became clear that, for both the nine older agencies, as well as the six founded since the 1960s, a major factor accounting for the current consensus among them was the shift in thinking by the 1960s about the nature and causes of poverty overseas. Several indicated that new emphases emerging among social scientists, the media, or government policymakers a generation ago on the need to attack the structural causes of underdevelopment rather than to alleviate symptoms convinced them to orient more of their own priorities in this direction.

However, in analyzing budgetary allocations and probing further in my interviews, I found that there were significant differences between official or-

[1] *CARE's Use of Food Aid*, p. 5.

[2] "The Charter of Catholic Relief Services (Revised April 1978)," in CRS, *CRS: Catholic Relief Services*.

[3] CWS, *Church World Service Annual Report, 1980*.

[4] FPP USA, *Journey*, p. 2.

ganizational rhetoric and style of performance. Some of the older and larger PVOs—namely CRS, CARE USA, and ADRA—despite a new language about fostering longer-term change, still rely predominantly on resources that are geared to short-term alleviation of suffering.

These agencies are among the largest PVOs today, and the ones that beginning in the 1950s linked themselves closely to the U.S. government's food surplus distribution program abroad. They still rely overwhelmingly (for 70 percent or more of their resources) on food to support overseas programs (see appendix C, table 1). Just as the U.S. government in the early 1960s began to change the rhetoric of its overseas food aid program (so as to make it fit new U.S. developmental objectives), so too the few large PVOs that became major networks for the distribution of these commodities abroad shifted their official mission definition.

The publications of most of these PVOs refer to the bulk of the material aid they send overseas as developmental assistance. A good deal of it is used in nutrition projects for mothers and their children under five, school-age children and elderly persons, and food-for-work projects (in construction, irrigation, and sanitation) administered by local governments. They also try, as one CRS spokesperson told me, to use food aid in such nonemergency circumstances to support new community organizations that emerge around feeding centers and food-for-work projects. In 1981, for example, CRS indicated that 65.8 percent of its total resources were devoted to human development as opposed to emergency relief, refugee aid, or humanitarian assistance to the aged, orphans, or handicapped.[5]

However, representatives whom I interviewed in these three organizations (two in CRS, three in CARE USA, and one in ADRA) did not use the development language emphasized in official publications. I asked them to prioritize six different goals for their organizations: (1) immediate alleviation of suffering; (2) increasing income and/or employment; (3) improvement of skills and problem-solving capacities; (4) enhancement of recipient bargaining power vis-à-vis local merchants, credit institutions, government agencies, etc.; (5) construction of new community-run institutions and networks; and (6) empowerment of the poor to challenge and change dominant political and economic structures. All respondents, despite the development rhetoric in their public documents, chose the first as the most important goal for their institutions in selecting projects to support abroad.

Dr. William M. Pruzensky, regional director for Central America and the Caribbean of CRS in 1983, indicated why a relief goal is still primary for his organization:

Most of the staff at CRS think they are development-oriented by using relief materials for development, but we may very well be primarily a relief organization. Most

[5] CRS, *Annual Report, 1981*, p. 35.

of our resources are relief in nature. We have a foot in both worlds, old and new. Some newer emphases in food aid are in development, i.e., encouraging new community organizations and work projects supported by food, but it is difficult to say how much of this is development. In Central America, probably not much of it is.[6]

Monsignor Roland Bordelon, Director for South America of CRS in 1983, gave some additional reasons as to why immediate relief of suffering is still dominant in the organization:

There is a difference between stated goals and resource allocations. Most in CRS would like to say we are a development agency because relief is no longer in vogue. Nevertheless, we jump when an emergency occurs. Moreover, food remains our main resource. Some would say food is development aid assistance, but this is not completely true since the priorities for food [outside of disaster situations] are feeding programs for mothers and children under five, food-for-work projects, and food for school children and older persons. . . . The bishops want to be seen as the biggest and best providers of the corporal works of mercy. Therefore, relief is stressed.[7]

George F. Kraus, regional program officer for Latin America of CARE USA until early 1983, voiced a similar judgment about his organization's actual priorities. He indicated that the orientation of the board of directors was still towards the immediate alleviation of human suffering:

The Board of Directors pushes towards relief. Several members date back to the 1940s in their experience with overseas aid and do not talk about poverty in the same way as structuralists. They believe it results from cataclysms. . . . Half are still concerned only with the delivery of goods to poor persons. Another board group wants to focus on emergencies. Short-run and long-term goals are not distinguished among board members.[8]

[6] Interview with Dr. William M. Pruzensky, CRS.

[7] Interview with Rev. Msgr. Roland Bordelon, CRS. Since 1983 there have been some major initiatives inside CRS to accelerate the organization's transition from relief to development. In July 1983 a new executive director was appointed, and for the first time in the organization's history he was a layman—Laurence A. Pezzulo, former U.S. ambassador to Nicaragua. He mandated that all the staff and field representatives prepare three-year phase-out plans for PL 480 Food for Peace programs in each country where CRS was administering such aid. He also expanded efforts to raise more cash resources for long-range development projects through direct mail appeals to individual Catholics in selected dioceses of the United States (to supplement income from the once-a-year Lenten donations made through collections in local churches). Given the long and excellent record CRS has had as a relief organization during disasters and the 1984–1985 famine in Ethiopia, where it administered the largest PL 480 food aid program of any PVO, it remains difficult to phase out food aid rapidly. Longer-term food phase-out plans have been prepared for Africa and Latin America, but in some of the countries (Haiti, Ethiopia) hunger and serious malnutrition will continue to be critical problems for some time to come. Interviews with Terence Martin, Lenny Vargas and Ronda Kogan, CRS.

[8] Interview with George F. Kraus, CARE USA. I interviewed Mr. Kraus one day after he had resigned from CARE USA.

Although the words have changed in some older PVOs regarding the causes of poverty and what constitutes their mission, several of the largest still concentrate their energies in areas where they have a proven track record—moving material assistance quickly to alleviate hunger and sickness. Some staff members (who write publicity materials) may prefer to be development-oriented, and this certainly is the image the U.S. government wants its surplus food program to have. When pushed, however, these representatives admit that immediate alleviation of suffering is still the primary goal. Their organizations' resource allocations (most of which are in the form of material supplies) still reflect a relief orientation rather than a structural focus.

The remainder of the overseas aid resources of these three agencies in 1981 was cash raised either from private sources or U.S. government grants ($61.2 million for CRS, $37.7 million for CARE USA, and $2.9 million for ADRA). It was spent mostly for technical assistance projects aimed at resource and production improvement or training—water development; natural resource conservation; the construction of schools, low-income housing, or health facilities; and the inculcation of better farming technologies. Hence, all six respondents from these three agencies prioritized as organizational goals—just after the immediate alleviation of suffering—increasing income and/or employment, and improving skills and problem-solving capacities of the poor.

The CRS, CARE USA, and ADRA are among the largest of all PVOs, and their combined overseas aid in 1981 totaled nearly one half ($712.2 million—or 48.4 percent) of the total aid of the eighty largest PVOs (see appendix C, table 1). As seen in table 5.1 below, the combined overseas aid of all twenty-three major relief-oriented PVOs reached $997.1 million, or 67.9 percent of the total foreign transfers ($1.47 billion) of the eighty largest PVOs. Moreover, $599.3 million (60.1 percent) was in the form of government subsidies,

TABLE 5.1
Statistics on PVOs with Largest Relief Programs, 1981 (in 1986 dollar values)

Overseas Aid of Largest Relief PVOs	$997.1 million
As Percentage of Total Aid of All Largest PVOs	67.9
Government Subsidies to Largest Relief PVOs	$599.3
As Percentage of Their Resources	60.1
As Percentage of Total Government Subsidies to All Largest PVOs	79.8
Food-Related Subsidies from Government to Largest Relief PVOs	$506.4
As Percentage of Their Overseas Aid	50.8
As Percentage of Total Government Aid to All Largest PVOs	67.4

Source: AID, Voluntary Foreign Aid Programs, 1982, pp. 21–27.
N = 23

and over one-half ($506.4 million) were PL 480 food commodities or payments to defray the cost of shipping them. Finally, 79.8 percent of all government aid ($599.3 million of $750.8 million) was given to these 23 agencies. Just food-related aid alone to these relief PVOs constituted 67.4 percent of all U.S. government assistance.

Despite new structural emphases in language among most PVO since the 1960s, in reality a relief focus still dominates those that account for nearly two-thirds of the resource transfers of the largest organizations. A major reason for this has been the size of food and food-related subsidies that are provided to just a few very large agencies. In the 1950s the government began using PVOs to help in the disposal abroad of food surpluses that the U.S. Department of Agriculture purchased from American farmers to keep domestic food prices high. This pattern accelerated in the 1960s and continues to be the thrust of overall resource allocations of the whole PVO community.

It also reflects the government's own priorities in implementing since 1973 its "new directions" in foreign aid through the U.S. transnational nonprofit network. Although government cash subsidies between 1973 and 1980 substantially increased, the food proportion remained about the same—accounting for 65.1 percent in 1973 and 66.1 percent in 1981.

It is also true that many private donors to U.S. PVOs prefer to give to these larger relief PVOs. Nearly two-fifths (39.9 percent—$397.8 million) of the overseas aid of the largest relief PVOs in 1980 originated from private donations. This accounted for well over one-half (55.6 percent) of all private contributions (716.1 million) to the eighty largest PVOs in 1981. It is not the U.S. government's agricultural policy alone that accounts for the predominance of a relief focus in overall PVO aid resources. It is also the preferences of Americans who want largely to contribute to those aid organizations that have a long reputation as being effective in the immediate relief of suffering abroad.

Technically Oriented PVOs

A second category of PVOs consists of those smaller organizations that concentrate primarily on technical training to improve basic skills or infrastructure in areas of health, education, or rural development. These outnumber thirty-two to twenty-three the larger relief agencies, but in 1981 accounted for only about one-fifth (22.8 percent—or $227.5 million of $997.1 million) of the resource transfers of these larger relief-type nonprofits. (See appendix C, table 2). All of their aid is in cash grants or technical equipment. They transfer no food.

The U.S. nonprofits in this category, therefore, tend to prioritize their objectives in longer-terms than do relief agencies. Representatives of the two technically oriented PVOs in my sample—AITEC and the Pan American Development Foundation (PADF)—ranked first and second as organizational goals improving the skills and problem-solving capacities of the poor and increasing income and/or employment opportunities.

Multiservice Institution Builders

The third category of PVOs engaged in overseas assistance also tends to stress long-term structural solutions to poverty. Rather than targeting their resources on predominantly technical problems, however, these PVOs tend to support a whole variety of intermediary indigenous Third World nonprofits who administer or support social services at the grass-roots level among the poor. These address basic health, nutrition, housing, education, income generation, and techniques of local community organizing.

Nearly one-third, twenty-five of eighty largest PVOs in 1981, belonged in this category. But, as in the case of technically oriented PVOs, their combined overseas aid in 1980 ($242.3 million) was less than one-fourth (24.3 percent) of the resources sent abroad by the twenty-three largest relief agencies ($997.1 million). As a group they receive proportionately much less U.S. government aid than either relief or technically oriented PVOs. Federal subsidies accounted for under one-third (31.2 percent) of their combined budgets in 1981—$75.6 million of $242.3 million (see appendix C, table 3).

Eighteen of twenty-five PVOs in category three, were founded prior to the 1960s, some dating back to the late eighteenth and nineteenth centuries and having religious affiliations. Most of these receive little or no U.S. government aid.

Some PVOs established primarily as relief agencies during or immediately after World War II—CWS, LWR, and the Unitarian Universalist Service Committee (UUSC)—in recent years have been de-emphasizing relief aid and concentrating instead on cash grants for social service projects carried out by indigenous church-affiliated and nonsectarian organizations abroad. They also support network-building by sponsoring regional and international meetings of representatives from Third World nonprofits to facilitate sharing of information and strategies of community-organizing.[9]

The SCF and FPP USA—both originally founded in the 1930s to care for orphans and children of destitute families in war-torn countries—now support local private community-development organizations in Asia, Africa, and Latin America that administer projects in health, education, nutrition, and employment. Although children benefit from such activities, they are no longer the direct targets or recipients of assistance. Instead, the social services of communities in which they live are being upgraded with significant voluntary commitments of time and manual labor by their parents.[10]

[9] Interviews with Rev. Oscar Bolioli, and Rev. Antonio Ramos, CWS; J. Robert Busche, LWR; Dr. Richard S. Scobie, UUSC.

[10] Interviews with John P. Grant, SCF, and Kenneth H. Phillips, FPP USA.

During the 1970s the Ford Foundation also shifted some of its resources to multiservice institution-building among low-income sectors abroad. Its original focus in developing countries in the 1950s and 1960s was on strengthening university institutions and social science research facilities (primarily of benefit to middle-class sectors), but over the past twenty years has focused more of its resources on rural community organizations among small farmers and on human rights groups providing legal information and social-service assistance to those in trouble with their respective governments. In both cases, this new thrust of the Ford Foundation is assisting many low-income rural and urban groups and is also fostering organizational networks that have grass-roots linkages.[11]

Several newer PVOs founded in the late 1960s and early 1970s, such as Oxfam America, Coordination in Development (CODEL) and Private Agencies Collaborating Together (PACT)—the latter two being federations of smaller PVOs—also emphasize strengthening local community organizations. The institutions they support abroad involve low-income people in designing and implementing service programs. They also provide participants with opportunities to discuss, and address, what they identify as the most pressing problems in their respective communities.[12]

Many of the indigenous Third World institutions supported by the U.S. PVOs in this third category finance technical components provided by local skilled personnel—e.g., improved agricultural techniques, prefabricated housing construction, the training of paramedical personnel, and credit advice. The emphasis, however, is not so much on the transfer of technology or equipment from abroad (as in the case of PVOs in category two) but on assisting intermediary and grass-roots organizations that in turn can help low-income people initiate and carry out programs in a wide variety of social services.

The PVOs in category three see as their major innovative thrust the dispelling of isolation and hopelessness among the poor in Third World countries by stimulating collective self-help action and community organization-building. Many of the projects carried out by indigenous nonprofits abroad in this area do, in fact, include a component of consciousness-raising among recipients. Literacy training, adult education, and women's solidarity groups are often associated with such service projects. They involve stimulating awareness of and discussion about the most urgent obstacles to economic and social improvement of their communities—many of which are the result of structural inequities, such as maldistribution of land, a monopoly over credit or market-

[11] Interview with Jeffrey M. Puryear, Ford Foundation.
[12] Interviews with Joseph Short, Oxfam America; Kenneth E. Brown, CODEL; James F. O'Brien, PACT.

ing facilities enjoyed by a few individuals, or a chronic neglect of the community by local government agencies.

Changing Political Structures Abroad Not an Explicit Goal of PVOs

Given these potentially controversial aspects of service support in Third World countries (especially when consciousness-raising of participants occurs), one might expect that some PVOs would endorse political change as part of their overseas mission. However, the overwhelming majority of respondents in all PVOs in my survey ranked very low (or excluded as a mission) empowerment of the poor to challenge and change dominant political and economic structures.

Respondents from the first two clusters of PVOs—the three that are predominantly relief (CRS, CARE USA, ADRA); and the two that are technically oriented (AITEC and PADF)—did not rank empowerment high on their list of priorities since they claimed their focus is clearly in a different direction. Of the eight persons prioritizing objectives from these five PVOs, five ranked empowerment last, one listed it fifth, and two explicitly rejected it as having any importance as an organizational objective.

Some of these spokespersons said it had no place in the scope of activities of a nonprofit organization in a developing country, since aiding the poor is essentially a humanitarian or technical issue and not related to politics. They claimed that the alleviation of immediate suffering or the building of a technical base to improve the lot of the poor could, and should, go on regardless of the ideology of a particular government. They said that their respective organizations work under all types of regimes since they are totally apolitical. Representatives of six PVOs in my sample took this position—all five that stress predominantly relief or technical aid (CRS, CARE USA, ADRA, AITEC, and PADF) and one that is predominantly a multiservice institution-builder (SCF).

Mario H. Ochoa, assistant executive director for ADRA, simply said: "By definition as a church we don't want to take political positions. Governments should be respected everywhere. We don't take a position on good or bad aspects of governments."[13]

John P. Grant, regional director for Latin America of SCF in 1983, also argued in favor of avoiding political involvement: "We are apolitical according to our status. We are also trying to work in a variety of political environments. There are frequent political fluctuations in Latin America. We have to be apolitical so as to survive in rapidly changing contexts."[14]

George F. Kraus, the regional program officer for Latin America in CARE

[13] Interview with Mario H. Ochoa, ADRA.
[14] Interview with John P. Grant, SCF.

USA until early 1983, expressed a similar view: "I did not support Pinochet's philosophy in Chile, or that of the generals in La Paz, Bolivia, but CARE can do its work on technical grounds—e.g., water projects—and operate in any type of regime for the long-range good of the people."[15]

This position is also in direct continuity with the situation in the 1950s and 1960s, when technically oriented PVOs began to fill gaps in social service delivery mechanisms in developing countries and act as articulators of local group interests to government agencies. Given this preference for practicality and system improvement that dates back thirty years among both relief and technically oriented PVOs, it is not surprising that they do not include controversial political objectives in their overseas mission objectives today.

What was somewhat surprising to find, however, was the fact that PVOs in category three—multiservice institution-building that claim to include an awareness-raising component among participants—also disclaim any political agenda abroad. All ten PVOs in this category that I interviewed ranked very high as their organizational goals items four and five on the list—enhancing recipient bargaining power vis-à-vis local merchants, credit institutions, government agencies, etc.; and building new participatory institutions and networks. Several of the twenty-one representatives interviewed from these ten PVOs (thirteen of whom ranked the six items) commented on how these two goals fit together. The creation of private participatory structures among the poor would lead to an enhancement of their bargaining position with other important social and economic groups or institutions that critically affect their lives. These PVO respondents did not, however, consider any of this to involve politics.

Many representatives of the PVOs in category three ranked empowerment of the poor quite low. Of the thirteen persons from these organizations who prioritized the six goals, two ranked it last, two placed it fifth, and two explicitly rejected it as a goal. Only two ranked it second, two placed it third, and three (all from PACT) listed it first. Hence, only among five of these ten PVOs in category three did respondents rate empowerment of the poor to challenge the dominant political and economic structures in their environment within the top three goals of their respective organizations.

Nine out of ten of the PVOs from my sample in this category did acknowledge that a totally apolitical position was impossible to maintain in their developmental objectives. However, all eighteen respondents in these nine PVOs distinguished between what they considered to be a political position, which they believed unavoidable given the nature of their work, and a partisan political position (involving close linkages with specific parties), which they believed to be harmful and which they claimed to avoid assiduously.

All eighteen respondents in this group of PVOs indicated that building

[15] Interview with George F. Kraus, CARE USA.

grass-roots institutions among the poor had political implications with a "small p" since, when these institutions were effective, they would eventually lead to a redistribution of power in society—economic and political—in favor of the poor. One PVO spokesperson said that participation of people in decision-making (a requirement his PVO demands of its Third World recipient counterparts) is at times political since it is based on an option for democracy, and some governments are against this.[16] Another respondent acknowledged that PVOs have a liberal bias since they encourage participation and collective action in addressing the causes of poverty. This, he said, entails an implicit political ideology.[17]

However, all PVO spokespersons who acknowledged some political implications in their work indicated that their organizations had policies of not giving aid to a Third World counterpart tied to one political party or ideology. Such aid, many argued, would undermine their credibility among the broad range of recipients abroad, would create serious problems with Third World governments, and would definitely upset their donors at home.

Several indicated that at times the overseas counterparts they supported had a political orientation, but were not explicitly tied to or controlled by a partisan organization. A spokesperson for PACT said that "we support a development process even if associated with a political tendency," provided that the recipient organization is not part of a political party or movement.[18] Another from CWS emphatically ruled out any support for groups closely identified with parties but stated that "a progressive political position can be maintained by working with groups seeking structural change."[19] A representative of LWR acknowledged that the "majority of indigenous agencies we support in Latin America are in opposition to the policies of those in power," but if they were part of a political organization, movement or party, they received no aid.[20]

It is largely because of this distinction between political levels in outlining their organizations' mission priorities that respondents in institution-building PVOs ruled out empowerment of the poor to challenge and change the dominant political and economic structures in their environment. Representatives in nine out of ten such PVOs associated this activity as having partisan overtones requiring links with specific political movements—and hence not something they would endorse as an official goal of their organizations.

Some admitted, however, that perhaps indirectly they may be contributing to significant political change, but never as an explicit goal. Reverend Boyd Lowry, executive director of CODEL, a consortium a forty U.S. aid-sending PVOs (thirty-five of them church-affiliated), affirmed this judgment: "We do

---

[16] Interview with Kenneth H. Phillips, FPP USA.
[17] Interview with Carlos Castillo, PACT.
[18] Interview with James F. O'Brien, PACT.
[19] Interview with Rev. Oscar Bolioli, CWS.
[20] Interview with J. Robert Busche, LWR.

not aim (in our criteria) to challenge or change dominate political and economic structures. However, the consequences of our acting within our guidelines (self-reliant, participatory projects among the poor) should have this as a byproduct.''[21]

Even the representative from SCF, John P. Grant, who claimed a totally apolitical position for his organization, admitted that empowerment of the poor might be an implicit part of the work supported by SCF overseas, albeit never part of the agency's goals: "We don't talk about this in our literature, but I am sure we do this quietly at the local level."[22]

A spokesperson for the one PVO in my sample that ranked empowerment first—Carlos Castillo, regional representative for Latin America in PACT in 1983—did not share the common view of most other multiservice institution-building PVOs that such a goal entailed a partisan political commitment. He did acknowledge, however, that this objective is often hard to operationalize for a variety of reasons:

> Only a small minority of our projects really address empowerment. About 10 percent include structural changes. . . . It is a slow process to affect power through nonformal education and collective action. . . . These projects are also hard to get through our project selection committee [constituted by a board of development experts outside the agency] since its members are still oriented towards income generation. Empowerment projects are also hard to evaluate since the normal indicators—income, production levels—don't capture the results.[23]

As in the cases of several relief agencies mentioned earlier, there is sometimes a divergence between rhetoric and reality regarding mission definition among U.S. multiservice institution-builders. Those who shun empowerment in their public statements because of what they feel to be unacceptable partisan political overtones acknowledge it may be a possible indirect consequence of their work overseas. Those who are more explicit about it being a goal, however, also recognize they may not be speaking for many others connected with their agency and that the bulk of their resource allocations may very well still be in other areas. What is clear, therefore, is that PVOs across the board either do not include as a primary objective changing political structures in developing countries, or that they believe it is a very difficult goal for them to acknowledge and to realize—even if some staff members personally see it as an important goal of their work overseas.

This position reflects the same ambiguity that exists in the public sector, as seen in chapter 3 when describing the evolution of rationales for U.S. bilateral foreign aid beginning in mid-1960s. Although the Congress explicitly en-

---

[21] Interview with Rev. Boyd Lowry, CODEL.
[22] Interview with John P. Grant, SCF.
[23] Interview with Carlos Castillo, PACT.

dorsed democratic political development as an objective for official U.S. aid to Third World countries in Title 9 of the Foreign Assistance Act of 1966, it later toned down this emphasis, subsuming it under the more politically neutral and humanitarian rubric of a BHN approach in the 1973 "new directions" mandate. It did not formally retreat from Title 9 but made it a more implicit rather than explicit focus of U.S. government aid objectives after 1973 so as to downplay the image of U.S. interventionism abroad.

The PVOs manifest similar caution about fostering democratic political change abroad, even those in category three—many of whom include as part of their activities the promotion of bargaining power, popular participation, and consciousness-raising among groups suffering economic and political inequities. Several PVO staff members and executives will admit it is or hope it will be an indirect consequence over the long term, but they agree with government policymakers in not making political change a direct and explicit goal of their overseas aid strategy.

CITIZEN ATTITUDES ABOUT DEVELOPMENT IN THE U.S.

It is not merely the fact that PVOs receive U.S. government aid that accounts for their ambiguity about espousing political change through their work. The attitudes and preferences of private contributors to PVOs also have a significant bearing on their reluctance to espouse political objectives abroad.

U.S. citizens tend to be relatively uninformed about developing countries. There is much less coverage in the U.S. media of economic and political problems in these countries than there is in Europe. The issues that receive the most attention are ones involving natural or human-made disasters requiring quick and effective international relief. As a result, public opinion surveys have shown Americans to be generally ignorant about developmental issues, but supportive of foreign assistance aimed at immediate alleviation of suffering, such as hunger, malnutrition, and disease.

A random stratified sample of twenty-four hundred Americans in 1972 commissioned by the ODC found that 36 percent of Americans were clearly uninformed about developing countries. Moreover, the survey also indicated that 64 percent believed that medical assistance was a very effective form of aid, and that 54 percent believed the same about food and clothing. A high percentage believed some forms of technical assistance were also very effective—teachers and books, 61 percent; training of foreign students in United States universities, 58 percent; tractors, fertilizers, and seed, 56 percent; birth control aid, 55 percent; and sending trainers and engineers, 52 percent. However, only 6 percent believed that the reason that people are poor in developing countries is that they are victims of the system, whether it be injustices due to social structures or repression by government. The study concluded that

Americans, therefore, do not understand the word "development" to mean liberation or freedom from oppression.[24]

The survey also found that PVOs are very popular among the Americans as more reliable channels of aid than government programs. U.S. citizens believe too much official aid is wasted in either our government's bureaucracy or that of host-country governments. When given a list of various nonprofit organizations to rate in terms of effectiveness, two of the top three were the American Red Cross (rated as very effective by 51 percent) and CARE USA (rated as very effective by 50 percent)—both predominantly relief agencies. The U.S. Peace Corps was the other one in the top three—a technically oriented, but government-sponsored organization—and 50 percent of respondents believed it to be very effective. The categories "religious groups," "YMCA/YWCA" and "private foundations," many of which are geared to multiservice institution-building, were rated much lower, with only 33 percent, 18 percent, and 17 percent respectively scoring them as very effective.[25]

While it may be true that respondents were unfamiliar with the overseas work of multiservice institution-building organizations (and many in the sample offered "not sure" answers for PVOs in these categories), this itself indicates why private cash contributions are more readily given to relief agencies. They are better known among the American populace. Their orientation also fits American preferences in aid-giving, which are predominantly oriented to the immediate relief of suffering and geared towards the replication of the American dream of self-help—neither of which includes a political focus or framework of analysis.

A 1986 random survey of twenty-four hundred Americans sponsored by both the ODC and INTERACTION pointed to the persistence of several of these same attitudinal patterns. Most Americans continue to be poorly informed about development issues and about U.S. relations with the Third World. Forty percent, for example, did not know whether the U.S. government supported the Contras or the Sandinistas in Nicaragua.[26]

Over three-fifths in the survey favored several forms of technical aid, such as health care (62 percent), education for population control (62 percent), and assistance to farmers to buy seeds and basic equipment (61 percent). Nearly three-fourths (74 percent), however, endorsed disaster relief as the highest priority for U.S. foreign aid. Just 28 percent believed political or strategic objectives to be the main reason for giving economic assistance, and only 3 percent felt the promotion of democracy, freedom, and social justice to be compelling reasons for sending economic aid abroad.[27]

Moreover, the vast majority of Americans surveyed in 1986 (85 percent)

---

[24] Laudicina, *World Poverty and Development*, pp. 11–13, 41, 69.

[25] Ibid., pp. 5, 47–48.

[26] Contee, *What Americans Think*, pp. 7, 51.

[27] Ibid., pp. 7–8, 47, 49.

believed that a large part of official aid is wasted in government bureaucracy (especially in the U.S. government). Most (59 percent), however, had some or a great deal of confidence that the money they donate to private organizations reaches needy people in developing countries.[28]

Hence, up to the mid-1980s Americans tended to espouse more humanitarian than political objectives for U.S. foreign aid, to favor relief and technical assistance as their preferred forms of assistance, and to have more faith in private than in public mechanisms for aid administration.

NONCONTROVERSIAL APPROACH BY PVOS AT HOME

Paralleling the reluctance of to avow goals directly threatening to the prevailing political or economic order abroad are the relatively noncontroversial strategies PVOs use at home to influence citizen attitudes and public policies towards developing countries. In fact, until the mid-1980s very few PVOs engaged in any extensive efforts to educate Americans about Third World needs or influence government foreign policies on issues other than those that directly affected their own institutional interests.

Thirteen of the fifteen PVOs in my 1982–1983 sample did not have formal development education programs either for their own donors or the wider public. The practice of the majority is to provide some information about projects in periodic mailings to donors, but normally neither these nor fund-raising messages in the media attempt to provide data or analysis about economic or political problems in developing countries, particularly those involving deeper structural causes of poverty and social inequity.

During my interviews, some PVO respondents indicated that a more effective way of getting Americans interested in overseas problems is a picture of an undernourished child rather than an explanation of structural issues underlying poverty. One said a letter from a child in an overseas village assisted by American private aid is more educational than all the books and articles on development.[29] Others stated that the controversial approach often taken by European and Canadian NGOs in their development education programs at home (described later in this chapter) simply would not work in the United States since Americans do not associate private aid with politics.[30] Lynn V. Marshall, in charge of community education affairs at CRS in 1982, told me: "U.S. people respond better to appeals to the heart than to the head. CRS has gotten a lot of negative feedback from individual donors when we have tried to make them aware of the deeper structural causes of injustice in Central

---

[28] Ibid., pp. 8, 51.
[29] Interview with Kenneth H. Phillips, FPP USA.
[30] Interview with Rev. Laurence M. Olszewski, C.S.C., CRS.

America. They have bought Reagan's argument that we have to stop communism there."[31]

Since the appointment of its first lay director in 1983, CRS has begun a more systematic attempt to inform selected groups of donors in various dioceses around the United States about some of the political dimensions of the situation in Central America. Terence Martin, regional director of South America in CRS in 1985, however, indicated this sort of approach, although necessary, is sensitive and problematic:

> Education is a difficult process. It requires self-education as well inside CRS to generate clear concepts of its development purpose. In the past our Catholic constituents have been close to ethnic immigrant customs, and this has meant identifying with the goals of the American government. This is changing now, but it is a slow process. We need to do more in education.
>
> This is a difficult issue to handle. Given our religious affiliation and values, we should be willing to speak out and challenge people. However, there is always the danger of turning people off and losing all your credibility. The incremental approach is more prudent, but here the danger is losing the moment and not meeting your responsibility to educate.[32]

Only two of the fifteen PVOs in my survey have given attention to the types of developmental education prevalent in most Canadian and European organizations—Oxfam America, and the UUSC. Oxfam prepares and distributes brochures and films among its three thousand affiliate groups in the U.S., which include critiques of policies of governments (e.g., impact audits of the repressive economic and political policies of the El Salvadoran and Guatemalan regimes). It also publicly advocates changes in U.S. policy toward developing countries (e.g., no military aid for Central America).[33]

The UUSC in the early 1980s organized bipartisan congressional fact-finding trips to Central America to raise awareness among policymakers about the continued repression being perpetrated by some governments that receive U.S. military and economic aid. The UUSC also has distributed findings from these trips (which normally are critical both of Central American governments and U.S. policies in the region) to its eight thousand member contributors and publicizes them in the media. The UUSC also included representatives from business, academia, the professions, and the media on some of these trips.[34]

The UUSC also maintains structures for education and advocacy on issues pertaining to both its international and domestic service programs. Its Volunteer Service Corps (unique among U.S. transnational development institutions) is similar to the volunteer networks of animators and affiliates operated

---

[31] Interview with Lynn V. Marshall, CRS.

[32] Interview with Terence Martin, CRS.

[33] Interview with Joseph Short, Oxfam America.

[34] Interview with Dr. Richard S. Scobie, UUSC.

by CCFD and CIMADE in France (described later). As of 1985 the UUSC had 649 members who engage in short-term education and advocacy activities among the one thousand local Unitarian Universalist congregations throughout the country. These focus on such issues as peace and disarmament, U.S. policies in Central America, sanctuary for Central American refugees, prison construction moratoriums, and elimination of the death penalty. The UUSC also supports units, or small groups, of Unitarian Universalists (about two hundred in each) in eleven different cities that engage in long-term study of these issues with documentation supplied by UUSC headquarters in Boston. The units also cooperate with other nonprofit organizations attempting to mobilize public opinion on these issues at the grass-roots level.[35]

These efforts by both Oxfam America and UUSC, however, are not typical of PVOs. Several are now beginning to move in the direction of formal developmental education, but the purpose of their efforts has not been to provide a political analysis of the causes of poverty or injustice in developing countries or to question U.S. government or business policies abroad.

In 1984 a document prepared for member organizations by a Joint Working Group on Development Education of the ACVAFS and Private Agencies in International Development (PAID)—a federation mainly of newer and smaller PVOs founded in 1980—laid down suggested guidelines for developmental education by PVOs. Although mentioning that information conveyed in such programs should familiarize "the public with transnational inequities and conflicts that inhibit people's capacity to achieve their own goals for a decent living," none of these injustices were named nor their underlying causes identified. The document emphasized that such programs must respect pluralism of approaches, "considering the variety and differences that exist among segments of the public and within the PVO community." Most of the examples as to what effective developmental education entails dealt with the problem of world hunger, and several involved suggestions for collecting food or donations for food to send overseas for those suffering from malnutrition.[36]

The lobbying activities of most PVOs have also tended to avoid controversial issues. Of the fifteen PVOs in my survey, representatives in nine said that their organizations (individually or collectively) do try to influence policies of the U.S. government. However, persons in six of the nine PVOs gave as examples efforts to impact on government decisions directly affecting the institutional interests of PVOs themselves—e.g., levels of cash or food subsidies to PVOs, regulations on their use, administrative oversight conditions on PVO activities, and waivers for using U.S. government aid in nations that are not AID country priorities.

[35] UUSC, *Report to the Membership, 1985*; Zimmerman, "Constituency Education Review."
[36] Joint Working Group on Development Education (ACVAFS/PAID), *Framework for Development Education*, pp. 3, 5, 7.

Representatives in only three PVOs in my sample—CWS, Oxfam America, and UUSC—indicated that their agencies try to influence aspects of U.S. foreign policy that extend beyond their own organization's operations—e.g., the lifting of U.S. government economic embargos against Cuba and Vietnam (CWS), the establishment of more equitable U.S. immigration policies for Haitian refugees (CWS), and the curtailment of U.S. military aid to Central America (Oxfam America and UUSC). The respondents in all three of these PVOs, however, admitted that their lobbying efforts in Congress or in executive agencies have not been effective in changing U.S. government policies on any of these issues.[37]

Since the early 1980s there have been indications that more PVOs are beginning to address wider foreign policy and developmental issues in their lobbying efforts, but thus far only with mixed results. In 1983 representatives of ACVAFS and PAID offered joint testimony before the presidentially appointed Commission on Security and Economic Assistance (the Carlucci Commission). They argued that the resource imbalance between U.S. security and economic assistance be adjusted and that bilateral and multilateral developmental aid be separated legislatively and administratively from military-related aid. The commission, however, in its final report to the president, rejected such a separation and indeed recommended even closer ties between official U.S. economic and military assistance than existed previously.[38]

After 1984, when ACVAFS and PAID merged to form a new federation of over one hundred PVOs—the American Council for Voluntary International Action (INTERACTION)—there have been some additional collective initiatives by U.S. nonprofits to impact on wider issues of foreign policy. The African Working Group inside INTERACTION actively (and successfully) lobbied in 1985 in favor of increased and long-term development aid to Africa from the U.S. government and for more U.S. public aid to African nations to be channeled through multilateral institutions. The Public Policy Committee of INTERACTION has also studied ways of making its members' views known to Congress more effectively through phone calls to key members and letter-writing campaigns.[39]

Nevertheless, the bulk of collective efforts to date by PVOs to influence U.S. government policies through INTERACTION still has been focused primarily on issues that directly affect their own institutional interests. In 1985 these included the share of U.S. foreign assistance to be channeled through PVOs, the level of government subsidies for their domestic education activi-

---

[37] Interviews with Rev. William Wipfler, NCC, Laurence Simon, Oxfam America, and Dr. Richard S. Scobie, UUSC.

[38] PAID and ACVAFS, "Testimony Submitted to the U.S. Commission on Security and Economic Assistance."

[39] Telephone interview with Robert J. Berg, ODC; INTERACTION, *Monday Developments*, 3, no. 11 (June 17, 1985): 3, and enclosure 1.

ties, proposed changes in charitable-contributions laws that could reduce private donations to the entire U.S. nonprofit sector, and the level of private contributions necessary to make PVOs eligible for continued public subsidies.

CAREER PATTERNS AND OVERLAPPING MEMBERSHIP OF PVO PERSONNEL

Although lobbying efforts to affect broad foreign policy issues may continue to expand in scope in the future, it is not likely that they will be given the prominence or ideological intensity in the PVO community that they are given by many European and Canadian NGOs. The PVOs involved in overseas aid activities traditionally have not attracted political activists into their ranks. Nor have they been linked directly, or indirectly through individual staff commitments, with other organizations in the United States agitating for political change.

The PVO personnel themselves have previous career patterns not closely associated with partisan political movements. Board members in large part come from business, professional, or religious organizations. Executive directors have either worked their way up the ranks in the same or other PVOs or have had previous administrative experience in business or government. In some instances, executive directors (in four out of fifteen U.S. PVOs in my 1982–1983 sample) have had long careers working for the U.S. government either as ambassadors (CRS, LWR, and PACT) or as AID officials (PADF). Project officers and field representatives frequently have had prior overseas experience either in the U.S. Peace Corps or in a private volunteer-sending agency.

Hence, prior career experiences of those working in PVOs would not orient them in a change-oriented political direction or encourage them to challenge U.S. government foreign policy in their work for nonprofits. Similar to the attitudinal patterns of U.S. citizens who contribute to PVOs, those administering such institutions are more humanitarian and pragmatic than political in their objectives. They are also, like most Americans, satisfied with the overall framework of current U.S. foreign policy, even if disagreeing at times with some specifics on the margins.

Relative Isolation of PVOs from Political Advocacy Groups

Not only does political debate in the United States about Third World issues focus on a narrower range of alternatives than is the case in Europe and Canada, but PVOs are seldom linked with the small minority in this country that does openly challenge U.S. foreign policy regarding trade agreements, immigration laws, defense strategies, MNC activities, or human rights violations in other countries. Nor do they form strategic or tactical alliances with those pressing for changes in domestic U.S. policies regarding ecology, gender equality, or racial discrimination.

Unlike the situation in Europe and Canada, these other policy issues are not normally linked conceptually or strategically with the development activities of PVOs. The PVO personnel perceive them as analytically and practically distinct, and the militants working for change on these other fronts seldom join PVOs in attempts to influence government policymaking on a broad range of issues.

When cooperation occurs among some advocacy groups—e.g., peace movement supporters and Latin American solidarity groups orchestrating joint demonstrations against the arms build-up in Central America—PVOs (with a few notable exceptions such as Oxfam America, AFSC, and UUSC) are not officially part of these efforts. The PVO executives and staffs are not only more relief and technically oriented, but they are also nonpolitical in their public posture for fear of offending private donors and the U.S. government. They are not attracted to the overt political strategy of U.S. advocacy organizations. In turn, these other groups tend to be critical of PVOs for being too narrow in their approach and too closely identified with the U.S. government.[40]

Given all of these domestic cultural and structural factors, it is not surprising that commitment to significant political changes either abroad or at home is generally submerged or almost nonexistent in the priority choices and mission definition of PVOs. In Europe and Canada, however, the case is different—and primarily because the domestic political culture, as well as the NGO location within it, is quite distinct from the U.S. pattern.

PRIORITIES OF EUROPEAN AND CANADIAN NGOs

Resource Allocations

As can be seen below in table 5.2, resource allocations of European and Canadian NGOs tend to cluster much more in the longer-term developmental activities than in the shorter-term relief category. Approximately three-fourths of the overseas aid of the 125 largest NGOs in 1980 was administered by NGOs that are predominantly technical assistance or multiservice institution-building agencies (as compared to less than one-third of PVO aid resources in these categories).

Part of the reason, as seen clearly in table 5.2, are differences in public subsidy patterns between the United States and other North Atlantic countries. Four-fifths (79.8 percent) of government grants to U.S. PVOs goes to those in the predominantly relief category, whereas well over four-fifths in Canada (84.9 percent) and Europe (91.3 percent) goes to NGOs supporting more long-

[40] Telephone interview with Douglas Hellinger, Development GAP.

TABLE 5.2
The Distribution of Aid Resources among the 205 Largest U.S. (1981), Canadian (1980), and European (1980) PVOs/NGOs (in 1986 dollar values)

PVO/NGO Type	U.S. (N = 80)			Canada (N = 45)			Europe (N = 80)		
	Private	Public	Total Aid	Private	Public	Total Aid	Private	Public	Total Aid
Predominantly Relief Assistance	55.6%	79.8%[a]	67.9%	30.0%	15.1%[b]	24.7%	36.9%	8.7%[c]	25.3%
Technical Assistance	21.2%	10.1%	15.5%	22.0%	23.7%	22.6%	26.6%	33.2%	29.3%
Multiservice Assistance	23.2%	10.1%	16.6%	48.0%	61.2%	52.7%	36.5%	58.1%	45.4%
Dollar Totals (in millions)	$716.1	$750.8	$1,466.9	$150.7	$83.4	$234.1	$674.3	$475.7	$1,150.0

Sources: AID, Voluntary Foreign Aid Programs, 1982, pp. 21–27; OECD, Directory of Nongovernmental Organizations, 1981; CCIC, Directory of Canadian Nongovernmental Organizations, passim.

[a] 67.4% of which was food.
[b] 0% of which was food.
[c] 7% of which was food.

term structural types of programs overseas—especially multiservice institution-building. It is food aid that accounts for such skewed patterns of public subsidies. In the United States 67.4 percent of all government aid to PVOs is food or food-related (and therefore earmarked for PVOs in category one), whereas no public food aid program for nonprofits exists in Canada and only a very small one (about 7 percent of total government aid to NGOs) in Europe (the FRG, the Netherlands, and the EEC).

However, table 5.2 also shows that it is not U.S. agricultural policy alone that accounts for the different PVO/NGO resource allocation priorities across the North Atlantic region. Patterns of private philanthropy are also quite different in Canada and Europe from those in the United States. Whereas well over one-half (55.6 percent) of private cash resources for overseas aid from the United States in 1981 were handled by relief PVOs, a much smaller percentage of private donations went through relief-type NGOs in Canada (30.0 percent) and Europe (36.9 percent). Sixty to seventy percent of philanthropy in these other North Atlantic countries was donated to NGOs with a more long-term development approach.

Explicit Political Goals of NGOs Overseas

Not only are NGO resource allocations geared much more toward structural rather than relief types of assistance, but they are also far more explicit than PVOs in defining as integral to their overseas objectives changing political and economic power distributions in favor of the poor. Only one out of the six Canadian agencies in my sample that ranked their priorities, and only three of nineteen in Europe that did so, ruled out empowerment of the poor to challenge and change the dominant political and economic institutions in their environments. Four of thirteen U.S. nonprofits who so ranked their priorities did so.

A proportionately greater number of European and Canadian respondents placed this goal among their top three priorities than did their American counterparts. Many, in fact, considered this objective to be part of a top cluster of priorities, closely related to promoting participatory organizations among the poor and increasing bargaining skills of low-income groups vis-à-vis significant elites who affect their lives.

By weighting in table 5.3 the responses of U.S. Canadian, and European respondents in my sample who ranked their mission priorities,[41] the differences in how they define their objectives are emphasized. The PVOs as a

[41] In constructing weighted scores for the priorities listed in table 5.3, I assigned points to each of the six items depending on how often it was mentioned first, second, third, etc., by respondents in my survey. First choice, six points; second choice, five points; third choice, four points; fourth choice, three points; fifth choice, two points; sixth choice, one point; not applicable or not ranked, no points.

TABLE 5.3
Weighted Ranks and Scores of Priorities of U.S., Canadian, and European PVOs/NGOs, 1982–1983

Priorities	U.S. (N=13) Rank (Score)	Canada (N=5) Rank (Score)	Europe (N=19) Rank (Score)
Immediate alleviation of human suffering (hunger, sickness, lack of shelter, etc.)	4 (48)	6 (5)	5 (37)
Increasing income and/or employment opportunities for poor people	2 (53)	5 (12)	6 (28)
Improving the skills, knowledge, and capacity of recipients to solve problems and manage programs	1 (57)	3 (20)	4 (71)
Building new institutions and networks of socioeconomic participation designed and operated primarily by the poor themselves.	3 (49)	1 (26)	1 (99)
Enhancing the bargaining power of recipients to secure equitable arrangements with important social and economic groups and institutions that can assist them—merchants, landlords, credit institutions, government agencies, etc.	5 (41)	4 (18)	3 (76)
Empowerment of the poor to challenge and change the dominant political and economic structures in their environment.	6 (22)	2 (24)	2 (80)

Source: Personal interviews
N=37

whole preferred technically oriented goals and ranked improvement of skills and increasing of income as their top two priorities. Although the building of participatory institutions ranked third among the Americans, it was not closely associated with political change in their consciousness. Empowerment of the poor to challenge and change dominant political and economic structures received less than half the weighted score (twenty-two) of participatory institution building (forty-nine) and finished in last place (well behind the alleviation of immediate suffering).

The Canadians and Europeans, however, both emphasized the building of new participatory institutions and empowerment of the poor to challenge and change dominant power structures as their top two—with enhancing bargaining skills of the poor as the third goal for the Europeans and the fourth for the Canadians. Hence, these other North Atlantic nonprofits clearly preferred objectives more directly oriented to political change in developing countries than did their American counterparts.

Since my sample of PVOs in the United States contained more organizations primarily focused on relief or technical assistance (five out of fifteen) than in Canada and Europe (four of thirty), the differences in table 5.3 might be a reflection of this disproportion. The PVOs in these two categories (relief and technical aid) do not include political change as an explicit or implicit institutional objective. Even when one focuses only on category three organizations—whose activities involve multiservice institution-building and the stimulation of a greater social awareness among project participants—one still finds, as seen in table 5.4, similar strong differences between PVOs and NGOs.

Among multiservice institution-building PVOs that ranked their priorities, enhancement of bargaining skills jumps from fifth to third place, but improvement of technical skills still remains first, and empowerment of the poor to challenge and change dominant power structures continues to be ranked last. Among Canadian and European organizations in category three, however, there is almost the same ranking of priorities as occured when all categories of NGOs were considered together. Hence, in the minds of representatives from other North Atlantic nonprofits, multiservice institution-building in developing countries is much more closely linked with the struggle for political change than it is for Americans from the same type of organizations.

Most Canadian and European NGO representatives in category three spoke very frankly about the explicit political (albeit non-party-affiliated) character of their organizations. They did not, as did the Americans, claim that empowerment of the poor to change their condition has to be only an indirect consequence of their work. In fact, several explicitly saw political empowerment as a central ingredient of development.

Lawrence S. Cumming, national secretary of Oxfam Canada in 1983, stated:

> We support certain causes in polarized situations—e.g., in Central America. You are on one side or another and this can't be avoided. . . . We now judge projects both on technical criteria (sound, self-sustaining, etc.) and on social-political criteria. Does the group have a vision for change and empowerment—i.e., some sort of structural analysis and mobilization of the people to change institutions.[42]

[42] Interview with Lawrence S. Cumming, Oxfam Canada.

TABLE 5.4

Weighted Ranks and Scores of U.S., Canadian, and European Institution and Network Building PVOs/NGOs, 1982–1983

Priorities	U.S. (N=8) Rank (Score)	Canada (N=5) Rank (Score)	Europe (N=16) Rank (Score)
Immediate alleviation of human suffering (hunger, sickness, lack of shelter, etc.)	5 (25)	6 (5)	5 (24)
Increasing income and/or employment opportunities for poor people	4 (29)	5 (12)	6 (23)
Improving the skills, knowledge, and capacity of recipients to solve problems and manage programs	1 (35)	3 (20)	4 (55)
Building new institutions and networks of socioeconomic participation designed and operated primarily by the poor themselves	2 (34)	4 (18)	3 (72)
Enhancing the bargaining power of recipients to secure equitable arrangements with important social and economic groups and institutions that can assist them—merchants, landlords, credit institutions, government agencies, etc	3 (32)	1 (26)	1 (89)
Empowerment of the poor to challenge and change the dominant political and economic structures in their environment	6 (19)	2 (24)	2 (77)

Source: Personal interviews.
N = 29

Tim Brodhead, executive director of INTER PARES in 1983, which supports overseas grass-roots programs and interchanges between Canadian and Third World community organizations, acknowledged that political motives shape his organization's decisions about taking on new overseas projects. He also said that development inherently requires working for empowerment of people:

We recently began working with refugees in Central America. We got into this work for political reasons—so as to be able to speak out in Canada on Central American issues. . . .

Development is not so much education and training, but analysis of currents of social change and finding ways to empower people to change structures and act collectively.[43]

Marlyse Strasser, director for Latin America in the Catholic Committee Against Hunger and for Development (CCFD) in France, indicated that the goal of CCFD's overseas multiservice institution-building has an explicit political dimension due to the type of groups it seeks to assist:

CCFD supports groups who are involved in the process of promoting change. These groups discover which structures favor just development and which do not, and they take action accordingly. CCFD is not party oriented but does include a political dimension in its work by supporting such progressive groups.[44]

Juan Josi, Project Officer in MISEREOR, the official Catholic development agency in the FRG, also indicated that there is a political perspective that his organization includes in project selection:

We also see projects in the function of social change—viz., on behalf of freedom and social rights. We look for integral human development, not just a technical goal. . . . We believe there is no peace without justice. We believe that capitalism can work in a humane way but justice must be done within it. Therefore, structural change is sometimes necessary to achieve this. Workers have a right to a decent standard of living, and our projects are aimed at achieving this. Our limit is that we aim to promote such changes peacefully. We do not support groups involved in armed revolution.[45]

In its official documents, the Interchurch Coordination Committee for Development Projects (ICCO), the development agency of the Dutch Protestant churches, mentions the promotion of human rights and the raising of awareness among the poor about the causes of injustice fundamental to its developmental work. Rev. S. S. van Dijk, head of ICCO's Latin American department, acknowledged the logical political implications of this official position:

We have no party affiliation, here or through the projects we support overseas, but political implications of our work exist. We support projects aimed at changing unjust structures and that conscienticize the poor. This is political.[46]

Political Education by NGOs at Home

Not only are nonprofit aid-sending organizations in Europe and Canada more explicitly political in defining their overseas goals, but in their attempts to

[43] Interview with Tim Brodhead, INTER PARES.
[44] Interview with Marlyse Strasser, CCFD.
[45] Interview with Juan Josi, MISEREOR.
[46] Interview with Rev. S. S. van Dijk, ICCO.

influence citizen attitudes and public policies at home, they also take very controversial positions. They have far more extensive and aggressive development education campaigns than do PVOs. They also engage in significant lobbying efforts against many of their respective governments' foreign policy positions, as well as some of those of MNCs based in their own countries.

Thirteen of fifteen (86.7 percent) of the PVOs in my sample had not yet begun a formal development education program at home by 1983. Two-thirds of the European and Canadian NGOs (twenty of thirty) by then were engaged in significant attempts to enlighten both donors and the wider public about the realities and needs of the Third World well byond the dissemination of information about the specific projects they support overseas. As indicated in chapter 4, this tradition began in the 1960s when many NGOs (e.g., during FAO's Freedom from Hunger Campaign) began to see as integral to their mission changing attitudes and policies at home regarding immigration, aid, and trade. This tradition has continued, and most governments in Europe and in Canada in the 1970s even began to subsidize such educational programs (despite their political content) to generate more public interest in developing countries and mobilize support for more foreign aid. These programs, however, also include political messages.

Canadian NGOs since 1968 have been distributing materials (including books, study guides, brochures, flyers, and film strips) via their own regional offices, thirty-five learning centers (partially funded by the government), schools, churches, unions, cooperatives, and community groups. These include basic information showing how developing countries are affected by decisions made in Canada. Sometimes these materials condemn specific policies, such as Canadian and U.S. government support for repressive Third World regimes (e.g., in Central America), arms sales to developing countries, and overseas investment and employment practices of MNCs. They also often recommend specific action to readers, such as letter-writing campaigns to governments and boycotts of targeted companies' products.[47]

On the average, from 2 to 20 percent of the total budget of Canadian NGOs is now allocated to education at home. The Canadian Catholic Organization for Development and Peace (CCODP), for example, allocates 20 percent of its resources and fifteen full-time staff members to domestic educational activities. Moreover, by the mid-1980s CIDA through its Public Participation Program (initiated in 1971) was allocating nearly $9 million annually for NGO development education.[48]

In Great Britain since the early 1970s, Development Education Centers (DECs, now numbering thirty) began to be set up in various cities and towns sponsored by a whole series of NGOs, including Oxfam UK, CA, CAFOD,

[47] CCIC, *Study of International Development Education in Canada*, pp. 10–21, 49–73.
[48] Interviews with Rev. C. William Smith, CCODP, and David Kardish, CCIC.

War on Want, and VSO. The DECs prepare materials to be used in schools, and they run in-service teacher training programs. They also offer courses, conferences, film presentations, theater, and exhibitions on a wide range of developmental issues for trade unions, political campaign organizations, adult education networks, churches, and other religious bodies.

Several of the British NGO contributors to these DECs carry out individual education efforts of their own. Oxfam UK dedicates 5 percent of its annual budget to such activities and targets youth, teachers, and schools with education materials on problems in Third World countries where it is supporting projects. In recent years, based on information from local counterpart groups abroad about the negative effects of infant formulas, drugs, and pesticides, Oxfam UK has joined or initiated campaigns and published books condemning abuses of these products in the Third World by MNCs based in Europe and the United States.[49]

Other British NGOs that support the DECs, such as CA and CAFOD, also carry out campaigns of their own to educate public opinion. In addition to making materials available throughout the DEC network, they circulate newsletters through Protestant and Catholic churches in Great Britain. They offer film strips, reading materials, and liturgical materials to be used by local congregations in social events and religious rituals. These materials also cover politically controversial issues, such as the repressive effects of martial law in the Philippines and the unequal distribution of resources in rural Brazil exacerbated by transnational agribusinesses.[50]

In France, the CCFD has made education at home equal in importance to raising funds for overseas projects. On the occasion of its twentieth anniversary in 1981, it invited over one hundred representatives from its counterpart groups in fifty-four countries to Paris to discuss their common struggle to change unjust structures in the world. The theme for its education in France that year was: "Solidarity: Nothing Will Ever Change in the Third World if Nothing Changes Here." It also stated, "This change, this questioning, calls for the transformation of the socio-economic and socio-political structures of domination which characterize the relations between the so-called 'developed' countries and the so-called 'developing' countries, a relationship which maintains a situation of underdevelopment and dependence."[51]

To accomplish this change it distributes a monthly magazine, *Faim-Développement* (Hunger-development) as well as a monthly newsletter, *CCFD-INFO*. The first includes sector studies on development abroad where progress is being made in meeting basic needs (e.g., in postrevolutionary Nicaragua) as well as criticisms of international trade and investment policies of France

[49] Whitaker, *Bridge of People*, p. 38.
[50] Interviews with Alonso Roberts, CA, and Claire Dixon, CAFOD.
[51] CCFD, *Getting to Know the CCFD*, p. 6.

and other industrialized countries as these negatively impact on the income of the Third World. The second presents brief factual information about CCFD's overseas projects and brief articles analyzing the causes of injustice in developing countries (e.g., oppressive social and political policies of right-wing authoritarian regimes). These periodicals are distributed monthly to over six thousand people who are either donors paying a voluntary tithe to CCFD or members of the twenty-four lay organizations that sponsor CCFD. Yearly, a "Dossier D'Amination" (education kit) with similar information is distributed to the ninety diocesan committees throughout France for use in local church education programs.[52]

The CCFD's Protestant counterpart—CIMADE—has a network of seven hundred animators (volunteers) throughout France who reach several thousand people (about twenty thousand in 1983). These volunteers and their clientele are targeted for CIMADE's educational materials, which include monthly dossiers (*CIMADE Informations*) with critiques of repressive Third World governments responsible for the creation of exiles or displaced persons (traditionally a major focus of CIMADE's work since its creation in 1939). The CIMADE also publishes materials on the legal, political, and social problems encountered by Third World immigrants in France who are the objects of much discrimination and racism.[53]

In the FRG, MISEREOR, the major Catholic development agency, each year during Lent chooses a theme for educating its donors. It prepares and circulates materials (primarily through Catholic churches and schools) about one particular area or country of the world in which there is intense and widespread suffering. The MISEREOR does not hesitate to denounce the root causes of injustice underlying some of these situations. It has strongly condemned the Brazilian model of development under the former military regime (1964–1985) for exacerbating poverty among peasants and workers and has denounced the apartheid regime in South Africa for severely discriminating against the black majority.[54]

One of MISEREOR's Protestant counterparts, *Brot für die Welt* (Bread for the World), prepares a manual each year with suggestions for local Protestant congregations throughout the FRG on how to run liturgical and educational programs about the Third World for adults as well as children. Like MISEREOR, it chooses annual themes that are controversial. The theme for 1982, for example, was "Hunger Through Abundance," and it argued in its educational materials that comfortable life-styles in rich countries and among Third World

---

[52] Ibid., p. 1; CCFD, *Faim-Développement*, pp. 11–14; *CCFD-INFO*, pp. 2–3.

[53] Interview with Rev. Maurice Barth, CIMADE. See also CIMADE, "Uruguay: Cris d'un peuple"; CIMADE, "Au Brésil"; and "Bolivie soutien une démocratie."

[54] MISEREOR, *Brasilien*; and MISEREOR, *Südafrika*.

elites perpetuate hunger and deprivation among the poor in developing countries.[55]

Both of the major FRG political foundations—the Friedrich Ebert Foundation (FES) and the Institute for International Partnership of the Konrad Adenauer Foundation (KAS)—run training programs for labor and political organizations affiliated with their respective parties. In such courses, information about the needs of developing countries is included. In FES' program for middle-level trade union leaders, for example, emphasis is given to a nonprotectionist approach to international trade and to the importance of allowing more Third World products into the FRG. The BMZ supports such development education projects among FRG NGOs, and in 1983 it spent $6.6 million in grants for NGO educational activities at home.[56]

In the Netherlands sixty NGOs administer an organization created by the Ministry of Development Cooperation in 1970—the National Committee for Information on Development (NCO), set up for the purpose of carrying out development education. The NCO's role is to approve proposals for public financing of projects by all NGOs. In 1974 its mandate was broadened to include dissemination not merely of information but also analyses about the causes of inequities between and within rich and poor nations. By 1983 the government was channeling approximately $7.7 million annually through the NCO for various NGO education projects in the Netherlands.[57]

Some NGOs also arrange trips to facilitate greater mutual understanding among groups in the First and Third Worlds. The Commission on Interchurch Aid, Refugees, and World Service (CICARWS) of the WCC sponsors visits by church leaders from North Atlantic to developing countries who report back home. An ecumenical delegation of nine persons sent by CICARWS to Nicaragua in 1983, for example, publicly condemned the terrorist activities of the Contras against civilians, urged more support by North Atlantic governments for the Contadora peace process, and asked for more economic assistance by North Atlantic churches for programs aiding the poor in Nicaragua.[58]

The ICCO in the Netherlands finances similar fact-finding missions of Dutch Protestant religious leaders. It regularly invites representatives from overseas organizations with projects it supports to visit the Netherlands. They spend some time with local Protestant congregations so as to explain the realities of their respective countries and regions to Dutch Christians.[59]

Oxfam Belgique sponsors and participates in disarmament campaigns at

[55] Brot für die Welt, *Hunger durch Überfluss.*

[56] Interviews with Klaus-Peter Treydte, FES; Herbert Kölsch, KAS; and Dr. Horst Breier, BMZ.

[57] Arnold, *Implementing Development Assistance*, pp. 78–79; interview with Teunis Kamper, Office of International Organizations and NGOs.

[58] *Informe de una visita a iglesias en Nicaragua* (Geneva: WCC, 1983).

[59] Interview with Rev. S. S. van Dijk, ICCO.

home and distributes materials on injustice abroad through its network of 120 World Shops in Belgium. From time to time it also sends experts to a crisis situation abroad to offer assistance and report back to the Belgian public on the conditions they have seen. In 1982, for example, it sent a team of doctors to Beirut to visit Palestinian refugee camps. When they returned to Brussels, they denounced the conditions they observed and strongly criticized the governments in the Middle East they believed responsible for circumstances creating such refugees.[60]

Not all NGOs emphasize politically controversial themes in their education campaigns. Hein P. Kolk, director of Foster Parents Plan (FPP) Netherlands, indicated his organization educates its donors through its regular mailings about overseas projects. Those mailings may include data about inequities, but they are not the major focus:

> We engage in education but not as some other Dutch NGOs do. We send 14 mailings a year to each Foster Parent in the Netherlands [numbering 105,000 in 1983]. We include information about projects benefiting their foster children and background information on the socioeconomic situation in the countries where they live. In these background papers and in the description of our projects we try to describe the needs of the people and so we do speak about skewed distribution of resources [e.g., land]. In this way we try to inform our contributors about structures and how our projects change them.[61]

While in the Netherlands in September 1983, I also observed an hour-long television documentary describing the work of FPP Netherlands in Tumaco, Colombia (referred to in chapter 8). Although mentioning neglect by local government agencies of the black majority in this Colombian city, the program focused on the positive impact of FPP's projects on the income and dignity of the people.

Thomas Kines, national director of CARE Canada, criticized the approach taken by many Canadian NGOs in the area of developmental education. He argued that education must aid in expanding NGO income if it is to be judged effective:

> We engage in education of our donors but not in the way CCIC suggests and other NGOs do it (e.g., Oxfam Canada, and the CCODP). They spend a good deal of money without knowing the impact it is having. They believe you must show to the public the links between what they are doing overseas and what is going on here in Canada. I think this is nonsense.
>
> We used to send out a lot of material to people and it never affected our income. We can measure through our computers exactly what we are bringing in. I believe your development education efforts must be positively related to your fundraising.

---

[60] Interview with Pierre Galand, Oxfam Belgique.
[61] Interview with Hein P. Kolk, director, FPP Netherlands.

People simply do not read many of the things they receive, especially if it has a political orientation.[62]

Hence, although the majority of NGOs in my European and Canadian sample include considerable political analysis and advocacy in their educational efforts, some purposely shun it. These concentrate on informing donors and the public about the specific projects they support overseas. In this way, they are much closer to their American counterparts.

Aggressive NGO Lobbying Campaigns

The lobbying efforts of most NGOs aimed at public policies at home also tend to be far more controversial than those of PVOs. They extend well beyond issues directly related to their own financial and administrative relations with home governments.

Representatives in six of the seven Canadian NGOs I interviewed not only acknowledged that part of their mission at home was to affect Canadian government foreign policymaking, but in every case the examples given were broad issues. These included (1) trying to get the Canadian government to renew aid to Cuba (Canadian Universities' Service Overseas, CUSO), and Vietnam and Kampuchea (CCIC); (2) pressuring CIDA to provide assistance to Nicaragua after the 1979 revolution (CCODP); (3) pushing for parliamentary restrictions on Canadian trade with South Africa (CCODP); (4) urging the Ministry of External Affairs to take a more independent stance from U.S. foreign policy towards Central America and Namibia (CCIC); (5) advocating that the Canadian government do something about political prisoners in Guatemala (Service Universitaire Canadien Outre-mer, SUCO); (6) asking the prime minister that import duties be lifted on certain goods from Tanzania, which were aimed at saving a handful of Canadian jobs at Exxon (INTER PARES); and (7) petitioning the government to place more emphasis on basic needs and human rights in its foreign aid programs (CCIC).[63]

Spokespersons from these Canadian NGOs acknowledged that success had been only marginal or not forthcoming on several of these issues. They pointed to some cases, however, where the government actually changed its policies after NGOs exerted direct pressure—the sending of Canadian government grain to Nicaragua as well as contributions to its literacy campaign; the lifting of import duties on the Tanzanian goods; the expression of concern for Guatemalan political prisoners by the Canadian ambassador.[64]

[62] Interview with Thomas Kines, CARE Canada.

[63] Interviews with Richard J. Harmston, CCIC; Rev. C. William Smith, CCODP; Jorge Rodríguez, CUSO; Enrique Ramírez, SUCO; Tim Brodhead, INTER PARES; and Lawrence S. Cumming, Oxfam Canada. See also, CCIC, "A Framework for Canada's Development Assistance."

[64] Ibid.

Nineteen of the twenty-three European NGOs in my sample also engage in efforts to influence broad government policies affecting developing countries. Some of them pressure their respective parliaments through publicity and appeals for citizen action. Others work behind the scenes through direct contacts with elected officials.

In the 1980s lobbying efforts by British NGOs (begun in the 1940s and 1950s) have continued. In 1981 Oxfam UK and several other NGOs organized the "Brandt lobby." This movement included ten thousand people who went to Westminster to urge MPs to substantially increase British foreign aid in accord with the recommendations of the Brandt Commission report published in 1980. As a follow-up, the World Development Movement, Oxfam UK, and CA contributed to the preparation of a critique of British foreign aid (published in 1982) by an independent group of experts on aid and development.

The report, *Real Aid: A Strategy for Great Britain*, strongly criticized the close ties between British aid and trade (a policy endorsed by the Conservative government of Margaret Thatcher), urged more official assistance for overseas projects that had an immediate effect on the living standards of the very poor, and demanded more public scrutiny of the government's Overseas Development Administration (ODA) in its handling of foreign aid. The World Development Movement circulated flyers summarizing the report and petitioning British citizens to write their MPs and the candidates of other parties during the next elections to express concern about British foreign aid and to solicit their positions on the recommendations in *Real Aid*.[65]

Along with Oxfam UK both of the major church-related NGOs in Great Britain—CA and the CAFOD—have engaged in other types of activities to influence official foreign policy. In the early 1980s the three paid for a trip to Nicaragua by several MPs. The NGOs hoped that they would be more open to the achievements of the Sandinistas and more critical of the official U.S. government positions on Central America once they had seen the situation in that country first hand. In 1985 the board of directors of CA published in the press a statement criticizing the Thatcher government for its unwillingness to apply economic sanctions against South Africa. It called upon citizens to write to both Parliament and British corporations demanding that they initiate sanctions in aid, trade, and investment.[66]

In the Netherlands both NOVIB and Ecumenical Action for Solidarity with Latin America also have engaged in open campaigns in the 1980s to pressure elected officials on broad foreign policy issues. In 1982 NOVIB held a press conference announcing that it was considering two projects in Cuba to be funded with Dutch government cofinancing assistance after the Dutch govern-

---

[65] Whitaker, *Bridge of People*, p. 38; World Development Movement, *Real Aid* and *Real Aid: A Briefing and Action Guide*.

[66] Interviews with Alonso Roberts, CA; and Claire Dixon, CAFOD.

ment itself had cut off all official bilateral aid to that country in 1977. The NOVIB was technically within its rights to consider (and even fund) such projects since, as explained in chapter 4, Dutch government cofunding criteria are quite flexible and leave much discretion to NGOs themselves. The NOVIB's announcement, however, precipitated a debate between members of the Christian Democratic administration (then moving closer to the Reagan positions on Central America and the Caribbean) and the Social Democratic opposition. The NOVIB, from its own perspective, was achieving its goal. Kees van Dongen, project officer for Latin America in NOVIB, explained: "One of our institutional aims is to foster pressure on the Dutch government. We look for publicity whereby to foster discussion in public on critical political issues."[67]

Most of the European NGOs in my sample also engage in lobbying efforts to affect public policies at home. Many do so, however, in a more quiet, less confrontational manner than the examples described in Canada, Great Britain, and the Netherlands. Representatives in the FRG NGOs whom I interviewed indicated that they normally express their views and try to influence attitudes of policymakers on some broad policy issues (such as government policies toward Central America). They do so almost exclusively through private contacts with government officials and other elites.[68]

The Catholic and Protestant churches in the FRG, for example, since 1977 have been participating in a formal "Dialogue Program" with representatives from government, political parties, trade unions, and professional associations on international development issues. The purpose is to explore possibilities for reaching a consensus among the participants (all of whom hold leadership positions in their respective organizations) for taking joint action to improve FRG foreign aid and trade policies towards developing countries.[69]

The NGOs headquartered in Geneva often take advantage of the presence of the offices of various intergovernmental organizations also located in that city to make their views known about critical global issues. For example, Lutheran World Federation (LWF), CICARWS, and ICVA—as well as CRS, the only PVO with an office in Geneva and category two status as an observer in the ECOSOC—all make regular representations to international organizations located nearby. These include the United Nations High Commission of Refugees (UNHCR), the United Nations Disaster Relief Office (UNDRO), the World Health Organization (WHO), and the League of Red Cross Societies (LORCS)—all which have central offices in Geneva. These NGOs pass on information and suggestions they have received through field staff or counter-

[67] Interview with Kees van Dongen, NOVIB.

[68] Interviews with Heinrich Stienhans, German Agro-Action; Jurgen Lieser and Martin Salm, German CARITAS Association (DCV); Werner Rostan, *Brot für die Welt*; Wolfgang Kaiser, Protestant Association for Cooperation in Development (EZE); and Juan Josi, MISEREOR.

[69] Schoonbrood, *Development as an International Social Issue*.

parts overseas. They also attempt to influence policy-making in these large public international agencies and make them more aware of the needs of groups at the grass-roots level in Third World countries.[70]

In the Netherlands, although neither of the two major church-related NGOs (CEBEMO and ICCO) have development education programs, they do engage in advocacy activities to influence public policymaking. The CEBEMO lobbies parliament members privately on Dutch development policies. It also puts visitors from overseas counterparts in contact with media persons in the Netherlands to speak on Dutch television and radio about the situation in their home countries. The ICCO invites officials of various Dutch political parties to its offices in Zeist from time to time to inform them on human rights abuses in Third World countries and discuss with them strategies the Dutch government can take to minimize such abuses.[71]

Hence, on the whole NGOs take a much more active—and sometimes very public—role in efforts to influence policies of their respective governments and corporations toward developing countries. This advocacy function in Europe and Canada is seen by many as an integral part of their developmental mission and directly related to the goal they support overseas of empowering the poor to challenge and change dominant power structures that are obstacles to equitable socioeconomic development. They have come to the conviction that unjust power structures abroad are supported by policies in North Atlantic countries (governmental and business) that must change if equity is to occur in the Third World.

WHY NGOs ARE POLITICAL

These dramatic differences between PVOs and NGOs in political posture are due to several distinctive features of political culture in these other North Atlantic societies and the location of NGOs within it. These include the tenor of public opinion about developing countries in Europe and Canada, the domestic social base of NGOs, the previous career patterns of NGO personnel, and the linkages these nonprofits have with political advocacy groups or parties in their home societies attempting to impact on a broad range of domestic and foreign policy issues.

Attentive and Politically Alert Publics

A random survey of over ninety-seven hundred persons in ten European countries in October 1983 sponsored by the CEC in its Euro-Barometer series indicated the following: (1) 10 percent of the population have had a direct personal experience in one or several Third World countries and have recently seen information on these nations in the media; (2) 22 percent have contact with Third World nationals and have recently seen information in the media; (3) 46 percent have no direct or indirect contact but have recently seen information in the media. Only 22 percent had no contact or access to information. Hence, almost four-fifths of European citizens have some exposure to Third World issues on a regular basis. Because of these and other responses, the survey concluded that most Europeans are aware of the severity of Third World problems.[72]

The survey also showed that most Europeans believe that injustices are causing global poverty. Over three-fifths (60.6 percent) agree that Third World countries are exploited by developed countries such as their own. Over four-fifths (83.8 percent) believe that a rich minority exploits the rest of the population in the Third World itself, whereas only 6 percent of Americans are of the opinion that the poor in these nations are victims of an unjust system.[73]

Both in terms of awareness of developing countries and perception of the causes of their problems, Europeans are quite different from Americans. A high proportion of citizens in these other North Atlantic countries receive more regular exposure to Third World problems, and the vast majority analyze the causes to be unfair structural imbalances at the international or national levels.

The type of foreign assistance that many Europeans endorse, therefore, are the ones geared to long-term change rather than relief forms of aid aimed at immediate alleviation of suffering (except during disasters). Well over one-half (53.5 percent) of the 1983 CEC-commissioned survey felt the most important thing their nation should do for developing countries was to send equipment and training to promote greater economic self-reliance among the poor. Nearly one-half (46.8 percent) also endorsed small projects that directly involved participants in planning and implementation, which would lead not only to greater self-help initiatives but enhance the dignity and confidence of the poor to solve problems. The sending of food aid, however, was ranked considerably lower. It was considered important as a regular means of assisting the poor by less than one-quarter (23.2 percent) of Europeans, compared to 54 percent of Americans who believed such type of assistance to be effective.[74]

The survey also indicated that there was a significant proportion of respon-

[72] Rabier, Riffault, and Inglehart, *Euro-Barometer 20*, pp. 77, 97–103. See also European Consortium for Agricultural Development (ECAD), *Europeans and Aid to Development*, pp. 83, 85.

[73] Rabier, Riffault, and Inglehart, *Euro-Barometer 20*, pp. 81, 84; Laudicina, *World Poverty and Development*, p. 11.

[74] Rabier, Riffault, and Inglehart, *Euro-Barometer 20*, pp. 92, 93, 96.

dents (26 percent) who defined themselves as being politically on the left or far left—a phenomenon nonexistent in the United States due to the narrower range of political debate and party choice. Moreover, there was a significant minority (15 percent)—made up predominantly of those with leftist sympathies—who were of the conviction that colonial policies held back Third World development, that Europeans consequently have a moral duty to help such nations, and that European foreign aid should be increased for developing countries. This group tended to be under forty years of age, well educated, of higher than average income, and acting as opinion leaders (i.e., they regularly discussed politics and tried to convince others of their political views).[75]

Hence, there is small, but politically active and acticulate, minority in Europe that consistently supports left-of-center parties in domestic politics and greater government commitments to Third World needs. It is this group that is also the most sympathetic to the goals of the NIEO agenda articulated by Third World leaders and supported by European intellectuals in the mid and late 1970s. They are also sympathetic to policies aimed at significant domestic and international power shifts to implement it (e.g., expanded concessional financial flows to developing countries and price guarantees for Third World export commodities). There is no evidence from the United States showing the existence of such a significant and outspoken minority favoring the NIEO agenda.

Political Support Bases of NGOs

Another important factor explaining the more overt political character of European and Canadian NGOs is the social bases that constitute their membership or primary elements of support. In the United States the boards of trustees of PVOs are made up of individuals who, although they came from other institutions (local church congregations, corporations, the professions, PVOs), are not chosen to represent formally such organizational interests on PVO boards. They bring with them views shaped by past organizational experiences, but these normally do not include strong political commitments—and certainly none identified with left-of-center movements.

Many NGOs, however, have as part of their official support bases other private domestic organizations which have official representatives on the NGO governing boards. Many NGOs are membership organizations in which institutions as well as individuals are responsible for governance. Often these contributing membership organizations themselves are either closely linked to political parties or are active political advocacy movements themselves in the domestic politics of their respective societies.

Oxfam Belgique and the three large Dutch NGOs—ICCO, CEBEMO, and NOVIB—all have on their general boards or assemblies official representatives of the major trade unions in their respective countries. These large con-

<hr>

[75] Ibid., pp. 215, 255; ECAD, *Europeans and Aid to Development*, pp. 47–48, 88.

federations, in turn, are formally or informally linked with Christian-inspired or Social Democratic parties in both countries and are very active in domestic electoral politics.

The CCFD in France and CCODP in Canada both have on their governing boards official representatives of a variety of Catholic lay organizations active in domestic cultural and social-service activities throughout France and Canada respectively. Moreover, some of these Catholic Action groups in both countries—e.g., the Young Christian Workers (JOC), Catholic Action for Workers (ACO), the Young Catholic Students (JEC), the Rural Christian Movement (CMR), Independent Catholic Action (ACI)—have since the 1960s become closely associated with leftist political movements in both countries.

Among Catholic Action militants in France (who as a group number in the several thousands) there was a significant number from the mid-1960s on who distanced themselves from official Church positions and became active participants in leftist political movements. Party memberships among French Catholic Action militants increased from 8 to 18 percent between 1968 and 1976, and most gravitated to the Socialist Party (PS). They also allied themselves with those inside the PS pushing for significant changes in French policy towards developing countries. These very same Catholic Action organizations now constitute part of the sponsoring organizational base of CCFD today, and many of the staff members of CCFD themselves have come out of such progressive Catholic lay associations.[76]

In Canada many of those active in these Catholic lay organizations were from Quebec. They experienced a weakening of commitment to official Church positions in the 1960s after the Church's institutional structures and privileges shrank dramatically in the wake of the provincial government's takeover of most of its educational and domestic social service functions. These Catholic lay activists then turned their attention to politics, and subsequently became involved in Quebec separatist movements. The Catholic Action organizations to which they belong also have come to reflect such views. As in the case of CCFD in France, many of the current staff of CCODP in Montreal have received their training in this Catholic milieu in Quebec, which has developed political ties to the left.[77]

In some instances, the social base of NGOs ties them directly, rather than indirectly, to political parties. This is the case with the major FRG foundations that were actually founded by political parties—the Friedrich Ebert Foundation (Social Democratic Party, SPD), the Konrad Adenauer Foundation (Christian Democratic Union, CDU), the Friedrich Naumann Foundation (Free Democratic Party, FDP), and the Hanns-Seidel Foundation (the Bavarian Christian Social Union, CSU). Although the foundations are legally auton-

[76] Berger, "Religious Transformation and the Future of Politics," pp. 37–41; Rousseau, "L'Action Catholique Ouvrière," pp. 70–71; CCFD, *Le defi de la solidarité*, p. 90; interviews with Rev. Henri Madelin, Society of Jesus in France; and Collette Dugua, CCFD.

[77] Interview with Rev. C. William Smith, CCODP.

150 · Chapter Five

omous organizations, they are each linked de facto to one of the four established parties. Many leading party figures are among their trustees, directors,
and staffs. They thus act in their overseas activities as instruments for explicit
political objectives by providing aid to strengthen indigenous trade unions and
political parties that espouse the same political ideology as their own parties
in the FRG.[78]

In the case of some NGOs in Europe and Canada, it is not so much the
organizational connections at the governing level that link them with a particular social base in society that is political. Rather, it is the primary class or
ethnic composition of their donors that gives them a political orientation. The
CAFOD in Great Britain and the SUCO in Canada appeal primarily to one
subgroup in their respective societies that in both cases is sympathetic to
movements abroad working for political change on behalf of oppressed minorities.

The overwhelming majority of private donors to CAFOD belongs to the
Catholic minority, most of whom (or whose predecessors) have immigrated to
British industrial areas from Ireland for economic reasons. They tend to be
moderate Labourites and have keenly felt the brunt of the unemployment crisis
of the early 1980s. They also are sensitive to what are presented to them as
injustices against oppressed minorities abroad due to their long-standing resentment of British treatment of Ireland. Hence, they are willing to listen to
aggressive development education campaigns of CAFOD on the plight of oppressed workers in Brazil under military rule or in the Philippines during the
martial law imposed by Marcos. They contribute money through CAFOD to
overseas NGO projects purportedly working to alleviate such injustices.[79]

The social support base for SUCO in Quebec had been predominantly constituted since the 1960s by French-speaking Canadians sympathetic to or actively engaged in Quebec separatist activities. Like the contributors to CA
FOD in Great Britain, they constitute a small but significant Canadian
minority favoring leftist domestic policies. Following the same pattern of governmental initiatives of Quebec Province itself since 1960, they have shown
themselves sympathetic to liberation movements abroad among groups being
treated unjustly in their own societies—e.g., blacks in South Africa and peasants in Central America.[80]

Previous Political Socialization of NGO Personnel

The staff background of many NGOs is also different from that of most PVOs,
and this often has already oriented them in a left-of-center political direction

[78] Forrester, "German Political Foundations."

[79] Interview with Claire Dixon, CAFOD.

[80] Interview with Enrique Ramírez, SUCO. See also Nossal, *Politics of Canadian Foreign Policy*, pp. 202–6.

well before they begin working for NGOs. As indicated earlier, the most common previous career patterns for PVO staff members is participation overseas in the U.S. Peace Corps or some private volunteer agency. Moreover, PVO executives either work their way up through the ranks inside the PVO community or come from administrative posts in the U.S. government or business community. In Europe and Canada it is very rare for an NGO executive to have been a previous government administrator. Only one of the thirty Canadian and European NGOs in my sample has an executive director who formerly worked in an administrative capacity in government. In contrast four of fifteen PVO chief executives have previous government administrative experience. Very few NGO administrative or staff personnel come from the business community either, although some (as in the United States) have previously served in a volunteer capacity overseas in a government or private nonprofit agency.

In addition, much more so than in American church-related PVOs, a significant percentage of European religiously affiliated NGOs are staffed by ex-missionaries who have served in Third World countries in a clerical or lay capacity since the 1960s. This includes CA and CAFOD in Great Britain, MISEREOR and Bread for the World in FRG, CEBEMO in the Netherlands, and CIMADE in France. The CIMADE also has on its staff several Third World citizens who left repressive regions in Latin America or Africa.

Returning missionaries and Third World émigrés in Europe have often served indigenous churches in Asia and Africa that have distanced themselves from the colonial era when they were instruments of European cultural control and not closely identified with the struggles of the poor. Many missionaries returning to Europe from Latin America have been involved in recent church commitments to alleviate chronic poverty or redress grievances of peasants and urban slum dwellers. Hence, some of the clerical and lay staff of church-related NGOs have had overseas experiences that alienate them against several North Atlantic government policies toward the Third World and in favor of major political change on behalf of marginal sectors inside developing countries.

Also unlike PVO executives, NGO administrators and project officers have had significant academic experience. In some organizations (e.g., NOVIB in the Netherlands), it is expected that project officers have university degrees in development-related subjects. In others several staff persons (Oxfam UK) or executive directors (EZE in the FRG, Oxfam Belgique, and ICCO in the Netherlands) have served previously as university professors at home or in a developing country. As a result, many NGOs maintain ongoing contacts with universities, especially with faculties and institutes dealing with development studies.[81]

[81] Interview with Christine Whitehead, Oxfam UK. Telephone interviews with Kees van

There are, moreover, several high-quality teaching and research institutes in Europe that specialize exclusively on Third World problems. These often provide training for NGO personnel or assist in preparation of NGO development education materials. These include the Institute for Development Studies at the British University of Sussex, the Ecole Pratique des Hautes Etudes in Paris, the Institute for Social Studies in the Hague, the Center for Development Studies at the University of Rotterdam, the Institute for Development Economics at the University of Breisgau in Freiburg, and the Free University of Berlin. Such institutes tend to be policy oriented (and therefore attractive to NGO practitioners), but they also are intellectual centers where NIEO strategies have often been articulated and defended—e.g., the Center for Development Studies at the University of Rotterdam headed by Jan Tinbergen, director of the RIO study.[82]

In addition, there are some NGO executives and project officers who previously were active in political movements on the left. The executive directors of both Oxfam UK and War on Want in Great Britain in the mid-1980s had been Labourite MPs prior to assuming top administrative responsibilities in these respective NGOs. In the case of both CAFOD in Great Britain and Oxfam Belgique, several staff persons had formerly been active in peace organizations—the Christian Peace Movement and Pax Christi in the case of CAFOD, and the disarmament movement for Oxfam Belgique. In fact, Oxfam Belgique was founded in 1964 by young Belgians involved in pacifist organizations, such as the "Stop War" movement, who perceived the rearmament in Europe of the 1950s and 1960s as a major obstacle to generating resources for Third World development.[83]

Finally, even in cases where NGO staff persons have similar past experiences to their American counterparts—e.g., serving as overseas volunteers—the type of exposure and the overall impact is sometimes different. In Canada, for example, it is quite common for current NGO executives or project officers to have served in the closest Canadian equivalent to the U.S. Peace Corps—viz., Canadian Universities Service Overseas (CUSO). Founded during the same year (1961) and with similar objectives as the Peace Corps, by 1986 CUSO had sent over nine thousand Canadian volunteers to engage in teaching and technical assistance in developing countries. The CUSO, however, is a private, not a public agency. Also, unlike the U.S. Peace Corps, it recruits host country nationals to serve both in administrative and volunteer service positions alongside or supervising Canadian expatriates abroad. The CUSO's

Dongen, NOVIB; Jan Reinders, EZE; Pierre Galand, Oxfam Belgique; and Rev. S. S. van Dijk, ICCO.

[82] Telephone interview with Hendrik van der Heijden, OECD.

[83] Telephone interviews with Alonso Roberts, CA; Claire Dixon, CAFOD; and Pierre Galand, Oxfam Belgique.

leadership over the years has taken positions in public criticizing the Canadian government's aid and trade policies toward developing countries.[84]

Hence, Canadian volunteers who have returned from serving in CUSO (a significant number of whom continue to work in development, and many in NGOs) have often had as part of their first experience overseas collegiality with or supervision by Third World counterparts. They have also been stimulated by CUSO to develop a critical attitude toward development strategies, even those of their own home government.

Linkages of NGOs with Domestic Political Movements

As a result of such prior career patterns and experiences of many NGO personnel, it is not surprising to find that they bring to their current developmental work a highly developed political awareness and, in many instances, a bias toward the left. Many NGO staff persons—and some executives as well—currently are active members in or strong sympathizers of other organizations in their home societies pressuring for significant changes in policy and attempting to shape public opinion accordingly.

In some cases NGO personnel are militants in political parties, mostly left-of-center parties. Although staff members and executives whom I interviewed indicated that this in no way ties the NGO officially to a party, since such activities involve individuals acting on their own time, it does reinforce the political ideology and orientation that many of these persons already bring to their developmental work and it shapes their decisions.

The majority of the project officers and those engaged in developmental education in CA in Great Britain, for example, are activists in the Labour Party, with a few in the Liberal Party as well. Several of the staff members of EZE in the FRG are militants in the Green Party that advocates nuclear disarmament and stricter environmental protection policies. Many of the respective staffs of the larger Canadian NGOs—CUSO, CCODP, and Oxfam Canada—are active members in, and in some cases close personal friends with leaders of, the leftist New Democratic Party—with a few also strong supporters of the Liberals.[85]

In the Netherlands, all major parties are represented on the respective boards of NOVIB and CEBEMO. Moreover, within each organization, those with administrative posts hold key positions in the specific party that represents the orientation of most of their respective staffs. The chairperson of the six-person general board of NOVIB, which acts in the name of the larger general assembly of membership organizations to oversee policy implementation, is himself the vice president of the Labour Party (Pvd A) in the Second Cham-

---

[84] Telephone interview with David Kardish, CUSO.

[85] Telephone interviews with Alonso Roberts, CA; Jan Reinders, EZE; and David Kardish, CUSO.

ber of the parliament. The director for international programs of CEBEMO, the Catholic NGO in the Netherlands, is the head of the International Development Commission of the Christian Democratic Appeal (the amalgam of the former Catholic and Protestant parties).[86]

In France, although the small Protestant minority of under 1 million tends to be located in the business and professional communities (and therefore normally right-of-center politically), the majority of the staff of the major Protestant NGO—CIMADE—gravitates towards the Socialist Party because of its strong official endorsement since the mid-1970s of many of the items on the NIEO agenda, which they personally favor. Moreover, after the Socialists came to power in 1981 members of the administration began to consult CIMADE (and other French NGOs) regularly for suggestions to reorient official French aid policy more toward helping the grass-roots poor overseas and assisting foreign political refugees in France (CIMADE's traditional priority).[87]

Aside from significant activism in or open sympathies for political parties (primarily of the left), many NGO staff persons are also participants in other political advocacy movements in their societies that have been expanding in popularity and significance over the past decade. These often are organizations created to lobby on specific domestic or international issues not yet being addressed comprehensively by the political party system. Such include disarmament groups, environmental protection advocates, human rights organizations in solidarity with Third World groups, and those working to end discriminatory policies and attitudes against Third World immigrants in their own societies.

In Great Britain, the FRG, Belgium, and the Netherlands, the antinuclear movement grew in strength in the early 1980s, largely as a result of the U.S. government's decision to pressure NATO allies to allow American-made Pershing II missiles on their soil and the Soviet Union's placing SS20 missiles in Eastern Europe. In each of these four countries several hundred thousand persons on several occasions between 1981 and 1983 participated in massive public demonstrations against such policies by the superpowers.

In each case the respective governments (all then dominated by right-of-center or conservative parties) rejected public pressure and allowed the deployment of American missiles (with the Soviets doing likewise in Eastern Europe). Unlike the Nuclear Freeze Movement in the United States, which lasted only for a short time in the early 1980s, these organizations in Europe did not disband and continued to exert pressure on other issues involving weapons spending and disarmament, even after such missiles were deployed. They continued to maintain a cross-class and cross-party base of support in

---

[86] Telephone interviews with Kees van Dongen, NOVIB; and Thom Kierstens, CEBEMO.
[87] Telephone interview with Marianne Hunziker, CIMADE.

their respective societies, including the Tories Against Cruise and Trident (TACT) in Great Britain.[88]

Many NGOs in these name countries have established links with these disarmament groups, either through overlapping memberships of their individual personnel or sometimes through staff meetings and exchanges with these other institutions. Several individual staff members of CA and CAFOD in Great Britain, EZE in the FRG, Oxfam Belgique, and ICCO and NOVIB in the Netherlands are active in antinuclear organizations in their respective societies. The executive director of Oxfam Belgique has for years been active in domestic peace organizations and during the early 1980s was president of the largest pacifist coalition opposing the deployment of Pershing II missiles on Belgian soil.[89]

Working for NOVIB in the Netherlands is recognized by the government as an official alternate to military service. In 1986 there were twenty Dutch conscientious objectors in home-office staff positions of NOVIB who were also active members of Dutch disarmament organizations. The CEBEMO in the Netherlands, although not having any formal ties to such groups, has set up meetings between its own staff and those of antinuclear associations to explore ways in which development and peace issues might be integrated in the respective public education and advocacy campaigns carried on by NGOs and pacifist groups in the Netherlands.[90]

Finally, NGO staff members belong to a whole series of other political advocacy organizations throughout Europe that try to influence public policies and citizen attitudes. Several of the staff members of the two major church-related NGOs in France—CCFD and CIMADE—are active in organizations calling for more flexible policies and laws affecting immigrants. These organizations also denounce private-sector racist policies that discriminate in employment and housing against African and Arab migrant workers or political refugees living in France.[91]

Environmental advocacy groups have also risen in Europe over the past decade (as in the United States) in reaction to greater public concern with air and water pollution and the lack of public access to scarce resources such as land. Unlike the situation in the United States, however, staff from NGOs are frequently involved in these campaigns as well. In the Netherlands, for example, several ICCO staff persons are active in environmental organizations attempting to effect stricter public controls on pollution and land use.

There are also a number of solidarity groups in Europe drawing attention to the needs of oppressed people abroad. They often include on their staffs polit-

[88] Interview with Dr. Jolyon Howarth, Harvard University.

[89] Telephone interviews with Alonso Roberts, CA; Claire Dixon, CAFOD; Jan Reinders, EZE; Pierre Galand, Oxfam Belgique; Rev. S. S. van Dijk, ICCO; and Kees van Dongen, NOVIB.

[90] Telephone interviews with Kees van Dongen, NOVIB; and Thom Kierstens, CEBEMO.

[91] Telephone interviews with Collette Dugua, CCFD; and Marianne Hunziker, CIMADE.

ical refugees from these nations working to educate Europeans, effect reductions of official aid to repressive governments in such societies, and raise money for those seeking to relocate elsewhere. These solidarity groups also attract the interest of NGO personnel, and sometimes formal exchanges and cooperation occur between them and NGOs on issues of mutual concern. When MISEREOR in the FRG centered on injustices in Brazil in 1979 and South Africa in 1983 during Lenten education campaigns, it established working relationships with the respective solidarity groups in the FRG working to highlight human rights violations in those countries so as to maximize its own information in preparing educational materials.[92]

It is also common for NGO project officers who are working in a particular Third World country (e.g., Chile, South Africa) to be active personally in solidarity groups in their own societies. The project director for Latin America in CAFOD in the early 1980s previously worked with the Chile Human Rights Committee assisting Chilean émigrés to Great Britain, and continued close cooperation and exchanges with this domestic British organization after coming to CA. In addition to commitments in the antinuclear movement, several staff members of Oxfam Belgique who are responsible for channeling funds to indigenous NGOs in Africa are active as well in the antiapartheid movement in Belgium. This group is pressuring for sanctions against South Africa by the Belgian government.[93]

Hence, throughout these other North Atlantic countries, NGOs are frequently enmeshed in a network of private organizations that have explicit political agendas regarding domestic and/or international issues. In most instances the ideology underlying these agendas is clearly left of center and is shared by many NGO personnel in large part due to their own previous educational or social experiences.

Participation in this domestic political subculture by many NGO personnel, however, does not always entail active membership in political parties of the left. Although this is the case for some, for others the network itself serves as a surrogate for party activism because they believe none of the major parties are adequately addressing critical domestic and international issues.

Pierre Galand, director of Oxfam Belgique, indicated that his NGO takes the place of a party for most of its staff members, since they are disenchanted with what they believe to be a failure by Belgian left-of-center parties (including Social Democrats) to offer programs fully consistent with their ideologies:

> Some of our staff are active in parties, but only a minority. Parties do not present an appealing vision of the world for us, nor an effective strategy to achieve it. Oxfam offers the possibility of political engagement compatible with the ideals of our staff. We are working through NGOs not merely for economic and political justice for the poor in developing countries but also, due to our close links with domestic organi-

[92] Telephone interview with Heinzberndt Krauskopf, MISEREOR.
[93] Telephone interviews with Claire Dixon, CAFOD; and Pierre Galand, Oxfam Belgique.

zations here at home (e.g., labor unions and the anti-nuclear movement), for a more just and less militarized Europe.[94]

Apolitical NGOs

There are NGOs in Canada and Europe that are not part of the leftist subculture in their domestic societies and, like many PVOs, their political character is much less clearly defined or at least not overtly manifested. As mentioned earlier in the chapter, some NGOs in my sample do not espouse as a goal the empowerment of the poor to challenge the dominant political and economic structures abroad. Nor do they engage in politically aggressive education campaigns at home.

In some instances this is due to the scope of appeal of an NGO resulting from the breadth of its support base. German Agro Action (*Deutsche Welthungerhilfe*), for example, was created as the official FFHC committee in the FRG in 1962. From the start it aimed at the broadest possible audience to maximize income. It has continued to enjoy widespread support and today is sponsored by a number of member organizations that cut across a variety of classes and political orientations—women's associations, small farmers' organizations, bakers' unions, and teacher federations. It also solicits funds from enlisted men in the armed forces through the Ministry of Defense.

Amidst such social diversity there is not a clear political consensus about what development requires. Military men tend to give for charitable purposes. Women's groups, the bakers, and small farmers (all three close to the CDU) are interested in noncontroversial but structural approaches to the alleviation of hunger. Students and professors tend to see political change as an essential ingredient in development. Hence, the staff of German Agro Action is cautious about expressing political change as an official goal due to the diverging orientations among member organizations and other donors.

Heinrich Stienhans, project officer in the Latin American Department of German Agro Action, indicated that although political and economic empowerment of the poor was a part of the staff's concerns, it had to remain officially unarticulated. "This concept is in the back of our minds," he said, "but it is never expressed by us as an official goal of the organization."[95]

There are other NGOs that also try to avoid politics not merely because they want to appeal to as many different groups as possible, but because they do not believe effective development requires the stimulation of a critical consciousness of the poor about power imbalances in their environment. Many of these NGOs are linked to those parts of the cultural and economic substratum in Europe and Canada not associated with the political left. A number of them also originated with significant support by patron organizations in the United

[94] Telephone interview with Pierre Galand, Oxfam Belgique.
[95] Interview with Heinrich Stienhans, German Agro-Action.

States that became known in Canada and Europe for their international work. They continue to share their names with their original U.S. sponsors. Some of them, moreover, are now among the largest Canadian and European NGOs in their respective societies.

Such NGOs include CARE Canada, CARE France, CARE Germany, FPP Canada, FPP Netherlands, Candian Save the Children (CANSAVE), and Save the Children Fund in Great Britain. All of these are now autonomous organizations but part of an international federation of nonprofits who drew their original inspiration and philosophy from PVOs of the same name. Although some now might differ with their American counterparts on specific policy issues (e.g., whether or how to use food aid), they continue to share with these PVOs the basic outlook that their mission is primarily apolitical. Moreover, in most instances the original sponsoring PVO continues to dominate those decisions that are made collectively, and usually is still financially the largest partner in the federation (e.g., CARE USA, and SCF in the United States).[96]

Hence, there are some NGOs that do not have a sharply defined political character and whose domestic support base or original sponsors are not closely identified with leftist political movements. Unlike the case in the United States, however, they are a minority among the largest nonprofits involved in overseas aid. Ironically they often are not as heavily dependent on public subsidies as many of the NGOs in their own societies espousing more overt political objectives, which are potentially more problematic for home-country and foreign governments. These NGOs thus do not present the same challenges to traditional theories about the function of the nonprofit sector or about nation-state sovereignty as do those who are overtly political in orientation (and who also are heavily subsidized by governments).

CONCLUSIONS

Some long-standing historical and critical differences between the United States and the other North Atlantic countries continue to play an important

---

[96] Most of the Canadian and European NGOs that do use an explicit political framework in analyzing and approaching the causes of poverty abroad are critical of the apolitical NGOs. They feel they are naive for not addressing what they consider the fundamental causes of human suffering in their overseas work. In some NGO federations in Canada (CCIC) and Europe (CIDSE), there is a clear division between these two groups of NGOs, and often there is little effort to cooperate except in times of disasters abroad. These same Canadian and European NGOs that espouse political empowerment of the poor as part of their objectives are also very suspicious of PVOs in this country. They not only believe that many U.S. nonprofits place too much emphasis on alleviating the symptoms of poverty (e.g., through food aid), but that PVOs as a whole are far too dependent on the U.S. government for their income. Most politically oriented NGOs in Canada and Europe feel, therefore, that PVOs are too closely associated with official U.S. foreign policy objectives (which they oppose). They are even more reluctant to establish cooperative arrangements with PVOs than with apolitical NGOs in their own societies.

role in shaping current resource allocations and mission priorities of international nonprofit aid organizations based in these societies. The abundance of surplus food commodities and the U.S. government's preference to make these the major part of its subsidies to PVOs, the lack of a significant political left in this country (narrowing the range of foreign policy debate), the primarily humanitarian and pragmatic approach to global poverty characteristic of most Americans, and the lack of insertion of development issues into a wider range of policy questions all continue to shape the orientation of PVOs. Relief and technical emphases characterize PVO priorities and mission definition, and a political dimension to their work abroad and at home is downplayed, although present under the surface.

The type of persons recruited into PVOs and the domestic alliances PVOs establish tend to reflect this nonpolitical approach to overseas development. The PVOs both historically and in their current self-definition thus strive to avoid a political profile abroad as well as alliances at home with groups advocating significant policy changes on other issues. Some do acknowledge, however, that indirect consequences of their work among the Third World poor could have political consequences.

All of these domestic historical and cultural factors have been different in Europe and Canada, and they have a direct bearing on how NGOs in these societies define their objectives today. The resource fulcrum of the NGO community does not lie on the relief side of the aid spectrum because domestic agricultural policies have not dominated government cofinancing arrangements with nonprofits engaged in foreign assistance. Given the long historical involvement of Europe with Asia, Africa, the Middle East, and Latin America during the colonial era, citizen awareness of Third World issues is broader than in the United States. There is greater awareness of the deeper structural and political dimensions underlying poverty. The membership or support bases of many NGOs are also frequently constituted by organizations or ethnic groups having strong political convictions about domestic or foreign policies.

Moreover, the debate about foreign policy toward poor nations is shaped by significant input from the political left due to the broader domestic electoral spectrum in North Atlantic countries other than the United States. Although leftist proposals for the NIEO cannot be implemented—even when leftist parties are in power—they are still on the agenda for public discussion, and there is an articulate minority that favors elements of the NIEO.

It is from this sector that the personnel in many NGOs originate or with whom they most closely identify—under 40, well educated, and politically active in leftist movements and causes. In fact, some gravitate to NGOs precisely because long-established leftist parties cannot consistently implement the NIEO agenda.

A significant number of the larger NGOs, therefore, have come to act as surrogates for an emerging number of Europeans and Canadians possessing what Ronald Inglehart has termed a "post-materialist" orientation. They value intellectual, aesthetic, and environmental advancement along with greater social, economic and political equity at both the domestic and international levels.[97] Many NGOs espouse economic and political objectives in overseas aid that resonate with values of this articulate minority and solicit their support. But these nonprofits are also linked into a domestic network of advocacy groups working on a range of issues that are perceived by postmaterialists as all being related—such as arms reduction, international human rights, and the protection of immigrants or political refugees. Postmaterialists and NGO personnel see development as part of this larger cluster of issues since, for them, it essentially involves enhancing long-term equity and peace within and among nations. For such people, development entails much more than the immediate alleviation of suffering and the broadening of technical skills to solve piecemeal problems—as it is commonly understood among the majority of Americans.

To be sure, there are postmaterialists in the United States as well who support an agenda for greater equity domestically and internationally.[98] When they focus on foreign policy issues, however, these tend to be in the areas of the arms race, U.S. military intervention overseas, and human rights violations in developing countries. Development policy as such is not often included on their agenda. Nor do they form strategic alliances with PVOs since the approach of most PVOs to foreign policy issues is much narrower and more relief or technical in orientation.

Although the espousal by European and Canadian nonprofits of explicit political means to achieve their development goals is understandable given this subcultural framework, the question arises why governments would continue to subsidize their activities abroad and at home—particularly if they appear to represent but one approach to development, and that preferred by a specific subgroup that does not constitute a majority of their respective populations.

Moreover, one would expect that the type of activities supported by such NGOs abroad and the controversial nature of their educational and lobbying efforts at home would precipitate strong punitive actions on the part of policymakers whose reasons for originating cofinancing arrangements with these nonprofits were quite different from current NGO political priorities. One would also expect Third World governments as well to place severe restrictions on, or even terminate, grass-roots projects supported by these transnational NGOs, due to their purported subversive roles in changing current power balances inside host countries.

The next three chapters will explore these apparent dilemmas. Although

---

[97] Inglehart, *Silent Revolution*, pp. 27–31, 40–46, 60–63.
[98] Ibid.

tensions do emerge between governments and NGOs from time to time because of diverse agendas, there is also a range of trade-offs that make ongoing collaboration possible and mutually appealing. There are also a number of formal conditions and informal understandings that act as boundaries for NGO activities both at home and abroad. Finally, while the nature of government-PVO relations is different and less politically delicate, in the United States trade-offs exist as well for both the public and nonprofit sectors for continuing collaboration in foreign aid.

CHAPTER SIX

Current Trade-offs among the American Partners: PVOs, the U.S. Government, and Private Donors

HISTORICALLY North Atlantic nonprofits engaged in foreign assistance have received support from both the private and the public sectors. For over four hundred years citizens and governments alike have found them attractive conduits to assist the needy abroad for reasons that include, but often go well beyond, altruism. Nonprofits have served as useful mechanisms for concerned citizens to alleviate suffering and promote development abroad. They have allowed citizens to export their preferred economic strategies or visions for more just society, which official aid channels are incapable of doing. North Atlantic governments likewise have historically relied on nonprofits to pursue interests abroad complementary to their own official foreign policy objectives. Nonprofits have often served as their surrogates when official government-to-government channels have been unable to accomplish all of their goals.

Moreover, host-country government officials have also found the international nonprofit network (even when channeling assistance from other governments) a helpful instrument in achieving objectives their own public sector is not yet able to fulfill. Such aid has traditionally filled gaps in public services and built communication links between government and the people. It has also been politically more palatable since it gave receiving countries an indirect means of accepting assistance from former colonial powers and was thus more acceptable to host-country leaders sensitive about protecting national sovereignty in the post independence era.

It is clear, however—especially given the evidence presented in chapter 5—that over the past decade apparent conflicts of interest have emerged in these triangular partnerships among nonprofits, private groups, and governments both in North Atlantic and developing nations. Gaps between official rhetoric and actual resource allocation, as well as lack of comprehensive evaluation to prove promised results, have characterized the performance of many PVOs in the 1960s and 1970s. These could create tense situations between them and their private and public donors. Thus far, however, no major conflicts have emerged among the three partners in the United States.

In Europe and Canada many NGOs have come to espouse explicitly political objectives abroad and at home—often in opposition to the official foreign policies of their home governments as well as to the political status quo in host countries. One would expect either that public policymakers at home and in host countries would terminate active or tacit support for nonprofits under such conditions or that nonprofits themselves would have to rely almost exclusively on private contributions from politically sympathetic cadres in their home societies to pursue their agendas. Neither scenario has been the pattern for European and Canadian NGOs.

The next three chapters will explore these apparent contradictions among the major partners in the transnational private aid network. My basic argument is that, despite perception gaps and tensions, there is a series of trade-offs among the major groups involved, allowing active or tacit collaboration to occur. None of the actors or their respective objectives are unitary. Clusters of interests are represented among private citizens and public sector agencies in sending and receiving countries. The nonprofit sector itself at both ends of the transnational spectrum often pursues multiple objectives, not always reflected accurately in official policy or rhetorical statements. Explicit as well as tacit rules of the game exist among the partners both in North Atlantic and developing countries. This prevents a breakdown of the network, and thus allows some important interests of each major participant to be achieved.

In this chapter I shall analyze the trade-offs that occur among PVOs, private donors, and the U.S. government. In chapter 7 I shall do the same for Europe and Canada. In chapter 8 I shall explore the corresponding trade-offs among indigenous nonprofits, public agencies, and recipient grass-roots groups in Latin America, with a special focus on Colombia.

ADVANTAGES OF PUBLIC SUBSIDIES FOR PVOS

Financial Benefits

The major advantage of government grants for PVOs is clearly financial. One of the strongest motives behind PVO lobbying efforts for public subsidies during the 1970s—the leveling off of U.S. philanthropy for international causes—continued into the early 1980s. As table 6.1 indicates, although the amount of government grants to nonprofits in the United States increased in real value by 17.6 percent between 1973 ($643 million) and 1983 ($756 mil-

TABLE 6.1
Private and Public Contributions to PVOs, 1973–1983 (in 1986 dollars)

	1973	1981	1983
Private Donations	$1.69 billion	$1.18 billion	$1.36 billion
Government Grants	0.64	0.89	0.75
Total	$2.33	$2.07	$2.11

Sources: AID, *Voluntary Foreign Aid Programs*, 1974, 1982, 1984.

lion), income from private contributions declined by about the same proportion, from \$1.69 billion in 1973 to \$1.36 billion in 1983—a fall in real value of 19.5 percent in ten years. Amidst such a sharp drop in the constant-value private contributions, public subsidies for PVOs became more essential in their attempt to maintain overseas commitments.

Another advantage for PVOs from increased public subsidies is greater financial security from one year to the next. Since the "new directions" mandate in 1973, AID has been willing to make multiyear commitments (up to three years) to PVO-sponsored projects that cannot be completed in one fiscal year. These arrangements provide PVOs with certainty in budgetary planning, especially when private contributions are harder to generate and have to be raised on an annual basis.

Improved Evaluation Procedures

A second major advantage of public subsidies to PVOs has been the upgrading of evaluation procedures among nonprofit organizations. The U.S. government has taken the initiative in this area—a chronic weakness for PVOs—and has provided both the stimulus and the resources for nonprofits to give more attention to professional evaluation techniques.

Between 1980 and 1982, AID funded a series of workshops in evaluation techniques for forty PVOs sponsored by the ACVAFS. One outcome of these workshops was the publication of a book aimed at helping PVOs improve their project assessment by using techniques suitable for small-scale grass-roots projects. The AID subsequently provided financial assistance and technical methodology to be used by PVOs in assessing cost effectiveness appropriate for small institutions.[1]

Judith Gilmore, senior evaluation officer in the Bureau for Food for Peace and Voluntary Assistance of AID in 1986, indicated that these government initiatives have stimulated greater interest and capacity among PVOs since the early 1980s to improve their evaluation processes:

> Several years ago the usual reason given in the PVO community for conducting project evaluation was: "We do it for the donors as a duty." Now PVOs are beginning to realize evaluations can help their staffs and boards to learn more about what they are actually accomplishing in development and also make more precise the rhetoric they use.
>
> Many nonprofits (especially those engaged in small scale business promotion) are developing collaborative evaluation mechanisms so as to share insights both in approaches to evaluation and in the subsequent use of the findings for program planning.[2]

---

[1] Santo Pietro, ed., *Approaches to Evaluation*; telephone interview with Judith W. Gilmore, Bureau for Food for Peace and Voluntary Assistance.

[2] Interviews with Judith W. Gilmore, AID.

The evaluations sponsored by government subsidies are beginning to generate empirical evidence that documents both the accomplishments and weaknesses of PVO performance. It is clear, as a result of these studies, that nonprofits do have definite comparative advantages over governments in developing water and sanitation facilities in remote rural areas; in assisting small business enterprises, the informal sector that constitutes between 40 and 50 percent of the economy in Third World countries; and in providing low-cost basic health facilities in rural villages.

Even in the area of food aid it is becoming evident that—although much work is still primarily relief since it frequently originates during moments of famine or natural disaster—some food-for-work projects have been effective in providing expanded income and training. They have also helped create permanent infrastructure (roads, wells, trees) necessary to the development process in Third World countries.[3]

These AID-assisted studies are also identifying specific weaknesses in PVO performance—such as chronic lack of sufficient management staff, the tendency for projects to be conceived and implemented individually rather than as parts of broader regional strategies in host countries, the lack of replicability of many nonprofit-sponsored projects, and the still underdeveloped mechanisms for information and evaluation feedback into future program planning. Some nonprofits are, however, taking serious steps to rectify these weaknesses, especially technically oriented PVOs. Those working in the areas of credit for small businesses and primary health, for example, have made significant headway in using what has been learned from government-funded evaluations to cut costs and improve future project design and monitoring.[4]

Upgrading Technical Capacities and Credibility

A final area where public subsidies have made significant contributions to nonprofits has been the expansion of their capacities to undertake larger and more professionally executed projects in the area of technical assistance. This is the result of the whole series of new institutional and expanded project grants inaugurated by AID after the passage of the "new directions" mandate by Congress in 1973.

These grants have especially helped the larger relief-oriented agencies, such as CRS and CARE USA, that already have well-developed overseas counterpart networks to expand into the area of technical assistance. Although the weight of such institutions is still on food delivery, over the past decade they have significantly upgraded their capacities and resources to support local efforts overseas in irrigation, reforestation, health, and credit.

[3] AID, *Development Effectiveness*, pp. 4–5, and AID, *Strengthening the Developmental Potential*, p. 1.

[4] AID, *Development Effectiveness*, pp. 6–7; telephone interview with Judith W. Gilmore, AID.

In some instances this has significantly enhanced PVO credibility among host-country governmental agencies that are taking them more seriously. George F. Kraus, former regional program officer for South America of CARE USA, indicated to me in 1983 that substantial U.S. government subsidies enhanced the possibilities for CARE to work with, not independent of, host-country public agencies, thereby maximizing, in his judgment, its positive impact on the developmental process:

> Not many people in CARE have problems with public aid. It enables CARE to be taken more seriously by host country groups (private and public). In Colombia a department governor won't speak to a representative of a foreign PVO if it is spending less than $1 million in his/her region.
>
> More can be accomplished in terms of putting together a network of partnership if large public funds are behind you. You can go to a counterpart and get its attention faster. You can get the top flight personnel of a counterpart who is part of local government to cooperate if you have $1 million for a technical project instead of $250,000.
>
> I have been on both sides—with U.S. government money behind me and without it. I clearly prefer to have it since it enhances larger spillover possibilities of projects.[5]

A large PVO with substantial U.S. government aid such as CARE USA is willing to work with governmental as well as private organizations abroad. In so doing it is clearly not attempting to subvert or radically alter existing power structures but is working within them to make the system work more effectively. "The host government wants votes," said Kraus, "and the local groups want services."[6] Thus CARE attempts to play a brokering role connecting such interests. Having substantial U.S. government resources to fund larger projects enhances the possibility for it to do so. Under such conditions, local government agencies in the host country are far more likely to take its efforts seriously.

ADVANTAGES FOR THE U.S. GOVERNMENT IN AIDING PVOs

There are also clear advantages for the U.S. government in continuing substantial assistance to PVOs. As indicated in chapter 5, one reason that the congressional "new directions" mandate in 1973 urged AID to assist PVOs more in their overseas work was the high esteem in which they were held by the American people and the desire by Congress to reinject a more popular and humanitarian image into the overall foreign aid program by assisting them. Public opinion surveys carried out in 1972 and 1986 by the ODC have

[5] Interview with George F. Kraus, CARE USA.
[6] Ibid.

confirmed that the popularity of PVOs has remained consistently high among Americans since the "new directions" legislation was passed. In fact, many Americans view nonprofits as more reliable conduits for overseas assistance than official government channels, which they feel are overburdened with wasteful bureaucratic procedures. Other opinion surveys in the early 1980s, for example, indicated that although 59 percent of U.S. citizens believe the United States should help feed hungry people in foreign countries, two thirds (66 percent) are opposed to increased long-range governmental developmental assistance to the Third World.[7]

One result of this continued low esteem for official aid among Americans has been difficulty in Congress in passing annual foreign aid legislation. Over the past decade there have been several occasions when continuing resolutions have had to be used by the congressional leadership to extend current year appropriations at the same level for the next fiscal year. They have not been able to muster enough votes in both chambers to draft new foreign aid legislation that could steadily increase foreign assistance due to a variety of objections from both conservatives (who are convinced much aid is wasted) and liberals (who oppose such a heavy emphasis on military assistance in foreign assistance and who still believe that much of government-to-government aid does not get to the people in need).[8]

Not only has the emerging data on PVOs in the last few years begun to confirm empirically that they are more cost-effective than governments in directly assisting the poor in developing countries, but they have also been acting as a more coordinated and visible force in Washington on behalf of overall foreign aid legislation. This is especially the case since the establishment in 1984 of the new federation representing all major PVOs—the American Council for Voluntary International Action (INTERACTION). Since 1984 the PVO community has also been willing to testify before Congress on issues that go beyond their own institutional interests. Its members have been allies of both

[7] Laudicina, *World Poverty and Development*, p. 5; Contee, *What Americans Think*; AID "USAID Workshop for Biden-Pell Project Directions," p. 3.

[8] Despite the "new directions" mandate that AID emphasize basic-needs projects among the poorest sectors in developing countries, after 1973 AID found it difficult to implement this directive due to administrative and political constraints. The bulk of U.S. bilateral economic assistance is still supporting large capital-intensive projects that benefit mostly the middle-income sectors. Sectoral shifts of aid to rural areas still must filter through host government structures allowing large and medium landholders (who exercise predominant political power in the agrarian sector) to benefit most from new services. While new aid flows are reaching low-income sectors in greater proportion now, early assessments of the basic-needs approach endorsed by both AID and the World Bank in 1983 indicate that most aid still benefits relatively well-off farmers and commercial middle agents since the hard-core poor and landless remain difficult to reach. Moreover, lack of appropriately trained staff, the difficulties of appraising viability and impact of small-scale projects, and length of implementation periods all continue to limit U.S. bilateral aid's impact on basic human needs of the poorest abroad. See Michalopoulos, "Basic Needs Strategy," pp. 248, 250–53; Tendler, *Inside Foreign Aid*, pp. 101, 108–99; Ayres, *Banking on the Poor*, pp. 134–37.

AID and the congressional leadership in pushing for more long-term official economic assistance for drought-stricken countries in Africa. In 1985, for the first time in several years, Congress was also able to pass new foreign aid legislation that the PVO community helped to support.

There is currently a sense in both AID and among congressional leaders that PVOs wield some influence among millions of Americans that can be harnessed by policymakers for their own agendas in foreign aid. Policymakers concerned with official aid have not only been counting on PVOs in recent years to mobilize their constituencies on behalf of both PVO and government objectives, but are now providing grants for them to do so.

In 1981 two strong senatorial advocates of PVOs—Claiborne Pell (D-R.I.) and Joseph Biden (D-Del.)—initiated legislation to support domestic development education efforts by PVOs. The purpose was to help create a better-informed public concerning issues of world hunger and poverty and thereby build a stronger constituency for U.S. government economic assistance abroad. By 1986 these matching grants to PVOs for domestic educational purposes amounted to $2.7 million. Several hundred thousand Americans thereby were being reached annually by brochures, newsletters, classroom presentations, and media messages designed by PVOs. As indicated in chapter 5, none of this PVO education work espouses positions critical of or contradictory to U.S. government policy, and none of these new federal funds may support projects presenting "politically partisan views." As a result of these and other government initiatives, favorable public inquiries about U.S. development assistance to AID's Bureau of External Affairs significantly have increased in the past few years.[9]

Moreover, although AID itself has not used any of the results of PVO project evaluations to alter the performance of its own bilateral aid programs, the positive image of PVOs emerging from such documentation in sectors where they seem to have a comparative advantage over government programs is providing additional justification to both AID officials and congressional leaders for continuing public subsidies to them. Some of the positive, but previously unverified beliefs about PVO performance are being confirmed by such studies, thereby establishing more solid empirically based arguments for the government's reliance on PVOs for implementing some of its "new directions" mandate (especially when there is growing evidence that government-to-government aid is not achieving much success in this area).

In the realm of food aid as well, evaluations that have begun to be more systematized since 1980 have reinforced the position of Congress (originally articulated in the 1960s) that Food-for-Peace should not be merely relief-ori-

[9] Telephone interview with Marian Chambers, House Foreign Affairs Committee; AID, "Guidelines for Development Education Project Grants, Fiscal Year 1985," p. 3; AID, "USAID Workshop for Biden-Pell Project Directors," p. 3.

ented but also developmental in its impact. These studies are demonstrating that much of the commodities being distributed abroad by PVOs is still primarily relief-oriented, since a good deal of such aid supports child feeding as well as material health and nutritional activities. In the area of food-for-work, however, AID-supported evaluations of PVO projects have begun to identify some long-term structural impacts when several ingredients other than food commodities are involved in the implementation—e.g., an education component for recipients, effective supervision and management techniques, and an appropriate program design that is linked to broader development strategies of local governmental institutions in the host country.[10] This evidence is, therefore, helping to prove that some forms of food aid can be developmental, and provides a justification for the U.S. government to continue relying on PVOs in an effort to give Food-for-Peace a more structural as opposed to merely relief image.

Moreover, evaluations of food aid are also showing that the vast majority of PVO food-related projects, whether relief or structural, are reaching the poorest sectors in developing countries. This is not necessarily true for the projects ultimately supported when AID relies on governmental channels to dispose of its surplus commodities abroad, since legislation for this (PL 480, Title 1) allows host country governments to sell the food inside their countries and use the local currency generated for whatever priorities they choose—usually to offset current cash flow imbalances in central government accounts.[11] Hence AID's reliance on PVOs as overseas food aid conduits (even when the ultimate impact is relief) not only assists U.S. farmers at home, but also helps preserve a clearly humanitarian thrust for the overall PL 480 program. This enhances its image in the eyes of the Americans who are desirous of feeding the hungry overseas, but who are skeptical about the capacity of public bureaucracies to do so.

Even the Reagan administration, which placed great emphasis on reducing overall government expenditures, found PVOs attractive for promoting some of its priorities in foreign assistance. It made one of its own objectives in foreign aid the stimulation of indigenous private business initiatives in developing countries. Many PVOs, based on the evidence from recent government-funded evaluations, directly (through credit assistance) or indirectly (through training programs) are making important contributions in this area—especially among very small entrepreneurs not yet reached either by AID-supported programs or by U.S. private investment in developing countries.[12]

Hence, they thereafter rose steadily—from $756 million in 1983 to over $1

---

[10] AID, "PL 480 Title II Evaluations, 1980–1985," p. 21.

[11] Telephone interview with Judith W. Gilmore, AID; AID, "PL 480 Title II Evaluations, 1980–1985," p. 9.

[12] Ibid.

billion (in 1986 dollars) in 1986[13]—even though government subsidies to PVOs dropped significantly in the early 1980s when the Reagan administration began vigorously pursuing major budget cuts. One reason was the growing awareness, both in AID and in the White House, that these agencies had certain comparative advantages over bilateral approaches in satisfying the Reagan administration's preferences for promoting private sector solutions to poverty in developing countries.

DISADVANTAGES OF GOVERNMENT AID FOR PVOs

Despite the benefits accruing to PVOs from substantial increases in public subsidies over the past decade, there are limitations on the use of this assistance and at times, because of it, a close identification with U.S. government foreign policy objectives. Such restrictions limit PVO freedom of choice in country focus and project selection and sometimes complicate their relationships with private counterparts in developing countries.

Twenty of the twenty-four persons I interviewed in the eleven PVOs in my survey receiving some form of U.S. government assistance indicated that there were definite restrictions. Thirteen stated that at one time or another their organizations were limited in the choice of projects they could support overseas.

Political and Economic Restrictions

Some of them said that these restrictions resulted from political considerations based on U.S. foreign policy objectives. Cuba, postrevolutionary Nicaragua, and pre-1984 Grenada are Latin American nations where no U.S. government subsidies could be used by PVOs due to the political nature of the regimes and the absence of U.S. bilateral assistance to such governments. For the same reasons, postwar Vietnam and North Korea are other countries off-limits to nonprofits using U.S. government aid.

In addition, PVOs cannot use government subsidies in many other nations for economic reasons—when AID has classified them middle-income nations based on comparative aggregate indicators. Such societies—which now include all of Latin America except Haiti—are not considered by AID as being in as much need of U.S. economic assistance as other nations having lower per capita incomes (e.g., in sub-Saharan Africa). Nevertheless, two-fifths or more of the respective populations of middle-income nations in Latin America often live well below the minimum poverty line as established by their own governments—as is the situation in Brazil, Mexico, Colombia, Chile, Peru, Venezuela, and Argentina.

[13] AID, *Voluntary Foreign Aid Programs*, 1984; AID, "Expenditure Report of Support."

The AID can waive country limits based on economic considerations. The PVOs must argue each case separately and on a project-by-project basis. This is time consuming and places added administrative burdens on PVOs, especially the smaller organizations that are chronically understaffed. Moreover, even in countries eligible for U.S. official aid, at times PVOs must use AID resources only in areas that are selected on the basis of criteria other than strict economic need—e.g., the "drug corridor" in Bolivia between Sucre and Cochabamba where both U.S. and host government officials want to woo family farms away from coca leaf production. These restrictions are must less negotiable for PVOs than country limits determined on the basis of macroeconomic indicators.[14]

Food aid is also affected by restrictions determined by political, economic, or administrative considerations. The PL 480, Title 2 programs often tend to be larger than the PVO development projects subsidized by cash grants from AID, and, having greater visibility, receive more attention of administrators in AID missions abroad. Ration rates are strictly enforced, and the target groups prioritized by AID mission directors. In the early 1970s in Bolivia (which was not considered a middle-income country at that time), AID ordered the locking of a warehouse where PL 480 food was stored to prevent PVOs and others from using any U.S. food to aid the families of striking miners, which could have caused problems for the U.S. government in its relations with the Bolivian military regime. Even when there are many malnourished children in a country, U.S. PVOs may use no food aid to assist them if that country is on the U.S. political black list (Nicaragua), or considered a middle-income nation on the basis of macroeconomic indicators (Colombia).

Rev. Monsignor Roland Bordelon, director for South America of CRS in 1983, in commenting on the consequences of relying on PL 480 food, said that one goal of the U.S. food aid program (explicitly mentioned in the original legislation creating it in 1954) was to develop markets for American grain and dairy products in developing countries. This at times can hinder the growth of indigenous agriculture and also limits the type of aid PVOs can offer to small farmers. He said the U.S. government has refused, for example, to help Third World countries expand their soybean production, in order to protect U.S. soybean exports.

Bordelon also indicated that the distribution of U.S. food aid was heavily determined according to security interests. It is easy for a U.S. PVO to get PL 480 food products for Egypt, but it is very hard to get them for Uruguay or Brazil. The AID sometimes requires noneconomic conditions for its food aid. For example, AID officials have hinted that if CRS promoted contraception as part of its health or nutritional program (something that is against the agency's

[14] Interviews with Rev. Msgr. Roland Bordelon, CRS, and Kenneth E. Brown, CODEL.

official position on moral grounds), it would then receive more food assistance from AID.

Moreover, Bordelon said people in the home office at CRS in New York are very conscious of U.S. government support, or potential support, in any decision they make. When CRS gets word of a national disaster overseas, before committing funds CRS headquarters always calls the U.S. State Department to learn whether the government will reimburse CRS for any resources spent since it has so little private funding in its overall budget. The AID will not act, however, until the host government itself declares a disaster in its territory, and sometimes governments are reluctant to do so for fear of appearing unable to care for their own populations. Therefore, according to Bordelon, CRS is paralyzed until governments act. The CRS's freedom to move quickly, he said, is hampered by such chronic heavy reliance on U.S. government food aid.[15]

Fending Off Government Pressures

In some instances, PVO respondents to my survey claimed they were able to resist AID pressures, especially when they were blatantly political and determined by short-term foreign policy goals. A PVO can sometimes protect its freedom, they said, by appealing to its own criteria for project selection (included in the guidelines of the AID grants they receive). These rule out support for certain types of projects—for example, those that are technically weak or which do not involve local recipients sufficiently in the operation of the project.

Rev. Oscar Bolioli, director of the Latin American Office of CWS, for example, indicated to me that in the early 1980s AID, which was providing some food subsidies to CWS for its counterparts in Peru and Haiti, began to pressure CWS to use some of its *own* money from private sources to support a conservative religious group in El Salvador working very closely with the local government. The CWS refused such pressures on administrative grounds, pointing out to AID officials that its written policies are (1) to work only with a religious counterpart group in a host country that is a member of the local council of churches, which the particular group in El Salvador was not, and (2) not to give support to local groups in a host country closely linked with government agencies, which the Salvadoran religious organization was.[16]

The CRS was able to use a similar argument in early 1985 after AID had been pressuring it to join in its "Plan Mil" resettlement program in El Salvador. This was a three-year multiservice program to aid displaced persons with food, medical care, and jobs. The AID had available $26 million in funds and

[15] Interview with Rev. Msgr. Roland Bordelon, CRS.
[16] Interview with Rev. Oscar Bolioli, CWS.

$60 million worth of food each year from 1985 through 1987. Given the Reagan administration's policies to bolster the private sector rather than state bureaucracies (and the amount of corruption in Salvadoran government agencies), AID wanted voluntary organizations involved to a maximum degree both in channeling the assistance from the United States and in administering the program in El Salvador. The local counterpart nonprofits in El Salvador, however, had to be approved by the Salvadoran government and work in only those areas allowed by the Salvadoran military.

The program had all the trappings of a political pacification strategy. No services or resources could be provided in contested areas of the country, despite the critical need of civilians there. The Salvadoran military claimed that the predominant population in those areas consisted of guerrillas, or guerrilla sympathizers, and that the safety of PVO representatives could not be guaranteed in a war zone.[17]

The AID wanted CRS to be one of the donor PVOs involved in "Plan Mil" to gain cooperation of the other PVOs that previously had refused U.S. funds for their programs in that country. In fact, AID circulated the plan listing several PVO partners, including CRS, before CRS gave its approval. The CRS resisted this pressure, arguing that its official policy required at least the local church's acquiescence in a host country before it could participate in a particular project.

However, the Catholic bishops in El Salvador, after considerable deliberation, finally refused to approve the arrangement. They also prohibited their own social services agency—CARITAS-El Salvador—to be an administering counterpart PVO. They rejected "Plan Mil" both because of its close identification with the political policies of the Salvadoran government and because of the army's refusal in the past to allow CARITAS to bring humanitarian aid to noncombatants suffering in contested areas of the country. The CRS, therefore, eventually refused to be part of "Plan Mil" since to do so would have violated one of its formal written criteria for overseas aid.[18]

In 1982 AID applied pressure on PACT to channel funds for a project through a PVO consortium in Haiti, the Haitian Association of Voluntary Agencies (HAVA). The PACT specializes in promoting the development of indigenous nonprofit consortia overseas, of which HAVA is one. The PACT is also dependent on AID for over 90 percent of its aid resources (see appendix C, table 3). The PACT, however, refused to act as the go-between (even though AID also offered PACT an additional $1 million for other projects if it agreed), since the board of HAVA at the time was dominated by foreign donor PVO representatives and English-speaking groups.

[17] Preston, "Humanitarian Gesture or 'Political Pacification'?"; Albarran, "El Salvador: U.S. Humanitarian Aid."
[18] Interview with Lenny Vargas, CRS.

Although HAVA had over one hundred Haitian nonprofits as members, they were a minority voice among its governing trustees. Because PACT has in its written criteria for supporting consortia that they be representative of local communities and that their projects involve recipients in design and operation, it refused to participate in the plan. There was also a division of opinion within the AID mission itself on HAVA over the merits of the project, and no further pressure was brought to bear on PACT. The HAVA's board subsequently did become more diversified, however, and PACT later agreed to support the project after changes were made in its composition.[19]

The CODEL was pressured by AID during the first year of the Reagan administration to stop supporting a training program for blacksmiths in Vietnam, despite the fact that only private funds were being used for the project. The CODEL refused to terminate its support, arguing that the intermediary groups through which it was working were church organizations based in Europe and that the funds involved were totally private and did not implicate the U.S. government. It also was able to prove to AID through contact church groups in France that its private funds were being spent as designated and not shunted into other programs in Vietnam manipulatable by the host government.[20]

Unavoidable Limitations

In other cases, in which the official project policies of the PVO receiving public subsidies are not threatened, resisting AID pressures is harder. U.S. PVO representatives in my sample indicated they do modify their positions when it does not involve a compromise of a formal principle—e.g., when a project suggested by AID is within the PVO's project priorities and technically sound.

The CRS, for example, despite serious reservations and opposition by lower-echelon staff, participated from 1975 through 1978 in the Minimum Employment Program (PEM) of the Chilean government by contributing food packages destined for workers in partial payment for their labor in public works projects. This program was highly exploitative of workers since it did not pay them the legal minimum wage and also used day laborers in primary (not merely marginal) jobs, thus replacing many full-time public employees. Moreover, none of the PEM laborers received social security or health care, nor were they guaranteed work on anything more permanent than a day-to-day basis. In the perspective of government critics in Chile, PEM has not been a service to the poor but one more repressive instrument of the regime being used against them.[21]

The CRS participated in PEM for three years because it felt it had no good

[19] Interview with Dr. Robert F. O'Brien, and telephone interview with James F. O'Brien, PACT.
[20] Interview with Rev. Boyd Lowry, CODEL.
[21] Aldunate, S.J., and Ruíz-Tagle P., "El empleo mínimo."

grounds on which to refuse according to its own criteria. The government of Chile argued strongly for the food, convincing U.S. government officials in 1975 that PEM was a step toward alleviating unemployment and hunger in Chile. The AID, in turn, urged officials of CRS in New York to contribute some PL 480 food to PEM, since AID bilateral assistance to the Chilean government was being reduced due to human rights violations. Moreover, the Chilean Catholic Church's local counterpart of CRS, CARITAS-Chile, was willing to act as the local conduit of the food packages for PEM since it would help alleviate at least some suffering among the unemployed.

Many Chileans in the working classes were scandalized by what they considered support for an exploitative policy of the government by local and international agencies of the Catholic Church. The CRS and CARITAS-Chile finally withdrew from PEM in 1978. They did so not because of the moral ambiguity and negative political uses of PEM, but because AID on economic grounds no longer considered Chile a priority area for its Food-for-Peace program and thus eliminated all food aid for that country.[22]

There is simply nothing a PVO can do to change some AID conditions or restrictions on its assistance. The prohibition of U.S. government aid to certain countries for political reasons cannot be negotiated. CARE USA, for example, after 1980 could no longer use AID funds on a school construction project in Nicaragua it had begun with U.S. government assistance before the Sandinistas came to power. It had to look to the Canadian government to obtain funds to complete its commitment.[23]

Population control PVOs—some of which have come to depend heavily on AID for resources since the 1960s—had serious problems with AID restrictions after the Reagan administration took office. These organizations support a whole range of activities in developing countries that assist in limiting population growth, including abortion. The Reagan administration forbade any federal funds to be used by PVOs to support the performance of abortions and also pressured PVOs that receive AID funds to cease using their own private resources for this purpose as well. Organizations such as the Population Council and the Planned Parenthood Federation of America experienced significant and abrupt cuts in federal subsidies by the mid-1980s (ranging from 10 to 24 percent) because of these restrictions.[24]

Several respondents who either indicated that their organizations had felt direct AID pressure or restrictions on specific projects, or found the country priorities a serious impediment, also pointed to AID administrative efforts in the early 1980s to exercise greater control over PVO activities. They claimed these included requests by AID personnel to visit at will any projects that

[22] Interview with Daniel Santo Pietro, CRS.
[23] Interview with Ray Rignall, CARE USA.
[24] AID, *Voluntary Foreign Aid Programs*, 1983, p. 26, and AID, *Voluntary Foreign Aid Programs*, 1984, pp. 26–27.

PVOs support overseas with government funds, suggestions that PVO representatives traveling from the home office to the field make it a point to meet with AID mission directors in U.S. embassies abroad, and petitions that overseas AID missions be given a role of prior approval of new PVO projects before they are submitted to AID in Washington.[25]

AID versus PVO Views on the Restrictions

From AID's perspective these restrictions made sense and are part of an effort, it claims, not so much to control PVOs but to put more coherence into AID-PVO relationships. A policy paper issued by AID in September 1982 stated that the "partnership as it has evolved has not brought with it clear AID policy governing its relationship with PVOs," and that "given the commitment of this [Reagan] Administration to facilitate the work of the private sector," it was time to put more order into its relations with PVOs. More data gathering and oversight responsibilities by AID missions were mandated as a means of improving the information exchange between AID and PVOs. In addition, PVO activities were to be integrated more into the overall development priorities of host countries (as identified by AID) to maximize their effectiveness.

The policy paper noted that AID "is an instrument of total U.S. foreign policy," and consequently, "in determining where it will concentrate its resources for development, it must factor in a wide range of considerations." It also recognized that the "motivations, interests and responsibilities" of private development agencies are not identical to its own.[26]

While such statements did not necessarily imply an effort by AID to manipulate PVOs for political reasons, they highlighted the role political factors play in the allocation of official U.S. developmental resources and AID's desire for PVOs to coordinate more of their activities with AID programs. These tendencies in AID, in fact, led some PVO respondents in my 1982–1983 sample to express judgments that the U.S. government after 1980 was making efforts to tie PVOs very closely to its foreign policy strategies.

One explicitly mentioned the 1982 AID guidelines as an impediment to PVOs since these, he claimed, "will also make every private agency an instrument of government."[27] Another said he felt that since his organization had signed a grant agreement with AID, "they seem to be trying to move in on us" and bring the organization more in line with AID developmental priorities.[28] A third respondent said that while AID appears to be supportive of PVOs as part of its commitment to the private sector, in return it wants to make

[25] Interview with Carlos Castillo, PACT; James F. O'Brien, PACT; and J. Robert Busche, LWR.

[26] AID, *AID Partnership in International Development*, pp. 103, 108.

[27] Interview with J. Robert Busche, LWR.

[28] Interview with Dr. Robert F. O'Brien, PACT.

PVOs "act in close concert with AID policy objectives."[29] A fourth said he felt AID had a confused notion about what the voluntary sector was and tended to identify PVOs with corporations.[30] "The basic problem" asserted a fifth, "is the close tie of economic and military aid with political objectives in U.S. assistance programs which PVOs must try to break."[31]

Several others also indicated that use of public subsidies in Central America was very sensitive and often compromised PVOs because of heavy U.S. military objectives in the region and AID's strong desire to use PVOs to pursue some of these goals (as was done in Vietnam). As a result, some PVOs—even those that would ordinarily accept AID assistance for other areas of the world—ruled it out in Central America in the early 1980s so as to avoid close identification with U.S. policies, which would be damaging to their credibility among many local counterparts in these countries.[32]

Some also said that throughout Latin America there are some counterpart groups that will not accept any U.S. government funds, even indirectly through PVOs, due to their opposition to official U.S. government policies in the Americas. These same indigenous PVOs have no questions, however, about taking money from NGOs that are cofinanced by their respective governments in Europe or Canada.[33]

One may be inclined to discount some of these PVO protestations due to the highly ideological character of the Reagan administration's foreign policy, especially during its first years in office when my PVO interviews occurred (1982–1983). The growing unpopularity of U.S. involvement in Central America in the early 1980s certainly was a factor as well. Nevertheless, as seen in chapters 2 and 3, close ties with U.S. foreign policy objectives have long been an integral part of PVO history. Throughout this century the U.S. government has not hesitated to impose restrictions on PVOs to guarantee this, especially when it considers major U.S. interests at stake. The pressures experienced by PVOs during the early 1980s, therefore, are not entirely due to the peculiar characteristics of the Reagan administration. They are part of a long-standing pattern that has characterized U.S. government–PVO relationships for three-quarters of a century.

The other most common complaint by PVO spokespersons during my interviews had to do with AID reporting or payment procedures—e.g., that AID missions overseas are slow in payment of grants, causing cash flow problems

[29] Interview with James F. O'Brien, PACT.
[30] Interview with Rev. Boyd Lowry, CODEL.
[31] Interview with Robert T. Quinlan, CRS.
[32] Interviews with Kenneth H. Phillips, FPP USA; Jeff Ash, AITEC; and Rev. Oscar Bolioli, CWS.
[33] Interviews with Rev. Oscar Bolioli, CWS; Kenneth E. Brown, CODEL; and Carlos Castillo, PACT.

for PVOs. Several also pointed to what they considered to be the cumbersome nature of government accountability requirements.

One said the number of reports, audits, and requirements for separate accounts for government funds added considerably to his organization's administrative costs.[34] Another said that the type of project proposals and reporting procedures demanded by the government made it hard for low-level staff and Third World recipient groups to be involved in their preparation.[35] One suggested that AID simply accept a PVO's own reporting procedures rather than impose more of its own, which demand too much staff time.[36]

Assimilating the Aid Mentality

Perhaps the most subtle but debilitating limitation resulting from public subsidies to U.S. PVOs is the subservient mentality that this can create among some PVO executives, making them more than willing to meet government wishes, even sometimes before these are expressed. Joseph Short, executive director in 1983 of Oxfam America—one of the four PVOs in my survey that did not receive any U.S. government aid—articulated this problem: "Groups which have contracted with the U.S. government for a long time, or who receive a large percentage of their budget from the U.S. government, have a government mentality. They think as the government does. They don't have to be told what to do by government."[37]

This problem was also illustrated by Thomas Kines, national director of CARE Canada. In viewing the position of his U.S. partner from a distance, Kines felt that despite the avowed apolitical stance of CARE USA and its belief that U.S. government assistance is always a definite asset to its overseas work, there are drawbacks. At times, he felt, there are clear limitations (albeit perhaps unconscious) on the decision-making process in CARE USA, resulting from the fact that it consistently receives nearly three-fourths of its overall resources from AID. Kines described the problem as follows:

> The U.S. branch of CARE is most sensitive to what the U.S. government wants. When we meet in New York to discuss worldwide CARE projects, sometimes when we seem to agree that CARE should not pursue some projects on technical grounds, the New York director says, "Wait a minute. AID wants us in there. Get AID on the phone right now and let's talk about this."
>
> When this happens I get angry, since CARE USA claims to be nonpolitical. It is political, and subject to U.S. government pressures.
>
> I have advised CARE USA to use the international board of CARE (which in-

---

[34] Interview with Dr. William M. Pruzensky, CRS.
[35] Interview with John P. Grant, SCF.
[36] Interview with Kenneth H. Phillips, FPP USA.
[37] Interview with Joseph Short, Oxfam America.

cludes representatives of CARE branches in Canada, Germany, England, and France) for decisionmaking so as to counterbalance U.S. government pressures by the views of those from other nations. Thus far, however, the New York office has refused to do this. I think it would be an important step toward more autonomy from political pressure from the U.S. government.[38]

One study in the mid-1980s of domestic influences on PVOs concluded that the problem of undermining the private nature of PVOs does not originate from the government:

Ironically, their battle is not against an implacable foe. Rather, AID resembles the flame that attracts and may consume a moth that finds its light irresistible. AID's "new directions" concern with micro-development, bottom-up development projects, and its resources may prove to be an overwhelmingly attractive combination for some PVOs. To the extent that it does, PVOs will become appendages of U.S. foreign policy and, concomitantly, will lose any claim to adhering to their "articles of faith."[39]

Emerging Concerns in the U.S. Congress about the Private Nature of PVOs

This same PVO concern about preserving their privateness finds resonances in the public sector as well. What makes PVOs popular among the American people—and therefore attractive to Congress—is the fact that they are private institutions, and hence presumed to be more flexible and independent of the bureaucratic and political limitations that impinge upon official aid policies. Moreover, one of the perennial hopes of the Congress in "priming the pump" with subsidies to PVOs is to stimulate greater citizen interest in—and even tax contributions to—economic development abroad.

In recent years, however, some members of Congress have become concerned that substantially increased government aid to PVOs over the past decade may very well be undermining their private nature and thus reducing their credibility and attraction to American citizens. The fact that private donations to nonprofits in constant value began to decrease steadily at about the time that Congress substantially increased public grants to PVOs in 1973 has confirmed this fear among some in Congress—especially on the Republican side.

What is particularly worrisome to those in Congress involved in the preparation of foreign aid legislation is the fact that many smaller PVOs have become chronically and heavily dependent on public subsidies. In 1981, for example, 12 PVOs with annual budgets ranging between $1.2 million and $13.2 million and that focus on technical aid or multiservice institution-building depended on AID cash grants for 80 percent or more of their overseas aid re-

[38] Interview with Thomas Kines, CARE Canada.
[39] Roberts, "Domestic Environment of AID-Registered PVOs," pp. 111–12.

sources, with 9 of them receiving over 90 percent of their finances from the government.[40] From a financial perspective, these have the appearance of being almost appendages of government, and as relatively small organizations very vulnerable to government domination.

Some of the largest PVOs engaged primarily in relief work—such as CRS and CARE USA, each spending over $300,000 in overseas aid by 1981—also have come to be chronically dependent on U.S. government subsidies for over 70 percent of their annual foreign assistance resources. Although perhaps not as vulnerable to government political pressures as many smaller institutions in a similar situation, some members of Congress have been concerned that they are not doing enough to generate more private contributions for their international work—especially for the new technically oriented tasks they have undertaken primarily with start-up funds from AID since the 1970s.

In the late 1970s as a result of this congressional concern, the Senate Appropriations Committee at the urging of Senator Robert Kasten (R-Wis.) began recommending that more aggressive private fund-raising attempts be used by PVOs so heavily dependent on AID. The trends continued, however, and further steps were taken in the House. In 1981 an amendment to the Foreign Assistance Act introduced in the House Foreign Affairs Committee stipulated that by fiscal year 1985 voluntary agencies that receive federal grants for overseas work must receive at least 20 percent of their total annual finances for international programs from sources other than the U.S. government. This amendment did not result only from the new movement to cut federal deficits in the early 1980s, but also from a growing concern by both fans and critics of PVOs in the Senate and House that the privateness of many PVOs (and therefore their usefulness to the government) was seriously in jeopardy.

The General Accounting Office (GAO) of the Congress reinforced these concerns in a study of PVOs released in May 1982. The document stated that "the independence of PVOs is undermined by over-reliance on AID funding" and that "financial dependency has led some PVOs to focus on what AID wants rather than independently identifying and responding to needs through their own networks." Several months later the 1982 AID policy paper on PVOs affirmed as the major purpose of the 20 percent privateness rule, ensuring that PVOs "maintain their independence of action" and "continue to leverage additional private financial resources for development."[41]

---

[40] In 1980 these twelve PVOs and the percentages of their aid resources originating from AID, were the following: Opportunities Industrialization Centers International (99.5 percent), PACT (97.8 percent), New Trans Century Foundation, NTF (97.7 percent), Asian American Free Labor Institute (97.5 percent), Asia Foundation (97.1 percent), International Medical and Research Foundation (96 percent), AIFLD (95.9 percent), Association for Voluntary Sterilization (95.6 percent), African-American Labor Center (94.6 percent), Agricultural Cooperative Development International (88 percent), CLUSA (84 percent), and the Pathfinder Fund (82.5 percent). See tables 2 and 3, appendix C.

[41] Telephone interview with Marian Chambers, House Foreign Affairs Committee; U.S. Gen-

Further efforts to extend the privateness rule from 20 to 25 percent were introduced from the Republican side by Congressman Jerry Lee Lewis of California in 1985, but they were defeated on the House floor by Democrats after intense lobbying efforts by PVOs. The implementation of the 20 percent rule itself was also delayed another year (until January 1986) due to PVO requests for more time to prepare for its impact.

By 1986 concern about protecting the private character of PVOs subsided among the sponsors of the privateness rule initiatives. Most members of Congress are, in fact, satisfied that the advantages government receives from its support to nonprofits for both overseas and domestic activities currently outweigh the dangers of reducing their incentives to search for greater private support. Criticisms in Congress could reemerge, particularly if the government continues to have difficulty in bringing the federal deficit under control and if the PVO community as a whole—especially those that depend predominantly on AID for their survival—do not begin to generate substantial real increases in private contributions.

TRADE-OFFS BETWEEN PVOs AND PRIVATE DONORS

Continued Decline in Private Philanthropy for Transnational PVOs

Increasing private contributions, however, will not be easy given trends that began in the early 1970s. Private donations to PVOs have been declining steadily since the early 1970s. As a percentage of GNP, private philanthropy for international relief and development dropped from 2.01 percent in 1972 to 1.83 percent in 1981. Between 1971 and 1986, only in 1974 did private contributions for PVOs exceed 7 percent of total dollars contributed to the U.S. charities as a whole. In 1983 the proportion was down to 4.4 percent.

When the combined private donations ($612.7 million) to the ten largest PVOs in 1982 are subtracted from the amount ($830.4 million) given to all 167 PVOs registered with AID in that year (those eligible for government subsidies), the private resources received by the remaining 157 was $217.7 million—creating a situation of intense competition for scarce resources among many small institutions. Although these smaller PVOs as a whole increased their combined publicity and fund-raising expenditures in real value between 1978 and 1982 by 78.3 percent (from $30 million to $53.5 million) this new administrative cost well exceeded their 7.5 percent real expansion in private donations during the same period. This suggests that there very well may be diminishing returns in sustained fund-raising efforts among the American public for the foreseeable future.[42]

---

eral Accounting Office (GAO), *Changes Needed to Forge an Effective Relationship*, pp. i, iii; AID, *AID Partnership in International Development*, p. 3.

[42] AID, *Voluntary Foreign Aid Programs*, 1979, pp. 20, 25; AID, *Voluntary Foreign Aid Programs*, 1983, pp. 21–27.

The only organizations that have been able to substantially increase their resources from the private sector in recent years have been those that emphasize in their fund-raising campaigns immediate alleviation of suffering as a major objective of their institution. In testimony before Congress in early 1985, Thomas H. Fox, vice president for International and Public Affairs of the Council on Foundations, indicated that private contributions for international development have not risen as quickly in recent years as those for relief. He also pointed out that "close to 50 percent of all giving in the United States is directed to religious or church-related institutions" and that PVOs that either have an emotional appeal or religious affiliation do far better than others in raising funds from Americans:

> While Americans are normally generous in response to an emergency wherever it arises, such generosity rarely translates into substantial contribution for economic development programs—despite PVO improved fund appeals. . . .
>
> . . . It is also clear from the data that programs which have some capacity to involve the donor emotionally or religiously are far more successful in attracting individuals' philanthropic support than those which simply articulate an economic or intellectual argument about the need for assistance to the third world. With very

Foundations and corporations—the other major sources of private income for PVOs—constituted only 10 percent of the total private revenues of PVOs in the mid-1980s, and there is not much possibility that their respective donations to transnational PVOs will increase in the near future. Most U.S. foundations do not have an international program of their own, and their current level of support for the international activities of other PVOs appears to be static or in decline.

Corporate giving to U.S. PVOs engaged in overseas work is constrained by pressures to donate to domestic constituencies and by the reluctance of companies to contribute to international causes that do not directly enhance their own markets and profits. Major U.S. MNCs have been increasingly supportive to PVOs in recent years, but mainly in those areas where they have something to gain directly from their philanthropy. The Fund for Multinational Management Education (FMME) in New York, for example (with the assistance of a grant from AID), in the mid-1980s sponsored a project to improve relationships between PVOs registered with AID and MNCs headquartered in the United States. This project was limited to those specific commercial areas where PVOs can decrease costs or enhance the image of MNCs abroad—such as fee-for-product or fee-for-service relationships in which a PVO sells a product or service to a third party, or targeted philanthropy where a corporate grant to a PVO helps meet the business's obligation of social responsibility in a given region where it is operating.

Even in the area of social responsibility, corporations prefer to concentrate on "safe" projects, such as hospitals and scholarships, rather than donate to innovative programs among the poor that entail more risk of failure—precisely the areas where many PVOs are now specializing. The number of corporations giving any kind of support for the overseas work of PVOs in the mid-1980s was also limited (approximately 150), and even these rarely give more than 1 or 2 percent of their total donations to Third World programs. Traditionally they also preferred (although there were some signs of change by 1986) to give a lot of small grants to many nonprofits rather than large grants that could make a significant impact on a major problem or on the income of any one PVO. See Avrin McLean, *U.S. Philanthropy*, pp. 21–33; Bolling, *Private Foreign Aid*, pp. 104, 119; INTERACTION, *Monday Developments* 3, no. 6 (March 25, 1985): 8; and INTERACTION, *Monday Developments* 3, no. 8 (April 22, 1985): 7.

few exceptions, organizations with a religious appeal or connection are particularly successful, as are those which appeal to the plight of children, particularly the child sponsorship programs. Such programs, of course, often are not the best possible long-term economic development programs.[43]

Cultivating a Relief Orientation to Attract Private Donations

Ironically, some of the child-sponsorship organizations themselves—e.g., SCF, FPP USA, World Vision Relief Organization, CCF—have moved beyond relief work. They now include a considerable emphasis on technical aid or multiservice institution-building in areas of basic health and education, low-income housing, sanitation, vocational training, small enterprise promotion, and community development. In fact, SCF and FPP USA now devote the vast majority of their resources to longer-term programs.

They engaged in expanded and aggressive fundraising campaigns after 1980 and experienced significant increases in private revenues as a result. In media campaigns, however, child-sponsorship organizations that are now predominantly in category three (multiservice institution-building)—namely, SCF and FPP USA—continue to cultivate a relief image to maximize donations. Their short advertisements on television or in newspapers emphasize starving or sick children overseas whom they are assisting. The public sometimes receives the impression that donor money will go directly to alleviate the immediate suffering of a specific child. In fact, sponsors are assigned individual children who send them periodic letters on how they are benefiting from contributions.

These two PVOs personalize the donor-recipient relationship, but they do not say that a contributor's dollar gets to the child he or she is sponsoring. It does go to the village or neighborhood where the child lives and is used for projects that will improve the socioeconomic condition of the whole community, not just the individual child. The SCF and FPP USA support primary health and educational facilities, small-scale agricultural development, credit unions, well-digging, and prefabricated home construction among their overseas commitments.

Although organizations such as SCF and FPP USA have in the past twenty years clearly moved them beyond relief to addressing more long-term causes of suffering, the impression given to the U.S. public at times is still the former image. A careful reading of the annual reports or newsletters of these agencies makes clear this new structural orientation, but television and magazine ads (which generate the largest number of new contributors) sometimes can project the former relief image.

PVOs besides child-sponsorship organizations that now focus almost completely on development rather than relief projects also do not want to disasso-

---

[43] Fox, "Private/Non-Governmental Support," pp. 7–10.

ciate themselves completely from their past, because it is in relief that they can still generate the most private resources. Such organizations are often most willing to become active in emergencies, especially if they are already supporting longer-term development projects in a particular country or region where disaster strikes. It is also becoming common for development-oriented PVOs, which do not have field representatives or counterpart groups in the area where an emergency occurs, to collect resources at home and channel them through a designated PVO "lead agency" that has experience and contacts and can serve as a conduit for their own aid to the affected region.[44]

The major reason for this part-time relief strategy is that during disasters a development-oriented PVO can rapidly expand the number of its donors. Many U.S. citizens want to contribute to the immediate alleviation of intense human suffering during a well-publicized emergency, and any PVO that commits itself to doing some relief work during the crisis has a good chance of attracting new supporters.

Oxfam America, for example, which focuses predominantly on multiservice institution-building, and which accepts no U.S. government assistance as a matter of policy, does act in time of emergencies—e.g., the 1974 drought in the Sahel and the plights of refugees in Cambodia, Lebanon, and El Salvador in the early 1980s. In assisting in the alleviation of massive suffering at such times, Oxfam America hopes to expand contributions to its overall overseas commitments. It includes in its fund raising in time of such crisis not merely appeals for donations of food, clothing, or medicine (to be sent directly or through other "lead agency" PVOs). It also stresses the necessity for longer-term solutions to the problems underlying drought, famine, or refugee disasters—such as improved agricultural techniques among small farmers, better systems of irrigation, and new income generating activities among refugees in the areas where they are resettled.

Later, after the crisis subsides, Oxfam America makes an effort to keep crisis donors as ongoing contributors to development programs it supports in the crisis region or in other parts of the world. As a result of special fund-raising campaigns for emergencies in Cambodia and Lebanon, its number of private donors jumped from seventy thousand to eighty thousand in one year (1980–1981). It was also able to keep at least 40 percent of them on as regular contributors to Oxfam's other overseas programs.[45]

The Ethiopian famine, widely publicized in the American media beginning in October 1984, was another case in which many PVOs not ordinarily involved in relief undertook significant fund raising. These included AFSC, CWS, Oxfam America, LWR, SCF, and the UUSC. These and several other PVOs (thirty-three in all), who are members of INTERACTION, raised

[44] Cuny, *Disasters and Development*, pp. 256–58.
[45] Interview with Joseph Short, Oxfam America.

$147.3 million between late October 1984 and July 1985, with several recording about a 50 percent increase in their overseas aid to Africa in 1985 as a result of such blitz fund-raising efforts. Following the publicity about drought in the Horn of Africa in late 1984 and 1985, overall PVO aid to Africa increased by almost two-thirds in two years—from $485.6 million in 1984 (one third of which was from private donations) to nearly $800 million by the end of 1986 (at least one-half of which was from private contributions).[46]

Pros and Cons of the Dual Orientation Strategy

The attempt by various PVOs to keep at least a partial relief orientation in image or fact has clear advantages for donors and the nonprofits themselves. Citizens who want to support PVOs primarily for charitable reasons are pleased that the strong tradition of nonprofits in past relief work is not being jettisoned. The PVOs, desirous of expanding their overall overseas activities (including development commitments) and feeling the pressures from Congress to increase their private resources, are also satisfied since fund raising around emergencies substantially increases their private income.

There are, however, definite disadvantages from such arrangements for both sides. Not all PVOs are able to cultivate a dual image, so not all benefit from blitz campaigns. In fact, many of the smaller PVOs that depend on AID for 80 percent or more of their resources and that have the greatest need of more private contributions are not beneficiaries of American generosity during disasters. The type of work they do is exclusively geared to longer-term issues— e.g., population control, leadership training, educational and cultural exchanges, and credit assistance.

Moreover, intense publicity about disasters in the media wanes quickly when the immediate crisis subsides and the survival needs of the victims begin to be met. The famine in Ethiopia, for example, subsided by 1986, as did publicity about overall African famine in the media. The PVOs, who capitalize on such disasters for new spurts of private income in the short run, simply cannot rely on this as a predictable basis of funds over the long haul.

From the donor side, there are also difficulties with this two-pronged publicity strategy. The motivation of the majority of new contributors during emergencies is immediate relief of suffering, not long-term development. Sometimes when it becomes clear that PVOs are not using all their donations for immediate victim relief, questions can arise among contributors.

In August 1985, for example, CRS was accused by several of its former African field representatives of misleading donors to its Ethiopian aid campaign in late 1984 and early 1985. The charge—given considerable coverage in the press—was that much of the money collected was not being spent on

[46] INTERACTION, *Diversity in Development*, pp. 35–36, 44–45.

immediate relief-type food projects in Ethiopia (as suggested in original fund-raising appeals) but was being deposited in U.S. banks to accrue interest.

Officials of CRS acknowledged that this was the case, and that only $9.3 million of the $51.9 million the agency had raised from October 1984 through July 1985 had been spent on transporting and distributing food to 1.8 million malnourished Ethiopians. The reasons for CRS's inability to spend more of these funds, they said, were logistical problems in Ethiopia itself and larger-than-expected donations during the appeals campaign. Not being able to utilize much of this windfall of generosity for immediate relief, the agency officials decided to bank the rest to support long-term agricultural and irrigation development in Ethiopia and in seventeen other African countries whose drought problems were also critical.[47]

The criticisms subsided after a thorough examination by a panel of Catholic bishops exonerated CRS from any wrongdoing under such circumstances. The CRS is also more careful now to explain in its fund raising for African famine relief that a significant portion of the contributions will be allocated for long-term projects aimed at alleviating the deeper structural causes of drought and hunger.[48]

The incident reveals, however, the problems that can occur—or can be created by potential critics—when massive fund-raising appeals occur during disasters. Given the American public's penchant for relief, many donors simply may not read the fine print in ads or realize that much discretion is employed by PVOs today in using funds raised during crises for other worthwhile causes later.

The media in 1986 also focused on the gap between the child-focused rhetoric in fund raising by SCF and the now predominant development focus of most of its overseas activities. Both *Forbes* magazine and NBC-TV in mid-1986 ran features describing SCF as a rapidly growing PVO due to private fund raising around child-sponsorship. Each story pointed out that SCF uses the bulk of its resources to support overseas counterparts that do not focus on children but on the wider socioeconomic needs of villages or neighborhoods where they live.[49]

Although these media presentations about SCF did not create the impression of serious malfeasance, they pointed to the gap between donor expectation and agency performance endemic to a two-track strategy of fund raising around needy children. Such publicity in the media can potentially diminish the credibility of PVOs among sponsors and perpetrate suspicions among the wider public that international charities as a whole are not accurately presenting themselves in appeals.

[47] Blumenthal, "Catholic Relief Services Involved in Dispute."

[48] Filiteau, "Famine Relief in Ethiopia."

[49] Behar, "SCF's Little Secret"; NBC-TV, *1986* (July 29, 1986).

The program on NBC-TV in 1986, in fact, indicated that the attorney general's office in Connecticut (where SCF is headquartered) was investigating whether misleading advertising was occurring. The issue was later resolved when SCF agreed to rework its TV ads. It agreed to explain more accurately that contributions would not necessarily go to sponsored children but would be pooled into a fund supporting community development in the village or neighborhood where the children reside.

PVO Fudging When Sensitive Political Implications Are Involved

There are other situations in which gaps exist between donor perceptions and PVO performance—especially when full disclosure of activities is not given to donors on the controversial political implications of their developmental work. A small minority of PVOs that focus on multiservice institution-building at times quietly try to promote empowerment-type projects by working with the politically left-of-center (albeit non-party-affiliated) counterpart organizations in developing countries (as described in chapter 5). In recent years, PVOs such as CWS and Oxfam America, in addition to supporting standard social service projects, have attempted to search out indigenous non-profits abroad that are assisting people being repressed by governments for their political views or associations. These indigenous organizations try to protect persecuted groups by strengthening their economic base of support or by providing them with basic survival assistance.

In some cases a PVO such as CWS or Oxfam America has supported what it considers politically sensitive but non-party affiliated groups abroad—e.g., local church agencies in Central America that in part help refugee families who have relatives fighting with the guerrillas, or social service projects in areas of El Salvador dominated by insurrectionary forces and administered by private organizations that may very well be sympathetic to the guerrillas. In such situations, there are perception gaps between a PVO's staff and the people who contribute to these overseas activities directly (Oxfam America) or through local church congregations (CWS). Rather than give detailed information to donors or even try to educate them about the political dimensions, CWS and Oxfam staffs have approved projects based on their own judgments (informed by personal travel and communication with local counterpart church groups) as to what is needed to improve the lot of the poor and oppressed.

The CWS also has provided (with private funds) relief assistance for the reconstruction of Vietnam after the war, arguing that to be truly credible a church-related PVO must be universal in its concern for human need. The National Council of Churches (NCC)—of which CWS is the overseas service arm—is also a member of the WCC, which established a Program to Combat Racism (PCR) in the early 1970s. One part of the PCR was a special fund created to provide humanitarian aid (social and medical services) to liberation groups fighting in the southern African region against the Portuguese colonial governments of Angola and Mozambique and the independent governments of Rhodesia and South Africa. Contributions to this special fund of the PCR had to be so earmarked by donors and no general funds of WCC member churches were diverted into this specific program. The assistance, however, was provided without rigorous control over the manner in which it was spent, and little prior consultation with WCC member churches was done before this part of the PCR was implemented.[50]

Politically conservative groups in this country long have been upset with CWS, NCC, and the WCC for all of these activities, arguing that they have provided important political legitimacy and economic benefits to armed resistance forces and other enemies of the United States in various parts of the world. In 1983 these critics (articulating their views in both the electronic and print media) strongly attacked CWS for actively supporting "Marxist-Leninist movements," for lying to donors by calling such projects "humanitarian," and for not giving full and accurate disclosure of all their activities in politically sensitive regions abroad.[51]

In fact, CBS-TV's *60 Minutes* in January 1983 devoted two-thirds of an hour-long program to CWS specifically. Politically conservative critics of CWS (some active church members) were given ample opportunity to make these charges before a national television audience of several million Americans. The CWS subsequently denied charges of supporting Marxism and revolution and of lying to donors. No evidence was presented by its critics of funds being used to support violence abroad.

Sometimes PVO staff do not make an effort in agency publications or reports to explain fully the nature of projects or the reasons for funding them. They do not want to scare off actual or potential donors, and they do want to protect confidentiality for recipients of their humanitarian aid in politically troubled areas overseas. However, this can create a perception gap between PVOs and their donors or between PVOs and sectors of the wider public. Angry critics can use these gaps in attempts to discredit such agencies.

The staff at CWS is better informed than the average churchgoer as to what is going on overseas, and it is in regular contact with Third World church groups that know well the needs of their people and ask for aid to help them. It is not, as suggested by one critic on the CBS-TV *60 Minutes* program, an issue of lying by church executives in the NCC to their people about some of the activities supported by CWS abroad. There may very well be, however, a perception gap between the agency's staff and many of its contributors.

One analyst of the uproar caused by the *60 Minutes* program, who is clearly

---

[50] Lissner, *Politics of Altruism*, pp. 257–61.

[51] Isaac, "Do You Know Where Your Church Offerings Go?"; CBS-TV, "The Gospel According to Whom?"; Brownfield, "Behind the Effort to Cut Off Aid to El Salvador."

sympathetic to the NCC staff, believes the overall effect of the CBS report was a distortion. However, journalist Rev. John Reedy, C.S.C., claims that the NCC does have a problem in the distance that has developed between its sponsoring church membership and the mentality of many of its professional staff who shape the programs and projects of its overseas aid-giving arm, CWS. Reedy writes:

I . . . concluded that the NCC does have a serious problem in the distance which has developed between its sponsoring membership and the mentality of many of those who work professionally to shape its programs and services.

I know and admire some of these people. Those whom I have met impressed me as being deeply committed Christians who are trying to do all they can to relieve human suffering and injustice. They have an instinctive sympathy for those who are struggling to change social, political, and economic conditions which are outrageously oppressive.

This sympathy can occasionally lead to recommendations which turn out to be unwise and embarrassing. But, for Christians, excessive caution can also lead to a morally offensive inertia in the presence of our neighbor's suffering.

Somehow, though, the officials and staff of the National Council of Churches have to maintain their links to the awareness and convictions of the sponsoring membership. They are representing these churches, these congregations, these people who join together for common efforts.

My impression is that a huge gulf separates the experience, the sensitivity, the judgments of many NCC staff members from the awareness and practical judgments of local clergymen and the members of their congregations.

The Council must do a better job of communicating to its constituency the experience and convictions of those who formulate the programs. The staff needs to be more sensitive to the level of understanding of the church members in formulating the various programs.

It is unhealthy—ultimately self-defeating—when a professional staff of any organization allows too much distance to develop between itself and its membership.

In the long run, that kind of a gap can be more damaging than the treatment you might get from the *60 Minutes* crew.[52]

Oxfam America also has discovered that there are differences between donor expectations and what it is trying to accomplish overseas and at home. It is one of the few PVOs, in fact, that has an aggressive development education program that challenges American public opinion. It also from time to time engages in lobbying efforts to influence foreign policymaking (e.g., against U.S. military aid to Central America).

However, in 1983 Oxfam America found in a random national survey of one thousand of its adult donors that there was a gap between their perception

---

[52] Reedy, "Council vs. 'Sixty Minutes.' "

and what the Oxfam staff was actually attempting to do at home and abroad. The survey revealed that the average adult who contributes to Oxfam America has had some college education, worked for a corporation or in one of the professions, and had fairly liberal political views. The majority of respondents agreed that social injustices (domestic and international) underlie many problems of Third World poverty and that U.S. foreign policy, as well as trade and business practices, sometimes exacerbate these injustices.

However, nearly three-fifths of the respondents also felt that it was not the proper function for Oxfam America to be attacking such problems directly, either overseas in the type of projects it funds through its counterparts or at home in its education and advocacy work. The sponsors felt that working to alter power structures abroad or to change U.S. government policies at home was political activity and beyond the legitimate scope of Oxfam's functions.

Respondents indicated that they contributed to Oxfam because they felt it was helping poor persons abroad become economically self-reliant through the various socioeconomic programs it supported. They manifested little awareness of some of Oxfam's controversial programs (especially in Central America), or of the significant educational and lobbying efforts Oxfam supports in the United States to change public as well as policymakers' opinion about U.S. foreign policy.[53]

Hence, just as there are gaps between image and reality for PVOs that work the two-track relief/development strategy, there are differences in donor perception and PVO performance for those nonprofits supporting politically sensitive projects abroad but who do not broadcast or emphasize this in their public relations. In both cases, gaps result from PVO efforts to maximize their private income while respecting current preferences of U.S. citizens who value relief over development and frown upon any political activities by PVOs.

Unless there are some changes in American attitudes toward the purpose of private foreign aid and significant, steady increases in their financial support for it, these gaps between donor perceptions and PVO performance will continue. When they are publicized, the PVOs involved risk paying a price in the area of credibility and reliability.

CONCLUSIONS

Despite the long history of very positive benefits resulting from cooperative arrangements among PVOs, the U.S. government, and private donors, it is becoming clear that there are now clear trade-offs in continuing this tripartite relationship for each of the parties involved. It is also evident that each of the partners represent clusters of subgroups, not all with similar interests. There

---

[53] Interview with Joseph Short, Oxfam America.

is, therefore, a delicate balancing act both among and within participating groups in the private aid partnership in the United States.

Within the PVO community, there are a few organizations that on principle reject government aid (e.g., Oxfam America and the AFSC on the grounds that it seriously damages PVO independence and distorts PVO perceptions and priorities). Another small group has come to depend on it for their institutional survival. The vast majority are in favor of public subsidies, but they are also now more critical of the conditions that come with them than in the past.

On the plus side, these grants have provided several important financial, administrative, and political benefits to PVOs who accept them: (1) they have helped to offset the steady decline in real value of private philanthropy for international aid since 1973; (2) they have expanded the amount of information available to PVOs about their own work, and these AID-sponsored evaluations have highlighted that some PVO "articles of faith" no longer have to be taken by government and citizens on faith alone; (3) they have bolstered technical and financial capacities, enabling PVOs (especially the older relief agencies) to include more development in their scope; (4) they have bolstered PVO interest in and ability to implement domestic educational activities concerning global poverty and development; and (5) they have enhanced the size and credibility of development projects some PVOs (especially the larger ones) are capable of supporting overseas, thus stimulating greater respect by host-government agencies for their work.

On the negative side, there have been limitations in recent years resulting from government grants, which PVOs do not like. These range from formal restrictions limiting where and how government funds can be used, administrative controls to ensure stricter accountability, and PVO credibility problems with private counterparts abroad due to identification with unpopular U.S. foreign policy objectives. Ironically, as described in chapters 2 and 3, U.S. government controls over PVO activities on several occasions in the past (especially during wartime) were far more extensive than they are at present—and in eras when no or very small public grants were available to PVOs.

Government restrictions, in fact, are more justified now than previously, due to the substantial public aid now given to PVOs and the corresponding right of government to get something in return that serves its own foreign policy interests. In the post-Vietnam era, however—when there has been more criticism and active opposition both here and abroad to U.S. government policies in the Third World—some PVO personnel are more conscious of government restrictions and sensitive about their organizations' image, which such restraints can create among some of their partners abroad.

Those PVO executives and staff members who dislike what they consider drawbacks of public subsidies are now faced with two choices. They can either continue to accept the aid and live with the trade-offs and ambiguities, or they can refuse further assistance and lose several or all of the financial, administrative, and political advantages it provides. Every indication at present is that they will continue with the first choice. Neither a dramatic steady upsurge in private donations or a significant shift of mentality among their boards of directors is likely in the near future. Hence, even inside PVOs when there is criticism of the consequences of government aid, there is a plurality of viewpoints. Those responsible for guaranteeing institutional continuity and growth (boards of directors) have the last say, and this reinforces the likelihood of the first choice for the foreseeable future.

From the government side, the choices are neither as clear-cut nor easy to predict. As in the PVO community, diverse views exist in the public sector. Although supporters of cofinancing arrangements with PVOs in Congress have the upper hand, formidable critics have emerged recently. If present circumstances change, they could gain the upper hand, thus reducing public sector enthusiasm about continuing subsidies to PVOs at the same level.

The PVOs have long enjoyed a good reputation in Congress due to their high popularity among Americans and their excellent track record in relief work. They have also long supported and complemented U.S. government objectives abroad—even becoming surrogates for foreign policy interests when the U.S. Department of State could not act on its own. All of this occurred during many years when PVOs received little government financial aid. They have a good deal of residual support they can draw upon, in both the executive and legislative branches of government.

Moreover, there is growing evidence in some areas that the government is, in fact, getting its money's worth out of its assistance to PVOs. Nonprofits appear to have some comparative advantages in achieving development objectives with both cash and food subsidies that official distribution cannot yet achieve. The PVOs have also begun to act in a more coordinated and vocal fashion as strong advocates for increased foreign aid and as educators on global issues among the American public.

They have exhibited a chameleonic usefulness for pursuing foreign policy objectives that change from one administration to the next. In the 1950s they were perceived by many in the Congress and executive branch as bulwarks against communism and exporters of the American dream, in the 1960s as implementers of participatory democracy at the grass-roots level, in the 1970s as humanitarian agents for basic-needs fulfillment among the poorest, and in the 1980s as a proof that privatization is an effective solution to the economic problems of developing countries. As a result, support for PVOs in government over time has been bipartisan and has cut across several critical committees, departments, agencies, and offices responsible for foreign policy-making and implementation.

Recently, however, several factors have converged to stimulate criticism of PVOs among some in Congress, and these have resulted in some limits on public subsidies to PVOs. These factors include the necessity to search annually for federal budget cuts amidst mounting deficit problems, increasing information about nonprofits (including their weaknesses) available to Congress resulting from evaluation and accountability requirements for subsidized PVOs, and the continuing real decline in the private philanthropy for international causes.

Doubts have emerged among budget-conscious members of Congress about whether the government is getting its money's worth on all fronts as a result of PVO cofinancing arrangements. In their minds, public subsidies to PVOs are meant to "prime the pump" for greater financial contributions from the private sector as well as stimulate greater citizen support for the government's own development assistance programs. In neither case has substantial progress yet been achieved.

The PVOs have made greater efforts in recent years to convince Americans both of the value of official foreign aid and of their own programs as a complement to it. Most citizens have not yet accepted their arguments, however, as reflected in the continued low popularity of governmental foreign aid and the steady decline in private contributions to the PVO community.

Thus far PVOs have been able to draw upon their long-standing support among the majority of Congress, have proven some of the rhetoric about their development contributions, and have ongoing support in AID desirous of keeping PVOs as allies in its battle in Congress on behalf of unpopular foreign aid legislation. They also have strong support among farm-bloc representatives and PL 480 officials in government as providing useful solutions for government food surpluses.

The 20 percent privateness rule, however, could be only the first legislative salvo across their bow. Even the supporters of PVOs in Congress will have a hard time preventing further initiatives along these lines if (1) the deficit continues to mount, (2) real private income of PVOs continues to decline, and (3) U.S. citizens remain unenthusiastic about foreign aid.

Each of these three *ifs* is very likely to continue as reality for the foreseeable future. Although these factors will probably not precipitate a termination of government aid to PVOs, more objections are likely to be voiced in Congress and in the office of the presidency by those carefully measuring the political cost-effectiveness of every federal dollar spent. Even the appeal of PVOs in the 1980s as fostering privatization in economic development has been tarnished due to the heavy public dole needed to maintain their initiatives abroad.

From the government side, therefore, the choices are to (1) accept the quasi-governmental characteristics of many PVOs in exchange for their domestic political support; (2) force them to become considerably more financially autonomous, thereby risking a loss of allies in the difficult effort to build a stronger constituency for foreign aid in American society; or (3) continue to apply piecemeal pressure on PVOs from time to time to improve their performance in private fund raising and consensus-building for foreign aid. The first choice is probably no longer feasible for anyone in government. The third choice is most likely in the foreseeable future, but the second cannot be ruled out if significant progress is not made in managing the government deficit by Congress and in stimulating greater citizen support for international development.

The third partner in this relationship is, in fact, precisely the American citizen. Unlike the early years of PVO growth, since the early 1970s Americans have been reducing their contributions to PVOs. The credibility of PVOs, however, remains quite high among the public. The potential is there for PVOs to rekindle private generosity to their causes.

As is the case with the other two partners, the private sector participant in nonprofit foreign aid is also diverse. There is a group of well-educated professional persons that is willing to contribute to PVOs working on long-term structural solutions to poverty. Oxfam America, for example, discovered these to be the hard-core of its steady support base. The vast majority of Americans, however, are more relief-oriented in their motives. They still look to PVOs as "humanitarian firefighters" ready to react quickly in times of overseas disasters. Not only are these people far more numerous than the first group, they also oscillate in their giving patterns to PVOs depending on the frequency of disasters, the extent of the human suffering involved, and the degree of media exposure the tragedies receive. Both groups of PVO donors are in agreement, however, that nonprofits should remain far removed from politics in their work.

This donor bifurcation has led to inconsistencies in PVO mission definition and self-presentation in fund-raising campaigns. It has led to firefighter-type reactions whenever the disaster bell rings regardless of other priorities of the moment. Some have also been less than forthright in their disclosure procedures for fear of seriously offending Americans who naively believe humanitarian work and politics are mutually exclusive.

Thus far the zig-zag strategy has worked for most PVOs. They have been increasing their income by disaster campaign blitzes and finessing potential blowups when they are involved in delicate situations abroad. Most donors have been satisfied with this approach since they do not read the fine print or ask probing questions. They are also satisfied that they have ready and willing outlets for their humanitarian impulses when overseas tragedy strikes.

Periodically, however, the weaknesses of this strategy are exposed. In fact, the greater public attention that is focused on PVOs due to more and better evaluations of their work and more vigorous PVO fund-raising and educational efforts, the greater the likelihood that this will occur. Both the media (which they use effectually to raise funds) and politically conservative groups (to whom they present themselves as primarily humanitarian and apolitical organizations) are becoming more aware of gaps between PVO rhetoric and performance that still exist, and they are voicing criticisms about them. No serious long-term damage has yet occurred for PVOs, but should criticisms become more heated and substantiated, the PVO community could experience serious credibility problems and a further real decline in private contributions.

Moreover, the two-track strategy in PVO fund raising is no lasting solution to their serious financial problems. There simply aren't enough disasters occurring on a regular basis that can provide them with a steady source of private income. Even if there were, their development-thrust would be seriously weakened, along with their attractiveness to many public sector policymakers.

The PVOs thus face a number of choices vis-à-vis their private donors, all of which carry difficult consequences: (1) they could opt for almost purely relief work, thus curing their institutional schizophrenia by running with what traditionally has been their strongest suit; (2) they could embark on more extensive and forthright disclosure and education campaigns, enlightening the American public about the need for structural solutions to poverty abroad and that humanitarian work in polarized contexts involves political choices and risks; or (3) they could continue to muddle through with their current multilayered approach to both overseas problems and domestic public relations.

The first choice is distasteful to most due to the prestige developmental work brings among their colleagues, public policymakers, and academics. It also would result in a significant reduction of their institutional apparatus during normal times when no overseas tragedies are occurring, something few board members or executives or large PVOs would accept.

The second choice is very risky given the long-established relief preferences among Americans. Even if successful in building a wider base of financial support for long-term development work, the short-run consequences of a more aggressive education would probably involve a loss of many donors who would walk away from PVOs bored, angry, or scandalized. The PVO boards and executives will not risk institutional suicide to change the way Americans think and act.

The third choice is the most likely since it is what many PVOs are now doing. It maximizes their options overseas and their income at home from both the public and private sectors. It does not, however, solve the problem of seesaw private financing that oscillates from peaks to troughs, nor does it allay congressional anxieties about the erosion of a strong private financial base for many PVOs. It also risks the likelihood of more public criticism the longer the ambiguities of this strategy continue and the more information about them becomes available.

How the three partners in American private foreign aid will solve these dilemmas remains to be seen. It is clear that the status quo in the current tripartite trade-offs is not stable. Nor are the choices open to resolving the underlying contradictions easy for any of the participating groups.

CHAPTER SEVEN

Current Trade-offs among the European and Canadian Partners: NGOs, Governments, and Private Donors

IT IS IN EUROPE AND CANADA that the sharpest apparent contradictions between nonprofits and their public- and private-sector supporters exist. Not only are many NGOs in these other North Atlantic societies more explicitly political in mission definition, but these political agendas often are in direct opposition to official government policy positions and the attitudes, lifestyles, and economic interests of many citizens.

Despite such contradictory interests, there are also shared objectives that cut across all three partner groups. In fact, a modus vivendi exists among NGOs, governments, and private donors allowing those in each cluster to pursue some of their core interests.

These trade-offs among partners are not exactly the same as in the United States due to the different domestic political context in Europe and Canada. As in the United States, however, sufficient overlapping concerns exist making ongoing collaboration among the partners feasible. The NGOs receive critical financial, administrative, and political benefits from public subsidies. Some party leaders and government bureaucrats find NGOs useful political allies in domestic political battles, while those engaged in foreign policymaking see them as alternate channels for diplomacy, thus allowing governments to pursue sensitive political objectives overseas with less accountability. There is a hard core of well-informed private donors that shares NGO ideological commitments and a larger number (less well informed) who look to NGOs to pursue development or humanitarian work in time of disasters in foreign countries.

Boundary lines—formal and informal—exist, however, on NGO activities. A variety of co-optive as well as punitive measures are used by policymakers to prevent NGO activities from creating serious political embarrassments for them at home and abroad. In turn, disclosure methods by NGOs to private donors vary in content and emphasis depending upon which cluster group of supporters is being addressed.

However, serious tensions arise when NGOs become drawn into partisan conflicts in domestic politics, or when their political objectives become known to private donors who support them for development or humanitarian reasons. Hence, as in the U.S., the tripartite relationships in private foreign aid involves tensions. The status quo is not stable, and for it to continue on present course caution, as well as a certain amount of secrecy, is essential.[1]

ADVANTAGES OF PUBLIC SUBSIDIES FOR NGOs

Financial Benefits

As mentioned in chapter 4, private donations to European and Canadian NGOs between 1973 and 1983 grew by 44 percent in real terms. Unlike the situation in the United States, therefore, NGOs were successful in this ten-year period in expanding significantly their financial base of support from private philanthropy.

This is a factor that has given NGOs as a whole greater flexibility in project decisions than their American counterparts. They are less susceptible to government restrictions than are PVOs in the United States, where the maintenance or even survival of nonprofits now depends very heavily on public subsidies.

It is also clear from table 7.1, however, that government aid to NGOs in Europe and Canada both absolutely and proportionately grew much more than private income over the entire ten-year period. Public assistance grew in real terms by over $520 million (325 percent) between 1973 and 1983. Moreover, more than three-fourths of the increase ($410 million) came between 1980 and 1983 alone. Hence, although not as crucial for nonprofit institutional maintenance or survival as in the U.S. case, government aid to NGOs has enabled them to expand commitments to overseas development and domestic education at a much faster pace than what they could have done by relying on private resources alone.

As in the U.S. case, government funding for nonprofits also can be author-

TABLE 7.1
Private and Public Contributions to Canadian and European NGOs, 1973–1983 (in 1986 dollars)

	1973	1980	1983
Private Donations	$0.84 billion	$1.11 billion	$1.21 billion
Government Grants	0.16	0.27	0.68
Total	$1.00	$1.38	$1.89

Sources: Van der Heijden, "Development Impact and Effectiveness of Nongovernmental Organizations," tables 2 and 3; AID, *Voluntary Foreign Aid Programs*, 1974, p. 12; CCIC, *Report of the Task Force on Government Funding*, p. 8.

[1] A shorter version of this chapter appears as "More Than Altruism: The Politics of European International Charities," in James, ed., *Nonprofit Sector in International Perspective*.

ized now on a multiyear basis, thus alleviating the pressures to raise funds annually for all of an agency's overseas commitments. The ODA in Great Britain, for example, is willing to provide block grants to British NGOs—especially to church-related agencies that work through well-established and broadly representative indigenous nonprofits in developing countries. The Ministry of Foreign Affairs in the Netherlands since 1980 has been approving three-year block grants, which the four major Dutch NGOs can distribute without prior approval for individual projects.[2]

Administrative Flexibility in Use of Government Funds

Even when projects must be approved on an individual basis, there is a great deal of flexibility permitted to NGOs in their reporting procedures. Except in the FRG where accountability procedures are as strict as in the United States, reporting requirements to governments allow much discretion for NGOs. Nonprofit executives and staffs, for example, can often omit information that they consider to be confidential in documents sent to their respective governments, such as the names of recipients in or explicit details about projects that could be politically sensitive.[3]

In some countries (e.g., Canada and Great Britain) country limits exist. These prohibit the use of public funds by NGOs in certain nations because of the political nature of the regimes or because of current political disagreements that a European government has with a Third-World government. In most European countries, however, such restrictions do not exist, and NGOs are free to use home-government aid wherever they choose.

Moreover, the foreign policy traditions and current interests in some European countries are more conducive to NGO empowerment goals. Sweden and the Netherlands, for example, do not have major security objectives abroad, and they are much less concerned about potential political unrest in developing countries. Sweden prides itself, in fact, for playing a role of international "conscience" among nations, and it is a major supporter of liberation movements in various parts of the world.[4]

Even larger European nations that have significant economic or military interests in the nature and pace of change in developing countries often use different measures to influence political dynamics in those countries then those used by the United States. The NGOs are sometimes seen as invaluable allies in accomplishing some of these aims. Rather than placing considerable restric-

[2] Alonzo Roberts, CA, letter to the author, May 1, 1986; Dr. J. E. Paulus, head, NGO Programme Coordination Division, Ministry of Foreign Affairs, the Netherlands, letter to the author, July 13, 1986.

[3] Interviews with Wolfgang Kaiser, EZE; Heinrich Stienhans, German Agro Action; Rev. S. S. van Dijk, ICCO; Christine Whitehead and Peter Sollis, Oxfam UK.

[4] Arnold, *Implementing Development Assistance*, pp. 172–73.

tions on the geographical scope of subsidized NGO activities or demanding detailed feedback from them, these governments find that allowing considerable flexibility to NGOs in country and project focus is to their advantage.

Improved Evaluation Procedures

As in the U.S., European and Canadian governments have provided both stimuli and incentives to NGOs to improve their evaluation mechanisms. By so doing, as with PVOs, NGOs have been able to prove some of their claims about making unique contributions to the development process.

In Canada and in the Netherlands, for example, increased government funds have been made available to NGOs since the early 1980s to pay for project evaluations done by professionals, either from the home or host country. At about the same time (1981), the CEC began its multiyear cooperative evaluation process of various types of small developmental projects supported bilaterally by European governments and jointly cofinanced by governments and NGOs.[5] These CEC-commissioned studies showed that the costs of NGOs are constantly lower than those funded by government-to-government arrangements in the same generic areas. They also indicated that at least half the projects examined to date have been successful in reaching the hard-core poor. The NGO-sponsored projects also made significant headway in improving primary health services, subsistence food production, and water supply for low-income groups.[6]

These evaluations also indicated that NGO-sponsored projects that involve explicit attempts to raise the awareness of grass-roots participants about the wider socioeconomic and political dynamics of their respective locales, in fact, have a higher rate of success in achieving technical and material gains for the local population than those projects that do not. The reason is that they tend to actively include the beneficiaries from the start in articulating their most pressing needs, prioritizing objectives and selecting strategies. They also better involve the poor in implementing and administering services through the life of the projects.[7]

The NGOs that stress political change "from the bottom up" as among their primary development objectives have interpreted these findings as a confirmation of the validity of their political approach. At the very least, the evaluations carried out by the CEC have not been critical of explicit attempts to sharpen the social and political awareness of the grass-roots poor.

[5] Interviews with Richard J. Harmston, CCIC; Kees van Dongen, NOVIB; and Dr. Helmut Eggers, CEC.
[6] CEC, *Comparative Evaluation of Projects Cofinanced with NGOs*, pp. iii, 2, 10; De Crombrugghe, Howes, and Nieuwkerk, *Evaluation of CEC Small Development Projects*, pp. 8, 19.
[7] De Crombrugghe, Howes, and Nieuwkerk, *Evaluation of CEC Small Development Projects*, p. 8.

ADVANTAGES OF NGO COFINANCING FOR GOVERNMENTS

Alternate Channels for Pursuing Sensitive Foreign Policy Objectives

Although NGOs publicly challenge some of the policy premises and specifics of their respective home governments, they can also be useful in pursuing overseas objectives when governments cannot take direct action themselves on certain fronts. Both left-of-center and right-of-center governments use NGOs as alternate conduits for influence in developing countries when their own official policy positions or the sensitivities of host country governments prevent them from pursuing certain agendas through normal state-to-state mechanisms.

Unlike the situation in the United States, where PVOs are forbidden to use government funds in certain countries because of the type of regime, in most of Europe these prohibitions do not exist or are not as strict. A European government (or the CEC) may sometimes refuse bilateral (or multilateral) aid to certain countries for political reasons. The FRG government, for example, cut off all bilateral economic aid to Chile when the military came to power in 1973. When the CEC inaugurated its multilateral aid program in the late 1970s, it did the same, and it also ruled out Haiti and Uganda for also being repressive authoritarian regimes.

In such cases, however, the respective aid agencies—the BMZ in the FRG and the Development Directorate of the CEC—allowed NGOs to use their funds to support private projects in these respective countries. In the judgment of policymakers in the FRG and the CEC, aid sent through NGOs had a much higher chance of benefiting those in need in these nations than did assistance sent to the respective governments. Moreover, such a strategy would also be a symbolic gesture of political support for the citizens in such countries suffering from repression and thus enhance their respect for European governments.[8]

In some instances, European government leaders share the specific political ideology of those suffering persecution under repressive regimes and want to provide them with financial support. But they need an intermediary or buffer to avoid severe diplomatic repercussions. In Chile, for example, after the military coup, the SPD government in the FRG actually increased its aid to German NGOs supporting socioeconomic projects in Chile. The German Social Democrats wanted to help those being persecuted by the Pinochet regime, not merely out of humanitarian concern but because those who bore the brunt of such repression in the early years of the Chilean military government were supporters or members of the previous socialist government of Salvador Allende which the SPD backed.

[8] Interviews with Klaus Peter Treydte, FES; Heinzberndt Krauskopf, MISEREOR; and Thom Kierstens, CEBEMO.

The FRG NGOs could reach such groups with aid, since in the period immediately following the coup they channeled their assistance almost exclusively through Chilean Protestant and Catholic church networks providing legal, economic, and social services to those most in need—the majority of whom were on the left politically. In fact, what made possible the rapid expansion of Chilean church-sponsored social services in this period was an influx of aid through both religious and secular NGOs. Many were channeling economic aid from their respective home governments that had been sympathetic to the Allende government (especially in the FRG, Sweden, Great Britain, the Netherlands, and Canada).[9]

In the late 1970s when socialist governments in Europe wanted to find ways to assist black liberation movements in southern Africa, NGOs again were useful conduits for unofficial foreign policy initiatives. They could act as buffers and surrogates for European policymakers without officially implicating them in the specific actions overseas.

In the mid-and-late 1970s, SPD Chancellor Helmut Schmidt was searching for ways to distance his government from the Republic of South Africa and also provide some support for black liberation movements working for the overthrow of white-dominated regimes in the region. Schmidt, however, did not want to risk losing critical raw materials and other reciprocal trade agreements with the Republic of South Africa. During a trip through Africa in July 1978 he met with Joshua Nkomo, head of the Patriotic Front opposing Ian Smith's government in Rhodesia, and he promised to provide assistance for its cause. Subsequently, the German Ministry of Foreign Affairs made good on this promise when it announced it was sending medical and sanitation supplies, as well as assistance for refugees, to the Patriotic Front through the Friedrich Ebert Foundation (FES), controlled by the SPD but legally separate from the government.[10]

Although the funds originated from the FRG government, they were administered by an NGO that legally is private and autonomous, albeit almost wholly funded by the government for its overseas activities. The FES, however, provided enough of a buffer between the governments involved (the FRG and Rhodesia) so as not to precipitate a serious diplomatic incident—as in the case of Herbert Hoover's ARA in the Soviet Union in the early 1920s. Schmidt's action was only a symbolic gesture, but its importance was not lost on other liberation movements in the region who were opposing the South African regime. Such a strategy also did not risk a loss of trade with the South African government since no aid was given (even indirectly) to the African National Congress (ANC).

Right-of-center and conservative governments have also found NGOs use-

[9] Brian H. Smith, *Church and Politics in Chile*, pp. 325–27.
[10] Braunthal, *West German Social Democrats*, p. 284.

ful instruments to keep open alternate channels of communication and influence abroad, even in cases when such governments might disagree with the leftist rhetoric and agenda of these same NGOs. For example, rightist governments in power in the FRG, the Netherlands, Belgium, and Canada in the mid-1980s had serious reservations about U.S. policies in Central America. They believed that heavy U.S. emphasis on military aid would not provide a lasting solution to the region's problems. They preferred instead a diplomatic resolution to tensions.[11]

In addition to giving rhetorical encouragement to the Contadora process, these governments also allowed NGOs to support projects (cofinanced by themselves) in contested areas of El Salvador, where the left had sympathies or control, and in Nicaragua among groups supportive of the Sandinistas. Nor did they object when these NGOs at home criticized U.S. policies in Central America in government-subsidized development education campaigns. In such a way, government leaders indirectly expressed opposition to U.S. policies without having to pay the price that direct action on their part would entail. Moreover, by keeping open channels of indirect communication with leftist groups abroad, European policymakers hoped to exercise a moderating influence on their political strategies and also be better able to deal with them should they ultimately gain power in the region.[12]

This gambit used in Central America, in fact, built upon a similar strategy used by European governments of the right and left in the late 1960s in Southeast Asia. During the Vietnam War, European governments subsidized and relied on NGOs to act on their behalf in North Vietnam. The NGOs provided relief and development assistance to those residing in the North when European governments could not risk doing so directly. The NGOs thus created a posture for Europe independent of U.S. objectives, but without officially implicating their home governments in such activities. This strategy also maximized the options for a quicker normalization of diplomatic and economic relations between Vietnam and European countries after the conflict.[13]

The conservative CDU government in power in the FRG after 1982 provides aid to Vietnam through FRG NGOs. Although not giving direct aid to the communist Vietnamese government, CDU policymakers allow church-related NGOs to use public funds in supporting socioeconomic projects in Vietnam despite the fact that no private counterpart NGOs exist in that country independent of government control.

The German Catholic CARITAS Association (DCV) works through the Archbishop of Ho Chi Minh City, even though in reality it is the Vietnamese government that administers the projects since the Catholic Church has no

[11] Pierce, ed., *Third-World Instability*.

[12] Interviews with Hendrik van der Heijden, OECD.

[13] Ibid.

social service organizations of its own in Vietnam. If the local archbishop approves the projects, however (designed and operated by the Vietnamese government), and they meet FRG government development criteria for cofinancing, the DCV can channel public funds to Vietnam to support them.[14]

In such a way, the CDU in the FRG is abetting the usefulness of the Catholic Church to the Vietnam government, thereby hoping to enhance the possibilities for greater religious freedom for the 3.5 million Catholics in that country (out of a population of 57 million). The Vietnamese government gains access to the FRG government funds it could not leverage directly on its own, and local Vietnamese citizens receive added economic services. Both governments save face by such a maneuver, local church attractiveness to Vietnamese policymakers increases, and Vietnamese citizens (regardless of religious creed or political ideology) materially benefit from the exchange.

Finally, even when a conservative government normally is critical of left-oriented NGOs, it can at times find them useful to keep open alternate channels for influence abroad. Since Margaret Thatcher came to power in Great Britain in 1979, NGO projects supported in Nicaragua have been scrutinized more carefully when submitted to the ODA for cofinancing, and approval takes much longer now than under the previous Labour government. Most are eventually cofunded by the ODA, however, even though ODA provides no bilateral economic assistance to Nicaragua. The NGOs have become careful to present only those that are ODA development priorities—such as community health, cooperative training, and agrarian development assistance.[15]

By giving financial aid to NGO-sponsored development projects in Nicaragua, the Conservative government in Great Britain gains in several ways. The delaying and scrutinizing tactics of ODA keep a close rein on British NGOs, forcing them to keep within strict development criteria and avoid supporting only counterparts who collaborate closely with the Nicaraguan government or who are tools for its domestic political agenda. Funding NGO-supported projects by the Thatcher government also keeps the Nicaraguan government from getting the credit for helping its people, since the aid goes through private channels. Moreover, by channeling aid through NGOs, the Thatcher government hopes to strengthen the economic viability and autonomy of the private sector in Nicaragua over the state, even if many in these grass-roots projects are sympathetic to Sandinistas ideologically.

Hence, when in power both the left and the right in Europe find NGOs useful instruments in pursuing some objectives abroad that normal diplomatic or bilateral aid channels cannot accomplish. Even when ideological disagreements exist between government leaders (especially on the right) and NGOs, collaboration between them is still possible under certain conditions, indicat-

---

[14] Interview with Dr. Franz-Josef Vollmer, DCV.

[15] Telephone interview with Claire Dixon, CAFOD.

ing the complexity government/NGO trade-offs involve in these other North Atlantic countries.

In the United States, straightforward and clear mechanisms of control are imposed by Congress or AID on PVOs that use public funds abroad. In Europe restrictions are fewer and demand for detailed information less, precisely because those who craft foreign policy in Europe often use NGOs as much for political as for developmental objectives abroad. Under such conditions, less, not more, accountability makes sense to provide respective ministries of foreign affairs more flexibility for what they are hoping to accomplish through NGOs. Less accountability also provides grounds for "plausible denial" if a host country should charge NGO action as intervention in its internal affairs.

As a matter of fact, there are few occasions when foreign governments do protest NGO activities to the European and Canadian governments who subsidize them. As we shall see in chapter 8, host country officials have their own mechanisms for controlling or pressuring indigenous nonprofits as well as NGOs who are giving them support. There are trade-offs for Third World leaders in confronting European governments over NGO activities. They risk losses on other fronts if they make European NGO resource transfers into their countries (relatively small in comparison to the value of trade and official aid) a major issue in bilateral relations with a North Atlantic government. Moreover, European and Canadian governments who subsidize NGOs do place some controls—explicit or implicit—on how their funds can be used abroad. This also reduces the risk that NGOs will precipitate serious diplomatic embarrassments for them with foreign governments.

Allies in Domestic Political Battles

Perhaps even more important than providing alternate channels of influence abroad is the role NGOs play in domestic political battles among or within various sectors—the ruling party, the loyal opposition, and public bureaucrats in foreign aid ministries. Both those on the left and the right try to solicit the aid of NGOs to pursue their respective agendas either within government or in their relations with political opponents. Moreover, some of the reasons behind using NGOs as alternate foreign policy conduits, in fact, are rooted in domestic political strategies.

Given their particular social and political bases in Europe and Canada, many NGOs represent important constituencies for party leaders. This is particularly true for the left, but also for the right when conservative parties possess leftist factions within their own ranks. In Great Britain, for example, both the Labour and Tory leaders periodically cultivate NGOs as part of their political strategies against one another or within their own parties.

In recent years, with chronic problems in the domestic economy, the Labour Party has downplayed its traditional positions of urging both greater foreign aid and aid on easier terms to developing countries. The mood of the nation in the mid-1980s did not resonate with these traditional Labour Party positions. The party, however, lost some of its support among small groups of intellectuals and others on the left who remain committed to Third World issues. The NGOs have attracted the attention and active commitment of these elites, and the Labour Party wants to win back their allegiances—especially during electoral campaigns. Hence, in Parliament, Labourites are strong advocates of maintaining levels of assistance to NGOs, not merely as a way of helping the poorest abroad but as a stratagem to allay the fears of those Labourites disenchanted with its silence on foreign aid in recent years and who also are fans of NGOs.[16]

There are groups in the Conservative Party as well—"Red Tories"—who are sympathetic to NGOs. Being in the left wing of their party led by former Prime Minister Edward Heath (a member of the Brandt Commission), they are uncomfortable with what has happened to official foreign aid during the Thatcher government. Not only has official aid leveled off, but it has become more closely tied to trade and investment objectives that benefit Great Britain. The "Red Tories" do not want to see a total disregard for a BHN approach in British foreign assistance. They support NGO cofinancing programs at least at existing levels even if domestic considerations dictate cuts in bilateral aid.

The Thatcher government, therefore, can achieve several important domestic political and economic goals by continuing grants to NGOs. It can satisfy the "Red Tories" in its own party and those in the Labour opposition at the same time, both of whom want some aspects of aid-to-the-poorest left in British foreign assistance. It can keep a BHN dimension present in British aid but at low cost, since the cofinancing budget for NGOs constitutes a very small fraction of official development assistance (0.27 percent in 1983, or $5.9 million).[17]

In the Nicaraguan case specifically, continued aid to NGOs working there—under tighter supervision—allows Prime Minister Thatcher to parry Labour charges that her government has been too hard on that country. When the opposition criticizes her for terminating all bilateral assistance to Nicaragua, she responds that Britain now, in fact, helps the people of Nicaragua more by channeling public resources through British NGOs. Britain, she claims, thus can be assured that those truly needy Nicaraguans benefit, since the Sandinistas are unable to manipulate the aid for their own political purposes.[18]

Similar intraparty and cross-party maneuvering through the use of NGOs occurs in the FRG. In the 1970s, Helmut Schmidt felt he had to take some initiative on behalf of southern African black liberation movements and the

---

[16] Cable, *British Interests and Third World Development*, pp. 23–25.

[17] Van der Heijden, "Development Impact and Effectiveness of Nongovernmental Organizations," tables 3 and 5.

[18] Telephone interview with Claire Dixon, CAFOD.

Chilean opposition. Pressure to do so was being applied within his own SPD, especially by the younger elements in the party—the JUSOS. In both cases the JUSOS wanted stronger action—recognition of the black liberation movements as the sole representatives of the people and cessation of formal diplomatic ties to the Pinochet regime. Through the use of FRG NGOs, not only was the chancellor finessing potential problems with other sovereign nation states but was also taking some action to placate groups to the left of him in his own party who wanted much stronger action that was unacceptable to him.[19]

The CDU government that followed the SPD into power in 1982 has also used NGOs—especially church-related organizations and the Institute for International Solidarity of the Konrad Adenauer Foundation—to neutralize critics within its own ranks. The government of Helmut Kohl has tried to gain important trade and investment concessions from developing countries through the use of FRG bilateral economic assistance—similar to the foreign aid strategy pursued by Margaret Thatcher's administration in Great Britain. The left wing of the CDU is upset with this tactic since it views it as a further step back from the official German commitment to a BHN approach in foreign aid endorsed in the mid-1970s. As a concession to it, the Kohl administration has not conditioned its aid to NGOs with such restrictions. It has also significantly increased its cofinancing support for nonprofits since 1982.

Picking up on this stratagem, the SPD in the mid-1980s has tried to push it further in order to embarrass the CDU. Since 1983, the Social Democrats and the Green Party both have urged strongly in the *Bundestag* for an overhaul in FRG foreign aid, arguing that the current economic restrictions placed on official German assistance are hurting the poor in developing countries. Both of these opposition parties have proposed a major privatization of foreign aid that would channel much more government resources through NGO channels since they are in a better position to reach the poor at the grass-roots level. The Green Party has also sought FRG NGOs' advice on Third World issues and has made part of its foreign policy platform elements of the NIEO agenda espoused by many German NGOs.[20]

The NGOs in the FRG have not been comfortable with such proposals by opposition parties, whose political ideology many nonprofits share. They are pleased with the praise, publicity, and added funds that are coming to them as a result of these current intraparty and cross-party political debates. However, they well know that they cannot manage massive amounts of resources that the privatization proposals of the SPD and the Greens imply. They also do not want to see the government shirk its own responsibilities to administer official aid in ways more oriented to basic-needs fulfillment abroad. Nor is the SPD

[19] Braunthal, *West German Social Democrats*, pp. 283–84.
[20] Telephone interview with Jan Reinders, EZE.

entirely sincere in presenting a privatization plan, since its orientation as a left-of-center party is in the opposite direction. Neither have the Social Democrats been fair in criticizing the CDU for tying foreign aid with economic conditions, since the SPD did the same while in power after the 1973 shock. What is clear, however, is that NGOs are very useful to sectors in several German parties in waging intraparty and cross-party political battles at home.

Finally, there are cases in which those within the official aid bureaucracy in European governments find NGOs useful allies in pursuing their own agendas. In both the FRG under Kohl and Great Britain under Thatcher, the official aid agencies (BMZ and ODA respectively) still have personnel who long predate current administrations. Many of these government officials began their terms during the heyday of expanding official aid commitments in the 1970s when a BHN thrust was endorsed by left-of-center governments in both countries. These bureaucrats in the FRG and Great Britain are frustrated with a redirection of official aid in each country. They see NGOs as carriers of the ideals of former government commitments. They channel the maximum amount of resources to them not merely for overseas programs focusing on basic human needs but also for development education programs at home. In such a way, these bureaucrats are helping to keep before the public elements of the NIEO agenda no longer in vogue among the rightist government leaders in each country.[21]

Hence, NGOs for some government civil servants are perceived (and assisted) as surrogates for their own dissent against official aid policies. The bureaucracy is much less permeable in Europe than in the United States, and visible, public alliances between bureaucrats and interest groups to pressure legislators openly is less frequent than in the United States. Dissenting bureaucrats in Europe play a more subtle game to blunt government policies with which they disagree. This is done by quietly supporting those groups in civil society that can trumpet causes on which they themselves must remain silent. In this way, they hope to create pressures on—or embarrassments for—higher government and party leaders, which they themselves cannot exert or risk exerting from within the bureaucracy.[22]

President Mitterrand appointed Jean-Pierre Côt (who represented sectors of the Socialist Party associated with a progressive policy towards the Third

[21] Telephone interview with Jan Reinders, EZE; and Claire Dixon, CAFOD.

[22] Parallels exist in Europe among civil servants responsible for environmental issues. Personnel in the Ministry of Environment in the FRG, for example, channel public funds to advocacy groups in societies that champion environmental causes. In such a way, these bureaucrats gain publicity, and they hope popularity, for their agendas for greater government action. Those in the Ministry of the Economy who carry more weight inside the government than they do, oppose such programs due to the economic or political costs involved. Telephone interview with Professor Russ Dalton, University of Florida. See also Kitschelt, "New Social Movements in West Germany and the United States."

World) as Minister for Cooperation and Development in 1981. Côt attempted to use French NGOs to shake up the French aid bureaucracy. He wanted to pressure them to implement the new agenda for French aid endorsed by the PS in the mid-1970s. This agenda included an increase in official development assistance; a geographical redirection of French aid away from a concentration on overseas departments, territories, and former colonies (several of which, such as Zaire, Gabon, and Chad, were under repressive authoritarian rule); an expansion of generalized trade preferences; and a greater focus on rural-development projects benefiting the poorest sectors in Third World countries.

Côt wanted to overcome resistance to the changes required by such an agenda (supported by left-wing secular Socialists and their progressive Catholic adherents) coming from entrenched bureaucrats in his own and other ministries dealing with official aid. He therefore established within the Ministry for Cooperation and Development two new structures that would allow formal NGO input into aid policy deliberations and also give NGOs greater publicity in French society. He hoped thereby to widen the constituency for this new direction in French policies toward developing countries.[23]

One structure, the Commission for Development Cooperation, included representatives from the various ministries responsible for aid policymaking and implementation (Foreign Affairs, the Economy, Overseas Departments and Territories, Cooperation and Development) as well as spokespersons from the NGO umbrella federation—the Intercollective of National Associations for Development Solidarity. The commission facilitated dialogue among NGOs and various government officials on aid policies, and gave NGOs some leverage in shaping priorities in French developmental assistance programs in 1981 and 1982.

The other structure—the Information and Liaison Service with NGOs (SI-LONG)—provided increased cofinancing for some NGO development education programs in France covering up to 50 percent of their costs. The SI-LONG also facilitated easy access by left-oriented NGOs to government-controlled television so that they might better argue their case publicly for NIEO-type changes in French posture toward Third World problems.[24]

Thus, pressures were created on the French aid bureaucracy both from within and without through clever use of NGOs by a newly appointed minister needing allies to carry out his agenda inside the traditional bureaucracy. In the first years of Mitterrand's administration, in fact, such strategies by Côt did stimulate a wider debate among government officials about new directions in foreign aid. More resources were also channeled into BHN projects abroad. French NGOs benefited as well, with government subsidies to them increasing

[23] Côt, À l'épreuve du pouvoir, pp. 93–102, 199–210; Hessel, "France and the Third World."
[24] Baile, Survey of European Nongovernmental Aid Organizations, p. 55.

from \$2.4 million in 1980, the last year of Giscard d'Estaing's presidency, to \$19.2 million in 1983.[25]

The fact that NGOs are closely tied in to domestic political networks in their home countries and also represent small, but critical, attentive publics on foreign policy issues, makes them particularly attractive to different sets of political elites competing among one another in shaping policy. Even when public policymakers do not agree with all NGOs objectives, they can use NGOs as useful instruments for finessing opponents, partially placating dissidents in their own ranks or introducing new agendas into policy debates when their own options or leverage on these fronts are limited.

LIMITS ON NGO ACTIVITIES

There are restrictions—both explicit and tacit—on NGO activities that provide some protection for governments against severe political embarrassments internationally and domestically. There are also enticements and penalties policymakers can and do use in attempts to modify or curtail NGO strategies.

In contrast to respondents to my PVO survey (reported in chapter 6), NGO respondents expressed very little concern over limitations on their organizational autonomy resulting from government subsidies. Of the thirty-five persons interviewed in thirty European and Canadian NGOs, only two (in two different British NGOs) felt that their respective institutions experienced significant restrictions resulting from public aid. None of the thirty-five indicated any image or credibility problems in Latin America for their organizations among actual or potential counterpart groups due to the government aid they receive. In fact, many confirmed what several PVO representatives had stated—namely, that money originating from governments in Europe and Canada does not cause the sense of alarm or caution among Latin American nonprofit groups working with the poor that funds coming from the U.S. government do, even when given indirectly through PVOs.

Legal Limits against Support for Armed Insurrection Abroad

There are restrictions, however—both formal and informal—even if NGOs claim not to find them burdensome. There is a mutual agreement, for example, between governments and NGOs that transnational nonprofits will not use public subsidies to support armed violence by foreign groups in attempts to overthrow legally constituted governments. Sometimes this kind of restriction, in fact, is explicitly written into law by parliaments.

In the Netherlands, this condition is part of the formal written agreement

[25] Van der Heijden, "Development Impact and Effectiveness of Nongovernmental Organizations," table 3.

between the Minister for Development Cooperation and the four large NGOs receiving three-year block grants. It states "that the Netherlands Government may be held responsible under international law for the implementation of the CFP [Cofinancing Programme]. You will therefore refrain from providing support for any activities aimed at undermining the political independence of any state or at bringing down a legal government by unlawful means."[26] Dutch NGOs are required by the agreement to consult with the minister "should there by any doubt surrounding the interpretation or appreciation" of this agreed upon restriction "or concerning any adverse consequences that the financing of particular projects could have" for the Dutch government.[27]

Given the increasing amount of private resources donated to NGOs in recent years (reported in table 7.1), nonprofits can use income from nongovernment sources to support overseas projects that are politically controversial. In fact, many NGO representatives told me they simply do not submit some projects to their governments for cofinancing but rather tap their private income for such activities.

Even this restriction against supporting armed insurrectionary movements has been interpreted rather broadly by NGOs and governments alike. The "reasonable doubt" clause requiring prior consultation with the Dutch government is very rarely used by NGOs. One Dutch NGO, for example, which is totally dependent on government funds for its overseas aid resources (ICCO), supports private organizations inside areas controlled by the guerrillas in El Salvador. Some of the project participants of such counterparts clearly have ties to or sympathies for the armed branch of the revolutionaries, but the services indigenous nonprofits provide are not of a military nature. Rather they are socioeconomic in scope. So long as the aid is not weapon-related, the Dutch government does not consider it a violation of the above cited restriction. Nor does it expect prior consultation.[28]

Oxfam Belgique similarly interprets its tacit agreement with the Belgian government not to support with public subsidies armed insurrection abroad. Like ICCO in the Netherlands, it channels government money for projects that may benefit those close to liberation movements, but it is not directly given to liberation groups themselves. Pierre Galand, Director of Oxfam Belgique, gave examples of this strategy and the purpose Oxfam has in using it:

We always try to challenge the Belgian government. We push our government to fund some controversial projects through us it would ordinarily avoid in its bilateral aid programs. We go to the government with projects within its own economic cri-

---

[26] Minister for Development Cooperation, Netherlands, official translation of the letter of November 21, 1983, by which the ministry formalized the renewed Programme Subsidy model to the four cofinancing organizations (CFOs), p. 1.

[27] Ibid., p. 4.

[28] Interview with Rev. S. S. van Dijk, ICCO; van Dijk, letter to author, Feb. 3, 1986.

teria, but carried out by groups with close ties to, but technically separate from, liberation groups—the Palestinian Red Crescent (close to PLO) and the Sahraoue Red Crescent in the Western Sahara (with affinities to the Polisario movement). The Belgian government sometimes says the project is too political, but in the past has normally backed down for fear of our mounting a major publicity campaign of protest here at home if it turns the project down.[29]

There are steps governments can use short of actually cutting off funds to make NGOs cease controversial actions abroad or at home that policymakers find particularly annoying. These involve providing incentives to NGOs to move in some directions and away from others, closer scrutiny of projects and delays in approving them, diversion of some subsidies away from troublesome nonprofits to more politically acceptable NGOs, and removing or threatening to remove the tax-exempt status of nonprofits that engage in unacceptable partisan political activity. Finally, as an extreme measure, if the NGO refuses to modify its behavior, governments will cut off funds for its activities.

Positive Enticements and Rewards by Government

In Canada, CIDA has definite preferences for how NGOs spend public resources in Latin America. It makes available more funds for some projects— e.g., well-digging—than for others. Some that can be politically sensitive— e.g., formation of labor leaders, human rights defense, publications by grassroots organizations presenting analyses by the poor of structural reasons for a lack of developmental progress in their respective locales—are not eligible for matching grants from CIDA since these are not part of its current development priorities.[30]

The Belgian government uses a mixture of measures to dissuade NGOs from moving in certain directions, rewarding some nonprofits and penalizing others. It is clear that NGOs that want to increase the political power of the grass-roots poor have more difficulty in getting their overseas projects approved for Belgian government cofinancing (and receive less in the overall distribution of public subsidies) than those that focus on relief or technical projects.

Between 1976 and 1981 Belgian NGOs stressing the necessity of political change in their overseas activities had 47 percent of their projects approved for government cofinancing. The approval rate for those emphasizing immediate alleviation of suffering was 56 percent, and 58 percent for NGOs supporting training or the building of physical infrastructure. Of the $76.7 million given the 103 Belgian NGOs for overseas development projects by the gov-

---

[29] Interviews with Pierre Galand, Oxfam Belgique.

[30] Interviews with Rev. C. William Smith, CCODP; René Guay, CCODP; and Richard J. Harmston, CCIC.

ernment between 1976 and 1981, only 22 percent ($16.9 million) went to those stressing popular mobilization and consciousness-raising among the poor by Third World counterparts.[31]

In the case of Oxfam Belgique, although the government has not cut off funds for any specific project it supports overseas, the amount of overall subsidies it gives has leveled off in recent years. A center-right coalition government headed by Christian Democrats came to power in 1982 (and was re-elected in early 1986). Its strategy has been to use foreign aid to promote greater commercial benefits in trade for Belgium. It has also steadily decreased aid for Oxfam since the early 1980s (although its cofinancing program for all NGOs has increased). The government can, therefore, claim that its commitment to a BHN strategy through aid to NGOs is increasing, but it can simultaneously distance itself gradually from Oxfam Belgique's controversial agenda. It can also accomplish this without ever having to single out for specific criticism or rejection Oxfam's support for groups such as the Palestinian Red Crescent or the Sahraoue Red Crescent since it provides an overall general subsidy for all of Oxfam's programs.[32]

The CEC also has clear but unwritten positive and negative incentives built into its cofinancing program with NGOs. These encourage them to move in certain directions and not in others. The commission has communicated informally with NGOs interested in receiving its aid that it will look favorably on projects from certain regions or countries, such as the West Bank, Zimbabwe, Mozambique, and Nicaragua. The Council of Ministers of the CEC has also concluded (although not putting its decision in writing) that no aid for NGO cofinancing is available for Israel (purportedly because of its high GNP level) or for Vietnam or Vietnam-controlled Kampuchea. Unlike country restrictions for PVOs by the United States government, however, CEC limitations on NGOs are unofficial and more easily subject to modification or relaxation.[33]

The Thatcher government in Great Britain has tended to scrutinize more carefully British NGO projects submitted to the ODA for cofinancing in Nicaragua. It does the same for projects in Vietnam and Kampuchea, although not ruling out in principle public subsidies to British NGOs for projects in any of these countries.

The British government has used another strategy since 1979 to discourage what it finds to be politically annoying campaigns at home by many NGOs. It has reduced significantly public aid for NGO developmental education (down from $6.7 million in 1978 to $275,148 in 1983). It has also redirected most of these subsidies for education away from the most outspoken groups, such as Oxfam UK, CA, and CAFOD. Ninety percent ($247,633) by 1983 was going

[31] Piret and Galand, *L'aide de la Belgique*, pp. 214–16, 221.

[32] Interview with Pierre Galand, Oxfam Belgique.

[33] Interview with W. Ködderitzsch, CEC.

to the Center for World Development Education. The CWDE is an organization that avoids controversial political messages in its literature and public advocacy. It also reaches out to groups, such as business organizations and school children, that are turned off by the confrontational approach of many other NGOs.[34]

Threats to NGO Tax Exemption Privileges

The Charity Commissioners in Great Britain have also increased their vigilance over British NGOs since Margaret Thatcher became prime minister. Warnings have been issued to NGOs, such as Oxfam UK, CA, and CAFOD on several occasions as a result of their public criticisms of official British policy towards Nicaragua and South Africa. Although none of these NGOs have lost their tax-exempt status, such strategies by the government have tended to make them more cautious in their advocacy campaigns at home.[35]

British NGOs do not want to provoke a formal trial since this could lead to a more strict interpretation of charity laws than exists at present. The language of these laws (written in the seventeenth century) forbids nonprofits from allocating funds to literature or activities wholly or substantially devoted to political persuasion. Rather than having to modify or give more specificity of interpretation to such laws, the Thatcher government appointed a charity commission chairperson who is willing to interpret them flexibly. This has allowed NGOs some leeway in advocacy provided they do not involve themselves too stridently or substantially in partisan political campaigns.[36]

Laws governing the behavior of charitable organizations have also been invoked in Canada (even under the Liberal administration of Pierre Trudeau) to slow down some of the domestic activities of NGOs in developmental education and lobbying. Revenue Canada in the early 1980s carried out investigations of several NGOs (including Oxfam Canada) to ascertain whether they had violated the Canadian Charities Act, which prohibits actions by nonprofits aimed primarily at influencing government policies. As in Great Britain, the language of the Canadian legislation is vague and allows Revenue Canada a great deal of discretion in determining when NGOs have violated it. Although no NGO has lost its tax-exempt status so far, investigations have made several uneasy. The NGO federation, CCIC, has asked the Conservative government of Brian Mulroney to make the wording more precise, but no change has been made by the parliament in the Charities Act. This leaves the government considerable flexibility in dealing with troublesome NGOs on a case-by-case basis

[34] Baile, *Survey of European Nongovernmental Aid Organizations*, pp. 8, 18.
[35] Interviews with Alonso Roberts, CA; and Claire Dixon, CAFOD.
[36] Baile, *Survey of European Nongovernmental Aid Organizations*, p. 7.

as it deems necessary (the same strategy employed by the Thatcher government in Great Britain).[37]

Curtailment or Cessation of Subsidies

In some cases, when other measures fail to modify or restrain political activities by NGOs, governments can and do take more drastic action. After repeated citizen complaints to the British Charity Commission about the overtly partisan political rhetoric and actions by War on Want (closely associated with the Labour Party) during Margaret Thatcher's first year in office (1980), the commission revoked its tax-exempt privilege. War on Want was forced to establish a new organization—War on Want Campaigns—separate from its aid-sending operations in order to continue its domestic political work. This new agency must pay taxes as any other partisan political organization, and contributions to it are not tax-exempt.[38]

In Canada all public subsidies to SUCO, the overseas volunteer-sending agency in Quebec province, were gradually phased out by the Trudeau government in the early 1980s. The SUCO supported liberation movements abroad, but what was more annoying to the government was its public support for French separatist movements in Canada itself. As part of its development education program, SUCO invited representatives of Third World liberation groups to Quebec who, while there, gave open support for Quebecois seeking political autonomy for their province from English-speaking Canada. This was done precisely at a time when separatism was a sensitive point of dispute between Quebec and Ottawa and receiving growing support among French-speaking Canadians.

The CIDA first cut out all cofinancing of SUCO's development education program. When this did not deter it from continuing to espouse openly the cause of separatism, CIDA terminated public subsidies for its overseas programs. Since SUCO was dependent on government aid for three-fourths of its resources, it gradually collapsed, and by 1986 ceased to exist.[39]

Narrow Target and Impact of NGO Development Education

The narrow targets of the most aggressive NGO education efforts and the negligible effect they seem to have on public attitudes keep much of their domestic advocacy work from annoying policymakers. Very often NGOs target their overtly political messages to their most consistent supporters, but these tend to be subgroups in the population already convinced of the validity of their

[37] Interviews with Robert Miller, Parliamentary Centre; and David Kardish, CCIC (telephone).
[38] Baile, *Survey of European Nongovernmental Aid Organizations*, p. 38.
[39] Telephone interviews with Rev. C. William Smith, CCODP; and David Kardish, CUSO.

political positions—the 12 to 15 percent identified with leftist political parties and causes mentioned in chapter 5.

To date there is no hard evidence that NGO development education work is significantly affecting opinion trends in wider society. Nor are NGO lobbying activities forcing government officials to alter major policy trends. In Great Britain, NGO advocacy work has had no visible effect on public opinion about policy toward the Third World, especially in the area of trade relations. Nor did a "Fight World Poverty" lobby organized by British NGOs in October 1985—mobilizing 20,000 people to visit or write their respective MPs—effect any important changes in government aid and trade policies then tailored to maximize British economic interests in developing countries.[40]

In the FRG a similar campaign was orchestrated by almost the entire NGO community in early 1985 to pressure the CDU government to alter its current trade policy towards developing countries. The NGOs as a group publicly challenged the government for tying its official aid so closely to trade and investment benefits for the FRG. They urged it to devote more bilateral resources to agricultural development abroad, as opposed to capital-intensive industrial development.

Such a coordinated campaign was successful in getting some public attention in the FRG. It forced the media to talk about the issues, and the government issued a statement explaining and justifying its position. No actual changes in aid policies, however, were effected by even such concerted NGO pressures.[41]

Policymakers are forced to modify their positions only when widespread public criticism is focused on a particular problem or issue over a sustained period of time—e.g., economic sanctions against South Africa. The NGOs are normally most influential in effecting changes only at the margins of critical policies or on less visible issues—e.g., minor trade adjustments and ambassadorial interventions on behalf of specific human rights grievances. On broader issues of foreign policy, in which more is at stake politically or economically for their respective home governments or business elites, NGO abilities to bring about change is very limited. Normally even the most coordinated efforts among nonprofits to gain maximum visibility and exert the most leverage at their disposal are neither sustained over time with intensity nor are they recipients of widespread public support.

Even parties of the left which rely on NGOs as allies in fighting foreign-policy political battles against the right, are not willing when in power to support the most critical NGO causes (e.g., the NIEO agenda on trade, aid, and investment) since the implementation of these could lose them much domestic

---

[40] Cable, *British Interests and Third World Development*, p. 25; Baile, *Survey of European Nongovernmental Aid Organizations*, p. 8.

[41] Baile, *Survey of European Nongovernmental Aid Organizations*, p. 45.

political support. As one commentator has observed, it is one thing for NGOs in the FRG to have good contacts with the SPD, but quite another to have actual influence in SPD decisions affecting its electoral viability.[42]

Hence, there are a range of limitations that minimize actual or potential political damage for policymakers and parties resulting from NGO political agendas. Some of these are based on legal requirements governing NGO activities at home and abroad. Others are positive or negative inducements crafted by policymakers to moderate NGO behavior. There are still others that result from the limited appeal NGO controversial domestic political agendas have among the wider public, thus limiting their potential for widespread and sustained mobilization against government policies.

DISADVANTAGES FOR GOVERNMENTS IN SUPPORTING NGOS

Despite the advantages in having NGOs as allies in domestic political battles or as surrogates for implementing sensitive foreign-policy agendas, there are some negative consequences for policymakers in continuing the current type of relationships with nonprofits. These involve their unimpressive record to date in helping to maintain public support for official foreign aid in those nations where it is declining, and occasional political backfirings for policymakers when using NGOs in heated partisan domestic struggles.

Narrow Scope of NGO Development Education

The drawback of the narrow targeting of overtly political development education of many NGOs is that they are not contributing significantly to one of the major objectives governments have in cofinancing programs—namely, building a broader constituency for overall foreign aid in domestic society. The majority of citizens in Europe and Canada are not identified with leftist parties, and thus are not impressed by the leftist agenda explicitly or implicitly articulated in many NGO education campaigns (described in chapter 5).

This has aroused concern among policymakers in some countries, who would like to see NGOs appeal to a wider audience in their government-supported education work so as to generate more public enthusiasm for overall foreign aid. Although public support for foreign aid in general tends to run much higher in Europe and Canada than in the United States, the declining trend that began during the domestic economic difficulties in the late 1970s has not been turned around substantially in all countries. Belgian polls during the 1980s have shown that public interest in development assistance remains low. In the Netherlands a national survey in 1980 indicated that 17 percent

---

[42] Ibid.

wanted the Dutch government to spend more on foreign assistance, as compared to 47 percent who supported aid increases in 1970.[43]

This lack of enthusiasm for greater commitments to the Third World has continued in the Netherlands. In the May 1986 parliamentary elections, aid and trade issues were not emphasized at all in party debates (as in the past), nor were they even given attention by the Pvd A—the traditional champion of more liberal policies in these areas. In those elections domestic economic growth, unemployment, and nuclear power dominated party platforms across the political spectrum.[44]

The center-right government of the Netherlands (reelected in 1986) in the early 1980s became concerned that many NGO education efforts were reaching only a limited number of people, especially those already convinced of the need for the Netherlands to maintain strong commitments in overseas aid. Therefore, public subsidies for NCO, the federation of NGOs that channels government funds to educational programs run by individual nonprofits, have leveled off in real value in recent years, remaining at approximately $5.7 million since 1982. This course of action has been taken by the government not merely because of the politically controversial nature of the campaigns that many NGOs carry out but also because a wider audience is not being reached or influenced.

In Canada similar concerns about the narrowness of NGO educational focus and appeal emerged when the Liberals were in power in the early 1980s. Romeo Maione, head of the NGO Division in the Special Programs Branch of CIDA in 1983, told me that a reassessment was going on among CIDA officials about the worth of some NGO development education programs due to what those in CIDA believed to be too narrow a target audience:

What many Canadian NGOs are doing is political activism, not education. For example, church-affiliated NGOs, such as CCODP, are reaching only 10 to 15 percent of their constituents who are politically aware. The other 85 percent of church people want to support development projects in areas such as water and health facilities. The churches in their political activism are losing contact with this 85 percent. . . .

CCODP should zero in on the 85 to 65 percent group and explain the systematic issues and political problems step by step rather than offering quick political solutions. Such an approach will gradually raise the consciousness of this next 20 percent of church constituents who are not yet politically aware.[45]

Neither the Dutch nor the Canadian governments are in a political position to reduce drastically cofinancing of NGO educational efforts as did the British government after Margaret Thatcher came to power. The pressing need to cut

[43] Baile, *Survey of European Nongovernmental Aid Organizations*, p. 75; NOVIB, *Steps Towards Each Other*, p. 125.

[44] Telephone interview with Professor Jan J. P. van Heemst, ISS.

[45] Interview with Romeo Maione, CIDA.

government spending amidst chronic recession has not given policymakers in these other two countries the plausible excuse to do so, as was the case in Great Britain. Moreover, aid to NGO development education in Great Britain had barely begun when Thatcher took office in 1979, whereas in both Canada and the Netherlands it was institutionalized in the early 1970s. In each of these countries, moreover, public aid to NGOs accounts for a much larger percentage of official aid—8.7 percent in Canada, and 7.2 percent in the Netherlands in 1983—than it does in Great Britain (under 1 percent even before the Conservative Party victory in 1979).[46] The NGOs as a group also are a more visible force in domestic politics in these other two countries than they have been in Great Britain. Hence, despite complaints by policymakers in Canada and the Netherlands, they do not have the strong support in their respective parliaments to scuttle NGO education programs even though these are not reaching the broad constituency that they had hoped to influence through NGOs.

Political Short-Circuits: The French Gambit Backfires

A second drawback for governments occurs when the strategies of policymakers who use some NGOs as surrogates or allies in domestic political battles backfire. Much of Jean-Pierre Côt's new agenda for French aid policy was thwarted when President Mitterrand, for economic and political considerations, continued to concentrate French economic assistance and trade preferences on former colonies in Africa—including Zaire, Gabon, the Central African Republic, and Chad, all of which were ruled by repressive governments. Although Côt resigned in disagreement with such policies in late 1983, the Mitterrand government did allow some of the left-oriented NGOs whom Côt had cultivated to have continued access to government-owned media. This was a concession to those in the sector of the PS who strongly advocated the NIEO agenda, little of which the government could implement.[47]

One such NGO, *Frères des Hommes* (Brothers of All People) was allowed regular participation in a half-hour daily program on government television presenting views on Third World needs. This NGO repeatedly accused French corporations on the program of exploiting Third World countries. It also urged significant changes in French life styles so as to benefit Third World countries—e.g., eating less so that more Third World agricultural production could be used in feeding the hungry inside developing countries.

The political right was angered at what it considered to be a simplistic analysis of Third World problems and the government's ploy of using an NGO as a surrogate to satisfy leftist sectors of the Socialist Party. At first the right was stymied. It had challenged government policies on all other fronts but found it

---

[46] Van der Heijden, "Development Impact and Effectiveness of Nongovernmental Organizations," table 5.

[47] Rondos, "Mitterrand's Two-Year Record"; Rudel, "Frères des Hommes."

difficult to do so in this area due to the moral credibility of *Frères des Hommes*—an NGO with over sixteen years of experience of aiding the poor overseas.

The opposition, however, found an effective solution when another NGO—*Medecins sans Frontières* (Doctors without Frontiers, MSF)—denounced *Frères des Hommes* publicly for propagating on national television a campaign of misplaced guilt and simplistic solutions for Third World problems. The MSF itself had impeccable moral credentials. It was a volunteer agency of French doctors and nurses that had an excellent track record overseas in assisting Third World countries in times of natural disasters (e.g., the Sahel and Ethiopia). It was also older and better known throughout France than *Frères des Hommes*. In its overseas work MSF had focused on humanitarian and technical aspects of development and normally eschewed political analysis or ideology in its fund-raising and education work at home—although some of its leaders personally were identified with rightist political parties in France.

The MSF attacked *Frères des Hommes* and other leftist French NGOs for placing too much of the blame for lack of Third World development on policies of industrialized countries and MNCs and for downplaying the responsibility of Third World leaders and elites themselves in prolonging poverty and perpetrating human rights abuses in their respective countries. The MSF called for a more objective and less ideological analysis of Third World issues. It subsequently set up its own foundation—*Liberté sans Frontières*—purportedly to promote this kind of objective research.

The political opposition and the media publications associated with the right capitalized on MSF's attacks, using them as surrogates to discredit *Frères des Hommes* and, through it, sectors of the PS identified with an NIEO agenda. Several of those in the French and British intellectual communities well known for their strong conservative positions on developmental issues—such as Jean François Revel, Pascal Bruckner, and Peter Bauer—were among the first invited to participate in activities sponsored by MSF's new foundation. They presented a public seminar in early 1985 strongly criticizing the ideology of leftist NGOs as being biased and empirically weak. The event took place in the French Senate building and received much public attention. It also precipitated bitter and ongoing exchanges for several months thereafter among NGO leaders caught in the midst of intense partisan entanglements.[48]

Through such a stratagem, the political opposition found a very respectable and effective surrogate in the NGO community to fight its battle against the Socialists on their own chosen ground. It also publicly uncovered divisions in the NGO community over approaches to development, thus neutralizing some of the impact of *Frères des Hommes* by showing its views not to be represen-

---

[48] Viratelle, "Au colloque"; Castel, "Débat: Le tiers-mondisme"; "Débat: Les tiers-mondistes."

tative of all nonprofits with experience in alleviating poverty abroad—especially some of the most respected, such as MSF.

Hence, when a political faction enlists the support of NGOs sharing its particular ideology, it is possible for its opponents to find other nonprofits who can act as surrogates for their cause as well—including NGOs that normally do not espouse overt political objectives in their work. Moreover, as the French case shows, this not only provides parties with useful surrogates in areas that are too sensitive to address directly themselves. It can also exacerbate latent divisions in the NGO community itself and weaken their appeal as a credible and unified community of advocates for global humanitarian issues.

TRADE-OFFS BETWEEN NGOS AND PRIVATE DONORS

Unlike PVOs, NGOs as a group have been successful in steadily expanding their private resources since 1980. The most dramatic increases of private contributions, however, have come as a result of the willingness of NGOs (like their U.S. counterparts) to become involved in alleviating the effects of famine in Ethiopia in 1984 and 1985. Moreover, many NGOs have multiple support bases and thus have developed different styles of information dissemination depending upon which set of donors they are approaching—well-informed regular contributors sharing their political commitments, those interested in promoting grass-roots development but unfamiliar with the politically sensitive agenda many NGOs espouse, and intermittent crisis supporters who give to alleviate suffering during natural disasters abroad. Hence, multitrack fundraising and reporting strategies exist among many NGOs. This at times, as in the U.S. case, can precipitate charges of duplicity—especially by those in the private sector who disagree with an NGO's political ideology.

Variegated Clusters of Private Donors

As indicated in chapter 5, many NGOs have elements in their support bases that espouse left-of-center political positions both domestically and internationally—trade unions, left-of-center parties, ethnic minorities, intellectuals, religious elites. These often are the most consistent and individually generous contributors to such NGOs and are the ones who are the targets of much of the most politically explicit and aggressive development education literature of the respective NGOs. These groups also receive the most complete information on the types of projects being supported overseas by the nonprofits.

There is normally, however, a wider circle of contributors to such NGOs who are less aware of the political orientation of the organizations. They are often larger in number than the hard-core politically committed supporters, but receive less explicit details both about overseas projects and the domestic agendas of these NGOs. They are reached through broad-based fund-raising appeals that tend to downplay political messages but emphasize the comparative advantages these NGOs have in reaching the poorest overseas and promoting low-cost solutions to their socioeconomic problems.

Finally, there is a third group of donors that gives primarily during moments of well-publicized disasters overseas. These are usually the largest in number but shortest in the duration of their giving. In recent years, as in the United States, more and more European and Canadian nonprofits that are technical or multiservice institution-builders—including those with explicit political agendas—are becoming active during emergency situations precisely to tap such crisis donors. These NGOs use the resources collected from new contributors to support relief activities in the affected regions abroad during the emergency, always hoping to keep at least some as ongoing supporters once the crisis has passed. As in the case of those reached by broad-based funding appeals, these crisis donors also receive very little information about the political agenda of NGOs that are appealing for their support primarily on humanitarian grounds.

The CA, for example, the major Protestant NGO in Great Britain, in 1985 had 12,600 people who made formal commitments (called "covenants") to contribute a fixed amount of money annually. These donations accounted for 6.3 percent of CA's 1985 income ($1.6 million of $25.4 million, in 1986 dollars). These donors received the most complete information about overseas projects and are well aware of the social-justice emphasis of CA and its denunciations of human rights abuses by repressive regimes.

The total number of donors to CA, however, amounts to several million. Many are reached by door-to-door appeals made by CA every May throughout the country. These people are much less aware of the political nature of some of the projects CA supports overseas (e.g., in Central America) or of its campaign at home in support of economic sanctions against South Africa. These aspects of CA's work are played down during door-to-door appeals. In 1985, however, they accounted for 32.7 percent ($8.3 million) of CA's income.

There were also special appeals in late 1984 and 1985 by CA in media campaigns (made jointly with CAFOD, Oxfam UK, and Save the Children Fund) to alleviate famine in Ethiopia. These ads emphasized exclusively immediate human need and avoided politics completely. These brought in $13 million in 1985, constituting 51.2 percent of CA's resources for that year.

Both of these fund-raising efforts by CA in 1985 (door-to-door requests for general contributions to development and media appeals for African famine relief) thus accounted for 83.9 percent of CA's resources that year. Aside from the 6.3 percent from the covenanters, the final 9.8 percent was obtained from government subsidies.

Hence, although donors reached by these wider appeals may give less individually than those who have made formal covenants with CA, as a group they are much larger and far more critical financially for the organization's maintenance and growth than the covenanters and the government combined.

Through these techniques of multiple targeting, CA has more than doubled its annual budget in real value in these years from $11.8 million in 1982 to $25.4 million in 1985—the largest increase coming from the windfall of support during the Ethiopian famine crisis.[49]

Other NGOs that espouse political change abroad and at home also have pluralistic private support bases. They thus tailor their financial appeal and information dissemination selectively. In the early 1980s Oxfam Belgique, for example, had twenty thousand donors, two thousand of whom committed themselves to giving 1 percent of their annual incomes to the organization. It is this smaller group constituting 10 percent of private contributors that receive all Oxfam materials, including specific information about overseas projects. They know every well that the organization is supporting groups sympathetic to the PLO in the Middle East and the Polisario movement in the Western Sahara. The other 90 percent receive only general reports that do not give much detail. These are told of the basic nature of the organization's work in different parts of the globe but not about the controversial aspects of some of the specific projects. Their prime concern is to support projects promoting socioeconomic development among the Third World poor, not to effect radical political change abroad. Their impression is that Oxfam Belgique is doing the first but not the second.

Moreover, after special appeals in 1984 and 1985 on behalf of the starving in Ethiopia, Oxfam Belgique picked up ten thousand new donors primarily interested in helping to alleviate famine. As a result of such multiple appeals, Oxfam Belgique increased its resources by almost 80 percent, from $2.3 million in 1982 to $4.1 million in 1985—precisely at the time when government subsidies to the organization were gradually declining because of its controversial activities overseas and at home.[50]

The CCFD, the major Catholic development agency in France, also has a small core of supporters reached through its local development education committees around the country. These are well aware of CCFD's commitment to liberation of the poor from oppression and its espousal of the NIEO agenda. The vast majority of its supporters however, (who account for 60 percent of its resources), are reached through special collections taken up at Sunday Mass during Lent. Since practicing Catholics in France tend to be on the right politically, they are not given as much information about CCFD's overseas work and ideology as are the smaller group. Their reasons for giving are also based on humanitarian motives, and they gave most generously during the Ethiopian famine crisis. As a result of this two-track fund-raising strategy, CCFD's income jumped by two-fifths between 1982 ($9.1 million) and 1984 ($12.7 million).[51]

[49] Telephone interview with Alonso Roberts, CA.

[50] Telephone interview with Pierre Galand, Oxfam Belgique.

[51] Telephone interview with Colette Dugua, CCFD; Baile, *Survey of European Nongovernmental Aid Organizations*, p. 56.

The Catholic-sponsored NGO in the FRG—MISEREOR—uses a similar strategy among its different sets of donors. During its major Lenten fund-raising campaigns in Catholic churches (whence comes most of its resources) it downplays controversy so as to maximize income, and it stresses the socio-economic aspects of its overseas work among the poor. During periodic disasters when it makes appeals to the general public, it emphasizes the need to alleviate immediate suffering. During its development education work throughout the year in parishes, in universities, and among labor groups, it includes information on human rights violations in countries such as Brazil and South Africa and stresses the need for policy changes abroad and at home to eradicate such structural inequities.

By conducting development education programs and fund-raising at different times, MISEREOR finds that more politically conservative donors are less likely to be turned off. Moreover, specialized groups that are more open to social-justice appeals—e.g., university students and union members—are targeted specifically for some of MISEREOR's more controversial messages. Its total income has also risen dramatically in recent years, growing by 40 percent between 1980 ($80.2 million) and 1985 ($112.1 million).[52]

These multiple appeals thus satisfy the various NGO support groups that feel their own particular interests are being met—whether they include political change benefiting the oppressed, socioeconomic development assisting low-income sectors, or alleviation of the suffering of disaster victims. Various groups within NGOs are also satisfied. Project officers and executives interested in promoting policy changes abroad and at home feel there are at least some donors who are aware of and committed to these causes. Fund-raising personnel are happy with steadily growing revenues. Board members are pleased due to institutional growth as well as with the flexibility of options a diversified funding base provides (including greater autonomy from government).

Periodic Disaffections and Exposés

Satisfying the multiple clusters of donors requires keeping many uninformed about some NGO work and about the political preferences of staff and executives, which shape decisions. Periodically, however, individual donors who give to these NGOs for development or humanitarian reasons become aware of political agendas and withdraw their support.

When some CA contributors read the advertisement paid for by CA in three major newspapers in November 1985—calling for British citizens to boycott South African goods and to write to their MPs in support of economic sanctions against that regime—they wrote angry letters terminating their donations to CA. MISEREOR in the FRG has also lost a number of contributors in the

---

[52] Telephone interview with Heinzberndt Krauskopf, MISEREOR.

pews when they have been exposed to some of its materials denouncing oppressive policies of governments in Latin America or Africa. Oxfam Belgique prior to the Ethiopian hunger crisis was finding it hard to expand its number of private contributors due to criticisms by some politically conservative Belgians that it was sympathetic to communism.[53]

Usually these withdrawals or criticisms involve a few individuals. They do not significantly hurt an NGO because the disaffection or anger receives little publicity. In some cases new contributors are gained by development education campaigns critical of home government policies. The MISEREOR in the FRG and CCODP in Canada have generated new contributors in recent years among university students (MISEREOR) or religious groups disillusioned with traditional forms of religious practice and almsgiving (CCODP among leftist Quebecois Catholics).[54]

There are, however, times when exposés occur in the media about politically sensitive projects supported by NGOs, especially overseas. Under such circumstances, the credibility of an NGO can be challenged if large numbers of citizens, including actual and potential donors, question whether the public is getting its money's worth from contributions to such nonprofits.

The battle in early 1985 between the French political left and right over development strategies, in which NGOs were used as surrogates, heightened public interest in and awareness of the political ideology of nonprofits. Later in 1985, and in 1986, several newspapers and journals with rightist political sympathies (such as *Le Figaro, Figaro-Magazine*, and *Le Quotidien de Paris*) published a series of articles mentioning several of the overseas projects supported by CCFD. They highlighted those that were politically controversial and mostly unknown to the average church-going Catholics contributing to the NGO.

The exposés in these newspapers and journals (well read by practicing Catholics who generally are politically conservative) revealed that CCFD gave support to government-controlled television programs in Vietnam about children (at the request of the Archbishop of Hanoi), refugee camps administered by the South West Africa People's Organization (SWAPO), and a newspaper and labor group in New Caledonia linked with FLNKS, the major political movement agitating for independence from France.

The series also identified some Chilean organizations with leftist political sympathies that had received CCFD assistance in the recent past—including secular journals, such as *APSI* and *La Bicecleta*, and the social science research center, FLACSO. The articles claimed that only five of the twenty-three projects in Chile that CCFD supported in 1985 were administered by

---

[53] Telephone interviews with Alonso Roberts, CA; and Heinzberndt Krauskopf, MISEREOR; interview with Pierre Galand, Oxfam Belgique.

[54] Telephone interview with Heinzberndt Krauskopf, MISEREOR; interview with Rev. C. William Smith, CCODP.

organizations under direct local church supervision. They concluded that approximately $173,275 of the $219,141 sent to Chile in 1985 went to political projects run by groups opposing the Chilean government.[55]

The themes of this exposé—repeated several times in the series—were that CCFD executives and staff have a leftist political agenda not representative of the majority of its French donors and that the NGO deceives most contributors by not giving them an accurate account of what it is actually doing with their funds overseas. The articles also claimed to be based on evidence provided by an on-site inspection of the projects CCFD supports in Chile, done by an independent group of interested French observers.

The CCFD strongly denounced such attacks as defamatory and fraught with distortions. It produced at a press conference in May 1986 several letters of support from prominent clerics and others in Chile denying any linkage of CCFD-supported projects with Marxism. The Chilean groups that had received CCFD aid also indicated that they had never been visited by any French delegation claiming to conduct an inspection of CCFD-aided projects. The CCFD spokesperson, however, did not deny having supported the television project in Vietnam or the journals and research center in Chile run by opponents of the regime.[56]

It is not clear how such an exposé will affect future private donations to CCFD. It is clear that the image of CCFD among French conservative Catholics (the main source of its private resources) was damaged. The French bishops subsequently received expressions of concern and outrage from lay persons about the type of work CCFD supports abroad, including a letter from two hundred Catholics in New Caledonia denouncing CCFD's contributions to organizations closely associated with political independence movements.

The hierarchy in France accordingly has taken steps to establish greater ecclesiastical control over CCFD activities, setting up a joint committee with episcopal and CCFD representation to revise the statutes of the organization. The changes also include more direct hierarchical involvement in the choice of CCFD's leadership (replacing the former practice of election by representatives of the twenty-five Catholic lay organizations constituting its membership). The French bishops also insisted that host-country bishops in the future always be consulted by CCFD before providing support for any project located in their respective dioceses.[57]

Hence, the strategy of double or triple reporting styles by NGOs to their multiple support bases in the private sector makes them vulnerable to exposés—especially if they are, in fact, supporting projects abroad or carrying

[55] Maury, "Charité chrétienne"; Bourdarias, "Chili"; Leclerc, "L'argent des chrétiens"; Bourdarias, "Une épine"; Maury, "CCFD."

[56] Holzer, "Intervention de Bernard Holzer"; Cool, "Le CCFD contre-attaque"; Tincq, "Le Comité catholique."

[57] Bourdarias, "Une épine"; Leclerc, "L'argent des chrétiens."

out advocacy campaigns at home with political orientations some donors do not share. Even if criticisms articulated in such exposés are not completely accurate and orchestrated for partisan political objectives—as the media attacks on CCFD were—they are not totally prefabricated. The half-truths contained in them are sufficient to tarnish an NGO's credibility—precisely when so little detail is given to the majority of donors about its controversial activities.

CONCLUSIONS

The relationships among NGOs, subsidizing governments, and private donors in Europe and Canada, as in the United States, involve a series of trade-offs. Often these are more complex than in the U.S. case due to the political agenda that different sectors in each group are pursuing. The delicate political game that is being played out requires a very careful balancing act within and across partner groups, and a certain amount of secrecy is an essential ingredient for maintaining the private aid system as it now functions.

Despite the clear left-of-center political priorities of executives and staffs in many of the largest NGOs, there is sufficient pluralism (or shrewdness) within these organizations to support multiple activities, including relief work during times of overseas disasters. This legitimates them in the eyes of many private donors (actual and potential) who do not share (and are not cognizant of) the political objectives of these organizations abroad or of their partisan work at home. Such multiple targeting of resources maximizes the opportunity for private income from diverse sources in society. It strengthens NGOs' credibility as humanitarian agents and their reputation for technical competence as development institutions. Both of these dimensions (reaffirmed by recent evaluations) are absolutely essential to provide a wider framework in which other more controversial agendas can be pursued.

So long as the humanitarian and development functions of NGOs are maintained at quality levels, government policymakers who are aware of their latent political agendas can use them to pursue other purposes. Were the political agendas the only objectives of NGOs, their partisan nature would be clear to all. Many host-country leaders would, in fact, see them as threats to national sovereignty, and their activities would be forbidden or tightly controlled. Home-government policymakers would, under such circumstances, no longer find NGOs attractive alternate conduits for sensitive foreign policy objectives, and public subsidies would be cut back or very restricted. Many private donors in Europe and Canada interested in the development or relief work of NGOs abroad would also cease supporting them if their partisan agendas were dominant or patent.

Hence, so long as a multiplicity of NGO activities is maintained, as well as "creative packaging" in reporting procedures to diverse groups in society,

NGO political work does not hurt their relationships with private donors or with home governments that subsidize them. The NGOs do criticize some home-government policies in their development education materials and attempt to alter them through lobbying campaigns. However, the advantages to policymakers, party leaders, and bureaucrats of being able to use these same nonprofits from time to time abroad or at home in pursuing their own political causes outweigh the annoyances such criticisms cause.

Both the left and right have discovered the usefulness of NGOs in contacting and assisting groups in Third World countries that the limits of national sovereignty and diplomatic protocol prevent them from dealing with directly. The flexibility that governments in Europe and Canada allow NGOs in reporting and accounting procedures is essential so that this delicate political work will not be traced back directly to themselves.

Both sides of the political spectrum in Europe and Canada have also found NGOs very helpful as surrogates and allies in appeasing dissidents within their own ranks or fending off the opposition. This is particularly true when such groups criticize official party or administration aid strategies that do not reach the hard-core poor abroad.

Moreover, there are a whole series of direct and indirect restrictions that government officials use to limit the potential political damage that may rebound from the controversial work of NGOs. There are also some in-built limits on NGO impact due to the narrow targets of their aggressive political messages at home.

There are, however, difficulties that make the status of these current relationships unstable and pressure points, that, if not handled very delicately, can cause the private aid system to break down. One of the original objectives of government policymakers in Europe and Canada (as in the United States) for expanding public subsidies to NGOs in the 1970s was to maintain a sagging consensus in society for continued and even expanded foreign-aid commitments. There is little evidence to date that NGOs have helped to achieve this goal, since much of their development education is politically partisan in nature and often narrowly targeted.

Policymakers, hence, are faced with a dilemma. The particular attractiveness of some NGOs to government officials—their ability to reach dissident groups abroad and to fight political battles at home—requires a partisan dimension. However, to educate and convince a broad spectrum of the domestic populace as to the importance of increasing government commitments in foreign aid, NGOs will have to shed their partisan political character. Government officials will have to decide which objective is more important for them, whether or not both can be achieved simultaneously, and what the trade-offs of a less partisan orientation in NGO development education will have in maintaining NGOs as allies or surrogates in other areas where their partisan commitments are useful.

Evidence from Canada, the Netherlands, and Great Britain indicates that policymakers are willing to pressure NGOs to be nonpartisan on the domestic education front through curtailing or diversifying cofunding for such operations. Most NGOs committed to a leftist political agenda, however, have been unwilling to alter the nature, focus, or intensity of their domestic advocacy work. How this will be resolved in the future and whether pressures from the political right will force governments to place even more controls over the partisan nature of NGO domestic educational activities remains to be seen.

What is clear is that groups on both the left and the right are drawing NGOs more and more into domestic political battles that are intense and in which the costs for NGOs are potentially quite high. In the FRG the gambit of left sectors of the SPD and the Greens to privatize official economic development assistance could place increasing amounts of public resources into their hands, which they cannot handle. An "embarrassment of riches" could be as costly as a cutting off of public funds entirely.

The subtle strategy of the FRG (under Kohl) and British (under Thatcher) political right has been to find ingenious ways of using even NGOs with leftist political agendas to serve their own conservative interests. This "cat and mouse" game has not seriously hampered or exposed the partisan agenda of these NGOs but rather cleverly harnessed it to the right's own use abroad and at home.

Far more damaging for NGOs, however, is the strategy to "fight fire with fire" crafted in France by the political right. Recent developments there indicate that the right, in response to blatant surrogate use of NGOs by the left, can readily find other NGOs as its allies in domestic partisan battles. This is partly as a result of the uneasiness that some NGOs have with the growing partisan work of others, partly a result of their own heretofore latent private sympathies for the right, which are becoming overt, and partly due to the clever strategies of conservative political leaders themselves in drawing these NGOs into the political fray.

Whatever the reason, two very critical consequences for NGOs of the French gambit are emerging. One is the creation of serious divisions within the nonprofit community that are being played out before a large public audience. As such differences emerge as part of larger partisan battles between the government and the opposition, the unity, credibility, and humanitarian character of the NGO community as a whole is being damaged. Secondly, as this occurs, the cover is being blown off the political orientation of NGOs, which is likely to precipitate disillusionment and anger on the part of many private donors who heretofore believed they were contributing to strictly humanitarian causes.

These consequences are the logical end point of a trajectory of close involvement by leftist NGOs in domestic European politics. Such NGOs do not speak for all international nonprofits based in their own societies. By attempting to place the moral legitimacy of the entire nonprofit sector behind their causes, however, they create frustration among some nonprofits who are not partisan and expose to the public the latent rightist sympathies of others.

If overt disunity along partisan political lines within the NGO community becomes more patent and prolonged—regardless who is to blame—the whole delicately balanced private aid system is likely to break down. Many citizens who perceive the NGO community to be nonpartisan are likely to curtail drastically their monetary support for nonprofits. They may also demand that governments do the same or take legal action to remove NGO tax-exempt privileges.

The relationships within and across partner groups involved in private foreign aid from Europe and Canada are not stable. Nor are the rules of the game fixed either for NGOs or for the various groups in government and the private sector who are using them as political surrogates or allies. The entire system depends upon keeping large numbers of citizens uninformed about some things that are transpiring, and having NGO and political leaders alike exercise self-restraint. When political stakes begin to escalate, however, these conditions are hard to maintain and the temptation to change these tacit rules grows strong.

It is not yet clear, therefore, whether the current trajectory is viable or whether the system is headed for a breakdown. Such will depend on the strategies chosen by subgroups within each partner group and on whether the public at large in Europe and Canada remains somewhat in the dark about the more-than-altruistic objectives being pursued in the private foreign aid network.

CHAPTER EIGHT

Threat or Support for Internal Stability in the Third
World? The Impact of Private Foreign Aid in
Latin America

THE LAST PIECES of the private foreign aid network that need to be explained
are the relationships within developing countries of indigenous nonprofits,
their clientele at the local level, and host country government officials. Although there are sufficient overlapping interests among donors, nonprofits,
and governments to sustain the private aid system in the North Atlantic region
(despite apparent contradictions and ongoing tensions), it is not clear why
those at the receiving end of the network can cooperate.

If many NGOs have as one of their prime goals the empowerment of the
poor in developing countries to push for a redistribution of economic and political power, why would host government officials allow them in—particularly when they serve as surrogates for foreign governments in assisting political dissidents? Why would policymakers in authoritarian or elite-controlled
regimes permit PVOs to operate if most espouse, at least as a latent agenda,
the enhancement of political pluralism through the promotion of autonomous
participatory organizations among marginal groups?

Why would indigenous nonprofit organizations—even if staffed by those
opposing dominant economic and political policies in their own countries—
risk taking money from foreign private sources that want the funds used for
politically sensitive activities? Such linkages with foreign groups trying to en-
gineer significant political change in Third World countries could very well
make indigenous nonprofits who accept such support appear as "trojan
horses" to their own governments.

It is also not clear why the third major actor at the receiving end of the
network—local recipients at the grass-roots level—would be eager to participate in projects challenging power elites and the government itself. Although
none of the aid coming from abroad can be given to armed insurrectionary
movements, there still could be considerable danger of repression against participants in projects designed to agitate for a redress of social and economic
grievances.

The purpose of this chapter is to explore these questions. I shall examine
whether multiple agendas characterize the partners in private foreign aid inside
developing countries, thus allowing for an overlap of interests as is the case at

the sending end of the network. I shall also explore the rules that allow private foreign aid to function in developing countries.

LATIN AMERICA: FOCUS OF ANALYSIS

Of the estimated ten thousand to twenty thousand development nonprofit organizations in Third World countries receiving assistance from NGOs/PVOs based in North Atlantic countries, more than four thousand are located in Latin America. Most of the larger Latin American countries have between two hundred and three hundred apiece. Brazil has over a thousand. Since the mid-1960s there has been a proliferation of such organizations throughout Latin America, and these now provide a variety of social services to low-income rural and urban workers. The majority originated under church auspices (and most still have some formal or informal church linkage), but over the past ten years a growing number have become independent secular institutions. The services they provide range from legal defense and assistance, technical training, credit, basic health, popular education, nutrition, the promotion of production and marketing cooperatives, technical aid for small artisanry and commerce and prefabricated housing, and applied research on critical socioeconomic problems affecting the poor.

Most of these nonprofits assist and support community organizations at the grass-roots level run by the poor, whom they are attempting to strengthen and make more self-sufficient. The majority of executives and staff persons in these developmental nonprofits are from the middle classes, however. They include intellectuals, professionals, clerics, political activists, and socially-concerned business leaders who are often dissatisfied with prevailing public policies for addressing the needs of low-income sectors. The amount of funding administered by these development nonprofits in Latin America (the overwhelming majority of which comes through the international private aid network) by 1986 was probably close to $1 billion annually and growing steadily.[1]

Particular cultural, economic, and political factors in Latin America over the past two decades have created the conditions for such a proliferation of developmental nonprofits serving the socioeconomic needs of low-income sectors. This region, therefore, will provide the primary area of focus in exploring trade-offs among the state, private organizations, and the poor. Colombia, since it reflects several of these dynamics and has a vigorous nonprofit sector, will serve as the central country case for analysis.

[1] Fernandes, "Las ONGs"; Padrón Castillo, *Cooperación al desarrollo y movimiento popular*; Arruda, "Role of Latin American Nongovernmental Organizations;" Landim, "Nongovernmental Organizations in Latin America."

GROWTH OF LATIN AMERICAN DEVELOPMENTAL NONPROFITS IN THE 1960s AND 1970s

The reasons for the growth of the nonprofit sector to serve the development needs of the poor during the last twenty years in Latin America have been due to changes in churches as well as in the domestic economic and political context. It has also been the result of new trends in international philanthropy described in earlier chapters.

Expanding Role of Churches

In the 1950s, various Catholic dioceses in Latin America set up their own charitable organizations—usually called CARITAS (Charity)—to alleviate some of the most severe symptoms of poverty with food, medicine, and clothing. The creation of these indigenous relief agencies was made possible by resources and personnel coming from North Atlantic countries (especially church-related PVOs home-based in the United States) who, after European recovery, began to turn some of their attention to other areas of the world.

In the 1960s, Latin American Catholic Church leaders began to focus more of their attention on structural solutions to the problems affecting those living below the poverty line in their respective societies—the bottom forty percent of the population, which earned less than the minimum wage. Competition emerged among Protestant and Catholic churches for the allegiances of peasants and urban workers (long on the margins of Catholic Church structures). New stimuli from the Vatican and various Catholic bishops' meetings ocurred to make social justice an integral part of the Church's mission (Second Vatican Council, social encyclicals of Popes John XXIII and Paul VI, the Medellín conference of Latin American bishops). These factors precipitated a new commitment by Catholic Church leaders to development, as opposed to relief, among the marginal groups in their societies.

From the secular side the growing attraction of Marxism among the poor— manifested in the growth of leftist parties, labor organizations, and guerrilla movements—also prodded the churches into playing a greater role in the developmental process among the poor. The Alliance for Progress also stimulated an air of urgency about development throughout Latin America in the 1960s.

Churches—due to their organizational outreach, credibility among the poor, and ideological antipathy toward Marxism—became important staging grounds for inaugurating new service programs by the mid- and late-1960s. Traditional religious charitable organizations expanded their focus, and new church-sponsored developmental activities were inaugurated. These were geared to addressing some of the deeper underlying causes of poverty rather than treating the symptoms and included rural cooperatives and labor associations, basic health projects, low-income housing assistance, and literacy training.[2] Almost 100 percent of the financial and material resources needed to mount such efforts came from the North Atlantic region. It was transmitted primarily through church-related nonprofits in the United States—as well as newly emerging NGOs in Canada and Europe—that were themselves starting to shift their focus away from relief toward development.

These new church-sponsored nonprofit organizations in Latin America in the 1960s were only one piece, and a minor one at that, in a whole range of new public and private efforts to address developmental problems in the region. Government efforts led the way in education, health, and training for the poor (assisted by AID during the Alliance for Progress) and far exceeded the expenditures of the church network. The private profitmaking sector, both indigenous and international, also expanded investments in manufacturing, agriculture, and extractive industries to stimulate accelerated economic growth in Latin America.

Limitations of Reformist Strategies to Alleviate Poverty

By the early-1970s, however, the nonprofit sector took on a more significant role in many Latin American countries. This was a result of economic and political obstacles that severely limited or terminated much of the social progress for low-income sectors begun in the 1960s by government.

The escalation of the Vietnam War in the late 1960s and early 1970s turned the attention of U.S. government policymakers away from Latin America toward Asia. This led to a drying up of much of the AID resources supporting expanded Latin American government services to the poor in their own societies.

The democratic governments in Latin America during the 1960s seldom had sufficient political support to carry out effective tax and agrarian reforms (called for by the Alliance) that would have provided them with increasing revenues to shoulder the costs for these new service projects themselves. They also invested the predominant part of the new loans and grants received during the Alliance in capital-intensive infrastructural projects not directly benefiting the poor, or, if so, only the relatively well-to-do low-income sectors.

Moreover, lack of price guarantees for primary product exports from Latin America to North Atlantic countries and continuing tariff barriers in Europe and the United States against manufacturing imports further reduced resources available to Latin American governments to continue these commitments to the poor made during the 1960s. The oil shocks in 1973 and 1978 further

[2] Brian H. Smith, "Religion and Social Change"; Brian Smith, *Church and Politics in Chile*, pp. 106–25; Bruneau, *Political Transformation of the Brazilian Catholic Church*; Levine, *Religion and Politics in Latin America*, pp. 70–96; Berryman, *Religious Roots of Rebellion*, pp. 25–32, 59–65, 98–106, 173–80, 223–25; Cleary, *Crisis and Change*, pp. 21–50.

exacerbated economic difficulties and, except in the case of oil-exporting Latin American nations (Venezuela, Mexico, and Ecuador) precipitated severe domestic austerity measures by the late 1970s. All of these domestic and international problems forced most governments to cut back drastically on public services in health, education, nutrition, credit, and training that had been set up to assist low-income sectors during the Alliance.

In addition, by the mid-1970s it was clear that the benefits from expanded private investment of the 1960s had not trickled down to the poor as expected. The predominant type of investments made were in the areas of capital-intensive manufacturing and agriculture, which provided almost no increased employment opportunities for unskilled laborers who made up the overwhelming majority of urban and rural workers. The economic miracle that emerged in Brazil in the late 1960s and early 1970s, for example, was fueled by such capital-intensive investments, as was the spurt of industrial growth in Mexico in the late 1970s. In neither country did the bottom 40 percent of the populations benefit significantly.

Amidst cutbacks in public services to the poor and the skewed distributions of the benefits of economic growth to upper-income sectors of the population, nonprofit organizations by the mid-1970s—both church-related and newly created secular ones—became increasingly important providers of social and economic services to the poor. Moreover, they were able to expand both in numbers and scope of activity precisely because they could tap into the international private aid network whose resources were beginning to grow significantly in the mid 1970s.

As described in chapters 3 and 4, it was at this time—the post-1973 period—when governments in Europe, Canada, and the United States were substantially increasing public subsidies to PVOs/NGOs based in their countries, which were eager to take on new commitments abroad. Hence, as indigenous Latin American nonprofits expanded in number and scope to fill gaps left by shrinking public social services and a lack of employment opportunities in the business sector, they were able to find new sources of financing abroad to do so.

Many of those who began working in administrative capacities for these rapidly expanding indigenous nonprofits—middle class professionals, intellectuals, clerics, former government social service personnel—did so out of a sense of frustration with the failure of governmental and profitmaking approaches to solving poverty. They were also searching for more effective strategies to meet the basic needs of low-income sectors. Many were convinced that significant political change in their own societies was necessary to achieve this.

In Colombia, for example, despite the relatively stable democratic system and competitive elections between two multiclass-based parties throughout the 1960s, by the 1970s many clerical, academic, professional, and socially concerned business leaders became disillusioned with government strategies designed to improve the economic conditions of the poor. Political parties and the government were controlled by landed, industrial, and commercial elites through a well-orchestrated patronage system. Agricultural and industrial reform policies designed during the Alliance for Progress reflected their interests since these were geared to assist those already possessing land or capital. New state subsidies and private investment in both industry and agriculture were capital-intensive, not labor-intensive, and did very little for the bottom 40 percent of the population possessing little resources and few skills.

Many of those seriously committed to the needs of the poorest in Colombia began to look to the nonprofit sector to develop more adequate economic and social strategies to fulfill them. A series of nonprofit foundations were set up by the indigenous business community to channel tax-exempt resources into service programs for urban and rural marginal groups. Professionals, clerics, and disaffected political leaders joined or created developmental nonprofit organizations, assisted by international private aid, to support training, credit, health, and educational programs among the hard-core poor.

A major goal of the indigenous nonprofit service organizations in Colombia (and several other Latin American countries) was to help create and support autonomous community organizations among the poor, independent of the party patronage system and capable of exerting leverage on the elite-dominated system. It was hoped that by exerting pressure from below the poor could not only gain greater access to economic resources but begin to open up the political system for more effective participation.

Growing Tendencies toward Authoritarianism in the 1970s

An additional factor that stimulated the expansion of the indigenous nonprofit sector in Latin America during the 1970s—and gave it an added political dimension—was the fallout from authoritarianism. A wave of military governments came to power in the late 1960s and early 1970s with Brazil leading the way in 1964. Peru, Panama, Honduras, Bolivia, Chile, Uruguay, and Argentina followed. Military regimes already in power in other countries (Paraguay, El Salvador, Guatemala, and Nicaragua) deepened their control over their respective societies in the same period.

In most cases (Peru, Ecuador, and Panama being the exceptions), these regimes used very repressive measures to curb growing economic demands and political mobilization of the poor by center-left and leftist groups during the 1960s. Such strategies sometimes involved armed insurrection led by Marxists, as was the case in several countries of Central America and the Southern Cone region. The military governments that came to power during this social upheaval suspended constitutional guarantees; arrested, tortured, and killed real or suspected insurgents; outlawed (or placed in recess) center and center-left political parties, trade unions, civic and professional associations; and intervened in universities to root out whomever they considered to be a subversive faculty member and to censor the curricula. They also cut drastically service benefits for low-income sectors so as to lower public spending, curb inflation, and satisfy foreign creditors.

With other forms of social, cultural, and political participation destroyed or severely curtailed, nonprofit organizations appeared as attractive surrogates for many intellectuals and professionals, as well as for political party and labor organizations leaders. All these groups were ousted from their former occupations and forbidden to engage in overt partisan politics. The private social service institutions became their means of continuing (or supplementing) their lost or diminished employment opportunities and of also maintaining some form of contact with low-income sectors of their populations.

Amidst such repression, new church-related nonprofits were created to provide legal and other types of assistance to those suffering human rights violations in Chile, Paraguay, Argentina, Brazil, Peru, El Salvador, and Nicaragua. These were often staffed by lawyers and social workers with leftist political sympathies or who were strongly critical of government policies. Foreign private assistance, especially from church-related NGOs in Europe and Canada, provided almost all of the finances necessary to create and maintain these new organizations.[3]

Independent research centers were also created—in Chile, Argentina, Uruguay, and Brazil—to provide a haven for social scientists and technical experts purged from universities and the professions because of their political views. Some of these centers were set up under church protection—such as the Academy of Christian Humanism in Chile. Others were created under secular leadership, such as CEBRAP in Brazil and CEDES in Argentina. The international private aid network again provided a substantial amount of assistance in making these centers possible, with the Ford Foundation alone donating $3.5 million to support eleven private research centers in Argentina, Chile, and Uruguay between 1975 and 1978.[4]

Not only did these independent research institutes make it possible for academics expelled from universities to remain in their countries instead of going into exile, but they sponsored policy-relevant research. They often examined in depth the worsening conditions of low-income sectors and explored alternate policies and strategies needed to make the cost of national economic and political recovery less burdensome for the poor. They also established contacts with grass-roots organizations and the expanding network of nonprofit service

[3] Brian H. Smith, "Churches and Human Rights in Latin America"; Frühling, "Nonprofit Organizations as Opposition to Authoritarian Rule."

[4] Puryear, "Higher Education, Development Assistance, and Repressive Regimes"; Frühling, "Nonprofit Organizations as Opposition to Authoritarian Rule."

organizations serving their needs, making the results of their own research useful to practitioners working to assist low-income sectors.

Unfinished Agenda for Equity during Redemocratization

Although many of these countries in the early 1980s underwent a return to formal democracy, there is little evidence that the expanded nonprofit network is experiencing any institutional shrinkage. The surrogate role of nonprofits for clerical, academic, professional, and political dissidents is no longer as critical given the opportunity for them to pursue their agendas through constitutional processes and electoral politics. Nonprofit service organizations and independent research institutes continue to function in countries such as Brazil and Peru, for example, given the limited economic resources available for social service expansion in the public sector. In both countries, leaders in the nonprofit sector have also criticized the slowness of these new governments in responding to low-income demands for greater equity. Austerity programs are being implemented by governments to curb inflation, repay mounting foreign debts, and maintain the confidence and critical support of middle- and upper-income sectors. The nonprofit sector, therefore, continues to offer important services to the poor whose economic needs are not adequately being met by new democratic regimes, and its leaders act as public critics of government performance.

It is not yet clear, therefore, how strong the support for new democratic governments will be in the nonprofit service sector accustomed under military rule to identifying strongly with the needs of low-income sectors. If policymakers do not spread the costs of economic recovery and debt repayment more evenly across classes than did former authoritarian regimes, these nonprofit organizations are likely to continue to play a role of political opposition to government policies.

Revolutionary Change in Central America

A final stimulus to the growth in number and importance of nonprofit organizations in Latin America during the 1970s was insurrectionary violence in Central America. In both Nicaragua during the revolution and currently in El Salvador, indigenous nonprofit organizations—especially church-related service organizations—played or continue to play a critical role in attempting to create means of survival for those caught in the conflict.

When basic services break down in contested regions of these nations, indigenous nonprofits with international assistance have provided services in basic health and education and have aided refugees seeking to escape danger. Often, more than relief work is being conducted. Many indigenous nonprofits—especially in El Salvador where the war has been prolonged—are attempting to carry out longer-term development efforts, especially for those in contested areas who wish to remain in their home territories.

As indicated in earlier chapters, some European NGOs support indigenous nonprofits that work in conflict areas of El Salvador in the hopes of aiding the insurrectionary struggle indirectly. Although the local private-service agencies remain formally neutral in the struggle, some they assist are clearly sympathetic, or related, to guerillas fighting against the government.

In postrevolutionary Nicaragua, indigenous nonprofits continue to play a role in economic and social reconstruction of the nation. Both supporters and opponents of the regime have set up private institutions to meet the needs of low-income sectors. Even those staffed by regime opponents are allowed to receive aid from international private organizations to support their activities.

Since the mid-1960s, development-oriented nonprofit organizations have expanded their activities in Latin America in a wide variety of political contexts—stable democratic systems, authoritarian military governments, redemocratizing societies, nations undergoing insurrection or civil war, and most recently a socialist-oriented regime. In all of these regimes, the work of many nonprofits has a political dimension due to the clientele they serve and the fact that their agenda frequently involves at least tacit opposition to government policies. International private organizations support their activities and host-government leaders permit this assistance to enter their borders despite its potential for disruption. Latin America, therefore, provides rich experiences for examining what trade-offs occur among the local partners in such transactions—i.e., among the state, nonprofit organizations, and grass-roots beneficiaries.

Colombia: Primary Country Case Study

In exploring the trade-offs, Colombia will be the centerpiece for this analysis. One reason Colombia was chosen as a place to explore the role of nonprofits was the number and variety of activities administered by its indigenous nonprofit sector. The majority (twenty-four of forty-five) of the PVOs/NGOs I surveyed in Europe, Canada, and the United States have been supporting development-oriented activities in Colombia for some time. Very few (five), however, have their own field representatives, and none administer their own programs. Rather, they fund a wide variety of Colombian nonprofit organizations that directly administer developmental programs among the poor or who oversee projects carried out by low-income groups themselves at the grass-roots level.

In the 1970s these nonprofit institutions in Colombia expanded both in quantity and diversity. They now include: (1) technical and leadership-training institutions for low-income groups run by professionals; (2) applied research institutes staffed by social scientists that have educational components for workers or peasants and act as advocates for better public policy toward these groups; (3) private foundations that channel contributions from business firms into self-help programs among the poor for housing, health, credit, and recreation; (4) credit institutions for those small businesspersons who do not have access to normal commercial channels of finance; (5) production, marketing, and consumer cooperatives in regions where private and public infrastructures and credit are not available; and (6) multiservice agencies providing health, housing, recreation, or popular education to local community groups.

While Colombia may not be unique in having such a variety of nonprofit service institutions, the societal context in which they operate is more advantageous for accomplishing social change than in many other Third World countries. The second reason, therefore, that Colombia was chosen as a case study was due to the political and economic characteristics that provide a relatively optimal environment for examining the possibilities for indigenous nonprofits to push effectively from below for significant changes in the distribution of power and resources in favor of the poor (an explicit objective of many of the European and Canadian NGOs and an implicit hope of some American PVOs).

Colombia's two-party system has traditionally been controlled by elites who have not encouraged widespread public input into decision-making in either their own vertically controlled party organizations or in governmental agencies that both Conservative and Liberal parties dominate. Paternalism and patronage have long characterized politics. Abstention rates in national elections have averaged close to 50 percent in the past thirty years, especially during the period of the National Front, 1958–1974, when a pact between the Conservative and Liberal parties guaranteed both an equal share in all legislative and executive organs and alternating terms in the presidency. The country has also been plagued by intermittent violence throughout its history, suffering almost ten years of internal strife in the late 1940s and early 1950s (*la violencia*). A significant threat from guerrilla organizations began in the late 1960s. Political corruption has grown in the wake of a burgeoning drug trade with an annual value of purportedly $4 billion by the early 1980s.[5]

Despite these negative factors, the political system permits peaceful competition for power. Interest groups operate relatively freely, and vigorous public debate occurs in the media and in academia over alternate public policies. Nonprofit organizations have grown in attractiveness in recent years as alternate forms of participation and expression among those disillusioned with the party system. Historically, there has been little governmental regulation of the nonprofit sector, and procedures for legal incorporation of such institutions have been quite loose.[6]

[5] Dix. *Colombia*; Bagley, "National Front and Beyond."
[6] Low Murtra, "Las sociedades y las entidades sin ánimo de lucro."

The Colombian economy is also such that overall resources have grown steadily. In comparison to most other Latin American economies, if is relatively sound. The annual growth rate averaged 5.5 percent throughout the 1970s, and although it slowed to an average of 1 percent during the height of the global recession in 1982 and 1983, by 1984 it rebounded to 3.2 percent. The government has not had to impose rigid austerity measures due to burdens of a mounting foreign debt and serious inflation, both of which now plague several other Latin nations such as Argentina, Brazil, Mexico, Peru, Bolivia, Chile, and Venezuela. This has been due to growing diversification of the Colombian domestic economy and of its exports, near self-sufficiency in energy production (including oil), wise policy choices in the 1970s not to escalate foreign borrowing, and crawling-peg monetary devaluations since the late 1960s.

In the administration of social services there is a significant role for private sector groups. Local community organizations have participated in carrying out public programs and in helping to defray costs through decentralized implementation of services, contributions of materials, and voluntary manual labor. Colombia has traditionally given the private sector a significant share in the design and implementation of public policies, especially in commerce, agriculture, industry, finance, and insurance. Although this tradition of *concertación* (harmonization) has led to expanding influence in critical public decisions by large profitmaking groups (such as producer associations and other business interests),[7] it also provides an opportunity for the nonprofit side of the private sector to have some input into shaping policies—especially those in the realm of social services.

The implications of these contextual factors are that there is some political space in Colombia to struggle for equity, there are expanding economic resources available to respond to pressures from neglected sectors, and private sector groups do shape public policy design and implementation. In authoritarian political systems dominated by the military (Chile) or one political party (postrevolution Nicaragua and Mexico), there is little or no open competition for power, and interest group pressures are restricted or carefully channeled. Under such circumstances, attempts to redress social or economic imbalances by openly opposing public policies are more easily deflected, co-opted, or repressed. In severely divided societies undergoing civil war (El Salvador and prerevolution Nicaragua), both developmental work and nonviolent political pressure to effect changes in government policies are difficult to sustain.

In some democratic societies there are chronic inequities but a scarcity of economic resources to address them adequately due to a lack of steady growth and the presence of sizable foreign debts (Brazil, Peru, Bolivia, Venezuela,

[7] Dix, *Colombia*, p. 353; Bagley, "National Front and Beyond," pp. 19–23; Hartlyn, "Producer Associations, the Political Regime, and Policy Processes."

and Argentina). In these countries the scope of political activity by the non-profit sector may not be as circumscribed, but the chances for nonprofits to bring about a significant redistribution of resources are very limited. Their advice and cooperation in social service design and implementation may be sought by policymakers under such circumstances, but the opportunities for them to influence economic policy are rather narrow given the grave economic challenges facing such democracies.

Hence, to assess whether the aims of many European and Canadian donor NGOs are being fulfilled by the counterparts they support in developing countries—namely, empowerment of marginal sectors to push for changes in the economic and political power structures—one should focus on a country where open dissent and competition for political power is allowed and where steady, balanced economic growth is occurring. If there are significant limits on nonprofits' mobilization strategies in such an optimum context, *a fortiori* there would be even more restrictions in authoritarian regimes and in societies undergoing economic crisis or civil war.

Although Colombia is far from being a perfect democracy or a country of advanced economic equity, neither does it resemble closed systems that allow little opposition to government policies or input into their formulation by private sector groups. Economic success relative to several of the other major Latin American nations also provides policymakers in Colombia with resources with which to meet some demands from the popular classes in the event that sustained and autonomous mobilization strategies from this sector arise. Colombia is, therefore, a good case in which to examine the upper range of probability that indigenous nonprofits will pursue significant changes in the distribution of economic and political power and have some success in their efforts.

I shall also deal briefly with several other country cases in Latin America. The opportunities for nonprofits in these other contexts to precipitate significant political and economic change in the short run may be more circumscribed than in Colombia. It is clear, however, that they are also playing a political role in their respective societies—and often in explicit or tacit opposition to prevailing public policies. Trade-offs, although different from those in Colombia, do exist. Development nonprofits are also allowed by the state to assist low-income sectors in these other regimes with significant support from the international private aid network.

Colombian Development Nonprofits

As indicated in appendix A, in conducting field research in Colombia in 1984 I used a variety of methods in constructing a sample of thirty-six indigenous nonprofits that spread across seven different departments (or states) and all six of the major service categories in which Colombian developmental nonprofits are currently active. Almost all the institutions selected were also acting as intermediaries between foreign private sources of funding (from PVOs/NGOs in North Atlantic countries) and local grass-roots community organizations working among the Colombian poor. Upon their creation in the 1970s, only twenty-one received some form of foreign assistance, but by the mid-1980s thirty were so financed. By 1984 in fact, twenty-two of these were dependent for 50 percent or more of their annual budgets on these North Atlantic PVOs/ NGOs.

Many of the European and Canadian NGOs in my sample that explicitly identified as one of their primary goals social and economic change through political empowerment of the poor have been providing the financial support for several of these and other development nonprofits in Colombia in recent years.[8] Several of the PVOs that had indicated that support for greater political pluralism and participation in social structures by the poor was an implicit, if unstated, objective of their overseas agenda also are major supporters of Colombian nonprofits, including many I interviewed.[9]

One-half (eighteen) of the Colombian nonprofits in my survey claimed that a majority of those benefiting from their aid at the grass-roots level are at, or below, the minimum wage level ($1,477 annually) and constitute the poorest 40 percent of the population. Another one-third (twelve) indicated that at least some of the grass-roots groups they assist are made up predominantly of persons in this category. Hence, representatives of nonprofits in over four fifths (thirty of thirty-six) of my Colombian sample stated that they were reaching those in chronic poverty. Spot visits I made to seven different grass-roots organizations supported by these Colombian nonprofits all confirmed the validity of these claims.

In Colombia one might expect, therefore, that many developmental nonprofits would include political and economic empowerment of the poor as one of their objectives. Not only do local nonprofits continue to rely heavily on foreign private donors that espouse such goals, but they themselves are working among the poorest in a formally democratic country with a relatively sound economy, albeit significant maldistribution of resources and power. In such a context, one might expect indigenous nonprofits to promote grass-roots organizations that push the system to be more responsive to the needs of the poor.

In fact, during the 1970s a series of independent organizations created by peasants, small farmers, and student groups emerged outside formal party or government-sponsored social organizations. Their strategy was to pressure for a redress of social grievances for low-income groups—e.g., greater access to services, implementation of agrarian reform, and more provision of public

---

[8] These NGOs include CCODP and CUSO in Canada, CAFOD in Great Britain, CCFD in France, Bread for the World, MISEREOR, and FES in the FRG, and CEBEMO, ICCO, and NOVIB in the Netherlands.

[9] These PVOs include CRS, PACT, SCF, and FPP USA.

credit. These new grass-roots movements organized a number of large public protests, or civic strikes *(paros cívicos)*, at the local level in various regions of the country. These involved the seizure of public facilities and service agencies. Between 1971 and 1980 there were 128 such demonstrations in communities with a combined population of over 4.4 million persons (about 18 percent of the national population).[10]

Hence, precisely at the time when many of the Colombian development-oriented nonprofits in my survey originated, there were parallel movements emerging among the same clientele and using political pressure to achieve greater equity for the poor. In fact, in all seven departments in which I interviewed indigenous nonprofits and visited grass-roots projects, significant popular protest movements occurred during the 1970s. In several instances, they occurred in the same regions where the nonprofits in my sample were located—Tumaco, Pasto, San Gil, and Bucaramanga.

Given the converging influences on Colombian nonprofits both from international donors and parallel movements in their own environment, one clearly would expect them to make part of their developmental strategy the mobilization of the poor to seek a redress of social grievances. I found, however— both in my interviews in headquarters and in field visits to grass-roots organizations administering the projects—that very little emphasis in word or deed was given to such an objective. Although acknowledging the long-range political consequences of their work and encouraging significant participation of the poor in running local organizations, Colombian development nonprofits shun confrontational tactics with regional power groups. Rather, they place great emphasis on concrete material improvements through community self-help and through brokering between the poor and local government agencies. Moreover, when nonprofits or the groups they support at the grass-roots level engage in pressure tactics, these are not sustained over time.

Implicit Political Emphasis among Colombian Developmental Nonprofits

Like the majority of donor PVOs/NGOs in the North Atlantic region, most Colombian nonprofits do not believe a strictly apolitical position is possible in their work. Over three-fourths of those in my Colombian sample (twenty-eight) indicated that it was impossible to avoid political implications since they are working to improve the situation for the poorest sectors in society who are at the margins of power. However, none of the executive or staff personnel I interviewed in the thirty-six Colombian organizations espoused a political position that would entail close identification with parties. Very few personally were active in political parties. Many criticized the party system (dominated

---

[10] Santana, *Desarrollo regional*, pp. 113–19, 155.

by Conservatives and Liberals) for not effectively representing the interests of the poor or allowing them a significant voice in party decisions.

The director of SEPAS of Pasto, a church-related agency that promotes community organizations and trains leaders in isolated Indian villages in Nariño, frankly admitted the political implications of his work. However, he shunned party linkages for his organization: "We do not work with political parties. We are against the system in general. Small meetings have political implications. We teach people in the meetings that services are an obligation of government, not a gift. We tell people that we must, therefore, demand these services from the government."[11]

The program director of SEPAS of San Gil, a church-sponsored service agency in Santander with ten years of experience in promoting rural cooperatives and associations among small farmers, also emphasized the importance in making such a distinction when defining the political character of his organization: "It is impossible to be politically neutral. Serving the poor necessitates politics. But it does not require party politics. The political power of organized peasants is greater than any party. Parties are nominal national entities, but at the local level do not represent the people."[12]

The executive director of the *Fundación Friedrich Ebert de Colombia* (FESCOL)—which engages in advocacy research for more equitable public policies and brings together social scientists, government officials, and representatives of labor to discuss alternate economic strategies—also underscored the importance of this distinction. Although supported by FES of the SPD in the FRG, FESCOL did not identify with any party in Colombia:

> We don't take any party positions, but the implications and consequences of our activities are political since we are trying to open the political system to more input by those who do not have much voice. We would lose our credibility as a platform for debate if we took partisan political positions.
>
> In Venezuela, Ecuador, and Chile we support base movements closely linked with parties. In Colombia, however, we are trying to promote a more effective and open democratic system—but not a Social Democratic system.[13]

These remarks were indicative of the general distaste among Colombian nonprofits in my survey for political parties as they are now constituted. It was not surprising to find, therefore, that they do encourage the formation of autonomous participatory grass-roots organizations run by the poor themselves, which have political, albeit not partisan, implications. Several nonprofits are

[11] Interview with Rev. Gonzalo Castro, S.J., SEPAS of Pasto.

[12] Interview with Miguel Fajardo, SEPAS of San Gil.

[13] Interview with Klaus Schubert, FESCOL. A major reason why FESCOL does not identify with any party organization is that—unlike the situation in Venezuela, Ecuador, and Chile—there are no local affiliates or counterparts to European Social Democratic parties in Colombia.

also focal points for networking among base organizations, and they facilitate coordination and communication among them.

The CENPRODES, an organization that is part of the Secretariat of the Catholic Episcopal Conference of Colombia, assists local groups in preparing funding proposals for European donor NGOs. It has helped over seven hundred grass-roots organizations obtain funding since its founding in 1974. The participatory nature of its client organizations has also risen dramatically over time. In the first three years of CENPRODES's existence (1974–1977), only 8 percent of the projects it assisted were designed and operated by local recipients themselves. But due to its own commitment and insistence by European donors, between 1981 and 1983, 29 percent of the projects it assisted were designed and administered by beneficiaries in their own autonomous organizations. Another 32 percent of these projects in the early 1980s had as their objective the stimulation of recipient participation in decision-making during the life of the projects.

Moreover, CENPRODES invites representatives of all current projects it assists throughout the country (one hundred in 1984) to come together four times a year to share experiences. These discussions often involve analyzing political and economic obstacles facing each group in their respective locale— such as lack of access to land, inadequate government services, or unjust treatment by commercial middlemen. There is also considerable sharing of information as to what strategies the various groups have used in trying to overcome these and other problems.[14]

Several of the other nonprofits in my Colombian survey promote similar strategies of participatory institution-building and networking among the urban and rural poor who are recipients of their aid. *Foro Nacional de Colombia*, a group of professional architects and housing experts who assist neighborhood associations on urban problems, participates in the National Coordinating Movement of Civic Strikes, which emerged out of the series of public demonstrations in the 1970s. It also convenes meetings twice a month for groups of forty to one hundred representatives of community organizations in Bogotá working to improve low-income housing and pressuring government agencies to provide more services in this area.[15]

The AITEC of Boston, which provides training and grants for revolving loan funds to groups that assist small street merchants and home-operated businesses among the hard-core poor, helps four such programs in Bogotá, Cali, and Cartagena. These reach over twelve hundred persons, all at or below the minimum wage level. Part of the conditions of AITEC's aid to nonprofit organizations in Colombia is that loans be given to clusters of small entrepre-

---

[14] CENPRODES, *Informativo CENPRODES*, p. 9; interview with Roberto de Mendoza, CENPRODES.

[15] Interview with Dr. Constantino Casasbuenas Morales, *Foro Nacional de Colombia*.

neurs, not individuals, to promote greater solidarity and cooperation among them. It also insists that active loan recipients participate in credit-screening procedures for future petitioners and also meet regularly in assemblies to discuss common problems in their small businesses. Every three months AITEC itself sponsors national meetings for representatives of its client organizations to share experiences. From time to time it brings in representatives from organizations it has assisted in other Latin American countries (e.g., the Dominican Republic) to meet with the Colombian groups.[16]

Both SEPAS of San Gil and CINEP, a Jesuit-sponsored research and popular education institute in Bogotá, have collaborated in forming a unified confederation (USITRAS) of unions among small farmers, landless workers, women's groups, and students in Santander. This umbrella institution is the first of its kind in the region. Its affiliates represent different political tendencies, including sympathies for the small Communist Party (which is legally recognized in Colombia and competes openly in elections).[17]

SEPAS of San Gil itself laid the groundwork for this confederation by helping form COOPCENTRAL—a federation of cooperatives, organizations of small farmers, and local unions that now include about two hundred thousand persons (or 40 percent of the population of the diocese of Socorro and San Gil). In addition to helping in the creation of the wider coordinating agency of unions (USITRAS), it continues to offer courses and training programs for COOPCENTRAL, runs a regional congress every two or three years for peasant leaders throughout the region, and publishes in collaboration with local organizations a widely read monthly newspaper, *José Antonio*, that expresses peasant views on local political and economic problems.[18]

My own visits, conversations, and participation and observation in local project meetings in various parts of the country confirmed that the grass-roots community organizations created or strengthened by Colombian development nonprofits in my survey were enhancing the self-confidence and articulation skills of participants. Workers and peasants discuss critical local problems, try to identify underlying causes, and cooperate in seeking collective solutions—including, in several instances, more effective dealings with local power structures.

Consumer and loan cooperatives run by Inga Indian women in the Sibundoy Valley of Putamayo now are able to bypass exploitative credit and marketing practices of traditional commercial middlemen, thanks to aid from the *Federación Juvenil de Desarrollo Comunitario* (supported by SCF in the United States). Moreover, both men and women leaders in Sibundoy are more active in articulating their demands in the presence of local government authorities

[16] Interview with Valdi de Araujo Dantas, AITEC.
[17] Interviews with Rev. Alejandro Angulo, S.J., CINEP.
[18] Interview with Miguel Fajardo, SEPAS of San Gil.

now that their community organizations have been strengthened by such out-side assistance.[19]

Several production and consumer cooperatives formerly sponsored by *Plan Padrinos–Tumaco* (an affiliate of Foster Parents Plan International) among low-income black residents now operate as independent institutions generating credit and job opportunities for persons previously unemployed or denied loans by private banks.[20] Prices for a whole variety of basic goods have been lowered and stabilized for rural residents in Santander as a result of the con-sumer cooperatives set up by COOPCENTRAL, the independent confedera-tion of cooperatives created by SEPAS of San Gil.[21] Community organizations in Jamundí in Valle del Cauca emerged as a result of project aid by *Plan Pa-drinos–Cali* (also affiliated with Foster Parents Plan International) and now are training grounds for local leaders independent of paternalistic party organiza-tions.[22]

It was clear to me both from interviews with executive and staff personnel in Colombian development nonprofits and conversations with project partici-pants in local organizations they support in various parts of Colombia that the activities involved extend well beyond the transfer of skills and income gen-eration. A major part of the work includes enhancement of autonomous insti-tutions run by the poor themselves that are increasing the self-confidence and bargaining skills of these low-income groups.

No Challenge by Colombian Nonprofits to the Political or Economic System

Despite the acknowledged political implications of their work, Colombian de-velopmental nonprofits do not define their objectives in terms of altering sub-stantially the economic and political power configurations of society. In or-dering their priorities from a list of six goals, the respondents in my survey consistently ranked this objective as last.

Table 8.1 gives the weighted scores of six priorities I presented to execu-tives in the thirty-six nonprofits.[23] They cut across a variety of emphases,

---

[19] Conversation with Jaime Victoria, *Federación Juvenil de Desarrollo Comunitario*; and Sal-vador Lasso, alternate for Senator Eduardo del Hierro Santacruz.

[20] Conversations with administrators and participants in COOPCOMOAPLAN and *Creaciones Negritas*, Tumaco, August 11, 1984. Both of these cooperatives were formerly part of *Plan Pa-drinos-Tumaco* but now are independent institutions legally and financially. They continue to receive some technical advice from *Plan* in administrative and bookkeeping matters.

[21] Conversations with administrators of the consumer market run by COOPCENTRAL, San Gil, Santander, July 10, 1984.

[22] Conversations with local training personnel of *Plan Padrinos-Cali*, Jamundí, Valle del Cauca, June 12, 1984.

[23] In constructing weighted scores for the priorities listed in table 8.1, I assigned points to each of the six items depending on how often it was mentioned first, second, third, etc. First choice,

TABLE 8.1
Weighted Scores of Priorities Ranked by Colombian Nonprofits, 1984

Priorities	Score
Improving technical and administrative skills of local groups to solve their own socioeconomic problems	132 points
Increasing income levels and/or employment opportunities for the poor	126
Strengthening networks of social participation created and managed by the poor themselves	119
Enhancing the ability of the poor to negotiate more effectively with the significant institutions in their region—e.g., commercial agents, landowners, banks, government agencies, etc.	112
Alleviating the most immediate causes of human suffering (hunger, malnutrition, sickness, lack of potable water or housing, etc.)	85
Helping the poor in their struggle to change the structures of political and economic power in their region	75

Source: Personal interviews.

ranging from traditional relief orientations to more recent technical aspects of training and income generation to wider social and political objectives, such as the promotion of participatory organizations and the implementation of strategies to change the dominant power structures in society. These are the same objectives ranked by respondents in the PVOs/NGOs I interviewed in Europe, Canada, and the United States. Although, as reported in table 5.3, North Atlantic nonprofit representatives (especially those in Europe and Canada) gave considerable weight to the last aspect—namely, changing the current power configurations in Third World societies—it is clear that their Colombian counterparts do not espouse such an emphasis in their work.

Although many of the European and Canadian donor-NGOs surveyed saw a clear link between strengthening networks of participation, enhancing the bargaining ability of the poor, and working to change political and economic structures (fifteen of twenty-nine European and Canadian NGOs in my survey ranked all of these in a cluster as their top three priorities); the Colombian recipients of their aid separated this last and more controversial aspect from the other two. Not only did Colombian nonprofits consistently rank technical and material improvements as their top priorities, but they did not closely associate promoting participatory organizations and bargaining capabilities

six points; second choice, five points; third choice, four points; fourth choice, three points; fifth choice, two points; sixth choice, one point; not applicable or not ranked, zero points.

among the poor with direct attempts to change political and economic structures. In fact, the "political-economic change" priority even ranked behind the "traditional humanitarian" objective—a goal the Colombian nonprofits in my sample no longer give much emphasis.

Of the thirty-two Colombian development nonprofit representatives who responded to this question,[24] over one-third (eleven) did not even rank assisting the poor to change political and economic structures as a goal. None of those from category five in my sample—credit institutions for small merchants or farmers—ranked political and economic change higher than fourth on their list. Four of the five private foundation representatives (category four) did not include it as a priority, and the one person who did listed it fifth. Finally, only one of three representatives of cooperatives (category three), and only four of nine executives in multiservice organizations (category six) included it in their spectrum of objectives.

Of the twenty-one nonprofits who did rank political and economic change as a priority, thirteen mentioned it as one of their top three choices. Nine of these thirteen persons, however, worked for nonprofits in categories one or two in my sample—namely, technical or leadership training organizations and applied research and advocacy institutions. These types of organizations are staffed by those with advanced educational degrees, some of whom continue to hold part-time university teaching positions. Hence, it was more the intellectuals and academics in my sample, rather than those with business backgrounds in foundations or the persons in direct constant contact with the poor in service-delivery organizations, who gave emphasis to a political priority in their work.

It is not surprising that intellectuals are more oriented toward changing the political and economic status quo than business leaders. What is most interesting is that those in Colombian developmental nonprofits engaged in supporting various types of cooperatives (category three), loan programs (category five), and social services (category six) showed very little interest in this objective. Despite the fact that many of the seventeen organizations in these three categories are receiving grants from European and Canadian NGOs who claim to be aiding the poor to change power structures, they themselves, as conduits and overseers of such assistance in Colombia, do not at all define their own goals in these terms. They are also the ones in my Colombian survey who have the most ongoing contact with low-income groups and who do not have a foot in academia or business.

[24] Four nonprofit representatives preferred not to choose among these priorities since they claimed their work purportedly does not fit into such a framework. They were FESCOL; *Coordinación Colombiana de Trabajo Voluntario* (CCTV); *Financiera para el Desarrollo Social* (FINSOCIAL); and *Corporación para la Recreación Popular*. See appendix E for a description of their major activities.

WHY COLOMBIAN NONPROFITS DO NOT THREATEN THE SYSTEM

I would argue that the explanation for a lack of interest in direct challenges to the political or economic system by Colombian developmental nonprofits is in part the fact that the poor whom they serve are not politically radical or aggressive. Rather, they want concrete improvements in the material quality of their lives. Moreover, the system itself does respond to their demands for increased access to resources with some, albeit limited, improvements. There are also some overt, as well as subtle, means of control that those with power in Colombia employ to curb direct challenges to their own interests. Finally, developmental nonprofits themselves seldom act in coordinated fashion since there is much institutional competition and dispersal of energy among them. This limits any potential impact they could have on the political system and dissuades them, as relatively small organizations, from confronting power elites alone on a regular basis.

Limited Objectives of Low-income Groups

In the vast majority of public protests that occurred in Colombia throughout the 1970s and early 1980s, the goals were limited to very specific material grievances. They arose primarily in regions where public services were relatively underdeveloped (medium-sized cities and rural areas in Santander, the Atlantic coast, and the far south). They demanded in nearly 90 percent of the cases potable water, electricity, sewage, good roads, adequate urban and intercity transportation, and properly staffed education facilities. Moreover, these demonstrations tended to be multiclass in nature, since more than one social group was affected by the scarcity of services to a whole area. Hence, such movements did not normally promote a sense of political awareness or solidarity among low-income sectors.[25]

One of the reasons for a year-long truce signed by the Colombian government and four major guerrilla organizations in 1984 was the lack of widespread support among the poor for radical tactics as a means for changing the political and economic system. Although leftist guerrillas had been battling the Colombian army for more than thirty years, and the Defense Ministry acknowledged their numbers to be in the range of thirty thousand, their popular support has never been widespread. In fact, it declined in recent years due to efforts by President Belisario Betancur (1982–1986) to increase housing and educational and job opportunities for the poor.

One interpretation of the left's willingness to lay down its arms in 1984 was that leaders of these militant organizations believed they might better succeed if they mobilized new organizations among low-income sectors that would

---

[25] Santana, *Desarrollo regional*, pp. 134–39.

compete for office and thus break the monopoly of the two dominant parties (Conservative and Liberal). In return, the government itself offered amnesty and land grants to those who laid down their arms and increased the availability of public services in areas where guerrillas have been most active (such as the Magdalena Valley located in Antioquia and Santander).[26]

The truce between the government and major guerrilla organizations was not renewed in 1985, and since then violence has erupted, largely as a result of assassinations carried out against leftist leaders by right-wing terrorists during the cease fire. The guerrillas, however, have yet to gain sufficient support of the rural or urban poor to establish a revolutionary force capable of overthrowing the government. The goals of low-income sectors, amidst mounting violence and terrorism, continue to focus on limited material improvement in their life-style rather than radical political change.

Clientelistic Strategies of Government

Offering the poor some material benefits and services rather than granting them significant input into decision-making has long characterized the policies of the Colombian government in the face of popular unrest. These have succeeded in preventing significant and sustained mobilization of low-income groups in opposition to the regime.

In the aftermath of the period of the widespread *violencia*, which ended in 1958 when the two parties formed a pact to share office for 26 years thereafter (the National Front), bipartisan administrations in the 1960s initiated a series of social reforms that included accelerated housing and school construction, increased teacher training, expanded public health clinics, and a tax burden shifted toward the rich. They also established a network of community action boards (*juntas de acción comunal*) throughout the country to participate in the implementation of government services. These boards were to petition for service programs from local public agencies, help oversee their administration, and stimulate self-help projects at the local level to complement and extend their reach.[27]

A major goal of such efforts at "reform from above" was to pacify rural areas in which violence had been severe. They also were to prevent Marxist guerrilla movements from reorienting what had been spasmodic and feudlike conflicts into a significant revolutionary movement with class overtones. When these new community organizations in rural areas began to overstep their original purpose in the mid-1960s and focus on wider and more contro-

[26] Interviews with Rev. Manuel Uribe, S.J., CINEP; Guillermo Jaramillo Restrepo, *Futuro para la Niñez.*
[27] Dix, *Colombia*, chap. 6.

versial issues such as land reform, the government quickly imposed tight centralized control over their operation and finances.[28]

These neighborhood organizations have continued to operate, and by 1979 there were thirty thousand *juntas* in the country (80 percent in rural areas), which included 2.2 million persons on their boards or in their ongoing committee activities. Throughout the course of various development plans in the 1970s and early 1980s,[29] over thirty thousand public service projects were constructed by the government in collaboration with these local community action boards, including schools, health clinics, public housing, water and sewage systems, and credit and public employment programs.[30]

Despite these increased services and continued economic growth throughout the 1970s, the net share of income of the bottom 40 percent of the population did not change (remaining at about 10 percent). A trend towards greater capital-intensive economic strategies in both agriculture and industry and the continuation of an elite-dominated political system maintained the skewed distribution of benefits toward the middle and upper classes.[31] However, the fact that some services and employment opportunities did "trickle down" to low-income groups kept these sectors from mounting any sustained opposition to the power structure.

Broker Role of Nonprofits

In my interviews with Colombian nonprofit representatives and during my field visits to grass-roots organizations, I found that both central office personnel and project leaders stress the improvements that had occurred in the ma-

[28] Bagley and Edel, "Popular Mobilization Programs," pp. 259–69.

[29] The development plan of President Misael Pastrana Borrero (1970–1974)—*Las Cuatro Estrategias*—included expanding housing investment, greater land distribution, and more progressive taxation policies so as to pay for these increased public services. The program of President Alfonso López Michelsen (1974–1978)—*Para Cerrar la Brecha*—aimed at creating new productive employment among the poorest 50 percent in Colombia by expanding rural and urban credit, food subsidies, educational and health programs, and family services. The four-year plan of President Julio César Turbay Ayala (1978–1982)—*Plan de Integración Nacional*—emphasized construction of more effective transportation and communication systems and some decentralization of services. The development plan of President Belisario Betancur Cuartos (1982–1986)—*Cambio con Equidad*—gave priority to low-income housing without down-payments by recipients, extension of educational opportunities outside the classroom, and the creation of new jobs in small businesses. Parra Escobar, *La economía colombiana*, pp. 72–92; *La República*, August 7, 1984, C1, C2.

[30] Fundación para la Educación Superior y Desarrollo (FEDESARROLLO), *Desarrollo Social*, pp. 132–33.

[31] Throughout the 1970s, the bottom 40 percent of the population in Colombia continued to receive 10 percent of national income, while the top 10 percent (upper class) received 45 percent, the next 20 percent (middle class) enjoyed 25 percent, and the final 30 percent in the lower-middle class and upper sectors of the working class received 20 percent. Berry and Sligo, "Distribution of Income in Colombia."

terial quality of life of the poor as a result of the projects they supported. A great deal of the credibility of the nonprofits in Colombia, in fact, depends on their meeting immediate needs of low-income sectors in health, education, credit, and basic infrastructure and on showing the local communities how these services can be maintained. Part of the strategy of Colombian development nonprofits is to act as brokers between local communities and government agencies, precisely to enhance the sustainability of such services when the nonprofit sector itself is no longer able to provide aid.

Twenty-eight of the thirty-six nonprofits in my sample (78 percent) indicated that they try to act as mediators between recipients of their aid and local government representatives or that they try to convince public agencies to expand public services for the poor. Eighteen nonprofit spokespersons (50 percent of my sample) indicated that they have had some success in getting government officials to listen to their advice or to expand public services on behalf of the poor in a particular locale. Hence, while these respondents indicated they shunned formal linkages with local political parties, they have no hesitation in working with established powers in the political and economic system on an ad hoc basis to enhance material benefits for their clients.

The *Fundación Carvajal* in Cali, a leading philanthropic foundation set up by the business sector in the 1960s to aid the poor, has been successful in getting the municipal government to give tax breaks for the small established businesses it assists. It has also convinced some large corporations in Cali to set up a free advisory service for these small enterprises. The AITEC is working with the Secretariat for Popular Integration in the office of the president, which coordinates public services for low-income areas in twenty-four cities in the country, to get this agency to channel some resources into credit and training for street merchants and small family businesses that operate out of homes. *Futuro para la Niñez* in Medellín has a representative on an interinstitutional committee in Antioquia made up of six different national and departmental government agencies. The nonprofit representative on the committee informs the others of the needs of the various rural villages where *Futuro para la Niñez* is training community organizers and tries to obtain more public services for these areas. SEPAS of San Gil has convinced the national government credit agency, FINACIACOOP, to make an exception in its policies (requiring borrowers to have an income of $19,000) and allow smaller cooperatives in Santander (federated in COOPCENTRAL) to be eligible for public loans.

A confirmation of this nonconflictual brokering strategy of nonprofits vis-à-vis the Colombian power structure is the fact that in very few instances have there been serious tensions between nonprofit developmental organizations and government and business elites. Only eight of thirty-six organizations in my sample (22.2 percent) indicated that they had experienced *any* conflicts or tensions in recent years with powerful public or private institutions in their respective regions as a result of the work. Moreover, seven of these eight said that they had suffered no serious limitations on their operations as a result of such tensions. In almost all cases when problems do arise, they are solved through dialogue or mutual accommodation.

Government Response to Confrontation: Co-optation or Repression

Even when local community organizations that remain free of party or government clientelism do engage in pressure tactics or mount public protests, they have not produced any fundamental reordering of power in society. A major factor in accounting for this has been the ability of the government to respond to some of their demands for increased services or to blunt their effectiveness with repressive strategies. Out of 128 cases of significant public protest in the 1970s, thirty-five culminated in agreements with government agencies that fully granted demands for increased services, and seventeen others produced negotiations that led to partial fulfillment of popular requests. Hence, in 40 percent of the cases government concessions were made. In these cases, regional and local protest movements subsided once government response was positive.

In forty-five other cases (35.2 percent), however, the government used a variety of repressive measures to put down protests, including massive detentions, military occupation of neighborhoods or regions, direct physical force against protesters, or takeover of the grass-roots organizations themselves. In thirty-six of those forty-five cases, arrests of significant numbers of persons occurred—in some cases surpassing one hundred individuals—and in twelve instances these confrontations resulted in physical injuries or even deaths.[32]

[32] Santana, *Desarrollo regional*, p. 155. One large organization that participated in several of these *paros cívicos* in the 1970s, and which experienced mounting repression from the government, was the *Asociación Nacional de Usuarios Campesinos* (ANUC)—a federation of about five hundred rural associations with nearly one million members who receive rural public services or assistance in credit, storage, extension, and marketing. Similar to the community action boards established in the 1960s, ANUC was set up in 1970 to organize the rural poor from above and give them a greater sense of loyalty to the system by allowing them some participation in the local regulation and management of the services they receive.

Although organized in an extremely hierarchical fashion with its national structures and finances controlled by vertical government agencies, ANUC groups at the local level gradually became more militant. They began to demand expropriation of large estates without indemnification, nationalization of credit, and legal recognition of peasant invasions of large vacant farms. Land invasions were, in fact, orchestrated by ANUC leaders throughout 1971 and 1972 in several rural departments where small farmers and landless peasants were being squeezed out by expanding, capital-intensive agribusinesses. Even after the government cut off all subsidies, removed some of ANUC's national leaders, and created parallel peasant organizations, protests continued and expanded into civic strikes, consumer boycotts, and work stoppages. ANUC groups stayed fiercely independent of party patronage, however, and imposed membership fees on participants. They thus became more autonomous of manipulation by the political and economic establishment

The demonstrations that ended peacefully and produced partial or full accords were situations in which no significant new investments had been made by government agencies. These focused on limitations of, or prices for, existing services, such as electricity and urban or intercity transportation. Issues that led to government intransigence and which tended toward extended confrontation and ultimately repression involved demands for significant new public investments or a reordering of set priorities—such as the construction of new facilities for potable water and highways or the reorientation of regional development plans (decided by government agencies and the largest property owners or commercial investors in rural and urban areas).[33]

In my own interviews with nonprofit representatives, I discovered that those organizations that had engaged in significant public protests or that had used other means to challenge the power structure experienced the same pattern of elite response—either some limited achievement of goals or overt repression. In neither situation did sustained political mobilization of the participants occur.

In January 1984 in Santander, for example, four thousand peasants—belonging to various popular organizations and cooperatives set up by SEPAS of San Gil during the 1970s—blocked the main highway between Bogotá and Bucaramanga, the departmental capital, and staged an invasion of unused private land in Charalá. They also sent a group to Bucaramanga, which seized the departmental capitol building. Peasant leaders had attempted through previous conversations with government officials to get them to fulfill long-standing promises regarding land reform in Charalá and aid to tobacco and hemp producers throughout the region. When such dialogue produced no action, peasants resorted to massive protest and indicated they would paralyze services in fifty municipalities if the government did not respond to their demands.

Within three days the government agreed to buy five large farms in Charalá, distribute twelve hundred hectares (twenty-nine hundred acres) to landless peasants, fix minimum prices for tobacco, and renew its contract to purchase hemp from local producers when prices were low.[34] Representatives of the peasant organizations were subsequently invited to Bogotá by President Betancur to discuss with him and cabinet members other needs of the area.

Although land reform did not go beyond the limited area of five farms, and although the government after the demonstration was slow to renew its pur-

than were the community action boards. Under such circumstances, the government resorted to more severe means of control. Bureaucratic noncooperation in service delivery, legal harassment, and jailings became commonplace by the mid-1970s. Several ANUC leaders (including a member of the national board) were assassinated by local party bosses and large landowners. Bagley and Edel, "Popular Mobilization Programs," pp. 270–80.

[33] Santana, *Desarrollo regional*, p. 156.
[34] "Acuerdo entre 'el Común,' " p. 1.

chase of hemp from local farmers suffering from depressed prices, the civic strike was short-lived. It did not lead to any sustained political action or linkages with leftist parties or guerrilla groups—both of which were present in nearby locales. The peasant leaders and participants of the protest were satisfied with the publicity and quick, respectful attention they received from high government officials and with at least partial fulfillment of their demands.

Reverend Ramón González Parra, the director of SEPAS of San Gil, told me in an interview in mid-1984 that this twenty-year experience in working to form cooperatives and train peasant leaders in the region convinced him that the rural poor in Colombia are not politically radical. He claimed that they are easily satisfied when the system makes at least some positive response to their demands, however piecemeal:

> It took a long time for peasant leaders in Santander to get to a position where they decided to demonstrate publicly demanding the implementation of existing land reform legislation. Last January when some moved in and started planting on a few vacant farms in Charalá, and others marched on the highway or seized the capitol, it was their own decision, not mine nor that of SEPAS. However, peasants are conservative in the sense that they do not move quickly to the next stage. They are pleased with their victory and not about to push for any fundamental political changes in the region.[35]

The government uses repressive tactics when it considers mobilization strategies by nonprofits threatening to the long-range stability of the status quo. The CINEP, the Jesuit-sponsored research and advocacy organization in Bogotá, has provided training for thirty-thousand peasants in various rural areas including Santander, Cauca, Huila, Caquetá, and the Atlantic coast. It has also provided assistance to 250 grass-roots urban organizations and base communities of the Catholic Church with a total membership of five thousand persons. In 1981 four of its staff members were arrested (including two priests). They were accused by the military of collaborating with guerrilla organizations active in Cauca, Huila, and Caquetá among the same peasants where CINEP was offering training courses. Although no formal charges were ever brought, they remained in jail for six months, and the bishops publicly disassociated the Church from the work of CINEP. After the incident, domestic private contributions to CINEP declined (forcing it to search for more foreign assistance), and bomb threats from anonymous phone callers arrived regularly at its headquarters in Bogotá.[36]

The hierarchy also exercises close vigilance over other church-related nonprofit organizations that engage in community organizing. SEPAS of San Gil is the social action agency of the Diocese of Socorro and San Gil in Santander

[35] Interview with Rev. Ramón González Parra, SEPAS of San Gil.
[36] Interview with Rev. Alejandro Angulo, CINEP.

and one of the most progressive of the various church-sponsored social action agencies in the country. It periodically holds meetings for church personnel from other dioceses engaged in leadership training and economic development among peasants. It shares with them its strategies and success stories. Some bishops are wary of these and other meetings with similar agendas, such as those sponsored by the Jesuit-supported *Instituto Maior Campesino* (IMCA) in Buga or CINEP in Bogotá. These bishops will not allow priests or laity from their own service organizations to attend such gatherings.

On one occasion in 1983, when SEPAS of San Gil had also invited a representative from a local church organization in Nicaragua sympathetic to the Sandinistas to participate in one of its conferences, the prestigious and conservative Cardinal of Medellín, Alfonso López Trujillo, phoned the bishop of Socorro and San Gil and tried to stop the meeting on grounds that it would be political and subversive. It is also common knowledge that progressive priests in many dioceses of Colombia who become active in promoting autonomous grass-roots movements among the rural or urban poor are moved quite frequently from parish to parish. This is done to limit possible political repercussions of their work for the church and to discourage priestly involvement in controversial social action.[37]

Through a variety of means, the power elite of Colombia in government, business, and the church can control challenges to the political and economic system made from below by autonomous grass-roots organizations. Using various forms of co-optation or repression, those with political, social, and religious authority have thus far been able to prevent any serious and sustained challenge to the status quo from popular sectors. In such a context, neither the attitudes nor actions of the majority of low-income groups are radical. Nor are the strategies of nonprofit developmental organizations working among them geared to challenging the system substantially.

Lack of Coordination among Nonprofits

A final factor that reduces the likelihood that the developmental nonprofit sector will mount a serious political challenge to government, party, or business

[37] Interviews with Rev. Ramón González Parra, SEPAS of San Gil; Rev. Gonzalo Castro, S.J., SEPAS of Pasto; Luz Zuluaga de Díaz, CARITAS of Cali. The Catholic Church in Colombia is still legally established by the constitution (written in 1886) and has one of the most conservative hierarchies in Latin America. While instituting a variety of social service programs for the poor since the 1960s, the bishops have never endorsed the formation of lay-led local base communities (*comunidades eclesiales de base*, CEBs) that bishops in Central America, Brazil, Chile, Peru, and Paraguay have supported in the post–Vatican II (1962–1965) and post-Medellín (1968) era. The bishops have also used their disciplinary power to curb public dissent within the Colombian church and have been quick to denounce publicly any efforts by clergy or laity to form linkages with leftist movements. Wilde, "The Contemporary Church." See also Levine, *Religion and Politics in Latin America.*

leaders is a lack of coordination. Currently there are approximately two hundred major nonprofit organizations assisting low-income sectors in Colombia. There is, however, no national organization that acts as a coordinating link among them or any significant sharing of information or strategies throughout the nonprofit community.

In my own sample of developmental nonprofits, four-fifths (twenty-nine of thirty-six) indicated that they maintained some cooperative links with other comparable organizations. The most common type of collaboration, however, tended to be ad hoc arrangements—sporadic meetings, exchanges of bulletins, some limited collaboration for specific projects. Nearly 90 percent of the respondents (twenty-three of twenty-six) indicated that the cooperation among development nonprofits was, however, very insufficient.

Different reasons were given for this lack of systematic cooperation—insufficient time, money, or information about one another; diversity of scope and function within the development nonprofit sector; the difficulty for small and relatively new organizations to coordinate their activities. The most common reasons given, however, and mentioned by over half of those asked (fifteen of twenty-six), involved competition, institutional jealousy, and concerns with "protecting one's turf."

The head of CODESARROLLO, an applied research institute in Medellín, emphasized the protective attitude Colombian nonprofits take toward their own programs and funding sources, which they are afraid of losing through mutual collaboration: "Each nonprofit wants to promote its own program. They lack facility in making joint decisions and sharing information about their financial resources."[38]

The Director of the Social Division of the *Fundación para Educación Superior*, a nonprofit that both supports social service programs among the poor and acts as investment company to multiply the assets of other nonprofits, pointed to the strong individualism and isolationism that characterizes development nonprofits in Colombia:

Cooperation is difficult to achieve among nonprofits. A strong individualism prevails in Colombia, and collaboration is foreign to our culture. People don't believe in it. Moreover, cooperative ventures among the poor have often failed, faring better among middle-class professionals.

We try to support multi-institutional projects with our matching grants but have not had much success. In the health area, for example, we are supporting four programs in primary health care run by nonprofits. Each group says its own philosophy is better.[39]

The one effort made in recent years toward forming a consortium among development nonprofits in Colombia failed for these reasons. The Office of

[38] Interview with Luis Alberto Gómez Ramírez, CODESARROLLO.
[39] Interview with Dr. Alex Cobo, *Fundación para la Educación Superior*.

Interinstitutional Cooperation (OCIT), set up in 1978 with foreign private funding, included seventeen nonprofit organizations engaged in a wide variety of development activities including research, training, education, and support for grass-roots service projects. Its goals were to promote greater uniformity and integration of program criteria, policies, and objectives; facilitate the exchange of development experiences and methodologies; effect a more rational utilization of local and international resources; and stimulate the development of collaborative projects.[40]

By the early 1980s, OCIT had ceased to function effectively. This was due partly to the heterogeneity of focus and methodology of members, and partly to the unwillingness of foreign donor nonprofits to pay many of the administrative costs identified as joint priorities by the members (common secretarial, accounting, reproduction, computer, travel, and employment services).[41] The most critical debilitating factor, however—which caused a breakdown of OCIT, according to Miguel Gómez, its former executive secretary—was a fear that coordination would cause a loss of funding for individual members obsessed with institutional identity and self-preservation: "There was a certain institutional jealousy among the groups. They were reluctant to share all their data for fear of losing their foreign financial support. Each did not want the other to know the source and the amount of foreign money it was receiving."[42]

Hence, concern for institutional identity and financial secrecy has thus far militated against any effective widespread collaboration among Colombian development nonprofits. This lack of cooperation is one more factor preventing a more concerted and sustained effort by these approximately two hundred institutions to confront the political system. They are relatively small units, and, without more collaboration, they are vulnerable to both co-optive and repressive strategies by the state.

BENEFITS TO THE COLOMBIAN PUBLIC SECTOR FROM DEVELOPMENTAL NONPROFITS

Not only are developmental nonprofits not a major threat to the political or economic status quo in Colombia, they actually enhance it. In addition to acting as mediators between government agencies and local groups, they serve as gap fillers when there are no public services available for low-income groups.

In the two geographical areas that I visited where Colombian development nonprofits are having the most visible and widespread impact—the southern part of Santander in the northeast and Tumaco on the southwest Pacific coast—they are clearly surrogates for the government. There is a wide variety of so-

[40] Hellinger, "Consortia Experience," pp. 11–12.
[41] Ibid., p. 13.
[42] Interview with Miguel Gómez, CRS.

cial services being offered both by SEPAS of San Gil in southern Santander and by *Plan Padrinos–Tumaco*, as well as by the spinoff organizations from both. In 1984 they had annual budgets of $253,351 and $1.2 million respectively, and for a long time have been the only sources of effective aid to surrounding residents in credit, training, health, and education. They are not third-party contractors for government agencies. Nor have they stimulated effective government responses to the needs of the populace in these two very poor areas of the country despite their long and serious commitment—since 1963 by *SEPAS* of San Gil, and since 1971 by *Plan Padrinos–Tumaco*. In these remote regions, government has been content to let nonprofits (well funded from abroad) fill in the gaps where its own service delivery system is weak or nonexistent.

In all seven departments that I visited, it was clear that even when government services were available they were often not designed to meet the needs of those living at or below the minimum wage level. For example, many of the specialized agencies created by the national government in the 1960s and 1970s to carry out agrarian and tax reforms, as well as new social services, gave large businesses and landholders a definitive voice in policy implementation. While this guaranteed important elite support for such reform efforts, it has also blunted their distributive impact.[43]

Much of the focus of the various development plans of the four presidential administrations between 1970 and 1986 (see footnote 29) has been on infrastructural assistance, credit, or subsidies that primarily benefit those with the greatest productive assets rather than the poorest groups in a target area. For example, the vast majority of funds available for credit and training under the Integrated Rural Development (DRI) and National Nutritional (PAN) programs begun in 1974 aided large farmers rather than the 47 percent of the agrarian population who own seven and a half acres of land or less. The National Integration Plan (PIN), begun in 1978, concentrated on the expansion of rural infrastructure (roads, irrigation, electricity), which primarily helps those who are linked to large national markets not small farmers.[44]

Although the government of Belisario Betancur (1982–1986) made greater employment and housing opportunities for low-income sectors two priorities in its own development plan, the poorest 40 percent of the population did not benefit substantially from such commitments. Very little new government resources were allocated for programs assisting small businesses. The administration earmarked those that were for established entrepreneurs in the lower middle classes with fixed places of business and some patrimony—not for those who make up the vast majority of the rural or urban poor who have little

---

[43] Hartlyn, "Producer Associations, the Political Regime, and Policy Processes."

[44] Bagley, "National Front and Beyond"; Parra Escobar, *La economía colombiana*, pp. 67–97; Speck, *Colombia*.

or no capital and who often are migrant workers or street merchants engaged in petty commerce.

Although the Betancur government also committed itself to construct four hundred thousand new housing units during its term of office and eliminated the requirement for an initial down payment of 30 percent of total cost, the price of even the cheapest publicly financed housing was nearly $7,900 per unit because the government continued to rely on private savings and loan associations and construction companies to implement its plan. As a result, these new dwelling units were well beyond the reach of the 40 percent of the population earning $1,477 or less annually.

In both credit and housing, therefore, nonprofits continued to act as surrogates for government among the hard-core poor despite new commitments by policymakers in the mid-1980s to do more for the poor on each of these fronts. The only institutions that take the risk in providing credit to those in subsistence agriculture or petty commerce (where the majority of hard-core poor are employed) are nonprofit organizations (with support from international PVOs/ NGOs). These institutions assist groups of self-employed workers or farmers at or below the minimum wage level with loans of up to $211 and with training and advice in management techniques appropriate for their small business ventures.

Over two-thirds of current urban housing in Colombia (especially among slum dwellers) is constructed by residents themselves and not purchased from construction companies. By 1984 there were over seven hundred community housing groups engaged in self-help housing. They get little or no public assistance for the construction but do receive help from nonprofit organizations in the areas of information, technical advice, legal aid, subsidized credit, and low-cost materials. The total cost of the most expensive house built under such circumstances in 1984 was under $3,166, and a prefabricated model was under $633.[45]

BENEFITS TO THE PROFITMAKING SECTOR BY DEVELOPMENTAL NONPROFITS IN COLOMBIA

There is a tradition of substantial philanthropy in Colombia relative to other countries of Latin America. Legislation in effect between the late 1950s and mid-1970s allowed the total amount donated to nonprofit organizations by individuals or corporations to be tax deductible. This stimulated the creation of several large foundations by corporations in various parts of Colombia in the 1960s and early 1970s, which channeled private resources into services for low-income sectors of the population.

---

[45] Santana Rodríguez and Casasbuenas Morales, "Hacia una política de vivienda popular en Colombia," p. 222; Sorock, "Self-Help Housing in Colombia," p. 49.

The earliest activities of such organizations were in the construction and maintenance of recreational facilities, but in recent years most have shifted more of their focus on longer-term structural programs in areas of low-income housing and credit for small businesses. In the early 1980s fourteen received substantial loans (from $330,000 to $550,000) from the Inter-American Development Bank (IDB) to provide credit and training to small entrepreneurs in Colombia.

The assistance such foundations provide, however, is not aimed at the poorest sectors of the Colombian population—the bottom 40 percent who live below the minimum wage level. Loans for housing construction and small business development by these foundations, as with government policies in these areas, assist those already possessing stable employment and a minimum of capital.

The loans to small businesses provided by these Colombian foundations are limited by requirements set down by the IDB. Eligibility is limited to enterprises in the production (not commercial) sector, and in 1983 these had to have fixed locations of business and a patrimony not exceeding $12,656. The average loan in 1984 was in the vicinity of $1,266 to $1,583. The vast majority of those in 1984 at the minimum wage level ($1,477 per year) or below who constitute the hard-core poor are in subsistence agriculture or engaged in urban enterprises not covered by IDB loan requirements. The poorest in cities have no fixed places of business since they work out of their own homes or on the street. They are also not involved in small-scale industry (as required by the IDB) but in commerce—selling small artifacts or food. Moreover, they have little or no patrimony, and in 1984 most had the financial capacity of repaying loans of about $211 maximum.

With the aid of both private domestic philanthropy and long-term, low-interest loans from the IDB, Colombian foundations set up by corporations are expanding their own fixed capital. Although they give credit to small established businesses that do not have access to regular commercial channels due to their risk profiles, the beneficiaries are not among the poorest in Colombia operating at the subsistence level or below. They are in the upper sectors of the working class or in the lower-middle class. They are not only much less of a credit risk than the hard-core poor, but their potential for stimulating demand for goods and capital from larger businesses is greater than those operating at the margins of, or outside, the regular market economy of the country.

The potential benefit to the established profitmaking sector by these relatively well-off poor is much larger than that of the bottom 40 percent. Hence, private foundations set up by corporate philanthropy in Colombia prefer to channel their assistance to groups who will add to the growth of the established business sector more quickly and reliablly.

In contrast, the development nonprofits that are servicing those who constitute the majority of the poor in subsistence agriculture or in urban petty commerce are organizations that continue to rely on international PVO/NGOs for their main source of support. For example, institutions such as *Crédito Familiar* of *Parroquia Nuestra Señora de Esperanza, Banco Mundial de la Mujer-Cali*, and FUNDAEC (all three in Cali) assist groups of self-employed workers or farmers at or below the minimum wage level with loans of up to $211. These were to be repaid at normal interest rates of 23 percent (in 1984). Such institutions also provide training and advice in management techniques appropriate for small businesses.

Unlike the IDB grants to the larger Colombian foundations, however, the international PVOs/NGOs (such as AITEC, CRS, the Women's World Bank, and PACT) that support these indigenous nonprofits made grants (not loans) in 1984 in the vicinity of $31,600 to $52,780. The IDB assistance, although substantially more, is not only in the form of loans that must be repaid, but it does not go to those Colombian nonprofits working with the smallest entrepreneurs in greatest financial need and who constitute the majority of the poor.

What is clear, therefore, is that developmental nonprofits in Colombia that assist the hard-core poor complement very well the work of government, private business, and intergovernmental organizations; and they do so at little economic cost to these other sectors. For the Colombian government, they are gap fillers for public service agencies. For the business community and the IDB, they take care of those who, from an economic perspective, are in high-risk categories and not likely to enhance significantly in the near future the production capacities of the country (and profits for the established private sector). Thus, government, business, and the IDB can focus their own resources on those with modest incomes who are more likely to contribute significantly to GNP growth rates in the short term if given some additional services or credit. They also can do so knowing that the poorest whom they are not aiding (the bottom 40 percent) are being taken care of by small development nonprofits.

Hence, in Colombia development nonprofits not only seldom attempt to mobilize the poor to confront political or economic elites, they also enhance social stability by meeting some of the basic needs of those who do not benefit significantly from the system. In so doing they actually lessen pressure on government, business, and multilateral agencies to do more for the poor in Colombia, and thus reduce the likelihood that the hard-core poor will become frustrated enough to confront the system with radical political strategies.

RELATIONS BETWEEN COLOMBIAN NONPROFITS AND INTERNATIONAL PVOs/ NGOs

If the activities of indigenous developmental nonprofits are not significantly challenging the political or economic status quo in Colombia, why do foreign private donor organizations (especially overtly political NGOs in Europe and

Canada) fund their activities? There are a series of factors explaining continuing foreign support. These include underdeveloped evaluation and reporting mechanisms between recipient and donor nonprofits, the paucity of overseas field representatives of North Atlantic nonprofits, the at least implicit change-oriented potential of the projects, and the need of donor PVOs/NGOs to have dependable counterparts in developing countries to use the money they are raising on programs that provide some concrete benefits for the poor.

Underdeveloped Evaluation Procedures

Despite the progress made in the early 1980s on project evaluation techniques, these processes are still at a very nascent stage of development in Colombia. One-quarter (nine of thirty-six) of the nonprofits in my Colombian sample in 1984 carried out very little evaluation of the projects they support at the grassroots level. Moreover, those that do conduct evaluations use very informal methods—conversations, casual visits, brief progress reports written by the project participants themselves. Another one-quarter contract periodically with outside professionals to do formal evaluations, but not on regular basis.

The vast majority of Colombian development nonprofits (including those who sporadically use experts) rely primarily on self-evaluations by project recipients and brief reports of their own staff personnel. Given the time and personnel constraints on these nonprofits, such studies often do not follow any consistent framework, nor is the information systematized. None of the thirty-six organizations I interviewed carried out or contracted for impact audits that assessed the amount and quality of changes occuring in the wider environment as a result of the projects they sponsored at the grass-roots level, including assessments of political consequences or economic spillover effects.

A representatiave of *Grupo* PROJECTOS, one of the two screening nonprofits in my sample (the other being CENPRODES), which has assisted over five hundred local projects in Colombia obtain European and Canadian nonprofit funding since its creation in 1974, indicated that part of the reason for insufficient project evaluations in Colombia is the fault of the foreign PVOs/NGOs who give the money: "We have done some evaluation of projects, but these are usually self-evaluations done by recipient groups themselves in which we collaborate. The donor agencies abroad have no clear evaluation criteria and leave groups free to do their own. We have had only three external evaluations done, and in each case we hired a professional."[46]

Moreover, there are tacit agreements between recipient and donor organizations that any information considered politically sensitive by Colombia nonprofits can be omitted in reports sent to North Atlantic nonprofit agencies. The purpose is to assure confidentiality and to minimize the dangers of governments using such written documents to launch derogatory campaigns against

---

[46] Interview with Humberto Rojas, *Grupo* PROJECTOS.

Colombian nonprofit organizations or the beneficiaries of their aid at the grass-roots level.

Scarcity of PVO/NGO Representatives in Colombia

Most PVOs/NGOs have no field representatives in Colombia. They rely on Colombian development nonprofits to advise them on what grass-roots projects to support and also to handle both reporting procedures and the evaluations that do occur. Only six of the forty-five PVOs/NGOs in my North Atlantic sample have personnel stationed in Colombia (three Americans, two Europeans, and one Canadian) to oversee the work they support. Home-office project officers of the others usually make trips to Colombia once a year but are not able to do in-depth analyses of projects. The combination of allowing maximum flexibility in project reporting and evaluation and a lack of continual on-site presence in Colombia by PVOs/NGOs allows perception gaps between the reality of the actual projects and the expectations of executives and staffs in the home offices of foreign donor agencies. Although those in foreign donor organizations (particularly in Europe and Canada) may hope to be promoting significant political and economic change in Colombia, they simply do not have sufficient information to confirm (or challenge) their expectations.

Long-Range Change Potential of Projects

As described earlier, there probably are implicit, if indirect, long-range political consequences of the work of many of the development nonprofits in Colombia. They support autonomous grass-roots organizations free of the clientelistic structures maintained by the dominant political parties and the government. These organizations are also providing training for new grass-roots leaders, as well as networking among them through regional meetings, workshops, and publications. In some instances, this has resulted in the formation of labor or cooperative federations (USITRAS and COOPCENTRAL in Santander) involving close to a quarter of a million participants. Even in smaller business and credit associations, participants are gaining self-confidence and enhancing their bargaining skills vis-à-vis local government agencies or commercial middlemen. Over the long haul, such type of activities could have an important impact on the political and economic status quo as now constituted.

These developmental nonprofits who act as intermediaries between foreign donor PVOs/NGOs and grass-roots organizations in Colombia are themselves often staffed by academics, professionals, and clerics who do have an agenda of furthering greater equity for low-income groups, but they must proceed in a cautious and piecemeal fashion. Given the configuration of economic and political power in Colombia, more confrontational approaches are not likely to succeed—as witnessed in the repression by the state of those *paros cívicos* demanding substantial redistributional policies, the absence of radical political attitudes among those in the bottom 40 percent in income, and the failure of an effective reform movement in politics beyond the two-party system. Hence, those progressive sectors of the Colombian middle class that work in development nonprofits can present themselves and their organizations to foreign PVOs/NGOs as the most feasible alternatives to develop the capacities of the poor to change the system, albeit slowly, from below.

Need for Foreign Donor Organizations to Work within the Restraints of the System

Finally, foreign nonprofits themselves—especially European and Canadian NGOs—need a plausible cover to pursue their own political goals. They cannot directly fund organizations in Colombia or any Third World country that have as their objective significant and sustained political mobilization of low-income groups. The vast majority of the poor in Colombia are not attracted to such strategies, and will only participate in programs that have some chance of improving in the short run their own material standard of living.

In short, foreign donor nonprofits need counterparts in Colombia who can operate within the constraints of the political and economic system. They are not in a position, as foreigners, to create new Colombian organizations in their own image, nor in the short run recast either the mentality of the poor or the power configurations of the country—even if their own long-range aspirations are to alter both of these patterns substantially. They must also show their own home governments and most private benefactors who subsidize them some evidence that socioeconomic improvement for the poor is occuring as a result of the projects they are supporting through intermediary counterparts in Colombia.

For all of these reasons, gaps exist between the more radical political preferences of many donor NGO executives and staffs in Europe and Canada and the actual impact of the grass-roots projects they support through Colombian development nonprofits. Over the long term, the piecemeal and indirect change that is occurring may precipitate more widespread economic equity, greater political participation, and better government services for the poor in Colombia. In the short-run, however, no perceptible change is occurring in larger economic and political structures because of the work of the international private aid network. It is for this reason that the network is allowed by the Colombian government to support and administer development programs in that country.

All Affected Groups in Colombia Gain Something

Each of the major groups on the receiving end of this private aid network in Colombia are gaining from its activities in the short term. The hard-core poor are receiving material resources and services not otherwise available to them, and without sustained confrontations with or political co-optation by power elites. Public policymakers are relieved of some of their responsibilities to deliver services to marginal groups both difficult to reach and politically inert or disaffected. The business community faces less pressure to direct its philanthropy to those low-income sectors where potential for adding to the production capacities of the profitmaking sector are less clear in the short-run and who are also incapable of managing large sums of assistance. Indigenous nonprofits in Colombia are given a rationale for existence by filling needed gaps in the economic system. They, in turn, provide both employment opportunities and a space for social action for idealistic sectors of the middle class frustrated with the constraints operating on larger economic and political institutions.

Rather than presenting a challenge to power configurations in Colombia, in the short run the international private aid network provides support for many of their dynamics. Even in helping those not benefiting from the system (the poor) or those hoping to change it (middle class reformists), private foreign aid is relieving some of the pressures on it. It channels potential dissent into economically constructive activities that in the short run are system-maintenance in their effect. The long-range implications of such activities remain to be seen. Those with predominant economic and political power, however, are not concerned about the possible future threats that private aid may create, so long as such aid and the development nonprofits it supports in Colombia are currently serving some of their own immediate interests.

DEVELOPMENTAL NONPROFITS IN OTHER LATIN AMERICAN CONTEXTS

Developmental nonprofits play important roles in several over Latin American countries whose regimes—authoritarian, revolutionary, one-party, redemocratizing—are different from that of Colombia. In these other cases, although nonprofit organizations play a political role that includes some opposition to government policies, they also serve some interests of public policymakers as well. Moreover, there are tacit or formal boundary lines that they may not cross in their actions without incurring a series of restrictions or penalties from government.

Authoritarian Military Regimes (Post-1973 Chile and Brazil, 1964–1985)

In these two cases, indigenous nonprofits (with significant aid from international private organizations) expanded their role to include a variety of economic, legal, and social services for the poor and for those bearing the brunt of repression. They provided a haven for dissident intellectuals by creating private research institutes that provided a critical perspective on regime policies. They offered employment and political opportunities for middle-class opponents to these regimes unable to find work or engage in overt opposition to these respective military governments. They often were a source of information for international human rights organizations or other foreign critics of repressive political and economic policies of their respective governments.[47]

Despite such activities, however, indigenous nonprofits provided no major threat to the stability of the respective military regimes in Chile and Brazil. In fact, in some ways they served the interests of those in power. The social services they provided to low-income sectors relieved the respective governments from taking care of groups not part of their core support base. Legal aid by nonprofits to those under arrest or to families of the disappeared also relieved the military governments from a humanitarian task they did not want to handle themselves.

Moreover, nonprofit organizations were often staffed by middle-class opponents of the regimes. They thus channeled the energies of dissidents into constructive gap-filling functions that at least indirectly enhanced regime stability. If such dissidents did not have these outlets, they might have been tempted to search for more radical and violent modes of expressing their dissatisfaction with regime policies.

Both the social service activities and intellectual research programs carried out by indigenous nonprofits were circumscribed by clear (if tacit) boundary lines established by government policymakers. No political mobilization of the poor to oppose openly regime policies was permitted in the nonprofit sector. All intellectual activities carried out by private research centers had to be of high academic caliber and manifest no explicit partisan orientation. If these rules of the game were violated, repressive measures were employed by the governments to curb or forbid continued activities by such nonprofits—including expulsion or internal exile of nonprofit personnel; government scrutiny or theft of their records; and torture or even killing of those working in nonprofit organizations or participating in the projects they supported at the grass-roots level.[48]

From the government perspective in authoritarian Chile and Brazil, the cost of destroying or forbidding all nonprofit service and research organizations outweighed the costs of allowing some to function under restriction. Military leaders in both countries had justified seizing power on the grounds of preventing the victory of leftist insurgents and the subsequent danger of a Leninist state. In each case, the military courted the favor of the church following the takeover in an effort to gain legitimacy. It was eager to present itself to its own citizens and other nations as the defender of Western cultural values.

[47] Brian H. Smith, *Church and Politics in Chile*, chap. 9; Frühling, "Nonprofit Organizations as Opposition to Authoritarian Rule"; Bruneau, *The Church in Brazil*; Stepan, *Rethinking Military Politics*; Moreira Alves, "Grassroots Organizations, Trade Unions, and the Church."

[48] Brian H. Smith, "Churches and Human Rights in Latin America"; Frühling, "Nonprofit Organizations as Opposition to Authoritarian Rule."

Under such circumstances, the military in both Chile or Brazil found it necessary to allow space in civil society for some private organizations to function with a degree of independence from the state. Many of the service and research institutions that emerged to assist the poor and the persecuted at the height of repression (Brazil between 1968 and 1973 and Chile between 1973 and 1978) were created and supported by the local churches with considerable international church support. Preventing the creation and operation of these institutions would have made it impossible for the military to gain the moral legitimacy of the hierarchy, given in both Chile and Brazil at the start of military rule and maintained throughout, despite some sharp criticisms from time to time by bishops of human rights abuses.[49]

Even the nonprofit service and research organizations not under church sponsorship (created after intense periods of repression subsided) also provided a useful ideological function for the regimes in both countries. Despite the necessity for them to operate under restriction, their very existence provided grounds for the military in both countries to argue that their authoritarian rule was qualitatively different from a Marxist-Leninist state in which virtually no autonomy was permitted for private organizations opposing state policies.

Hence, for both pragmatic as well as ideological reasons, nonprofit organizations, albeit their antiregime bias, survived in authoritarian Chile and Brazil. In the judgment of the military in both countries, their contributions to regime stability and legitimacy outweighed any annoyance or embarrassment they created for the respective regimes at home or abroad.

Conflict Situations in Divided Societies (Nicaragua and El Salvador during Insurrection)

During the civil wars in El Salvador in the 1980s and in pre-1979 Nicaragua, governments in power needed as much international assistance as possible to support war-torn economies. They also did not want to alienate any major North Atlantic government whose aid and trade they needed to maintain (or obtain).

International private aid, heavily subsidized as it is by North Atlantic governments, was therefore allowed to enter El Salvador and Nicaragua during the respective civil wars as part of an overall foreign policy of maximizing the chances for good relations with Europe, Canada, and the United States. In monetary terms, the aid channeled through the transnational nonprofit sector into El Salvador and Nicaragua was very small (several hundred thousand dollars a year) in comparison to the millions of dollars to be maintained, or gained, in public aid and commercial trade with these same North Atlantic countries annually. A reduction of these larger and more essential monetary

---

[49] Brian H. Smith, *Church and Politics in Chile*, chap. 9; Bruneau, *The Church in Brazil*.

flows was too great a risk to justify cutting off very small amounts coming through the private aid network—even if some of it was eventually benefiting the guerrillas. The guerrillas themselves had other and far larger sources of foreign monetary assistance than that which came indirectly through the private aid network (Cuba, Soviet Union, and political solidarity movements in other Latin American countries).

Moreover, in both countries during insurrection, indigenous nonprofit organizations used much of their foreign aid for needed tasks the respective governments could not adequately carry out themselves. In conflict regions, government personnel who tried to maintain or expand public social services to the populace were likely to be assassinated by the guerrillas for purportedly representing a repressive government. Indigenous nonprofits, not identified with the government (and often staffed by personnel opposed to many government policies), often were able to function in these contested areas. They were popular among the people due to the services they provided and the independence they maintained from the government. The guerrillas often tended to let them alone in order not to risk the wrath of the local populace, whose good will they also wanted to win. Guerrillas also knew that these nonprofits often were sympathetic (at least unofficially) to their cause and might be useful potential allies for recruiting local support.[50]

The local residents received badly needed services, even if on a more limited basis than what the government potentially could provide due to its larger resources. At least these services by nonprofits were steady and relatively uninterrupted by the conflict.

The respective governments also benefited in the short run from such arrangements. Although some private aid might ultimately fall into guerrilla hands, the bulk of it was going for needed services in regions where public officials had little or no direct influence. The local people—whose allegiances were up for grabs—benefited, however. From the perspective of government policymakers, this kept them minimally satisfied and reduced the chances that they would become frustrated enough to throw in their lot with the guerrillas.

Indigenous nonprofit organizations thus could continue to carry out work amidst conflict and reduce some of the suffering for civilians caught between the contending parties in pre-1979 Nicaragua and in El Salvador in the 1980s. Foreign donor NGOs with sympathies for the guerrillas in both countries could thus continue to fund activities in conflict zones with the hope that such aid would eventually benefit the guerrilla cause at least indirectly, since they aided many people neglected or sometimes persecuted by the respective governments in power.

However, if indigenous nonprofits were suspected by government officials

---

[50] Michael Dodson, "Nicaragua: The Struggle for the Church," in Levine, ed., *Religion and Political Conflict*, pp. 79–105; Philip Berryman, "El Salvador: From Evangelization to Insurrection," in Levine, ed., *Religion and Political Conflict*, pp. 58–78.

of directly abetting the guerrilla cause, their personnel were subject to arrest, torture, expulsion, or death in both El Salvador and pre-1979 Nicaragua. Death squads, tacitly if not officially supported by the military, periodically carried out harassment, arrests, or execution of nonprofit personnel with some semblance of plausible denial by government leaders who refused any official link with such repression.

Hence, even in contexts of intense political polarization or civil war, indigenous nonprofits serve multiple interests. They are allowed by all major affected parties—host government, guerrillas, the poor—to carry out activities with international private aid. Here again, however, there are rules of the game that must be observed, and some interests of each of the major groups affected by nonprofit activities must be met, at least in part, for the nonprofit sector to function without severe penalties for its personnel.

One-Party States (Post-1979 Nicaragua and Mexico)

The Sandinista government in Nicaragua allows the international private aid network to bring in assistance both to supporters and opponents of the regime. In either case, the government gains some important objectives.

The government has created a purportedly autonomous nonprofit organization—the Augusto Sandino Foundation—to channel private foreign aid to grass-roots organizations in Nicaragua. Although technically a private organization, this foundation and the local groups it serves are predominantly constituted by sympathizers of the regime and they closely coordinate their activities with overall government development plans.

Foreign NGOs from Europe and Canada with leftist political sympathies can channel money to the Augusto Sandino Foundation without officially giving aid to the government. They are assured, however, that their resources will be used to help regime supporters. The Sandinistas are thus able both to leverage additional foreign resources they might not be able to get directly and also maintain control over how it is used inside their country. Those poor who are sympathizers to the regime receive additional resources that the government itself does not have to generate.

There are also indigenous nonprofits in Nicaragua not linked to the Augusto Sandino Foundation, many of whom are closely associated with opponents of the regime (e.g., some official service agencies of the Archdiocese of Nicaragua). These other nonprofits (both religious and secular) bring in resources from foreign public and private groups opposed to the Sandinistas or politically neutral. They channel such aid to those in Nicaragua linked to the private sector of the economy—which in the mid-1980s still accounts for 60 percent of overall production in the country.[51]

[51] Tendler, Crindle, and Hatch, "FUNDE: An Evaluation."

The activities they support, even if carried out among those Nicaraguans critical or opposed to regime policies, must be restricted to activities that are economically or socially constructive—credit, technical training, basic health, etc. Such indigenous organizations are not permitted to engage in political mobilization against the regime or assist the armed resistance, the Contras. If they are caught doing so, their staffs are arrested or expelled and their operations closed down.

Since the Sandinistas want to attract foreign assistance from a variety of North Atlantic sources and formally maintain a mixed economy, even those indigenous nonprofits not enthusiastic about their policies are allowed to function. Such nonprofits, even if supported by foreign donor organizations with money from Sandinista critics (e.g., the Thatcher government in Great Britain), contribute to Sandinista objectives by expanding the technical expertise and production capacities in the overall economy. Provided they do not engage in overt political opposition to the government, such nonprofits are permitted to operate—even if their long-range hopes are to weaken the regime by bolstering private sector initiatives among its opponents.

For the moment they also serve some important regime objectives. They are a sign to the world of pluralism inside Nicaragua, and they leverage money from abroad not available either to the government or the Augusto Sandino Foundation. By 1986 approximately 35 percent of Nicaragua's foreign exchange currency entered the country through the international private aid network.

As in the case of the Soviet Union and the ARA in 1921, sectors of the international private aid network assist those in Nicaragua that are not at the moment a government priority since they are not staunch regime supporters. This saves scarce government resources, keeps these opponents from making more demands on government services, and occupies them with some constructive, if politically harmless, economic activities.

In Mexico, given the strong one-party system of patronage controlled by the Institutionalized Revolutionary Party (PRI), no organization can avoid dealing with the system. However, nonprofits that are autonomous of PRI control and supported by international private aid provide a space for those critical or opposed to the system to work for the poor. However, as in Colombia, the majority of poor themselves do not have a radical political agenda. They want to obtain more services for themselves and their locales.

Thus, nonprofits in Mexico, as in Colombia, perform two important functions. They fill gaps in the system when no or insufficient public services exist. They act as brokers between local groups and the government to stimulate greater regime responsiveness to local needs.

In the aftermath of the September 1985 earthquake, for example, these private organizations played both roles. In the immediate wake of a disaster too massive for the government to handle alone (five thousand killed, forty thousand injured, and 350,000 homeless), nonprofit organizations with access to the International Red Cross and various church-related PVOs/NGOs in North Atlantic countries brought in millions of dollars for immediate relief. As time went on, new local community organizations emerged (spawned by nonprofit relief work) and organized urban residents to pressure the government to rebuild their homes for a price they could afford.[52]

Although these new local organizations and the nonprofit service agencies that continue to support them are not linked to the PRI (and, in fact, sometimes staffed by opposition political activists), the PRI and the government have dealt with them carefully and even acquiesced to some of their demands for more citizen input into public housing reconstruction. By negotiating with the government instead of protesting and by mobilizing considerable voluntary labor in site-and-service housing reconstruction, these organizations have helped ward off more radical forms of political expression.

Like their counterparts in Colombia, many Mexican nonprofit institutions at the regional and grass-roots level that are critical of the patronage system have played a broker role to gain better quality services from public agencies for their low-income clientele. The demands of the poor are concrete, and the best way for nonprofits to meet these (and thus enhance their own legitimacy) is to get the public sector to be more responsive. In turn, the public sector has channeled some resources through these new private organizations to low-income groups (not closely bound to the PRI or even strongly adverse to its patronizing style) so as to gain (or regain) legitimacy for itself through more effective service delivery to these disaffected or previously unorganized groups.[53]

As in Colombia, the nonprofits in Mexico ironically have become less a political threat to the system as they have become more successful in social and economic terms. As their social prestige among the poor has grown, their political power is being harnessed by the government and the PRI to enhance societal stability and regime legitimacy. Co-optation, rather than repression, has channeled nonprofit energies into an overall system-maintenance direction even if such organizations remain formally independent of government control.

Redemocratizing Contexts (Post-1980 Peru and Post-1985 Brazil)

Under regimes recently returned to democracy after long periods of military rule—such as Peru after 1980 and Brazil after 1985—nonprofit organizations continue to play important economic and political roles, albeit different from their former functions. Their focus during previous authoritarian periods was on meeting the minimal social and economic needs of low-income sectors

[52] Bennett, "Mexico City."
[53] Annis, "NGOs in Mexico City;" Koldewyn, "Mexican Voluntary Associations."

neglected or repressed by military governments. They also were holding operations for intellectual and political dissidents, providing them with both employment opportunities and legitimacy to continue their contact with grass-roots groups.

Newly emerging democratic regimes have committed themselves to upgrading services and employment opportunities for these same poor. However, given the abysmal state of the economy in both countries (with inflation in triple digits and mounting foreign debts), these governments do not have adequate resources to do so.[54] Moreover, many civilian leaders elected in the mid-1980s (especially at the state and local levels) have come out of nonprofit organizations where they worked, full or part time, during military rule. They are thus open to collaboration and input into policymaking by their former colleagues still working for nonprofits.[55]

Nonprofit organizations in such contexts are faced with difficult challenges. They are welcomed and encouraged by public policymakers more than they ever were under military rule. Their continued efforts to provide resources and training for low-income sectors is still sorely needed given the lack of adequate public resources to fulfill the high expectations the poor have of these newly elected governments. The stability of democratic rule in part requires the continued, if not expanded, ability of indigenous nonprofits to leverage foreign aid not directly available to political leaders themselves. In both Peru and Brazil, in fact, local government policymakers have sought out the advice and assistance of their former colleagues in the nonprofit sector on how to meet the needs of the poor. One-third of municipal governments in Peru by 1986 included former leaders of indigenous nonprofits in executive positions.[56]

Nonprofits, however, do not want to be co-opted by policymakers. Their goal, long postponed during military rule, is social and economic equity for the poor, which only massive government commitments can provide. They have strong credibility among the poor due to their past performance during authoritarian rule and do not want recently elected leaders (even if their friends) to steal this mantle of credibility for their own public policies (by association)—especially if such policies provide far less than what is needed to make a significant dent in poverty.

Nonprofit leaders want to see democracy succeed and commitments by recently elected leaders to be met, but they also want to maintain a critical distance from government. They want to play a collaborating role but also act as constructive critics and as a loyal opposition so that equity agendas will not be

[54] Riding, "Ailing Brazil is Divided"; Pang, "The Darker Side of Brazil's Democracy"; Bridges, "Peru"; Werlich, "Peru."

[55] Fernandes, "Las ONGs"; Padrón, "Redes y agrupaciones nacionales"; Arruda, "Role of Latin American Nongovernmental Organizations."

[56] Interviews with Hans Hoyer, LWR; and with Dr. Mario Padrón Castillo, DESCO.

further postponed. Such a balancing act is difficult to maintain if nonprofits are both to play a positive role in consolidating democratic rule and also to maintain their credibility in the eyes of their primary clientele—the poor.

It is too early to ascertain how this delicate balance will be worked out. Nonprofits want to collaborate in rebuilding debt-ridden economies in Brazil and Peru, but they need to maintain their autonomy and capacity to be critical. Newly elected governments, in turn, want to take advantage of nonprofit services and money to provide palliatives to the poor as austerity measures are imposed to control inflation and satisfy foreign creditors. The respective agendas are clearly not identical.

Although there is no immediate danger that democratic governments in these countries will impose the type of restrictions on nonprofits that authoritarian regimes are prone to, tensions between the private nonprofit and public sectors are likely to mount if government officials are unable to manage inflation and debt repayments and simultaneously make serious headway on equity for the poor. Thus far, achieving both of these goals together has not been possible for redemocratizing nations in Latin America, nor are the probabilities high that they will be able to do so for the foreseeable future.

CONCLUSIONS

Over the past twenty years, indigenous nonprofit organizations have grown in number, size, and importance in a wide variety of political contexts in Latin America. In all these regimes—long-standing democratic, authoritarian, revolutionary, one-party, and redemocratizing—these organizations have come to play important social roles due to their capacities to reach sectors of the respective populations who have long been marginalized and to support the creation of new community organizations articulating their needs. In each of these different contexts, they have also played an important economic role due to their ability to leverage increasing amounts of international resources and use these to provide social services to low-income groups (many in the bottom 40 percent in income).

In all of these different regime types, nonprofit development institutions have also played an important political role. What is common to most situations is their attractiveness to middle-class leaders disgruntled with regime performance in making significant headway in achieving economic equity and political participation for the poor. Unable to promote their equity agenda through established public or profitmaking institutions in their respective societies, many intellectuals and professionals over the past generation have gravitated to nonprofits as laboratories where they have been experimenting with new strategies for greater equity at the grass-roots level. In many cases, they have assisted those overlooked, exploited, or even persecuted by governments and profitmaking groups.

They have enabled oppressed groups to survive in authoritarian Chile and Brazil, as well as in revolutionary Nicaragua and El Salvador. They have also assisted those neglected or exploited by the system to gain greater bargaining power with government and business leaders under elite-dominated systems, whether competitive two-party (Colombia) or one-party regimes (Mexico). In countries undergoing a process of redemocratization in the 1980s (Peru and Brazil), nonprofits, with the support of many of the poor, have been outspoken critics of newly elected governments that are imposing austerity measures to control soaring inflation and meet interest payments on large foreign debts.

Despite the change-oriented social, economic, and political thrust of Latin American nonprofits in various regime types, they are not a significant threat to established interests in any country at present. They are too small individually and uncoordinated collectively to present a serious challenge to those with economic and political power. The clientele whom they serve at the grass-roots level, whether in repressive or formally democratic regimes, do not have a radical political agenda, but normally aspire to a greater stake in the system if at all possible. Under such conditions, government and business elites can often use a variety of co-optive, restrictive, or even repressive strategies to curb the impact of indigenous nonprofits whenever they do become politically annoying.

Paradoxically, these private organizations can also serve some of the immediate interests of governments and businesses in Latin America, even in situations when they are pursuing policies in clear opposition to the established order (e.g., caring for the persecuted in authoritarian regimes; working in areas favorable to guerrillas, or in neutral zones, in civil-war contexts; serving the needs of the poor who are disenchanted with public bureaucracies in one-party states). They can harness the energies of regime opponents from the middle class, which might have been channeled into more radically political or even revolutionary alternatives. They help placate working-class sectors and give them a sense of hope that the system is malleable and responsive to their needs. They are signs to foreign critics that authoritarian, one-party, or elite-controlled democratic governments allow a certain degree of pluralism and space for private initiative in their societies, thus countering charges that such countries are as statist as Marxist-dominated regimes. They leverage funds from foreign sources, including opposition groups abroad, for social and economic projects in their societies that local governments cannot obtain on their own.

Undoubtedly, over the long-term, the political impact of development-oriented nonprofit organizations in Latin America could be quite significant. The sense of autonomy and confidence growing among grass-roots groups whom they serve in a variety of political contexts cannot but enhance their bargaining power vis-à-vis the economic and political elites. Under certain circumstances (e.g., open disunity among ruling classes, the emergence of strong revolutionary movements, concerted international sanctions against repressive governments), this quiet but steady growth in self-confidence and autonomy among beneficiaries might spill over into more overt political opposition—especially if there is greater cooperation within the nonprofit sector and if nonprofits eventually forge alliances with partisan political movements.

There is no evidence, however, that any of these dynamics are yet present. Moreover, some of the characteristics of the nonprofit development sector (smallness, fierce competitiveness, fear of co-optation, lack of coordination) militate against closer collaboration among nonprofits. The shrewd orchestration of reward and punishment strategies for nonprofits by both the public and profitmaking sectors in various Latin American states, and the reluctance of North Atlantic institutions—especially corporations and banks—to use economic or political sanctions against Latin American regimes with poor records of social justice and human rights, also indicate that conditions favoring a significant political opposition role for nonprofits are not on the horizon.[57]

Clear trade-offs, therefore, exist at present among the three major groups involved in the receiving end of the international private aid—indigenous non-

[57] Although this chapter has exclusively focused on Latin America, evidence from Africa and Asia suggests that indigenous nonprofits that receive international assistance in these areas are also not a significant threat to the political system, but in fact actually enhance social stability.

In much of Africa both governmental and nongovernmental service organizations are still relatively underdeveloped in comparison to Latin America. Thus far, however, there is no indication that nonprofits will become serious opponents to governmental organizations as they grow and as public sector organizations also develop. At present, governments tend to tolerate the economic and social activities of nonprofits, since these often service groups and areas that governmental agencies thus far do not reach. Both authoritarian (Nigeria, Zaire, Togo) and democratic (Kenya, Zimbabwe) regimes, however, are very wary about any private groups that engage in community mobilization efforts not under governmental or party control and tend to monitor closely organizations that make such attempts. Tighter public restrictions and closer coordination between governmental and nonprofit service agencies are the likely future pattern in Africa as both public and private sector service organizations grow in size and scope. Bratton, "Politics of Government-NGO Relations"; Anheier, "Private Voluntary Organizations"; Johnson and Johnson, "Relations between Governments and Voluntary Development Organizations."

In many parts of Asia, nonprofits are also useful complements to government social services in health, credit, and technical training. In countries where they have exhibited the potential of becoming competitors or opponents of public sector institutions (India, Bangladesh, Nepal, Indonesia), governments have used a combination of financial co-optation, legal controls, or periodic repression to limit their political impact. In South Korea and the Philippines in the 1980s, however, these private organizations (mostly under church sponsorship) were training grounds for new leaders who have helped mobilize opposition to martial law. Since the overthrow of the authoritarian regime in the Philippines in 1986, many of the leaders in nonprofit service organizations (as in Peru after 1980 and Brazil after 1985) have joined the new democratic government to work for public agencies in land reform, refugee resettlement, and rural employment generation. What the long-term political impact will be of these new political strategies of nonprofit organizations remains to be seen. Cheema, "Role of Voluntary Organizations"; Garilao, "Indigenous NGOs as Strategic Institutions"; Sivaraksa, "Rural Poverty and Peasant Development"; Sethi, "Groups in a New Politics of Transformation"; Sheth, "Grassroots Initiatives in India."

profits, host governments, and the grass-roots poor—which make the system viable at present. Idealists and politically disaffected groups from the middle classes expand their income opportunities and also work for an equitable and participatory social system, but they do so in the short-run by making the present unjust order a bit more humane. Government officials allow space for such dissidents to operate (sometimes even to their own embarrassment), but they see gaps filled in services (at no cost to themselves) for low-income groups that make these recipients more acquiescent to the present order.

The grass-roots poor perhaps receive the greatest net gain from their own perspective. The natural quality of life is improving for them as a result of such arrangements, as is their own self-esteem due to the voice they frequently have in designing and implementing projects and in creating or strengthening their own community-run organizations. Moreover, all of this is gained without major confrontations with economic and political power elites.

Some might feel these recipients lose the possibility of forging among themselves a more cohesive and radical class consciousness by receiving assistance under such conditions, and that thereby the potential for popular revolution is significantly diminished or at best postponed. This may be true from a Marxist or utopian socialist perspective, but it simply is not felt as an important loss by the vast majority of the 150 million in Latin America who are in the bottom 40 percent in income. They are conservative and pragmatic. They know that successful revolutions are scarce, and that even the four that have occurred in Latin America in this century (Mexico in 1917, Bolivia in 1952, Cuba in 1959, and Nicaragua in 1979) have not eliminated poverty or produced fully participatory political systems. As a result, most of the poor only desire a somewhat better life for themselves and their children without risking the little that they have.

The private aid network as it now functions presents a reasonable chance that some of their hopes can be realized, if only in a small way. It may be supportive in the short run to the existing economic and political order (and therefore acceptable to major powerholders), but to the poor it also offers the possibility that their material and social conditions can improve in the short run. Even if they have never heard of Lord Keynes, they know that for most people on the planet in difficult straits it is the short run that is the critical challenge. If that challenge can be met with at least a modicum of success and minimal risk, what it may lead to in terms of future possibilities (even if vague at present) is far more attractive to them than grim, bloody confrontation.

CHAPTER NINE

Conclusions

MANIFEST AND LATENT FUNCTIONS OF THE PRIVATE AID NETWORK

The apparent paradoxes involved in the transnational private aid network presented in chapter 1 do have an underlying rationality. This makes it possible for the six major partner groups (private donors, North Atlantic PVOs/NGOs, North Atlantic governments, Third World nonprofits, host country governments, grass-roots recipients) with seemingly contradictory agendas to collaborate in making the system work. There are multiple agendas being pursued by several groups at once, and several of the actors are not unitary but made up of clusters of subgroups with different objectives that must be balanced, sometimes in creative tension. This is particularly true for private donors, governments, and PVOs/NGOs in the North Atlantic region, and to a lesser extent it is characteristic of the three partner groups in developing nations as well.

Moreover, some of the multiple goals of the actors are manifest and public, while others are latent and sometimes hidden to public view—even to other partner groups in the system. This factor helps keep potentially explosive differences from becoming overt and therefore disruptive to the network's viability.

The network is able to function since there are overlapping interests among the six partners to provide a common ground of consensus. These interests relate to publicly acknowledged goals on which considerable consensus exists among the various groups—namely, moving resources across country borders through cost-effective channels to alleviate human suffering in crises and to enable the hard-core poor in developing countries to better themselves in some significant, if limited, way. All major partners and subgroups agree that this should be done, and mounting evidence indicates it is being done. It is clear that the international private aid network has some comparative advantages over governmental aid and profitmaking institutions in accomplishing these objectives. They often exhibit great imagination and creativity in the process.

The latent, or secondary, agendas are the areas where tension and disagreement normally exists, since these often involve sensitive political objectives over which a common consensus throughout the network is harder to achieve—e.g., enhancing the political power of the poor in the third world, assisting political dissidents in developing countries, challenging and changing of foreign policy priorities of North Atlantic countries, harnessing, or taming, the energies of potentially radical political groups both in the North Atlantic and developing world to serve the interests of policymakers or political and economic elites, presenting a "good face" of North Atlantic societies to the developing world when concessions on more critical fronts (e.g., the NIEO agenda) cannot be made. So long as these more controversial and political objectives of different actors or their subgroups remain in the background to the public objective of improving the material lot of the Third World poor, trade-offs and flexibility among and within the partners is possible. This maintains the system even when some open clashes occur on the secondary objectives.

Moreover, where specific information about these hidden agendas is less available to many in the system and to the public at large, the network is more viable at the donor and recipient ends. Some basic disclosure is necessary, and evaluation and reporting processes are essential to prove that the manifest goals of the network are being accomplished—namely, assisting the poor in developing countries to improve their material condition not otherwise possible through government-to-government programs.

Much, however, needs to remain unwritten about the latent and more sensitive goals (e.g., aiding political dissidents or working to empower the poor to challenge and change unjust political and economic structures in developing countries). Relative silence about these sensitive political goals of some of the actors or their subgroups in the system (e.g., European and Canadian NGO executives and staffs, left-of-center party leaders) is necessary in order not to offend or embarrass another partner's subgroups (politically conservative private donors, and right-of-center parliamentarians in European and Canadian governments).

Vagueness is also necessary at times to prevent those committed to some controversial political goals not to become disillusioned if they are not being realized in the way they expect. For example, the core interests of most grassroots poor in developing countries are not politically radical at all, and many Third World indigenous nonprofits acting as intermediaries between them and foreign donors know this (even when they themselves are politically on the left). Explicitly telling European and Canadian donor NGOs, often staffed by those with socialist sympathies, that what they are actually supporting is petty capitalism could precipitate a curtailment of funds from such NGOs. This would reduce resources for the politically cautious Third World poor who participate in projects and for middle class political dissidents who oversee them through indigenous nonprofits.

Assistance of specific hungry children overseas who are individually sponsored by U.S. private donors may also not be occuring as directly as contributors think, since child-sponsorship PVOs are shifting more of their resources toward community development work abroad. Clearly and fully disclosing this to large numbers of actual and potential private donors in the United States could reduce private contributions to such PVOs or limit the possibilities of attracting new ones through a "hungry child" in short media messages.

Some myths, therefore, are essential for the private aid network to function. These allow some subgroups among the partner clusters to believe their secondary goals are being realized or have a chance of being fulfilled. Too much disclosure or evaluation of actual project performance could be frustrating to subgroups for whom the myths are important and could create serious obstacles for their continuing commitments to make the system work.

VULNERABILITIES OF THE SYSTEM

It is clear, however, that given the sensitive political nature of some of these secondary or latent goals and the distance between donor expectations and the actual character of the projects themselves, serious tensions or credibility crises can occur. When nonprofits engage in open and sustained partisan political activities in North Atlantic or developing countries, and when these threaten core interests of political or economic elites, they risk severe penalties ranging from significant loss of public subsidies, manipulation by political leaders for their own partisan purposes, growing disunity among themselves, or even outright repression by governments. When exposures occur in the media revealing some of these sensitive latent functions or questioning the validity of some claims of nonprofits, their credibility is called into question and private donor commitments are jeopardized. When evaluations uncover some weaknesses in nonprofit performance (e.g., the inability to increase citizen support for overall foreign aid or the poor record of nonprofits in generating more private support for their work), policymakers with other pressing agendas are forced to ask whether their governments are getting their money's worth by cofinancing nonprofits.

The system itself—relying as it does on the cooperation of many groups with differing agendas and a certain amount of vagueness to keep these in balance—is not stable. It requires a willingness to postpone some goals (or achieve them only partially) on the part of several of the key actor groups, as well as self-restraint across the board in keeping various latent agendas from coming fully into the open. Some partisan activity is acceptable, but not too much, and a certain amount of pluralistic ignorance is necessary among many of those participating in the network and among the public at large.

Based on evidence from Latin America, these tacit rules are currently being observed the best at the receiving end of the network—despite tensions and periodic clashes. Perhaps it is because in many developing countries the stakes are higher for those participating in or affected by the network (governments, nonprofits, and the poor), and the penalties for overstepping the tacit boundaries quite high.

In the North Atlantic region, however, the relationships among private donors, public policymakers, and PVOs/NGOs are facing significant challenges since some subgroups in each partner cluster (budget-conscious legislators, NGOs with latent conservative sympathies) as well as groups in society at large (the media, the political right) are beginning to question or challenge the validity of some of the secondary and latent functions of the system. If such continues, the future viability of the donor end of the network as now constituted could be undermined. If it breaks down, the receiving end of the network will be seriously hampered, since it cannot function at the same level without continuous resource flows from North Atlantic countries.

REEXAMINING THEORIES ABOUT NONPROFITS AND NATIONAL SOVEREIGNTY

The evidence emerging from the international private aid network confirms the basic thrust of many of the classical theories about the role of the nonprofit sector described in chapter 1. As it now functions, the network also does not threaten nation state sovereignty and will not in the foreseeable future. In fact, its very existence—even with its latent functions that threaten nation state interests—actually enhances in the short run the political and economic stability of governments at both the sending and receiving ends of the spectrum.

The classical religious and secular justifications for the nonprofit sector in Western societies are still quite valid. Human suffering is being alleviated and the poor are being helped (Jewish and Christian ethical demands), although the work being done goes well beyond mere treatment of symptoms, on which traditional religious charitable activities focused. The private aid network is also an expression of basic humanitarian sympathy (as Adam Smith described it) on the part of large numbers of concerned citizens in developed countries for the poor in developing societies. Moreover, this network is helping some to become economically more productive and self-reliant, and hence less prone to crime and other forms of violence (as Georg Simmel predicted would happen if charity functioned effectively).

The network preserves, at least in the short run, a differentiation among social classes within developing countries and among rich and poor nations, since it alleviates some of the pressures for more radical restructuring of the international economic system as called for by the NIEO. It also harnesses the energies of some middle class idealists and political dissidents both in the North Atlantic region and in developing countries and keeps them from more radical political or even revolutionary activities.

The network, therefore, performs a system-maintenance function, both at the international level among nations and within rich and poor countries themselves. As currently constituted, it presents no major threat to nation-state sovereignty. It actually enhances the political and economic stability of both donor and recipient societies.

The manner in which the private aid network functions both confirms and modifies contemporary theories about nonprofits as described in the last generation by economists and political theorists. It is clear the system delivers goods and services to certain sectors in developing countries that profitmaking institutions and the formal market system (both international and inside these countries) cannot or will not. It assures distant donors that their contributions will reach the poor in developing countries, whom they will never see, something which market transactions cannot guarantee (as Hansmann argues). It is also evident that nonprofit organizations in international aid are able to carry out tasks governmental institutions (bilaterally or multilaterally) are not equipped politically, economically, or administratively to handle, since they often reach the poorest in the Third World with a minimum of overhead costs and imaginative and flexible service delivery mechanisms. As Weisbrod has observed, they have a comparative advantage over governments in delivering certain services for which there is not yet a public mandate.

The international nonprofit network is not laboring under the categorical and majoritarian constraints limiting public sector institutions in foreign aid, as Douglas has observed. It can choose to work with groups that governmental organizations cannot (or will not) single out for special treatment, and it is not restricted by the consensus of a majority of citizens (in either sending or receiving countries) as to what services it can offer.

However, Douglas' two conditions for legitimately getting around the majoritarian constraint are not being met by all international nonprofits, especially those who have latent controversial political agendas. What some of them are hoping to achieve (mobilizing the poor in developing countries to challenge dominant economic and political policies in those societies) or actually doing (providing employment opportunities and cover for middle-class political dissidents abroad, and engaging in lobbying activities at home demanding significant changes in foreign and domestic public policies) are not necessarily what the majority of citizens in their home societies would see as reasonable pursuits for tax-exempt organizations. There are minorities who strongly disagree with such activities by PVOs/NGOs, and they vigorously protest such agendas when they come to light.

What Douglas and other theorists also see as an essential justification for the tax-exempt privileges of nonprofits—namely, a nonpartisan political position—is not being met by most nonprofits engaged in international aid. Many of the European and Canadian NGOs have clear leftist political sympathies and express these by working closely with leftist partners and movements in their home societies. They are also beginning to stimulate by such public alliances the latent conservative political preferences of other NGOs that are also now starting to enter the partisan political battles at home over foreign policy issues. In the United States many PVOs, if not overtly partisan, harbor latent liberal preferences since they quietly hope to check the political authoritarianism of the left and the right in developing countries. In developing countries nonprofits often house and protect opponents of such regimes, who are struggling to survive and prepare the conditions for a better political order.

Because many nonprofits in the international private aid network do not meet the conditions laid down by Douglas for legitimate dispensation from both the majoritarian constraint and the payment of taxes, a certain amount of vagueness is necessary to keep both citizens and policymakers alike in developed and developing countries from putting stricter legal, financial, and political limits on their activities. Both political groups and governments are using nonprofits, aided by taxpayers money, to pursue goals not necessarily supported by a majority of citizens in either developed or developing countries. For these reasons, clear accountability and full disclosure to the public at large, as well as to governments, are not always forthcoming.

The private aid network may in the short run perform a system-maintenance function internationally and within nations, but it clearly is not apolitical or even nonpartisan. In fact, part of its system-maintenance contribution depends upon its political character (albeit latent), since it is an outlet for potentially subversive political energies in both sending and receiving countries. It channels these into activities that serve some of the immediate interests of dominant political and economic elites in these respective societies, even if nurturing processes that in the long run may threaten them.

However, such latent functions and the way they are performed are not necessarily seen as legitimate by large numbers of citizens in sending and receiving societies, which makes some secrecy a necessary part of the network. It also makes the network vulnerable to criticism and attack by those who are upset with the privileges tax-exempt and government-subsidized organizations enjoy in pursuing their latent political agendas (whether they are successful in accomplishing them or not).

That these tensions and dilemmas are being handled relatively well at present is clear. If the theories about nonprofits in democratic societies are correct, however, there are inevitable mounting problems for the network in the years ahead. Ironically, they very well may arise not in developing countries where many of the most controversial goals are supposed to be accomplished but in North Atlantic societies where the donors (public and private) are located. The reason is that the sending countries are open, competitive democracies. Nonprofits, according to the contemporary political theories, need to be accountable to the public in such societies, and their activities need to be accepted by a wide citizen consensus so they can continue to enjoy tax-exempt status. It is from such societies that significant challenges to the international private aid network may arise in the years ahead as more becomes known about their latent functions and if various groups across the political spectrum continue to exploit them for their own partisan purposes.

Research Methodology

DONOR NONPROFITS from North Atlantic countries to be interviewed were not chosen randomly but in a purposive manner with the choices based primarily on size, scope, function, and geographical distribution. The sample was created to represent a cross section of the various types and categories of PVOs/NGOs that are now in operation—large and small; older and newer; partially relief oriented and exclusively development oriented; secular and religiously affiliated; with overseas field representatives and without; working as consortia and individual organizations; significantly subsidized by government and supported predominantly or exclusively by private philanthropy; based in a variety of the major aid-sending North Atlantic countries.

Although there are over forty-six hundred North Atlantic private organizations involved in some form of international assistance, in 1980, 205 accounted for 64 percent of the resource transfers ($2.9 billion of $4.5 billion in total aid). The vast majority of nonprofits engaged in overseas activities are quite small. Moreover, not all of these organizations are engaged in development-oriented work but in a variety of other activities (many of them dating to an earlier period), such as religious evangelization, cultural exchange, the promotion of professional associations.

In selecting the nonprofits for my sample, I chose mainly from those largest 205 who profess to be engaged in socioeconomic development and who have the resources to be able to make the most significant impact (a 1980 annual budget of $500,000 or more). I also selected some from among those with older relief orientations that are now shifting more emphasis to longer-term solutions, since those often tend to have access to the greatest resources (especially in the United States). I also chose from among those that are of more recent origin but that are focusing predominantly on structural issues underlying poverty—unemployment; lack of technical skills or basic services in health, housing, or education; weak community organizational structures; lack of effective participation and bargaining power.

I made sure that adequate representation was given to two other important variables—sectarian character and national origin—since these have been important distinguishing characteristics among North Atlantic nonprofits historically. I did not choose missionary societies as such since, although they are carrying out social welfare activities, budget allocations are sometimes not calibrated to separate evangelization from social service. I included, however, several of those newer church-affiliated institutions created since World War II, which focus exclusively on social services abroad, as well as many with a nonconfessional status of secular origin.

Finally, I wanted to be sure that the sample was a cross-section of major private aid-sending organizations in several different North Atlantic countries so as to assess the impact nationality had on style and objective. Hence, I selected nonprofits with headquarters in eight different North Atlantic countries—the United States, Canada, Great Britain, France, Switzerland, the FRG, Belgium, and the Netherlands.

Using these criteria, the final list was put together from PVOs/NGO listings in standard directories (the OECD 1981 directory, the TAICH 1983 directory, the AID *Voluntary Foreign Aid Programs* summaries [1979–1984], and the Canadian Council for International Cooperation 1982 directory.)[1] I also relied on information I gathered from those in the academic community in the various countries as well as from some government policymakers.

The sample contained forty-five North Atlantic nonprofits, representing 22 percent of the largest 205 in 1980 but accounting for nearly one-half (48.1 percent) of the overseas aid resources of these 205 largest private institutions. Fifteen were from the United States, seven were Canadian, and twenty-three were based in the six West European countries.

I normally interviewed in each of these PVOs/NGOs the persons most responsible for the oversight of projects the organizations supported in Latin America. In some of the larger institutions I also conducted interviews with those having other responsibilities and different perspectives (often the executive director). For a list of the forty-five North Atlantic nonprofits in my survey, see appendix B.

During these interviews (usually lasting from two to three hours) I used a pretested instrument of forty-seven open-ended and closed questions that focused on five critical issues: (1) mission definition and the ranking of current priorities; (2) sources and consequences of financing; (3) whether the organization attempts to influence public opinion and policymaking at home and the repercussions for its relationships with private donors and home government; (4) the methods of evaluating the effectiveness of its overseas activities and the feedback such evaluation provides to the organizations; and (5) its governance, including structure, process of decision-making, relations with overseas counterpart nonprofits who are recipients of its aid, and its cooperative relationships with other North Atlantic private organizations. A copy of the questionnaire is included in appendix D.

One reason Colombia was chosen as a place to explore PVO/NGO impact

[1] OECD, *Directory of Non-Governmental Organizations*, 1981; TAICH, *U.S. Nonprofit Organizations*; AID, *Voluntary Foreign Aid Programs*, 1979, 1982, 1983, 1984; CCIC, *Directory of Canadian Non-Governmental Organizations*.

abroad was because of the number and variety of development-oriented activities administered by its nonprofit sector. The majority (twenty-four of forty-five) of the PVOs/NGOs I surveyed in the United States, Canada, and Europe have been supporting development-oriented activities in Colombia for some time. Only five, however, have their own field representatives. Rather, they fund Colombian nonprofit organizations that act as their counterparts and which use their funding to administer development-oriented programs among the poor or facilitate projects carried out by low-income groups themselves at the grass-roots level.

In the 1970s such intermediary nonprofit institutions in Colombia expanded both in quantity and diversity, and now include (1) technical and leadership-training institutions for low income groups run by professionals; (2) applied research institutes run by social scientists, which have educational components for workers or peasants that also act as advocates for better public policy toward these groups; (3) private foundations that channel contributions from business firms into self-help programs among the poor in housing, health, credits and recreation; (4) credit institutions for small businesspersons who do not have access to normal commercial channels of finance; (5) production, marketing, and consumer cooperatives in regions where private and public infrastructures and credit are not available; (6) multiservice agencies providing resources for health, housing, recreation, or popular education to local community groups.

There is no national directory or federation of Colombian nonprofits that includes information on the overall activities on the nonprofit sector. The national government itself lacks comprehensive data on nonprofits since up until December 1984 (after my field research in Colombia was completed) there was no requirement that all such groups submit annual reports to the government. Once the government has granted them a juridicial personality as nonprofit institutions upon their establishment, they have provided further data on their agency activities only on a sporadic basis.

According to estimates in the mid-1980s, the total number of nonprofit organizations of all types that have been granted legal status by the Colombian government is close to six thousand.[2] The government believes that the number is closer to five thousand. This is based on information released in 1984 by the ministries of Government, Health, Education, and Justice, which listed the names of 1,665 current tax-exempt institutions, including corporations, associations, foundations, funds, societies, institutes, labor unions, federations, and cultural clubs.[3] In addition, the National Department for the Administration of Cooperatives published some statistics in 1981 on 3,483 other

---

[2] Low Murtra, "Las sociedades y las entidades sin ánimo de lucro."

[3] Only the names of these 1,665 tax-exempt organizations (with no description of their activities) were printed serially in the official government newspaper, La República, during the last week of August 1984 (August 22–30, 1984) after I had completed my research.

nonprofit institutions that cover cooperatives, employee funds, and mutual societies—all of which also enjoy legal and tax-exempt status in the country.[4]

However, such lists and summary statistics did not provide me with an adequate data base to construct a random sample for my own study. This information did not adequately disaggregate the tax-exempt sector so as to separate those organizations that are engaged primarily in development activities, as opposed to relief-type assistance, formal education, cultural promotion, professional activities, or partisan political work. Several persons whom I interviewed in various departments of the executive branch of government told me the data in government files on the nonprofit sector were still very uneven and unsystematized, and certainly not adequate to make a selection of the kind of development-oriented nonprofits useful for my purposes.[5]

Hence, to create a sample of Colombian nonprofit organizations that are focusing on the development issues I wanted to analyze, I had to rely on several different sources of information. These included international funding organizations; knowledgeable experts on Colombian nonprofits in government, business, and academia in Colombia; and suggestions within the Colombian nonprofit community itself. I indicated to persons in all of these groups the major critical areas of development upon which I was focusing, and asked each of these various sources of information for names of organizations that they knew were attempting to affect these issues.

The international nonprofits that I interviewed in Europe, Canada, and the United States provided me with a list of counterpart private organizations they fund in Colombia. International governmental agencies that channel resources into private grass-roots develoment programs in Colombia—namely, the IAF and the Small Projects Program of the IDB—provided additional names of such development-oriented nonprofit organizations in Colombia.

I also consulted a number of U.S., European, and Colombian experts (including social scientists, independent development consultants, persons working in governmental agencies, ex-PVO/NGO staff personnel) who were knowledgeable about development work by the nonprofit sector in Colombia. Finally, I relied on contacts given to me in the Colombian nonprofit community itself to identify other private organizations engaged in development-oriented work.

In selecting the specific Colombian organizations to study from those mentioned by all these resource persons and organizations, I used the following two additional criteria:

[4] *Colombia Estadística 1983*, p. 503.

[5] Interviews by the author with Alba Lucía Orozco de Tirana, director of the Administration of National Revenue, Bogotá, August 2, 1984; Diego Pizano Salazar, secretary for economic affairs, Office of the President, Bogotá, August 13, 1984; Rafael Prieto Durán, director of the Department of Economic Research, Bank of the Republic of Colombia, Bogotá, July 19, 1984.

1. Geographical distribution in the country, so as to avoid concentration in any one region.
2. Focus distribution, so as to include a cross-section of organizations working on different aspects of development issues.

My final list of organizations to study included thirty-six nonprofits located in seven different departments (states) of the country. These included four of the five major urban areas (Bogotá, Cali, Medellín, and Bucaramanga) as well as several of the predominantly rural areas such as Antioquia, Santander, Cauca, Nariño, and Putamayo (see appendix E for the names, descriptions, and locations of the organizations). The 36 organizations were spread across six different areas of activity:

1. Technical advisory and leadership training (seven).
2. Applied research on structural causes of poverty with adult popular education and public advocacy components, through conferences, meetings, courses, and publications (seven).
3. Cooperatives specializing in production, marketing, or consumption among small farmers, especially in isolated or poor regions of the country (three).
4. Private foundations sponsored by business groups providing support for multi-purpose activities, including aid to small business establishments (five).
5. Small credit institutions providing loans to low-income street merchants and home-operated businesses who do not have access to regular channels of finance (five).
6. Traditional social service organizations, now orienting their resources toward stimulating self-help, community development programs among the poor (nine).

I carried out structured interviews with one person in an executive position in each of these 36 organizations (normally the executive director or one of the principal administrative officers). These conversations normally lasted from two to three hours and were guided by a formal survey instrument in Spanish of sixty-two open-ended and closed questions (an English version of which is included in appendix F).

These questions were designed to generate information on the following topics: (1) the origin, character, and current goals of the organization; (2) sources of financing and relations with donors; (3) whether progress is being made toward self-financing both by the organization and by the low-income groups it assists; (4) interactions with governmental agencies and business organizations, and attempts by the nonprofit to affect their respective policies; (5) cooperation and coordination with other nonprofit organizations that engage in similar activities; and (6) internal administrative procedures, such as evaluation and planning. Many of these questions paralleled (or in some cases replicated) those used in my interviews with representatives of donor nonprofits in Europe, Canada, and the United States, thus allowing for some comparative analysis across levels of the international nonprofit development community.

In addition to these structured interviews with executives or administrative personnel, I also carried out on-site visits to, and conversations with, local community groups engaged in the projects sponsored by seven of these thirty-six Colombian nonprofits, cutting across four of the six categories of activity outlined above. In such a way, I was able to complement and corroborate information generated in interviews and documents available in central offices with more direct personal observations of project activities.

Finally, I also conducted interviews with eighteen representatives of various international and domestic governmental agencies active in Colombian development and with twenty-seven persons in different parts of the Colombian private sector—business, academia, and other nonprofits not in my survey. All of these persons were chosen for their knowledge of or ongoing contact with development-oriented nonprofits in Colombia. In conversations, I sought their opinions (as knowledgeable outside observers of groups included in my survey) regarding the effectiveness of such organizations in promoting sustainable development programs and affecting the policies of larger social institutions. Hence, in no way did I rely for information only on what the spokespersons for nonprofits in my survey told me.

While my methodology lacked the rigor of an exact random sample, such was not possible given the present scarcity of information on the nonprofit sector in Colombia. By relying on a variety of persons knowledgeable about Colombian development, however, I believe I was able to create a purposive sample designed to generate representative answers to my research questions.[6] In addition, by gathering considerable information from sources external to the organizations selected for my sample (forty-five of my eighty-one interviews in Colombia were with outside observers), I believe I minimized the danger of relying only on the views of those directly responsible for managing such institutions. Finally, so as to maximize the possibility of seeing the upper range of impact of Colombian nonprofits on socioeconomic development, I specifically weighted my sample toward those that have a reputation for making some headway on meeting the basic needs of the poorest and having visibility in the areas where they are operating.

[6] An eye scan of the names of the 1,665 Colombian institutions that were identified by the government in 1984 as functioning with tax-exempt status indicates that approximately 182 (or 12 percent of the total) are likely to be engaged in development work among the poor as opposed to other types of nonprofit activities. Since the government's information on the precise activities of such organizations has not been published, the names are the only clues to their focus. Leaving aside the remaining area of tax-exempt organizations not included in this list—the 3,483 cooperatives, whose class composition is difficult to ascertain from public information, I conclude that the thirty-three of thirty-six organizations in my sample that are *not* cooperatives represent about 18 percent of the 182 development-oriented nonprofits currently enjoying tax-exempt legal status in Colombia.

U.S., Canadian, and European Nonprofit Organizations in Survey

PVOs INTERVIEWED IN THE U.S.

CARE USA (New York)

Catholic Relief Services, CRS (New York)

Church World Service, CWS (New York)

Lutheran World Relief, LWR (New York)

Ford Foundation (New York)

Rockefeller Foundation (New York)

Private Agencies Collaborating Together, PACT (New York)

Coordination in Development, CODEL (New York)

Pan American Development Foundation, PADF (Washington, D.C.)

Adventist Development and Relief Agency, ADRA (Washington, D.C.)

Oxfam America (Boston)

Unitarian Universalist Service Committee, UUSC (Boston)

International Action for Appropriate Technology, AITEC (Boston)

Save the Children Federation, SCF (Westport, Conn.)

Foster Parents Plan, United States of America, FPP USA (Warwick, R.I.)

NGOs INTERVIEWED IN CANADA

Canadian Catholic Organization for Development and Peace, CCODP (Montreal)

Service Universitaire Canadien Outre-mer, SUCO (Montreal)

Canadian Council for International Cooperation, CCIC (Ottawa)

Canadian Universities Service Overseas, CUSO (Ottawa)

CARE Canada (Ottawa)

Oxfam Canada (Ottawa)

Among Equals, INTER PARES (Ottawa)

NGOs INTERVIEWED IN WESTERN EUROPE

Oxford Committee against Hunger of the United Kingdom, Oxfam UK (Oxford)

Catholic Fund for Overseas Development, CAFOD (London)

Christian Aid, CA (London)

Catholic Committee against Hunger and for Development, CCFD (Paris)

Ecumenical Aid Service, CIMADE (Paris)

CARE France (Paris)

International Cooperation for Socioeconomic Development, CIDSE (Brussels)

Oxford Committee against Hunger of Belgium, Oxfam Belgique (Brussels)

Ecumenical Action for Solidarity with Latin America (The Hague)

Central Agency for Joint Financing and Development, CEBEMO (Oegstgeest, the Netherlands)

Netherlands Organization for International Development, NOVIB (The Hague)

Interchurch Coordination Committee for Development Projects, ICCO (Zeist, the Netherlands)

Foster Parents Plan of the Netherlands, FPP Netherlands (Amsterdam)

International Council of Voluntary Agencies, ICVA (Geneva)

Commission on Interchurch Aid, Refugees, and World Service of the World Council of Churches, CICARWS (Geneva)

Department of World Service of the Lutheran World Federation, LWF (Geneva)

Protestant Association for Cooperation in Development, EZE (Bonn)

Friedrich Ebert Foundation, FES (Bonn)

Institute for International Partnership of the Konrad Adenauer Foundation, KAS (Sankt Augustin, FRG)

German Agro Action (Bonn)

Campaign against Hunger and Disease in the World, MISEREOR (Aachen, FRG)

Brot für die Welt (Stuttgart)

German CARITAS Association, DCV (Freiburg im Breisgau, FRG)

Aid Resources of 205 Largest U.S. (1981), Canadian (1980), and European (1980) Nonprofit Organizations

1. OVERSEAS AID AND PERCENTAGE FROM U.S. GOVERNMENT SUBSIDIES OF
THE EIGHTY LARGEST PVOs, 1981 (IN 1986 DOLLARS)

Total aid: $1.47 billion
Government subsidies: $750.8 million (51.1 percent)

TABLE 1
Predominantly Relief Aid, in Millions of Dollars
(Food, Clothing, Medicines, Disaster Help, Aid for Handicapped, Etc.)[a]

	Founded	Overseas Aid	PL 480 Food Related	% Government Subsidies
Catholic Relief Services (CRS)	1943	$384.1	$256.1	72.2
CARE USA	1945	309.7	238.3	77.8
World Vision Relief Organization	1962	72.3		6.0
American Jewish Joint Distribution Committee (JDC)	1914	58.8	0.156	26.9
Christian Children's Fund (CCF)	1938	39.2		0.0
International Rescue Committee	1933	24.2		98.5
Medical Assistance Program International	1954	20.5		1.9
Adventist Development and Relief Agency (ADRA)	1956	18.4	11.8	77.7
World Relief Corporation	1944	11.0		54.9
Catholic Medical Mission Board	1924	10.5		0.0
American Red Cross	1881	8.9		54.0
Christian and Missionary Alliance	1887	8.8		0.0
Direct Relief International	1948	6.5		0.05
Food for the Hungry International	1971	5.6		0.0
Mission Aviation Fellowship	1944	5.2		0.0
International Eye Foundation	1961	3.2		42.3
American Near East Refugee Aid	1968	1.9		81.3
Pearl Buck Foundation	1964	1.7		22.7
Brother's Brother Foundation	1963	1.6		0.3

TABLE 1 *(cont.)*

	Founded	Overseas Aid	PL 480 Food Related	% Government Subsidies
Helen Keller International	1915	1.3		38.9
American Leprosy Missions	1906	1.3		2.7
World Rehabilitation Fund	1955	1.2		37.6
Holt International Children's Services	1956	1.2		1.4
TOTAL 23 agencies		$997.1	$506.4	60.1[b]

Sources: AID, *Voluntary Foreign Aid Programs,* 1982; TAICH, *U.S. Nonprofit Organizations;* OECD, *Directory of Nongovernmental Organisations,* vol. 1, 1981.

[a] Represents 67.9 percent of all PVO aid.

[b] $599.3 million. This also represents 79.8 percent of all U.S. government subsidies to PVOs.

TABLE 2
Predominantly Technical Aid, in Millions of Dollars
(Training, Equipment, Building of Physical Infrastructure)[a]

	Founded	Overseas Aid	% Government Subsidies
Institute of International Education	1919	$42.1	47.2
Summer Institute of Linguistics	1934	29.8	2.8
Planned Parenthood Federation of America	1922	20.3	70.9
International Executive Service Corps	1964	15.8	32.8
Association for Voluntary Sterilization	1937	13.2	95.6
People-to-People Health Foundation/ Project HOPE	1958	11.3	27.9
Sudan Interior Mission	1893	10.8	3.0
Evangelical Alliance Mission	1890	9.8	0.0
American Federation for Rehabilitation through Training (American ORT)	1922	8.3	21.7
Pan American Development Foundation (PADF)	1962	5.9	22.4
Pathfinder Fund	1957	5.2	82.5
National Rural Electric Cooperation Association	1942	4.6	44.7
Population Council	1952	4.5	48.0
AFRICARE	1971	4.2	69.6
Experiment in International Living	1932	4.2	34.3
World Radio Mission Fellowship	1931	4.0	0.0
Opportunities Industrial Centers International		3.7	99.5
Overseas Missionary Fellowship	1901	3.6	0.0
New Trans Century Foundation (NTF)	1968	3.5	97.7
Project Concern International	1961	2.7	26.8
International Planned Parenthood Federation/Western Hemisphere	1922	2.5	0.0
Credit Union National Association (CUNA)	1934	2.4	75.0
Heifer Project International	1944	2.3	10.4
International Voluntary Services (IVS)	1953	2.2	66.7
Technoserve	1968	2.0	70.6
Winrock International Livestock Research & Training Center		1.6	32.1
National Association of Partners of the Alliance (NAPA)	1964	1.6	78.6
Overseas Education Fund of the League of Women Voters		1.3	77.8
International Medical and Research Foundation	1957	1.2	96.0

TABLE 2 (*cont.*)

	Founded	Overseas Aid	% Government Subsidies
Meals for Millions/Freedom from			
Hunger	1946	1.1	42.2
AITEC	1974	0.9	70.0
Institute for International Development	1971	0.9	62.5
TOTAL 32 agencies		$227.5	33.4%[b]

Sources: AID, *Voluntary Foreign Aid Programs*, 1982; TAICH, *U.S. Nonprofit Organizations*; OECD, *Directory of Nongovernmental Organisations*, vol. 1, 1981.

[a] Represents 15.5 percent of all PVO aid.

[b] $75.9 million. This also represents 10.1 percent of all U.S. government subsidies to PVOs.

TABLE 3
Predominantly Multiservice Institution-Building, in Millions of Dollars[a]

	Founded	Overseas Aid	PL 480 Food Related	% Government Subsidies
Church World Service (CWS)	1946	$42.3	$9.3	75.1
Ford Foundation	1936	24.7		0.0
Mennonite Central Committee	1920	18.6		2.1
Rockefeller Foundation	1913	15.8		0.0
United Methodist Church, Board of Global Ministries	1941	19.9		0.0
Domestic & Foreign Mission Society/Protestant Episcopalian Church	1789	14.6		5.8
Save the Children Federation (SCF)	1932	12.9		35.3
Lutheran World Relief	1945	11.2	2.9	34.3
United Presbyterian Church in the USA	1837	9.0		0.0
Foster Parents Plan USA	1937	8.9		1.6
Asia Foundation	1951	8.3		97.1
National Board of YMCAs	1883	7.7		45.3
American Institute for Free Labor Development	1961	7.7		95.9
International Human Assistance Programs	1952	7.6		19.0
United Church Board for World Ministries	1810	6.4		0.0
American Friends Service Committee (AFSC)	1917	5.5		12.9
Society of St. Columban	1918	3.6		0.0
African American Labor Center	1964	3.4		94.6
Private Agencies Collaborating Together (PACT)	1972	2.8		97.8
Oxfam America	1970	2.4		0.0
Agricultural Cooperative Development International	1963	2.4		88.0
Cooperative League/USA	1916	2.2		84.0
Coordination in Development (CODEL)	1969	2.2		66.7
Asian American Free Labor Institute	1968	1.7		97.5
Unitarian Universalist Service Committee (UUSC)	1939	0.5		0.0
TOTAL 25 agencies		$242.3	$12.2	31.2[b]

Sources: AID, *Voluntary Foreign Aid Programs*, 1982; TAICH, *U.S. Nonprofit Organizations*; OECD, *Directory of Nongovernmental Organisations*, vol. 1, 1981.

[a] Represents 16.6 percent of all PVO aid.

[b] $75.6 million. This also represents 10.1 percent of all government subsidies to PVOs.

2. OVERSEAS AID AND PERCENTAGE FROM CANADIAN GOVERNMENT
SUBSIDIES OF THE FORTY-FIVE LARGEST CANANDIAN NGOs, 1980
(IN 1986 DOLLARS)

Total aid: $234.1 million
Government subsidies: $83.4 million (35.6 percent)

TABLE 4
Predominantly Relief, in Millions of Dollars
(Food, Clothing, Medicines, Disaster Help, Aid for Handicapped, Etc.)[a]

	Founded	Overseas Aid	% Government Subsidies
World Vision of Canada	1954	$21.0	10.1
Canadian Red Cross	1909	12.3	63.0
Christian Children's Fund of Canada	1960	4.7	2.9
Mennonite Brethren Mission/Services	1898	4.5	7.4
Compassion of Canada	1964	2.8	7.1
Leprosy Relief/Canada	1961	2.8	6.8
International Medical Assistance	1967	2.0	2.3
Operation Eyesight Universal	1963	1.7	49.8
International Child Care/Canada	1973	1.6	10.4
Christian Reformed World Relief Committee/Canada	1968	1.6	18.8
Save a Family Plan	1965	1.6	6.0
Fame Pereo Institute	1962	1.2	18.5
TOTAL 12 agencies		$57.8	21.8[b]

Sources: CCIC, Directory of Canadian Nongovernmental Organisations; OECD, Directory of
Nongovernmental Organisations, vol. 1, 1981.

[a] Represents 24.7 percent of all NGO aid.

[b] $12.6 million. This represents 15.1 percent of all Canadian government subsidies to NGOs.

TABLE 5
Predominantly Technical Aid, in Millions of Dollars
(Training, Equipment, Building of Physical Infrastructure)[a]

	Founded	Overseas Aid	% Government Subsidies
Canadian UNICEF Committee	1955	$10.1	39.5
CARE Canada	1946	7.7	36.2
Centre for International Programs, University of Guelph	1967	5.2	58.9
Overseas Book Centre	1960	4.9	21.6
Sudan Interior Mission	1893	4.4	9.8
Canadian Baptist Overseas Mission Board	1911	2.9	2.3
Canadian Executive Service Overseas	1967	2.8	95.2
Association of Canadian Community Colleges	1978	2.7	60.0
Centre for Study and International Cooperation	1968	2.4	10.6
Canadian Organization for Rehabilitation through Training	1940	2.4	34.4
Food for the Hungry/Canada	1975	1.7	65.4
Canadian Teachers' Federation	1962	1.6	43.3
Foundation for International Training	1977	1.5	50.9
Oxfam Quebec	1973	1.3	16.0
Africa Inland Mission	1953	1.3	18.2
TOTAL 15 agencies		$52.9	37.4[b]

Sources: CCIC, *Directory of Canadian Nongovernmental Organisations*; OECD, *Directory of Nongovernmental Organisations*, vol. 1, 1981.

[a] Represents 22.6 percent of all NGO aid.

[b] $19.8 million. This also represents 23.7 percent of all Canadian government subsidies to NGOs.

TABLE 6
Predominantly Multiservice Institution-Building, in Millions of Dollars[a]

	Founded	Overseas Aid	% Government Subsidies
Canadian Universities Service Overseas (CUSO)	1961	$26.1	40.3
Foster Parents Plan/Canada (FPP Canada)	1937	21.3	13.8
Canadian Catholic Organization for Development and Peace (CCODP)	1967	17.6	54.7
Mennonite Central Committee	1963	10.6	70.0
Service Universitaire Canadien Outre-mer (SUCO)	1961	10.4	41.0
United Church/Canada		6.3	13.6
Canadian Unitarian Service Committee	1945	5.2	25.6
Canadian Lutheran World Relief	1946	4.7	60.0
Canadian Save the Children (CANSAVE)	1923	3.7	28.2
World University Service of Canada	1939	2.9	86.4
Cooperative Development Foundation of Canada	1947	2.8	90.5
Anglican Church of Canada	1959	2.6	31.5
Interchurch Fund for International Development	1974	2.3	76.5
Saskatchewan Council for International Cooperation	1974	2.3	14.7
National Council of YMCAs of Canada	1912	1.7	46.2
Canadian Jesuit Missions	1955	1.2	11.1
Oxfam Canada	1966	0.9	71.4
INTER PARES	1976	0.8	80.0
TOTAL 18 agencies		$123.4	41.3[b]

Sources: CCIC, Directory of Canadian Nongovernmental Organisations; OECD, Directory of Nongovernmental Organisations, vol. 1, 1981.

[a] Represents 52.7 percent of all NGO aid.

[b] $51.0 million. This also represents 61.2 percent of all Canadian government subsidies to NGOs.

3. OVERSEAS AID AND PERCENTAGE FROM HOME GOVERNMENT SUBSIDIES OF THE EIGHTY LARGEST EUROPEAN NGOs, 1980 (IN 1986 DOLLARS)

Total aid: $1.15 billion
Government subsidies: $475.7 million (41.4 percent)

TABLE 7
Predominantly Relief Aid, in Millions of Dollars
(Food, Clothing, Medicines, Disaster Help, Aid to Handicapped, etc.)[a]

	Founded	Country	Overseas Aid	% Government Subsidies
International Confederation of Catholic Charities	1950	Vatican	$73.6	0.0%
Swiss Red Cross International	1866	Switzerland	53.2	60.0
Save the Children Fund	1919	Great Britain	24.0	0.03
German CARITAS Association (DCV)	1897	FRG	16.6	13.0
Les Hommes pour les Hommes	1968	Belgium	16.4	0.0
British Red Cross	1870	Great Britain	13.3	22.0
Village of Children/Pestalozzi Trogen	1946	Switzerland	12.5[b]	0.0
Emergency Aid to Children	1959	FRG	12.4	0.0
CARITAS Netherlands	1914	Netherlands	9.7	0.0
Help the Aged	1962	Great Britain	9.3	5.0
Medical Mission Action	1925	Netherlands	9.2	0.0
Danish Refugee Council	1956	Denmark	8.6[b]	0.0
Human Earth	1960	Switzerland	8.0	20.0
Finnish Central Association of the Blind	1928	Finland	7.5[b]	31.0
Leprosy Mission International	1874	Great Britain	6.3	0.0
Evangelical Mission Against Leprosy	1874	Switzerland	5.3	0.0
Luxembourg Red Cross	1914	Luxemburg	4.5[b]	0.0
TOTAL 17 agencies		9 countries	$290.4	14.3[c]

Source: OECD, *Directory of Nongovernmental Organisations*, vol. 1, 1981.

[a] Represents 25.3 percent of all NGO aid.

[b] Total budget (overseas aid amount not given).

[c] $41.4 million. This represents 8.7 percent of all European government subsidies to NGOs.

TABLE 8
Predominantly Technical Aid, in Millions of Dollars
(Training, Equipment, Building of Physical Infrastructure)[a]

	Founded	Country	Overseas Aid	% Government Subsidies
Technological Institute	1906	Denmark	$33.3[b]	40.0%
International Committee for Development of Cultural and Educational Activities in Africa	1959	Italy	26.6	100.0
German Volunteer Service	1963	FRG	19.8	100.0
German Agro Action	1962	FRG	19.8	40.0
Norwegian Church Aid	1947	Norway	19.6	34.0
World Organization for Rehabilitation through Training	1880	Switzerland	16.2	70.0
French Association/Volunteers/ Program	1963	France	15.8	70.0
Organization of Netherlands' Volunteers	1965	Netherlands	15.3	100.0
Christian Aid/Belfast	1946	Great Britain	13.0	0.0
International Association for Rural Development	1964	Belgium	12.8	96.0
Swedish Save the Children (Redda Barnen)	1919	Sweden	10.1	17.0
Missionary Cooperation for Development	1969	Belgium	9.7[b]	0.0
YMCA, French Branch	1855	France	8.8[b]	0.0
Calouste Gulbenkian Foundation	1956	Portugal	8.6	0.0
Danish Church Aid (DANCHURCHAID)	1922	Denmark	8.3	38.0
Committee of Protestant Churches in Germany for Service Overseas	1975	FRG	8.0	36.0
Catholic Committee/Freedom From Hunger (Joint Hands)	1959	Spain	7.9	0.0
Swedish Free Mission	1965	Sweden	6.7	5.0
Danish Association for International Cooperation	1944	Denmark	6.5	0.0
Swiss Association for Technical Assistance		Switzerland	6.5	66.0
Swiss Association of Aid to Developing Countries	1948	Switzerland	5.3	38.0
Evangelical Mission Society	1856	Sweden	5.3	10.0
Finnish Missionary Society	1859	Finland	5.2	20.0
Catholic Relief/France		France	5.2	0.0

TABLE 8 (*cont.*)

	Founded	Country	Overseas Aid	% Government Subsidies
Tear Fund	1968	Great Britain	4.8	0.0
Pan African Institute for Development	1965	Switzerland	4.7	85.0
Voluntary Service Overseas (VSO)	1958	Great Britain	4.5	90.0
Society for Rural Development	1961	FRG	4.0	84.0
Norwegian Save the Children (Redda Barnen)	1946	Norway	4.0	8.0
Human Earth, German Section	1967	FRG	3.9	0.0
German Adult Education Association	1953	FRG	3.7	0.0
Workers' Educational Association	1919	Finland	3.3[b]	72.0
Institute of Cultural Affairs	1954	Belgium	3.3	30.0
Netherlands Universities' Foundation for International Cooperation	1952	Netherlands	3.3	100.0
Methodist Church/Overseas (Methodist Missionary Society)		Great Britain	3.2	0.0
TOTAL 35 agencies		13 countries	$336.9	46.8[c]

Source: OECD, *Directory of Nongovernmental Organisations*, vol. 1, 1981.

[a] Represents 29.3 percent of all NGO aid.

[b] Total budget (overseas aid amount not given).

[c] $157.7 million. This represents 33.2 percent of all European government subsidies to NGOs.

TABLE 9
Predominantly Multiservice Institution-Building, in Millions of Dollars[a]

	Founded	Country	Overseas Aid	% Government Subsidies
Campaign against Hunger and Disease in the World (MISEREOR)	1958	FRG	$73.7	40.0
Protestant Association for Cooperation in Development	1962	FRG	66.5[b]	90.0
Interchurch Coordination Committee for Development Projects (ICCO)	1964	Netherlands	46.6	95.0
Lutheran World Federation (LWF)	1947	Switzerland	41.3	0.0
Central Agency for Joint Financing and Development (CEBEMO)	1969	Netherlands	39.9	100.0
Brot für die Welt	1959	FRG	36.1	0.0
Friedrich Ebert Foundation (FES)	1925	FRG	29.3	90.0
Institute for International Partnership of the Konrad Adenauer Foundation (KAS)	1964	FRG	29.3	98.0
Pontifical Mission Aid Society	1838	FRG	18.8	0.0
Oxfam UK	1942	Great Britain	18.6	12.0
Friedrich Naumann Foundation	1958	FRG	14.6	90.0
Department of World Mission of Evangelical Lutheran Church of Bavaria	1972	FRG	11.3[b]	0.0
Catholic Committee Against Hunger and for Development (CCFD)	1961	France	11.5	16.0
Netherlands Organization for International Development (NOVIB)	1956	Netherlands	11.3[b]	80.0
Swiss Protestant Aid	1945	Switzerland	10.5	10.0
Broederlijk Delen	1961	Belgium	7.9	22.0
Christian Aid (CA)	1942	Great Britain	7.7	3.0
Oxfam Belgique	1964	Belgium	7.4	66.0
Institute for Research and Implementation of Development Methods	1958	France	5.3[b]	0.0
Humanistic Institute for Cooperation with Developing Countries (HIVOS)	1968	Netherlands	5.1	100.0
Ecumenical Aid Service (CIMADE)	1939	France	4.7[b]	10.0

306 · Appendix C

TABLE 9 (*cont.*)

	Founded	Country	Overseas Aid	% Government Subsidies
International Confederation of Free Trade Unions	1949	Belgium	4.5	25.0
World University Service	1920	Switzerland	4.3	93.0
Euro Action Agency for Cooperation & Research in Development	1976	Great Britain	3.9	0.0
Catholic Fund for Overseas Development (CAFOD)	1962	Great Britain	3.5	17.0
Netherlands' Trade Union Confederation	1976	Netherlands	3.3	0.0
Swedish Cooperative Centre	1958	Sweden	3.1	72.0
Entraide et Fraternité	1961	Belgium	2.9	20.0
TOTAL 28 agencies		7 countries	$522.7	52.9c

Source: OECD, *Directory of Nongovernmental Organisations*, vol. I, 1981.

a Represents 45.4 percent of all NGO aid.

b Total budget (overseas aid amount not given).

c $276.6 million. This also represents 58.1 percent of all European government subsidies to NGOs.

Questionnaire Administered to Policymakers in Forty-five U.S., Canadian, and European Nonprofit Organizations Supporting Programs in Latin America (October 1982–September 1983)

A. MISSION CHALLENGE

1. What does your organization see as the principal causes of poverty, and how does it define development?
2. What are the major short-run and long-run objectives of your organization?
3. Could you please rank the following goals in term of their importance to your organization when selecting projects to support in Latin America:
   (Please rank order from 1 to 6)

   _____ immediate alleviation of human suffering (hunger, sickness, lack of shelter, etc.).

   _____ increasing income and/or employment opportunities for poor people.

   _____ improving the skills, knowledge, and capacity of recipients to solve problems and manage programs.

   _____ enhancing the bargaining power of recipients to secure equitable arrangements with important social and economic groups and institutions that can assist them—merchants, landlords, credit institutions, government agencies, etc.

   _____ building new institutions and networks of socioeconomic participation designed and operated primarily by the poor themselves.

   _____ empowering the poor to challenge and change the dominant political and economic structures in their environment.

4. Can you describe some new programs or projects you have recently undertaken in Latin America? What accounts for your moving in this direction?

If Religiously Affiliated (5–6)

5. How does the religious affiliation of your organization affect its goals and style of operation? What is the relation between the socioeconomic projects you support and the evangelization programs of the church to which you are affiliated?
6. What do you consider major differences between your organization and that of the other major religiously affiliated institutions based in this country that support social service programs in Latin America?

B. Financial Challenge

7. What are the annual financial expenditures of your organization for the following:

_____ total operating budget

_____ overhead costs (staff, travel, etc.)

_____ overseas material support (e.g., food)

_____ overseas project support

_____ material support to Latin America (e.g., food)

_____ project support in Latin America

(If this information is available in your agency's annual reports, may I have copies of the ones from the last few years?)

8. Does your organization receive some funding, material support, or reimbursement from your own or any other government? If so, approximately what is the dollar value of such aid and for what purposes is it used?

If Receiving Some Public Funds (9–17)

9. What do you believe to be the major benefits to your overseas work that public aid provides?

10. Are there some types of programs or projects for which you would like to have (or have more) public funds and presently do not? If so, which ones?

11. Are there some areas in which you do not (or would not) use public funds? If so, for what programs, and why not?

12. Does your organization experience any problems in the scope or purpose of your overseas activities resulting from the use of public funds?

13. Do you feel your image or credibility has ever been damaged among recipients of your aid in Latin America because of your use of public funds? Why, or why not? Can you give any specific examples?

14. Do you believe the public funds you receive are too restricted in how they can be used?

15. Were you to have more discretion in the dispersal of government resources, how would you use them?

16. Have you ever felt any governmental pressure to support, or not support, overseas programs? If so, how did you respond?

17. Do you feel aid from certain governments is less problematic than from others? If so, please explain.

18. What are your major sources of support from the private sector? Have these changed in recent years in origins or amounts?

19. Has your organization ever rejected private support on the grounds that it was too restrictive?

20. Do you include public education campaigns as part of your fund raising that inform the public in your home country about the causes of poverty in Latin

America and needed strategies to eradicate or alleviate it? If so, please explain how you do this. Could I see some of your brochures and other printed materials from these programs?

If Organization Receives Little or No Public Funds (21–22)

21. Is the fact that your organization receives little or no governmental support an explicit choice on your part? If so, what are the reasons?
22. Do you believe other nonprofit agencies that receive substantial amounts of public aid for overseas activities are positively or negatively affected by this? In what ways, and which agencies?

C. POWER CHALLENGE

23. Do you believe a strictly nonpartisan political position is desirable for a nonprofit agency in its overseas activities? Why or why not?
24. What are the costs and benefits of a PVO/NGO sometimes showing political bias or identification in the types of projects it supports or objectives it seeks in its overseas activities?
25. How does the type of political regime under which you are supporting overseas programs affect your operations or projects? Are some regimes easier to deal with than others? If so, why?
26. Do you believe that to do effective relief and/or development work a foreign donor agency must be working toward some fundamental change in the distribution of power inside Latin American countries through the activities it supports in such societies? If so, please explain.
27. Does your organization try to cooperate or maintain close communication with your own government's agencies that also support projects in the same Latin American countries where you send aid? If so, in what ways are such relationships mutually beneficial?
28. If your organization purposely avoids such cooperative or communicative relations with your government, what are the reasons behind such a decision? Has your agency, or any other nonprofit you know, had negative experiences from such relationships in the past? Explain.
29. Does your organization ever try to affect or change the policies of your home government in its overseas objectives or activities? If so, how and with what success?
30. Has your organization experienced any tension with host governments in Latin America over the past decade as a result of programs/projects you have supported in such societies? If so, please describe. How was the issue resolved?
31. Do you encourage recipients of your aid in Latin America to cooperate or communicate regularly with agencies in their own governments? If so, why and

which agencies? What have been the results of such relationships for their own ongoing programs? If not, why not?

D. EFFECTIVENESS CHALLENGE

32. What processes and methods does your organization use to evaluate the effectiveness of projects you support in Latin America while they are under way? When they are completed?
33. How are the recipients of your aid in Latin America involved in deciding what constitutes program effectiveness and in evaluating programs?
34. Can you describe a case in which your organization insisted on significant modifications or termination of a project you originally supported in Latin America?
35. How does what you have learned from past program evaluations affect your current operations and future planning?
36. With whom and how does your organization share what you have learned from evaluations of programs you support in Latin America?

E. GOVERNANCE CHALLENGE

37. To whom is your organization accountable in its use of resources? How is such accountability maintained?
38. In what ways are recipients of your overseas aid accountable to your organization? Who decides the terms of accountability?
39. Describe the typical decision-making process your organization uses in initiating new projects in Latin America.
40. Do you normally deal directly with groups carrying out their own projects in Latin America or do you usually channel your aid through local, regional, or national intermediary agencies? What are the reasons for your choice?
41. How does planning occur in your organization? Who is involved and how often does the process occur? Can you give an example from recent past history where planning in your organization significantly affected the subsequent style of operation or allocation of resources for overseas activities?
42. Does your organization maintain a local field staff in countries or regions of Latin America where you support projects? If so, is it made up predominantly of foreigners, host country nationals, or about an equal mixture?
43. If you do not maintain a local or regional field staff overseas, whom do you rely on for information and input in deciding on what projects to support?

If Organization Has a Field Staff Overseas (44)

44. Please describe the types of contacts between your home and field-office personnel. What are the major delineations of functions and responsibilities between home and field representatives?

If Religiously Affiliated (45–47)

45. In the dispersal of your overseas aid, do you deal only (or mainly) with religiously affiliated groups in Latin America? What proportion of your aid goes to nonchurch related recipient groups?
46. Do church leaders at home or in Latin America have a role in approving new projects before you support them?
47. Do ecclesiastical leaders sit on the governing board of your organization? If so, what percentage of the membership do they constitute?

Colombian Nonprofit Organizations in Survey

1984 BUDGET   A. TECHNICAL ASSISTANCE AND/OR LEADERSHIP TRAINING ORGANIZATIONS

$33,669   1. *Amigos de las Américas* in Medellín—affiliate of Partners of the Americas, Washington, D.C. (business volunteers who provide advice and leadership training for low-income entrepreneurs and youth).

$63,338   2. *Centro de Estudios Comunitarios Aplicados* (CECA) in Bogotá (technical assistance for private persons constructing their own low-income housing).

3. *CÁRITAS of Cali* in Cali (provides training for peasant leaders in isolated villages in Valle del Cauca in health service and community organization skills).

4. *SEPAS* of Pasto (gives training for community leaders in rural areas of Nariño, and supports small businesses of laundresses in Pasto).

$42,225   5. *Centro de Promoción de Projectos de Desarrollo* (CENPRODES) in Bogotá (gives assistance to grass-roots groups in preparing project proposals and in finding grants from foreign PVOs/NGOs to finance them; does evaluation of projects for international PVO/NGO donors).

$26,391   6. *Grupo PROJECTOS* in Bogotá (provides same services as CENPRODES for other local Colombian groups).

7. *Coordinación Colombiana de Trabajo Voluntario* (CCTV) in Bogotá (facilitates cooperation among regional associations of volunteers throughout Colombia engaged in health, education, and rehabilitation services; trains and advises volunteers in service programs; provides loans to small urban businesses of women).

1984 BUDGET   B. INSTITUTIONS ENGAGED IN APPLIED SOCIAL RESEARCH WITH EDUCATIONAL AND/OR ADVOCACY COMPONENT

$263,908   1. *Centro de Investigación Nacional y Educación Popular* (CINEP) in Bogotá (conducts research on urban and labor problems; provides education, advice, and training for neighborhood associations, peasant organizations, and labor unions; publishes critical analyses of contemporary political and economic issues in Colombia that also propose improved public policies in these areas).

2. *Fundación Friedrich Ebert de Colombia* (FESCOL) in Bogotá—affiliate of Friedrich Ebert Foundation in Bonn, FRG (sponsors research and conferences on economic and political problems in Colombia; brings together government policymakers and social scientists to discuss results of such research; provides advice to labor organizations on current economic trends).

$202,681
3. *Corporación Integral para el Desarrollo Cultural y Social* (CODECAL) in Bogotá (produces materials for adult education in low-income areas; provides training for urban and rural community leaders and aid to community organizations engaged in popular education).

$12,668
4. *Foro Nacional de Colombia* in Bogotá (carries out research on urban problems, especially low-income housing, and gives courses for leaders of grass-roots organizations).

$147,788
5. *Fundación para la Educación Permanente en Colombia y Centro para el Desarrollo de la Educación No-Formal* (FEPEC-CEDEN) in Bogotá (conducts research and publishing, and carries out pilot projects of informal education for low-income families in areas of basic health, nutrition, and early childhood development).

$316,690
6. *Fundación para la Aplicación y Enseñanza de las Ciencias* (FUNDAEC) in Cali (conducts research and training in appropriate technology, health, and education for small farmers in Cauca; sponsors cooperatives and gives loans for small family businesses in countryside).

$475,034
7. *Corporación de Desarrollo* (CODESARROLLO) in Medellín (carries out research on problems of poverty and unemployment in Antioquia, and implements pilot projects that generate employment and construction among poor urban and rural sectors).

1984 SALES
C. PRODUCTION, MARKETING, AND TRAINING COOPERATIVES

$42.2 million
1. *Cooperativa Lechera de Antioquia, Ltda.* (COLANTA) in Medellín (cooperative of small milk producers in Antioquia,

providing services to members in marketing, training, credit, and construction of rural infrastructure).

$1.8 million   2. *Talleres Rurales Industriales del Valle, Ltda.* in Valle del Cauca (production cooperative in ten villages for women who make clothing and shoes to supplement small-farm family incomes; goods marketed by Catalina through assistance by the regional Coffee Producers Federation; cooperative also provides services in day care, education, and materials for housing construction).

3. *Sindicato de Cultivadores y Procesadores del Fique en Santander* (SINTRAPROFISAN) in Santander (marketing association of hemp producers; provides training in crop diversification among poor farmers; mobilizes small farmers to push for implementation of land reform legislation).

1984 BUDGET   D. PRIVATE FOUNDATIONS

$2.9 million   1. *Fundación Carvajal* in Cali (supports five large multiservice centers in low-income areas of Cali; sells materials for low-income housing construction—at cost—in Cali; provides advice, training, and loans for small urban businesses in Cali with patrimonies and fixed places of negotiation).

$633,379   2. *Fundación Carlos Sarmiento Lora* in Cali (supports a large recreational facility in Tuluá; provides advice, training, and loans to small businesses that have patrimonies and fixed places of negotiation in several small cities in Valle del Cauca).

$295,577   3. *Fundación para el Desarrollo de Santander* (FUNDE-SAN) in Bucaramanga (supports cooperatives, teacher training, and appropriate technology programs in rural areas of Santander; runs a public school in a poor area of Bucaramanga, and provides aid to upgrade emergency room facilities at a rural public hospital; gives advice, training, and loans to small businesses with patrimonies and fixed places of negotiation).

$11.6 million   4. *Fundación para la Educación Superior* (FES) in Cali (manages capital investments [from grants] of over four hundred nonprofit organizations, funds of several large intergovernmental organizations active in Colombian development, and investments of private citizens and companies; provides matching grants from its own earnings for socially productive enterprises in education, health, nutrition, and ecology).

$496,147   5. *Corporación para el Financiamiento del Desarrollo Social* (FINSOCIAL) in Medellín (manages capital investments [from grants] for 250 nonprofit organizations in Antioquia and handles investments for over fifteen hundred private individuals and businesses).

1984 BUDGET   E. CREDIT INSTITUTIONS

$295,577   1. AITEC of Boston—regional office in Bogotá (provides advice and grants to small nonprofit credit institutions serving groups of small, urban street merchants in nine cities of Colombia).

$73,894   2. *Banco Mundial de la Mujer–Cali* in Cali (provides advice and loans to groups of small businesses of various sizes in Cali, including mobile street markets run by low-income women).

$40,114   3. *Crédito Familiar de la Parroquia Nuestra Señora de la Esperanza* in Cali (provides advice and loans to groups of small street merchants in slum areas of Cali).

$401,140   4. *Corporación Acción por Antioquia* (ACTUAR) in Medellín (provides advice and loans for small family businesses in urban and rural poor areas in Antioquia).

$422,253   5. *Microempresas de Antioquia* in Medellín (provides advice, training, and loans for small businesses with patrimonies and fixed places of negotiation in urban and rural areas of Antioquia).

1984 BUDGET   F. MULTIPURPOSE SOCIAL SERVICE ORGANIZATIONS

$182,624   1. *Corporación para la Recreación Popular* in Cali (provides matching grants to local communities to construct, with the aid of government and private business, park facilities in eight slum areas of Cali, which also include health and preschool services for residents).

438,087   2. *Federación de Desarrollo Juvenil Comunitario* in Bogotá—affiliate of Save the Children Federation (provides training for rural community leaders; gives aid to construct health centers in rural areas and to upgrade the skills and teaching materials in rural public schools; supports revolving loan funds for small family businesses in rural areas).

$316,690
3. *Catholic Relief Services USA*—regional office in Bogotá (provides grants for technical and leadership training, production and marketing cooperatives, health and water facilities, and programs to protect Indian culture).

4. *Fundación para el Servicio de la Vivienda Popular Integral* (SERVIVIENDA) in Bogotá (runs factories in four cities that sell—at cost—pre-fabricated materials for low-income housing; also provides loans to buyers of such materials).

$527,816
5. *Plan Padrinos-Cali* in Cali—affiliate of Foster Parents Plan International (provides grants for income supplements, for health centers, and for education and housing facilities in poor urban rural areas near Cali).

$1.2 million
6. *Plan Padrinos-Tumaco* in Tumaco—affiliate of Foster Parents Plan International (provides social services and family income supplements to poor black families in Tumaco; constructs and operates rural health stations and literacy training programs, and gives advice to a series of cooperatives that are now independent of its sponsorship).

$105,563
7. *Futuro para la Niñez* in Medellín—affiliate of Children's Futures USA (provides training for community leaders in isolated rural villages of Antioquia to organize their people and identify collective needs; acts as broker between such community groups and local government agencies that can provide the services that the communities identify as priorities).

$253,352
8. *SEPAS* of San Gil (provides training for peasant leaders and groups in technical, organizational, and communication skills; provides technical advice for a federation of rural cooperatives (COOPCENTRAL), which it founded but which is now independent; runs a rural newspaper focusing on peasant problems in Santander).

9. *Fundación Santa Fe de Bogotá* in Bogotá (hospital-based out-patient clinic for ten thousand residents in a low-income area in northern Bogotá; provides training for medical paraprofessionals from the same area, and offers free backup in-patient services for residents when medically indicated).

APPENDIX F

Questionnaire Administered to Policymakers in Thirty-six Colombian Nonprofit Organizations (June–August 1984)

A. ORIGIN, CHARACTER, AND GOALS

1. What kind of organization is this?
   _____ cooperative
   _____ charitable institution
   _____ private foundation
   _____ social service agency
   _____ educational and/or research organization
   _____ other (please explain)
2. What are the principal activities of the organization?
3. When and how did the organization begin? Please explain the circumstances, the principal objectives, the key persons, etc., at the beginning?
4. What kind of financing did the organization have at the start? What were its principal sources of support—e.g., local community, foreign donors, etc.?
5. How many persons actually benefit from the activities or services of the organization?
6. What class of persons benefit from the activities of the organization (e.g., residents in a specific region or neighborhood, small farmers, youth, women, etc.)?
7. What is the income level of the majority of the beneficiaries of its activities?
8. Do you believe it is possible to help the poorest residents of the region (neighborhood)? Why, or why not?
9. Do you believe that the activities of your organization have an impact on persons or groups who are *not* members or beneficiaries? If yes, what is this impact and who are those affected?
10. In the perspective of the organization, what are the principal causes of poverty? What is the meaning of socioeconomic development?
11. What priority do the following goals have for your organization (please rank in order)?
    _____ alleviate the most immediate causes of human suffering (hunger, malnutrition, sickness, lack of potable water or shelter, etc.)
    _____ raise the level of income and/or employment for the poor
    _____ improve the technical and administrative capacities of local organizations or their members to solve their own socioeconomic problems

_____ strengthen a network of social participation created and managed by the poor themselves

_____ increase the influence of the poor to negotiate more effectively with other significant social groups or institutions in their region—commercial middlemen, landowners, banks, government agencies, etc.

_____ help the poor in their struggle to change the structures of political and economic power in their region

_____ other (please explain)

Has the priority among these goals changed since the beginning of the organization?

12. What has been the most successful activity or project that the organization has supported or carried out? Why?

13. What activity or project of the organization has been the least successful? Why?

If Religiously Affiliated (14–15)

14. Is there a link between the organization's socioeconomic activities or projects and the religious efforts of the church? If so, what is it?

15. Do beneficiaries of the organization's work have to be active members of the church? What percentage are not?

B. FINANCIAL ASPECTS AND RESOURCES

16. What is the annual budget of the organization, and how is it divided among major activities (including administrative costs)?

    Could you please give me a copy of the present budget or the last annual report of the organization?

17. Here is a list of the financial sources from among which organizations such as yours frequently receive support. Could you please indicate the approximate amount of aid your organization is receiving from each of these in the current year (1984)?

SOURCE	Total
a. national government	
ministry of _____	_____
ministry of _____	_____
b. departmental government	
office of _____	_____
office of _____	_____
c. municipal government	
office of _____	_____
office of _____	_____

d. international organizations
   governmental _____

   private _____

e. private domestic organizations or groups/individuals
   profitmaking _____

   nonprofit _____

f. contributions of members or participants in the organization's projects _____
g. sale of products, service fees, etc. _____
h. other sources _____ _____

18. In recent years has there been a change proportionately in the amount of support received from these different sources? If yes, what and where have been the changes?

19. Do you think that in recent years the possibilities of finding domestic financial support for your organization have increased? Why or why not, and please give examples.

20. In your opinion, what are the advantages and disadvantages for nonprofit organizations of receiving aid from each of the following sources?

SOURCE	*Advantages*	*Disadvantages*
a. Ministries or agencies of the national government	_____	_____
b. Divisions of state government	_____	_____
c. Offices of municipal government	_____	_____
d. International Organizations		
Private Profitmaking	_____	_____
Nonprofit	_____	_____
Governmental	_____	_____
e. Domestic Private Organizations		
Profitmaking	_____	_____
Nonprofit	_____	_____

If Receiving Aid from International Organizations (21)

21. How would you best characterize relations between yourselves and your international donors?

_____ They treat us as colleagues—we share in the definition of priorities of these international organizations and in the selection of projects they support.

_____ They give us block grants, which we freely assign to projects that we choose.

_____ They leave us much liberty to design and implement projects, but it is necessary to present each specific new project for their approval.

_____ We do not have much discretion either in the formulation or in the execution of projects because the donor organizations have their own priorities and very strict conditions.

_____ Other (please explain).

22. According to your experience, do domestic or international sources of aid place more conditions on their assistance? What type of restrictions?

23. Is there excessive pressure on you by your financial donors to diversify your sources of support? Please explain.

24. Are there any negative consequences in accepting aid from international organizations that are financed by governments in developed countries?
If there are, could you please explain what these are and give the names of the organizations and governments you have in mind?

25. What are the usual ways in which your organization identifies financial resources?

_____ We approach a potential domestic private donor.

_____ We approach a domestic governmental agency.

_____ We approach an international agency.

_____ A potential domestic private donor approaches us.

_____ A domestic governmental agency approaches us.

_____ An international organization approaches us.

_____ Other (please explain).

Of the above mentioned methods; which is the most frequent? Which is the least frequent?

26. Has it ever happened that a source of financial assistance has offered your organization resources subject to excessive conditions or restrictions?
If yes, can you please explain the circumstances and the response of your organization?

27. Is financial self-sufficiency a reality or a goal for your organization?

_____ It is a reality (or almost a reality) at present.

_____ It is a goal, and will be feasible in the near future.

_____ It is desirable, but not feasible in the foreseeable future because . . . (explain reasons).

_____ It is not a goal because . . . (please explain).

28. Is financial self-sufficiency a goal for the local projects or groups your organization supports?

_____ It is a goal, and for some it is currently a reality (or almost a reality).

_____ It is a goal, and will be feasible for the majority in the foreseeable future.

_____ It is desirable, but not feasible for the great majority in the foreseeable future because . . . (please explain).

_____ It is not a goal because . . . (please explain).

29. What would be the consequences of achieving financial self-sufficiency at some point in the future both for your organization and for the projects or groups it supports?

   a. Consequences (positive and negative) for the organization:

   b. Consequences (positive and negative) for the projects or groups you support:

C. SOCIAL, ECONOMIC, AND POLITICAL CONTEXT AND RELATIONS WITH OTHER ORGANIZATIONS

30. In your opinion, what are the *three* most urgent national problems now facing Colombia?

   What are the *three* most urgent problems in your region (or the region where the majority of the projects or groups supported by your organization are located)?

31. What will be necessary to solve these problems at the national level? At the regional level?

32. Is your organization contributing to the resolution of these problems? How, and with what results?

	Our Strategy	Results to Date
a. National level	_____	_____
b. Regional level	_____	_____

33. Do you believe an apolitical position is desirable and possible for a nonprofit organization that tries to promote socioeconomic development "from blow" in Colombia today?

_____ Yes, it is desirable and possible.

_____ It is desirable, but frequently is not possible because . . . (please explain).

_____ No, because to support the process of socioeconomic development it is necessary to bring about political changes and to associate with political movements.

_____ It is impossible to avoid politics, but it is necessary to distinguish between acceptable and unacceptable political activities for a nonprofit organization that works at the local level . . . (please explain).

34. Does your organization cooperate with any Colombian governmental agencies? If so, with which ones and with what results?

Agency	Type of Cooperation	Results
a.		
b.		
c.		
d.		

35. In your opinion, is there a danger of too close cooperation between a private organization such as yours and agencies of the government? If there is, what should be the limits to such cooperation?

36. If your organization does *not* cooperate with any governmental agencies, what are its reasons for not doing so?

37. Has your organization ever tried to influence decision-making of agencies or ministries of the government? If so, please explain the circumstances. What were the results?

38. Has your organization ever tried to influence decisions of private organizations or groups with significant economic power in your region? If so, how and with what results?

39. What are the Colombian organizations most critical for your work, and do these impact (positively or negatively) on your organization's activities?

40. Have there been conflicts or tensions in recent years between your organization and powerful institutions in the region? If there have been, how have they been resolved?

41. Are there other Colombian private groups or organizations who are carrying out similar activities as those of your organization? If so, what are those organizations?

42. Has your organization tried to establish methods of cooperation with these other private groups? With which ones, and with what results?

Organization	Type of Cooperation	Results
a.		
b.		
c.		
d.		

43. In general, would you say that there is sufficient cooperation among Colombian nonprofit organizations that work in the same areas of activity?

44. If not, what changes would be necessary to promote effective cooperation among them?
Do you think such changes can be brought about in the near future? Why or why not?

45. In your perspective, what has been the most important impact your organization has had in the region or field of activity where you operate?

46. Have any ideas or strategies of your organization with respect to socioeconomic

development been replicated by any governmental agencies or other private organizations? If so, what idea or strategy?

47. If your organization's strategies have been replicated by institutions with more resources than its own, what have been the results?

_____ These other organizations are now offering the services to more persons than we could do and, as a result, we are reorienting our resources and energies toward other problems.

_____ These other organizations that have tried to replicate our approach are not having much success because they are less capable or committed than we are.

_____ It is almost impossible to replicate our programs on a wider level, despite good intentions of organizations with more resources than ours.

_____ This duplication of our work by other institutions has brought on a crisis for us and has precipitated conflicts between us and other organizations.

_____ Other (please explain).

D. INTERNAL ADMINISTRATIVE CHARACTERISTICS

48. Could you please describe the administrative structure of your organization (e.g., how many divisions, departments, committees, etc.)?

49. Does your organization work only in one region or community, or does it have offices in various areas?

If there are other offices, how many are there and what are their interrelations?

50. Do you yourself participate in other organizations? If so, which ones?

social _____

economic _____

political _____

51. How many persons (and of what nationalities) work in each sector of your organization?

	Colombians	Foreigners (Nationality?)
board of directors	_____	_____
executive committee	_____	_____
director(s)	_____	_____
department heads	_____	_____
administrative staff	_____	_____

52. How is personnel selected for different administrative responsibilities in the organization, and what are their respective salary levels?

	Method of Selection	Average Salary Level
board of directors	_____	_____
executive committee	_____	_____

director(s)   _____   _____
department heads   _____   _____
administrative staff   _____   _____

If Religiously Affiliated (53–54)

53. How many church leaders (bishops, clerics, religious) serve in the following capacities?

	Numbers	Percent of Total
board of directors	_____	_____
executive committee	_____	_____
director(s)	_____	_____
department heads	_____	_____
administrative staff	_____	_____

54. What other functions do ecclesiastical personnel or leaders play in the organization?

_____ They have no other functions.

_____ New projects must be approved by them.

_____ They help obtain foreign resources for the organization.

_____ Other (please explain).

55. What are the principal responsibilities of each one of the following offices in the organization:

Office	Responsibility
board of directors	_____
executive committee	_____
director(s)	_____
department heads	_____
administrative staff	_____

56. How many persons work gratis as volunteers in your organization, and what are their responsibilities?

57. Could you please describe the usual procedure that the organization uses to select new activities and projects?

58. Do the persons who are beneficiaries of its activities or services participate in the critical decisions of the organization?

_____ Yes. In what ways do they participate?

_____ No.

59. What is the methodology used by the organization in evaluating projects?

60. Have evaluations ever precipitated changes in the procedures of the organization? If so, could you give an example of this?

61. Does the organization share results of evaluation of its activities or projects with other persons or institutions? If so, with which ones?

If they are shared, could you give me copies of some completed evaluations?

62. What methodology do you use to evaluate the impact of your activities or projects on the wider environment—e.g., on the social or economic structures in the region, or on the activities of other organizations, etc.?

63. Does the organization have a formal planning process? Do beneficiaries of projects take part in the process? If so, in what ways?

Bibliography

INTERVIEWS BY THE AUTHOR

Angulo, Rev. Alejandro, S.J. Director of Publications, National Center for Research and Popular Education (CINEP). Bogotá, Colombia, July 19, 1984, and August 3, 1984.

Ash, Jeff. Chief Project Officer, International Action for Appropriate Technology (AITEC). Cambridge, Mass., November 29, 1982.

Barth, Rev. Maurice, O.P. Assistant for Human Rights, General Secretariat, Ecumenical Aid Service (CIMADE). Paris, France, September 12, 1983.

Berg, Robert J. Senior Fellow, Overseas Development Council (ODC). Washington, D.C., January 20, 1986 (telephone).

Bolioli, Rev. Oscar. Director, Latin American Office, Church World Service (CWS). New York, January 6, 1983.

Bond, Jim. Staff Consultant, Appropriations Committee, U.S. Senate. Washington, D.C., March 17, 1986.

Bordelon, Rev. Msgr. Roland. Regional Director for South America, Catholic Relief Services (CRS). New York, October 12, 1982.

Breier, Dr. Horst. Press Officer, German Ministry for Economic Cooperation (BMZ), Bonn, FRG, September 20, 1983.

Brodhead, Tim. Executive Director, Among Equals (INTER PARES). Ottawa, Canada, May 31, 1983.

Brown, Kenneth E. Coordinator for Latin America and the Caribbean, Coordination in Development (CODEL). New York, January 7, 1983.

Busche, J. Robert. Assistant Executive Director, Lutheran World Relief (LWR), New York, January 5, 1983.

Casasbuenas Morales, Dr. Constantino. Member, Executive Board and Core Staff, *Foro Nacional de Colombia*. Bogotá, Colombia, June 6, 1984.

Castillo, Carlos. Regional Representative for Latin America, Private Agencies Collaborating Together (PACT). New York, January 6, 1983.

Castro, Rev. Gonzalo, S.J. Director, Evangelical Service for Social Action (SEPAS) of Pasto. Pasto, Colombia, July 29, 1984.

Chambers, Marian. Staff Consultant, Foreign Affairs Committee, U.S. House of Representatives. Washington, D.C., August 7, 1986 (telephone).

Cobo, Dr. Alex. Director, Social Division, *Fundación para la Educación Superior*. Cali, Colombia, June 12, 1984.

Confers, Bernard. Former Executive Director (1946–1981), Lutheran World Relief (LWR). March 3, 1986 (telephone).

Coolen, Antonio. Project Officer, Latin American Department, Central Agency for Joint Financing and Development (CEBEMO). Oegstgeest, the Netherlands, September 28, 1983.

Cumming, Lawrence S. National Secretary, Oxford Committee against Hunger of Canada (Oxfam Canada). Ottawa, Canada, June 2, 1983.

Dalton, Russ. Professor, Department of Political Science, University of Florida. Gainesville, Fla., May 13, 1986 (telephone).

De Araujo Dantas, Valdi. Representative of International Action for Appropriate Technology (AITEC) in Colombia. Bogotá, Colombia, August 3, 1984.

De Mendoza, Roberto. Assistant Director, Center for the Promotion of Development, Secretariat of the Catholic Episcopal Conference of Colombia. (CENPRODES), Bogotá, Colombia, June 7, 1984.

Del Hierro Santacruz, Senator Eduardo. Several conversations during June, July, and August, 1984 in Bogotá, Colombia, Pasto, Colombia, and Tumaco, Colombia.

Dixon, Claire. Project Officer for Latin America, Catholic Fund for Overseas Development (CAFOD). London, United Kingdom, September 9, 1983 and April 22, 1986 (telephone).

Dugua, Collette. Assistant to the Director, Latin American Department, Catholic Committee Against Hunger and for Development (CCFD). Paris, France, April 21, 1986 (telephone).

Eggers, Dr. Helmut. Director, Programming and Coordination of Evaluations, Directorate General for Development, Commission of the European Community (CEC). Brussels, Belgium, September 26, 1983.

Fajardo, Miguel. Program Director, Evangelical Service for Social Action (SEPAS) of San Gil. San Gil, Colombia, July 11, 1984.

Feldman, Dr. Lilli. Department of Political Science, Tufts University. Medford, Mass., May 6, 1986.

Frado, Dennis W. Secretary for Communication and Documentation, Department of World Service, Lutheran World Federation (LWF). Geneva, Switzerland, September 14, 1983.

Galand, Pierre. Director, Oxford Committee against Hunger of Belgium (Oxfam Belgique). Brussels, Belgium, September 27, 1983, and May 5, 1986 (telephone).

Giesler, Heidi. Community Development Service, Department of World Service, Lutheran World Federation (LWF), Geneva, Switzerland, September 14, 1983.

Gilmore, Judith W. Senior Evaluation Officer, Office of Private and Voluntary Cooperation, Bureau for Food for Peace and Voluntary Assistance, U.S. Agency for International Development (AID). Rosslyn, Va., May 17, 1983, and August 4, 1986 (telephone).

Gómez, Miguel. Assistant Director, Catholic Relief Services (CRS) in Colombia, and former Executive Director, Office of Interinstitutional Cooperation (OCIT). Bogotá, July 19, 1984.

Gómez Ramírez, Luis Alberto. Executive Director, Corporation for Development (CODESARROLLO). Medellín, Colombia, July 24, 1984.

González Parra, Rev. Ramón. Executive Director, Evangelical Service for Social Action (SEPAS) of San Gil. San Gil, Colombia, July 12, 1984.

Grant, John P. Regional Director for Latin America, Save the Children Federation (SCF). Westport, Conn., March 25, 1983.

Guay, René. Director for South America, Canadian Catholic Organization for Development and Peace (CCODP). Montreal, Canada, February 21, 1983.

Harmston, Richard J. Executive Director, Canadian Council for International Cooperation (CCIC). Ottawa, Canada, January 21, 1983.

Hellinger, Douglas. Codirector, Development Group for Alternate Policies (Development GAP). Washington, D.C., March 3, 1986 (telephone).

Howarth, Dr. Jolyon. (University of Bath, United Kingdom). Visiting Scholar, Center for European Studies, Harvard University. Cambridge, Mass., January 6, 1986.

Hoyer, Hans. Latin American Field Representative, Lutheran World Relief (LWR), Lima, Peru, January 7, 1986 (in Cambridge, Mass.).

Hunziker, Marianne. Director for International Relations, Ecumenical Aid Service (CIMADE), Paris, France, September 12, 1983, and March 27, 1986 (telephone).

Jaramillo Restrepo, Guillermo. Executive Director, *Futuro para la Niñez*. Medellín, Colombia, July 25, 1984.

Josi, Juan. Project Officer, Latin American Department, Campaign against Hunger and Disease in the World (MISEREOR). Aachen, FRG, September 22, 1983.

Kaiser, Wolfgang. Project Officer for Central America and the Caribbean, Protestant Association for Cooperation in Development (EZE). Bonn, FRG, September 20, 1983.

Kamper, Teunis. Office of International Organizations and NGOs, Ministry of Foreign Affairs, Government of the Netherlands. The Hague, September 30, 1983.

Kardish, David. Government Relations Officer, Canadian Council for International Cooperation (CCIC), Ottawa, Canada, August 6, 1985 (telephone). Public Relations Department, Canadian Universities Service Overseas (CUSO), Ottawa, Canada, March 3, 1986 (telephone).

Kierstens, Thom. Director of International Programs, Central Agency for Joint Financing and Development (CEBEMO). Oegstgeest, the Netherlands, April 1, 1986 (telephone).

Kines, Thomas. National Director, Canadian Cooperative Assistance for Relief Everywhere (CARE Canada), Ottawa, Canada, May 31, 1983.

Ködderitzsch, W. Head, Specialized Service, Directorate General for Development, Commission of the European Community (CEC). Brussels, Belgium, September 26, 1983.

Kogan, Ronda. Project Officer, South American Region, Catholic Relief Services (CRS). New York, June 18, 1985.

Kolk, Hein P. Director, Foster Parents Plan, the Netherlands (FPP Netherlands). Amsterdam, the Netherlands, September 29, 1983.

Kölsch, Herbert. Representative for Venezuela and Central America, Institute for International Partnership, Konrad Adenauer Foundation (KAS). Sankt Augustin, FRG, September 21, 1983.

Kozlowski, Anthony J. Executive Director, International Council of Voluntary Agencies (ICVA). Geneva, Switzerland, September 15, 1983.

Krashinsky, Dr. Michael. Department of Economics, Scarborough College, University of Toronto, Toronto, Canada, November 18, 1985 (telephone).

Kraus, George F. Regional Program Director for Latin America, U. S. Cooperative Assistance for Relief Everywhere (CARE USA). New York, January 4, 1983.

Krauskopf, Heinzberndt. Head, Latin American Department, Campaign Against Hunger and Disease in the World (MISEREOR), Aachen, FRG, April 21, 1986 (telephone).

Lasso, Salvador. Alternate for Senator Eduardo del Hierro Santacruz. Pasto, Colombia, July 7, 1984 (in Sibundoy, Colombia).

Lieser, Jurgen. Project Officer, Latin American Department, German CARITAS Association (DCV), Freiburg im Breisgau, FRG, September 16, 1983.

Lowry, Rev. Boyd. Executive Director, Corodination in Development (CODEL). New York, February 14, 1983.

Madelin, Rev. Henri, S. J. Former provincial superior of the Society of Jesus in France. Cambridge, Mass., January 25, 1986.

Maione, Romeo. Head, NGO Division, Special Programs Branch, Canadian International Development Agency (CIDA). Hull, Canada, February 22, 1983.

Marshall, Lynn V. Director, Community Education Affairs, Catholic Relief Services (CRS), New York, October 12, 1982.

Martin, Terence. Regional Director for South America, Catholic Relief Services (CRS). New York, June 18, 1985.

Merckaert, Jacques. Project Officer, Latin American Department, Central Agency for Joint Financing and Development (CEBEMO). Oegstgeest, the Netherlands, September 28, 1983.

Miller, Robert. Research Associate, Parliamentary Centre, Ottawa, Canada, June 1, 1983 (in Montreal, Canada).

Nichols, Bruce. Director, Project on Church and State Abroad, Carnegie Council on Ethics and International Affairs, New York, March 10, 1986 (telephone).

O'Brien, James F. Director, Project Fund, Private Agencies Collaborating Together (PACT). New York, December 30, 1982 and August 18, 1986 (telephone).

O'Brien, Dr. Robert F. Executive Director, Private Agencies Collaborating Together (PACT). New York, January 6, 1983.

Ochoa, Mario H. Assistant Executive Director, Adventist Development and Relief Agency (ADRA). Washington, D.C., February 7, 1983.

Olszewski, Rev. Laurence M., C.S.C. Coordinator of Diocesan Affairs, Catholic Relief Services (CRS). New York, October 12, 1982.

Padrón Castillo, Dr. Mario. Research Associate, Center for the Study and Promotion of Development (DESCO). Lima, Peru, October 21, 1986.

Peiró, Angel. Project Officer for Latin America, Commission on Interchurch Aid, Refugees, and World Service, World Council of Churches (CICARWS). Geneva, Switzerland, September 14, 1983.

Phillips, Kenneth H. National Executive Director, Foster Parents Plan, United States of America (FPP USA). Warwick, R.I., June 10, 1983.

Pruzensky, Dr. William. Regional Director for Central America and the Caribbean, Catholic Relief Services (CRS). New York, October 12, 1982.

Puryear, Jeffrey M. Program Officer, Developing Country Programs, Ford Foundation. New York, January 14, 1983.

Quinlan, Robert T. Director, International Office, Catholic Relief Services (CRS). Geneva, Switzerland, September 14, 1983.

Ramírez, Enrique. Assistant Director, Latin American Department, Service Universitaire Canadien Outre-mer (SUCO). Montreal, Canada, February 21, 1983.

Ramos, Rev. Antonio. Assistant Director, Latin American Office, Church World Service (CWS). New York, January 6, 1983.

Reinders, Jan. Assistant Director, Protestant Association for Cooperation in Development (EZE). Bonn, FRG, September 20, 1983 and March 26, 1986 (telephone).

Rignall, Ray. Director, Program Department, U.S. Cooperative Assistance for Relief Everywhere (CARE USA). New York, February 14, 1983.

Roberts, Alonso. Project Officer for Latin America and the Caribbean, Christian Aid (CA). London, September 9, 1983 and May 12, 1986 (telephone).

Rodríguez, Jorgé. Coordinator, Americas Program, Canadian Universities Service Overseas (CUSO). Ottawa, Canada, January 21, 1983.

Rojas, Humberto. Member of the Board of Directors, Projects Group (*Grupo* PRO-JECTOS). Bogotá, August 6, 1984.

Rostan, Werner. Director, Latin American Section, *Brot für die Welt*. Stuttgart, FRG, September 19, 1983.

Salm, Martin. Project Officer, Latin American Department, German CARITAS Association (DCV). Freiburg im Breisgau, FRG, September 16, 1983.

Santo Pietro, Daniel. Project Officer, South American Region, Catholic Relief Services (CRS). New York, August 13, 1981.

Schubert, Klaus. Executive Director, Friedrich Ebert Foundation of Colombia (FES-COL). Bogotá, Colombia, July 18, 1984.

Scobie, Dr. Richard S. Executive Director, Unitarian Universalist Service Committee (UUSC). Boston, October 25, 1982.

Short, Joseph. Executive Director, Oxford Committee Against Hunger of America (Oxfam America). Boston, April 1, 1983.

Simon, Laurence. Director, Policy Analysis Department, Oxford Committee Against Hunger of America (Oxfam America). Boston, March 8, 1983.

Smith, Rev. C. William. Project Director for Central America, the Caribbean, and Brazil, Canadian Catholic Organization for Development and Peace (CCODP). Montreal, Canada, December 16, 1982, February 21, 1983, and March 11, 1986 (telephone).

Sollis, Peter. Project Officer, Latin American Department, Oxford Committee Against Hunger of the United Kingdom (Oxfam UK). Oxford, United Kingdom, September 9, 1983.

Stienhans, Heinrich. Project Officer, Latin American Department, German Agro Action. Bonn, FRG, September 21, 1983.

Strasser, Marlyse. Director, Latin American Department, Catholic Committee Against Hunger and for Development (CCFD). Paris, September 12, 1983.

Treydte, Klaus-Peter. Director, Department of Development Research, Friedrich Ebert Foundation (FES), Bonn, FRG, September 21, 1983.

Uribe, Rev. Manuel, S.J. Executive Director, National Center for Research and Popular Education (CINEP). Bogotá, June 1, 1984.

Van der Heijden. Head, Aid Management Division, Development Cooperation Directorate, Organization for Economic Cooperation and Development (OECD). Paris, France, April 6, 1986; and May 12, 1986 (telephone).

Van Dijk, Rev. S. S. Head, Latin American Department, Interchurch Coordination Committee for Development Projects (ICCO). Zeist, the Netherlands, September 30, 1983, and April 29, 1986 (telephone).

Van Dongen, Kees. Project Officer, Latin American Department, Netherlands Organization for International Development (NOVIB). The Hague, the Netherlands, September 28, 1983, and April 15, 1986 (telephone).

Van Heemst, Dr. Jan J. P. Institute of Social Studies (ISS). The Hague, the Netherlands, May 20, 1986 (telephone).

Vargas, Lenny. Project Officer, South American Region, Catholic Relief Services (CRS). New York, June 18, 1985.

Victoria, Jaimé. Executive Director, *Federación Juvenil de Desarrollo Comunitario.* Bogotá, July 7, 1984 (in Sibundoy, Colombia).

Vollmer, Dr. Franz-Josef. Director, Overseas Projects Department. German CARITAS Association (DCV), Freiburg im Breisgau, FRG, September 16, 1983.

Whitehead, Christine. Project Officer, Latin American Department, Oxford Committee Against Hunger of the United Kingdom (Oxfam UK). Oxford, United Kingdom, September 9, 1983.

Wipfler, Rev. William. Director, Office of Human Rights, Division of Overseas Ministries, National Council of Churches (NCC). New York, January 27, 1983.

Zuluaga de Díaz, Luz. Assistant Director, Catholic Charities (CARITAS) of Cali. Cali, Colombia, June 15, 1984.

OTHER SOURCES

Abbott, Walter M., S.J., *The Documents of Vatican II.* New York: America Press, 1966.

"Acuerdo entre 'el Común' y el gobierno." *José Antonio* (San Gil, Colombia), February 1984.

Adelman, Irma, and Cynthia Taft Morris. *Economic Growth and Social Equity in Developing Countries.* Stanford, Calif.: Stanford University Press, 1973.

Agency for International Development (AID). Advisory Council on Voluntary Foreign Aid. *A Look to the Future: The Role of Voluntary Agencies in International Assistance.* Washington, D.C.: AID, 1974.

———. Bureau for Food for Peace and Voluntary Assistance, Office of Private and Voluntary Cooperation. *Development Effectiveness of Private Voluntary Organizations (PVOs).* Washington, D.C.: AID, February 1986.

———. "Guidelines for Development Education Project Grants, Fiscal Year 1985." Washington, D.C.: AID, December 1984. Mimeographed.

———. "PL 480 Title II Evaluations, 1980–1985: The Lessons of Experience." Washington, D.C.: AID, June 1985. Mimeographed.

———. *PVO Institutional Development Evaluation Series: Interim Report.* Washington, D.C.: AID, 1986.

———. *Strengthening the Developmental Potential of Food for Work.* Washington, D.C.: AID, April 1986.

———. "USAID Workshop for Biden-Pell Project Directors," Hilltop House, Harpers Ferry, W.Va., October 29–31, 1984. Mimeographed.

———. *Voluntary Foreign Aid Programs.* Washington, D.C.: AID, 1974, 1979, 1982, 1983, 1984, 1986.

———. Bureau for Program Policy Coordination. *AID Partnership in International Development with Private and Voluntary Organizations.* Washington, D.C.: AID, 1982.

————. Office of Private and Voluntary Cooperation. "Expenditure Report of Support and Revenue for U.S. PVOs Registered with A.I.D." Mimeographed. Washington, D.C.: AID, 1988.

Albarran, Luis. "El Salvador: U.S. Humanitarian Aid Said Linked to Counterinsurgency." *Interlink Press Service Reports*, February 1985, pp. 3–4.

Aldunate, Rev. José, S.J., and Jaime Ruíz-Tagle P. "El empleo mínimo: ¿Ayuda social o verguenza nacional?" *Mensaje* (Santiago) 29 (June 1980): 257–63.

Alger, Chadwick F. "Bridging the Micro and the Macro in International Relations Research." *Alternatives* 10, no. 3 (Winter 1984/1985): 319–44.

Alliband, Terry. *Catalysts of Development: Voluntary Agencies in India*. West Hartford, Conn.: Kumarian Press, 1988.

American Council for Voluntary International Action (INTERACTION). *Diversity in Development: U.S. Voluntary Assistance to Africa*. Washington, D.C.: INTERACTION, 1985.

Anheier, Helmut. "Private Voluntary Organizations and Development Organizations in West Africa: Comparative Perspectives." New Brunswick, N.J.: Rutgers University Department of Sociology, 1987. Mimeographed.

Annis, Sheldon. "NGOs in Mexico City." Mimeographed. Washington, D.C., ODC, August 1, 1986.

Arnold, Steven A. *Implementing Development Assistance: European Approaches to Basic Needs*. Boulder, Colo.: Westview, 1982.

Arnove, Robert F., ed., *Philanthropy and Cultural Imperialism: The Foundations at Home and Abroad*. Boston: G. K. Hall and Co., 1980.

Arruda, Marcos. "The Role of Latin American Nongovernmental Organizations in the Perspective of Participatory Democracy." Paper presented at the Third International FFHC/AD Consultation, FAO, Rome, September 3–6, 1985.

Asher, Robert A. *Development Assistance in the Seventies: Alternatives for the United States*. Washington D.C.: Brookings Institution, 1970.

Avrin McLean, Sheila. *U.S. Philanthropy: Grantmaking for International Purposes*. Washington, D.C.: Council on Foundations, 1982.

Ayres, Robert. *Banking on the Poor: The World Bank and World Poverty*. Cambridge, Mass.: M.I.T. Press, 1983.

Bagley, Bruce M. "The National Front and Beyond: Politics, Power, and Public Policy in an Inclusionary Authoritarian Regime." Occasional Paper no. 4, Washington, D.C.: Johns Hopkins School for Advanced International Studies (SAIS), June 1984. Mimeographed.

Bagley, Bruce M., and Matthew Edel. "Popular Mobilization Programs of the National Front: Cooptation and Radicalization." In *Politics of Compromise*, edited by R. A. Berry, R. G. Hellman, and M. Solaún, pp. 257–84.

Baile, Stephanie. *Survey of European Nongovernmental Aid Organizations: A Guide to NGOs and Their Perception of the World Bank*. Washington, D.C.: International Bank for Reconstruction and Development (IBRD), 1986.

Behar, Richard. "SCF's Little Secret." *Forbes*, April 21, 1986, pp. 106–7.

Bennett, Philip. "Mexico City Is Rising From the Ruins." *Boston Globe*, September 21, 1986, p. A9.

Berger, Suzanne. "Religious Transformation and the Future of Politics." *European Sociological Review* 1, no. 1 (May 1985): 23–45.

Berman, Edward H. "Educational Colonialism in Africa: The Role of American Foundations, 1910–1945." In *Philanthropy and Cultural Imperialism*, edited by R. F. Arnove, pp. 179–201.

———. "The Foundations' Role in American Foreign Policy: The Case of Africa, Post 1945." In *Philanthropy and Cultural Imperialism*, edited by R. F. Arnove, pp. 203–32.

———. *The Influence of the Carnegie, Ford and Rockefeller Foundations on American Foreign Policy: The Ideology of Philanthropy.* Albany: State University of New York Press, 1983.

Berry, R. Albert, Ronald G. Hellman, and Mauricio Solaún, eds. *The Politics of Compromise: Coalition Government in Colombia.* New Brunswick, N.J.: Transaction Books, 1980.

Berry, R. Albert, and Ronald Sligo. "The Distribution of Income in Colombia: An Overview." In *Economic Policy and Income Distribution in Colombia*, edited by R. A. Berry and R. Sligo. Boulder, Colo.: Westview Press, 1980, pp. 1–45.

Berryman, Phillip. *The Religious Roots of Rebellion: Christians in Central American Revolutions.* Maryknoll, N.Y.: Orbis Books, 1984.

Betts, T. F. "Development Aid from Voluntary Agencies to the Least Developed Countries." *Africa Today* 25, no. 4 (October-December 1978): 47–68.

Blumenthal, Ralph. "Catholic Relief Services Involved in Dispute over Spending in Ethiopia Aid." *New York Times*, August 7, 1985, p. A8.

Bock, Edwin A. *Fifty Years of Technical Assistance: Some Administrative Experiences of U.S. Voluntary Agencies.* Chicago: Public Administration Clearing House, 1954.

Bolling, Landrum. *Private Foreign Aid: U.S. Philanthropy for Relief and Development.* Boulder, Colo.: Westview Press, 1982.

Bourdarias, Jean. "Chili: L'engagement politique du CCFD." *Le Figaro* (Paris), March 25, 1986, p. 2.

———. "Une épine dans la chair de l'Église." *Le Figaro*, March 25, 1986, p. 2.

Bourges, Hervé. *The French Student Revolt: The Leaders Speak.* New York: Hill and Wang, 1968.

Bratton, Michael. "The Politics of Government-NGO Relations in Africa." *World Development* 17 (April 1989): 569–87.

Braunthal, Gerhard. *The West German Social Democrats, 1969–1982: Profile of a Party in Power.* Boulder, Colo.: Westview Press, 1983.

Bridges, Tyler. "Peru: After Some Good Times, Austerity around Corner." *Boston Globe*, April 19, 1987, p. A8.

Brittain, Vera. "Massacre by Bombing", *Fellowship* 10 (March 1944).

Brodhead, Tim, and Brent Herbert-Copley. *Bridges of Hope? Canadian Voluntary Agencies and the Third World.* Ottawa: North-South Institute, 1988.

Brot für die Welt. *Hunger durch Überfluss.* Stuttgart: Brot für die Welt, 1982.

Brown, E. Richard. "Rockefeller Medicine in China: Professionalism and Imperialism." In R. F. Arnove, ed., *Philanthropy and Cultural Imperialism*, pp. 123–46.

Brownfield, Alan. "Behind the Effort to Cut Off Aid to El Salvador." *Washington Times*, February 24, 1983.

Bruneau, Thomas C. *The Political Transformation of the Brazilian Catholic Church.* Cambridge: Cambridge University Press, 1974.

———. *The Church in Brazil: The Politics of Religion.* Austin: University of Texas Press, 1982.

Bruneau, Thomas, C., Jan J., Jorgensen, and J. O. Ramsay. "CIDA: The Organization of Canadian Overseas Assistance." Working Paper No. 24, Centre for Developing Area Studies, McGill University, Montreal, July 1979. Mimeographed.

Brusasco, Amedeo. "Cooperation between NGOs and the EEC." In OECD, *The Role of Nongovernmental Organisations in Development Cooperation.* Paris: OECD Development Centre, 1983, pp. 55–57.

Bullock, Mary Brown. *An American Transplant: The Rockefeller Foundation and PUMC.* Berkeley: University of California Press, 1980.

Cable, Vincent. *British Interests and Third World Development.* London: Overseas Development Institute (ODI), 1980.

Campaign against Hunger and Disease in the World (MISEREOR). *Brasilien.* Aachen, FRG: MISEREOR, 1979.

———. *Sudafrika.* Aachen, FRG: MISEREOR, 1983.

Canadian Council for International Cooperation (CCIC). *Directory of Canadian Nongovernmental Organizations Engaged in International Development.* Ottawa: CCIC, 1982.

———. "Framework for Canada's Development Assistance." Policy Paper of CCIC, Ottawa, November 1979. Mimeographed.

———. *I.D. Profile: A Who's Who and What's What of International Development.* Ottawa: CCIC, 1986.

———. *Report of the Task Force on Government Funding.* Ottawa: CCIC, June 1982.

———. *Study of International Development Education in Canada, Final Report.* Montreal: Cooperative d'animation et de consultation, May 1982.

CARE's Use of Food Aid: Policy and Guidelines. New York: CARE USA, 1984.

Castel, Pierre. "Débat: Le tiers-mondisme au rancart?" *Croissance des Jeunes Nations* (Paris), No. 270, March 1985, pp. 10–13.

Catholic Committee against Hunger and for Development (CCFD). *Getting to Know the CCFD: On the Occasion of the 1981 Meeting* Paris: CCFD, 1981.

———. *Le defi de la solidarité: La pratique du CCFD.* Paris: CCFD, 1982.

———. *Faim-Développement* 83 (June–July 1983).

———. *CCFD-INFO* No. 18, September 1983.

Catholic Relief Services (CRS). *CRS: Catholic Relief Services.* New York: CRS, 1983.

———. *Annual Report, 1981.* New York: CRS, 1982.

CBS-TV. "The Gospel According to Whom?" *60 Minutes*, January 23, 1983.

Center for the Promotion of Development, Secretariat of the Catholic Episcopal Conference of Colombia (CENPRODES). *Informativo CENPRODES* (Bogotá), Boletin No. 2, May 1984.

Cheema, G. Chabbir. "The Role of Voluntary Organizations." In *Decentralization and Development*, edited by G. C. Cheema and Dennis Rondinelli. Beverly Hills, Calif.: Sage Publications, 1983, pp. 209–29.

Church World Service (CWS). *The Church World Service Annual Report, 1980.* New York: CWS, 1981.

Clarkson, Stephen, ed. *An Independent Foreign Policy for Canada?* Toronto: Mc-Clelland and Stewart, 1968.

Cleary, Edward., O.P. *Crisis and Change: The Church in Latin America Today.* Maryknoll, N.Y.: Orbis Books, 1985.

Cloward, Richard A., and Frances Fox Piven. *The Politics of Turmoil.* New York: Pantheon Books, 1974.

Colombia Estadística, 1983. Bogotá: Departamento Administrativo Nacional de Estadística (DANE), 1983.

Commission of Appraisal (William Ernest Hocking, Chairman). *Rethinking Missions: A Laymen's Inquiry after One Hundred Years.* New York: Harper, 1932.

Commission of the European Community (CEC). *Comparative Evaluation of Projects Cofinanced with NGOs and Microprojects: Indicative Synthesis.* Brussels: CEC, 1981.

Commission on Private Philanthropy and Public Needs (Filer Commission). *Giving in America.* Washington, D.C.: Commission on Private Philanthropy and Public Needs, 1975.

Considine, John J., M.M. *Technical Assistance Activities by Christian Missionary Groups: Role of Churches.* New York: American Council of Voluntary Agencies for Foreign Service (ACVAFS), 1958.

Contee, Christine E. *What Americans Think: Views on Development and U.S.–Third World Relations.* New York and Washington, D.C.: INTERACTION and Overseas Development Council (ODC), 1987.

Cool, Michel. "Le CCFD contre-attaque." *La Vie* (Paris), No. 2124, 15–21 May 1986, pp. 27–28.

Côt, Jean-Pierre. *À l'épreuve du pouvoir: Le tiers-mondisme, pour quoi faire?* Paris: Éditions du Seuil, 1984.

Cuny, Frederick C. *Disasters and Development.* New York: Oxford University Press, 1983.

Curti, Merle. *American Philanthropy Abroad: A History.* New Brunswick, N.J.: Rutgers University Press, 1963.

Cziempiel, Ernst-Otto. "Germany and the Third World: The Politics of Free Trade and the Free Hand." In *West German Foreign Policy: 1949–1979*, edited by Wolfram F. Hanrieder. Boulder, Colo.: Westview Press, 1980, pp. 181–96.

Dams, Theodor. "The 'Third Avenue' for Development: The Role of Nongovernmental Organizations." University of Freiburg, Institute for Development Economics (IFEP), June 1987. Mimeographed.

"Débat: les tiers-mondistes contre-attaquent." *Croissance des Jeunes Nations* (Paris), No. 271, April 1985, pp. 9–11.

De Crombrugghe, Genevieve, Mick Howes, and Mark Nieuwkerk. *An Evaluation of CEC Small Development Projects.* Brussels: CEC, December 1985.

Dix, Robert. *Colombia: The Political Dimensions of Change.* New Haven: Yale University Press, 1967.

"Doing Good Abroad." *The Economist* 189 (October 11, 1958): 141; and 189 (December 27, 1958): 1158–59.

D'Orfeuil, Henri Rouille. *Cooperer autrement: L'engagement des organizations non gouvernementales aujourd'hui.* Paris: Éditions l'Hamattan, 1984.

Douglas, James. *Why Charity? The Case for a Third Sector.* Beverly Hills, Calif.: Sage Publications, 1983.

Dussel, Enrique. *History and the Theology of Liberation.* Maryknoll, N.Y.: Orbis Books, 1976.

Ecumenical Aid Service (CIMADE). "Au Brésil, un peuple se lève." *CIMADE Informations*, No. 12, December 1982, pp. 1–24.

———. "Bolivie soutien une démocratie encore fragile." *CIMADE Informations*, No. 5, May 1983, pp. 1–18.

———. "La CIMADE a 40 ans." *CIMADE Informations*, No. 10, October, 1980, pp. 3–15.

———. "Uruguay: Cris d'un peuple contre la tyrannie." *CIMADE Informations*, No. 1, 1979, pp. 1–50.

Emerson, Rupert. *From Empire to Nation: The Rise of Self-Assertion of Asian and African Peoples.* Boston: Beacon Press, 1960.

European Consortium for Agricultural Development (ECAD). *Europeans and Aid to Development.* Milan: ECAD, 1984.

Evers, Tilman. "European Social Democracy in Latin America: The Case of West Germany." In *The European Challenge: Europe's New Role in Latin America*, edited by Jenny Pearce. London: Latin American Bureau, 1982, pp. 80–129.

Federal Ministry for Economic Cooperation (BMZ), Public Relations Section, Federal Republic of Germany. *Development Policy Concept of the Federal Republic of Germany.* Bonn: BMZ, November 1975.

Fernandes, Rubem César. "Las ONGs: Una nueva realidad institucional en América Latina." Preparatory Seminar to the Third International Consultation of the Freedom From Hunger/Action for Development Campaign (FFH/AD) of the Food and Agricultural Organization (FAO), Rio de Janeiro, July 1985. Mimeographed.

Fernandez, Rubem César, and Leilah Landim. "Um perfil dos ONGs no Brasil." *Comunicacões do Iser* (Rio de Janeiro) 5, no. 22 (November 1986): 44–56.

Filiteau, Jerry. "Famine Relief in Ethiopia: CRS Has Nothing to Hide." *The Witness* (Dubuque, Iowa) 65, no. 39 (November 24, 1985): 1.

Fisher, Julie. "Development From Below: Neighborhood Improvement Associations in Latin American Squatter Settlements." *Studies in Comparative International Development* 19, no. 1 (Spring, 1984): 61–85.

Ford, Rev. John C., S.J. "The Morality of Obliteration Bombing." *Theological Studies* (Washington, D.C.) 5 (1944): 261–309.

Forrester, Veronica. "The German Political Foundations." In *Pressure Groups, Policies, and Development*, edited by C. Stevens and J. V. van Themaat, pp. 40–60.

Forsythe, David P. *Humanitarian Politics: The International Committee of the Red Cross.* Baltimore: Johns Hopkins University Press, 1977.

Foster Parents Plan, United States of America (FPP USA). *Journey*, Winter, 1984.

Fox, Thomas H. "Private/Non-Governmental Support for Third World Development." Testimony to the Subcommittee on Foreign Operations, Committee on Appropriations, House, 99th Cong., 1st sess., March 28, 1985.

Frühling, Hugo. "Nonprofit Organizations as Opposition to Authoritarian Rule: The Case of Human Rights Organizations and Private Research Centers in Chile."

PONPO Working Paper No. 96, Program on Nonprofit Organizations, Institution for Social and Policy Studies, Yale University, 1985. Mimeographed.

Fundación para la Educación Superior y Desarrollo (FEDESARROLLO). *Desarrollo social en la década de 70.* Bogotá: UNICEF, 1984.

Galtung, Johan. "Nonterritorial Actors and the Problem of Peace." In *On the Creation of a Just World Order: Preferred Worlds for the 1980s,* edited by Saul H. Mendlovitz. New York: Free Press, 1975, pp. 151–88.

———. *The True Worlds.* New York: Free Press, 1980.

Garilao, Ernesto. "Indigenous NGOs as Strategic Institutions: Managing the Relationship with Government and Resource Agencies." *World Development* 15, no. 10 (Autumn 1987, supplement): 113–20.

Gorman, Robert F., ed. *Private Voluntary Organizations as Agents of Development.* Boulder, Colo.: Westview Press, 1984.

Gordon, Walter. *A Choice for Canada: Independent or Colonial Status.* Toronto: McClelland and Stewart, 1966.

Goulet, Denis, and Michael Hudson. *The Myth of Aid: The Hidden Agenda of Development Reports.* New York: International Documentation (IDOC) North America, 1971.

Gruhn, Isebill. "The Lomé Convention: Inching Towards Interdependence." *International Organization* 30, no. 2 (Spring 1976): 421–62.

Haas, Ernst. *Beyond the Nation State: Functionalism and International Organization.* Stanford: Stanford University Press, 1964.

Hanrieder, Wolfram F., and Graeme P. Auton. *The Foreign Policies of West Germany, France and Britain.* Englewood Cliffs, N.J.: Prentice-Hall, 1980.

Hansmann, Henry. "The Role of Nonprofit Enterprise." *Yale Law Journal* 89, no. 5 (April 1980): 835–901.

Hapgood, David., ed. *The Role of Popular Participation in Development.* M.I.T. Report No. 17. Cambridge, Mass.: Center for International Studies, Massachusetts Institute of Technology, 1968.

Hartlyn, Jonathan. "Producer Associations, the Political Regime, and Policy Processes in Contemporary Colombia." *Latin American Research Review* 20, no. 3 (1985): 111–38.

Hartz, Louis. *The Liberal Tradition in America: An Interpretation of American Political Thought Since the Revolution.* New York: Harcourt, Brace, and World, 1955.

Hastings, Adrian. *A History of African Christianity, 1950–1975.* Cambridge: Cambridge University Press, 1979.

Hellinger, Douglas. "The Consortia Experience of Private Development Organizations in Latin America." Washington, D.C.: Development GAP, May 1983. Mimeographed.

Hessel, Stephane. "France and the Third World." Paper presented at the Conference, "Continuity and Change in Mitterrand's France," Center for European Studies, Harvard University, Cambridge, Mass., December 5–7, 1985.

Holzer, Bernard (President of CCFD). "Intervention de Bernard Holzer a la conference de presse du 5 Mai 1986: Le CCFD répond et dénonce." Mimeographed. 11 pp.

Horowitz, David. "Billion Dollar Brains." *Ramparts* (Berkeley, Ca.) 7 (1969): 23–33.

Horowitz, Irving Louis., ed. *The Rise and Fall of Project Camelot*. Cambridge: M.I.T. Press, 1967.

Hoskins, Lewis M. "Voluntary Agencies and Foundations in International Aid." *Annals of the American Academy of Political and Social Science* 329 (May 1960): 57–68.

Hunzinger, Jacques. "La politique étrangère du parti socialiste." *Politique Étrangère* (Paris) 2 (1975): 177–99.

Hutchison, William. *Errand into the World: American Protestant Thought and Foreign Missions*. Chicago: University of Chicago Press, 1987.

Independent Commission on International Development Issues (Brandt Commission). *North-South: A Programme for Survival*. Cambridge, Mass.: M.I.T. Press, 1980.

Independent Group on British Aid. *Real Aid: A Strategy for Great Britain*. London: The Independent Group on British Aid, 1982.

Inglehart, Ronald. *The Silent Revolution: Changing Values and Political Styles Among Western Publics*. Princeton: Princeton University Press, 1977.

International Bank for Reconstruction and Development (IBRD). *Cooperation between the World Bank and Nongovernmental Organizations (NGOs)*. Washington, D.C.: IBRD, 1984.

International Labour Organization (ILO). *Employment, Growth, and Basic Needs: A One-World Problem*. New York: Praeger, 1977.

Isaac, Rael Jean. "Do You Know Where Your Church Offerings Go?" *Reader's Digest*, January 1983, pp. 120–25.

James, Estelle, ed. *The Nonprofit Sector in International Perspective: Studies in Comparative Culture and Policy*. New York: Oxford University Press, 1989.

Johnson, Willard R., and Vivian R. Johnson. "Relations between Governments and Voluntary Development Organizations in Selected West African Countries." Center for International Studies, Massachusetts Institute of Technology, 1988. Mimeographed.

Joint Working Group on Development Education (ACVAFS/PAID). *A Framework for Development Education in the United States*. New York and Washington: ACVAFS and PAID, 1984.

Jones, Merwyn. *In Famine's Shadow: A Private War on Hunger*. Boston: Beacon Press, 1965.

Kierstens, Thom G. K. *Are NGOs In? The Role of the Development of Nongovernmental Organizations in the Netherlands*. Soesterberg, The Netherlands: Centrum Kontakt der Kontinenten, 1981.

Kitschelt, Herbert. "New Social Movements in West Germany and the United States." In *Political Power and Social Theory*, vol. 5, edited by Maurice Zeitlin. Greenwich, Conn.: JAI Press, 1985, pp. 273–324.

Knusel, Jack L. *West German Aid to Developing Nations*. New York: Praeger, 1968.

Koldewyn, Phillip. "Mexican Voluntary Associations: A Community Study." *Journal of Voluntary Action Research* 15, no. 1 (1986).

Kramer, Ralph M. *Voluntary Agencies in the Welfare State*. Berkeley: University of California Press, 1981.

Lador-Lederer, J. J. *International Nongovernmental Organizations and Economic Entities*. Leyden: A. W. Sythoff, 1962.

Landes, Ronald G. *The Canadian Polity: A Comparative Introduction*. Scarborough, Ont.: Prentice-Hall Canada, 1983.

Lamberton, Mary. *St. John's University of Shanghai, 1879–1952*. New York: United Board for Christian Colleges in China, 1955.

Landim, Leilah. "Nongovernmental Organizations in Latin America." *World Development* 15 (Autumn 1987, supplement): 29–38.

Lappé, Frances Moore, Joseph Collins, and David Kinley. *Aid as Obstacle*. San Francisco: Institute for Food and Development Policy, 1980.

La República (Bogotá), August 7, 1984.

Latourette, Kenneth Scott. *Christianity in a Revolutionary Age: A History of Christianity in the Nineteenth and Twentieth Centuries*. 5 vols. New York: Harper and Brothers, 1958–1962.

Laudicina, Paul A. *World Poverty and Development: A Survey of American Public Opinion*. Washington, D.C.: ODC, 1973.

Leclerc, Gerard. "L'argent des chrétiens au service de la révolution." *Quotidien de Paris* (Paris), March 25, 1986, p. 23.

Levine, Daniel H. *Religion and Politics in Latin America: The Catholic Church in Venezuela and Colombia*. Princeton: Princeton University Press, 1981.

Levine, Daniel H., ed. *Religion and Political Conflict in Latin America*. Chapel Hill: University of North Carolina Press, 1986.

Levinson, Jerome, and Juan de Onis. *The Alliance that Lost Its Way: A Critical Report on the Alliance for Progress*. Chicago: Quadrangle Books, 1970.

Linden, Eugene. *The Alms Race: The Impact of American Voluntary Aid Abroad*. New York: Random House, 1976.

Lissner, Jorgen. *The Politics of Altruism: A Study of the Political Behaviour of Voluntary Development Agencies*. Geneva: Lutheran World Federation, 1977.

Low Murtra, Enrique. "Las sociedades y las entidades sin ánimo de lucro como alternativos para el desarrollo." *Sociedades comerciales: Ponencias del primer simposio nacional sobre sociedades*. Bogotá: Cámara de Comercio de Bogotá, 1983, pp. 13–27.

McCarthy, Kathleen D. "The Voluntary Sector Overseas: Notes from the Field." Working Paper, Center for the Study of Philanthropy, Graduate School and University Center, City University of New York, 1988.

Mansbach, Richard W., and John A. Vasquez. *In Search of Theory: A New Paradigm for Global Politics*. New York: Columbia University Press, 1981.

Marris, Peter, and Martin Rein. *Dilemmas of Social Reform: Poverty and Community Action in the United States*. New York: Atherton Press, 1967.

Mashek, Robert. *The Inter-American Foundation in the Making*. Rosslyn, Va.: Inter-American Foundation, 1981.

Masoni, Vittorio. "Nongovernmental Organizations and Development." *Finance and Development*, 22, no. 3 (September 1985): 38–41.

Maury, Guillaume. "CCFD: C'est de plus en plus inquiétant!" *Figaro-Magazine* (Paris), April 19, 1986, pp. 21–24.

———. "Charité chrétienne ou subversion marxiste?" *Figaro-Magazine* October 26, 1985, pp. 25–34.

Meehan, Eugene J. *In Partnership With People: An Alternative Development Strategy.* Rosslyn, Va.: Inter-American Foundation, 1979.

Mecham, J. Lloyd. *Church and State In Latin America: A History of Politico-ecclesiastical Relations.* 2nd ed. rev. Chapel Hill: University of North Carolina Press, 1966.

Michalopoulos, Constantine. "Basic Needs Strategy: Some Policy Implementation Issues of the U.S. Bilateral Assistance Program." In *Human Rights and Basic Needs in the Americas*, edited by Margaret C. Crahan. Washington, D.C.: Georgetown University Press, 1982, pp. 239–59.

Michanek, Ernst. *The Role of Swedish NGOs in International Development Cooperation.* Stockholm: Swedish International Development Authority (SIDA), 1977.

Minear, Larry. "Reflections on Development Policy: A View From the Private Voluntary Sector." In *Private Voluntary Organizations*, edited by R. F. Gorman, pp. 13–39.

Ministry of Overseas Development, United Kingdom. *The Changing Emphasis in British Aid Policies: More Help for the Poorest.* London: HMSO, October 1975.

Moreira Alves, Maria Helena. "Grassroots Organizations, Trade Unions, and the Church: A Challenge to Controlled *Abertura* in Brazil." *Latin American Perspectives* 11, no. 1 (Winter 1984): 73–102.

Morris, Robert C. *Overseas Volunteer Programs: Their Evolution and the Role of Governments in Their Support.* Lexington, Mass.: D. C. Heath, 1973.

Mutuale-Balume, Ya. *Workers for Development: The Case of Volunteers from Nongovernmental Organizations within the European Community.* Brussels: Liaison Committee of Nongovernmental Organizations for Development in the European Economic Community, 1985.

NBC-TV. *1986* (July 29, 1986).

Nelson, Joan M. *Aid, Influence and Foreign Policy.* New York: Macmillan, 1968.

Netherlands Organization for International Development (NOVIB). *Steps Towards Each Other: Passing a Landmark.* The Hague: NOVIB, 1982.

Neusner, Jacob. "Righteousness—Not Charity: The Jewish Tradition." *Foundation News* 25, no. 5 (September/October 1984): 38–41.

Nichols, J. Bruce, *The Uneasy Alliance: Religion, Refugee Work, and U.S. Foreign Policy.* New York: Oxford University Press, 1988.

Nightingale, Benedict. *Charities.* London: Allen Lane, 1973.

Ninkovich, Frank. *The Diplomacy of Ideas: U.S. Foreign Policy and Cultural Relations, 1938–1950.* Cambridge: Cambridge University Press, 1981.

Nossal, Kim Richard. "Personal Diplomacy and National Behavior: Trudeau's North-South Initiatives and Canadian Development Assistance Policy." *Dalhousie Review* (Summer 1982): 278–91.

———. *The Politics of Canadian Foreign Policy.* Scarborough, Ont.: Prentice-Hall Canada, 1985.

Organization for Economic Cooperation and Development (OECD). *Collaboration between Official Development Cooperation Agencies and Nongovernmental Organisations.* Paris: OECD, 1981.

———. *Development Assistance Efforts and Policies of the Members of the Development Assistance Committee, 1967 Review.* Paris: OECD, 1967.

————. *Development Cooperation, 1979 Review*. Paris: OECD, 1979.

————. *Directory of Nongovernmental Organisations in OECD Member Countries Active in Development Cooperation*. 2 vols. Paris: OECD Development Centre, 1981 (1989, 2d edition revised).

————. "Government Subsidies to Voluntary Agencies Active in Development Assistance." Paris: OECD, 1975. Mimeographed.

————. *The Role of Nongovernmental Organizations in Development Cooperation*. Paris: OECD Development Centre, 1983.

————. *Twenty-five Years of Development Cooperation: Efforts and Policies of the Members of the Development Assistance Committee*. Paris: OECD, 1985.

Overseas Development Institute (ODI). *Not By Government Alone: Nongovernmental Organisations in the Development Decade*. London: ODI, 1964.

Packenham, Robert A. *Liberal America and the Third World: Political Development Ideas in Foreign Aid and Social Science*. Princeton: Princeton University Press, 1973.

Paddock, William, and Elizabeth Paddock. *We Don't Know How: An Independent Audit of What They Call Success in Foreign Assistance*. Ames, Iowa: Iowa State University Press, 1973.

Padrón Castillo, Mario. *Cooperación al desarrollo y movimiento popular: Las asociaciones privadas de desarrollo*. Lima: Centro de Estudios y Promoción del Desarrollo (DESCO), 1982.

————. "NGOs and Grassroots Development in Latin America." Paper presented at the Thirteenth International Congress of the Latin American Studies Association (LASA), Boston, October 22–26, 1986.

————. "Nongovernmental Development Organizations: From Development Aid to Development Cooperation." *World Development* 15 (Autumn 1987, supplement): 69–77.

————. "Redes y agrupaciones nacionales de organizaciones no gubernamentales de desarrollo en América Latina: El caso de Peru." Lima: DESCO, March 1985. Mimeographed.

Pang, Eul-Soo. "The Darker Side of Brazil's Democracy." *Current History* 87 (January 1988): 21–24, 40–41.

Parra Escobar, Ernesto. *La economía colombiana, 1971–1981*. Bogotá: CINEP, 1982.

Pierce, Andrew J., ed. *Third-World Instability: Central America as a European-American Issue*. New York: Council on Foreign Relations, 1985.

Piret, Baudoin, and Pierre Galand. *L'aide de la Belgique aux pays en développement*. Brussels, Contradictions and Vie Ouvrière, 1983.

Preston, Julia. "Humanitarian Gesture or 'Political Pacification'?" *Boston Globe*, December 16, 1984, p. A18.

Private Agencies in International Development (PAID) and the American Council of Voluntary Agencies for Foreign Service (ACVAFS). "Testimony Submitted to the U.S. Commission on Security and Economic Assistance." (Carlucci Commission). Mimeographed. Washington, D.C. July 11, 1983. 7 pp.

Puryear, Jeffrey M. "Higher Education, Development Assistance, and Repressive Regimes." *Studies in Comparative International Development* 17, no. 2 (Summer 1982): 3–35.

Rabier, Jacques-Rene, Helene Riffault, and Ronald Inglehart. *Euro-Barometer 20: Aid to Developing Nations, October 1983*. Ann Arbor: Inter-University Consortium for Political and Social Research, University of Michigan, 1985.

Rashke, Richard. "GVN/CRS/USAID." *National Catholic Reporter*, December 17, 1976, p. 1.

Real Aid: A Strategy for Great Britain. London: World Development Movement, 1982.

Reedy, C.S.C., Rev. John. "Council vs. 'Sixty Minutes.' " *The Witness (Dubuque, Iowa), July 17, 1983, p. 4*.

Riding, Alan. "Ailing Brazil Is Divided on Economy." *New York Times* (National Edition), June 1, 1988, p. 29.

Ringland, Arthur C. "The Organization of Voluntary Foreign Aid, 1939–1953." *Department of State Bulletin* 30, no. 768 (March 15, 1954): 383–93.

Roberts, Hibbert R. "The Domestic Environment of AID-Registered PVOs: Characteristics and Impact." In *Private Voluntary Organizations*, edited by R. F. Gorman, pp. 99–114.

————. "Meals for Millions: Limits and Potential for International Aid." *International Journal of Comparative Sociology* 21, no. 3–4 (September–December 1980): 182–95.

Rondos, Alex. "Mitterrand's Two-Year Record." *Africa Report*, May–June 1983, pp. 8–11.

Rosenberg, Emily. *Spreading the American Dream*. New York: Hill and Wang, 1982.

Ross, Franklin A. C., Luther Fry, and Elbridge Sibley. *The Near East and American Philanthropy*. New York: Columbia University Press, 1929.

Rousseau, André. "L'Action Catholique Ouvrière." *Acts de la recherche en sciences sociales*, 44–45 (November 1982).

Rudel, Christian. "Frères des Hommes: Contre le mal-développement." *La Croix* (Paris), December 20, 1983.

Santana, Pedro. *Desarrollo regional y paros cívicos en Colombia*. Bogotá: CINEP, 1983.

Santana Rodríguez, Pedro, and Constantino Casasbuenas Morales. "Hacia una política de vivienda popular en Colombia." In *La vivenda popular hoy en Colombia*, edited by P. Santana Rodríguez. Bogotá: CINEP, 1983, pp. 191–282.

Santo Pietro, Daniel., ed. *Approaches to Evaluation: Sourcebook for the PVO Community*. New York: ACVAFS, 1983.

Schoonbrood, Michel. *Development as an International Social Issue: A Dialogue Program of the Churches in the Federal Republic of Germany*. Bonn: Prospective International, Ecumenical Working Group on Church and Development, 1981.

Schwartz, Elliot. "Private and Voluntary Organizations in Foreign Aid." Washington D.C.: Office of Management and the Budget (OMB), Special Studies Division, November 15, 1978. Mimeographed.

Sethi, Harsh. "Groups in a New Politics of Transformation." *Economic Political Weekly* (Bombay) 19 (January–March 1984): 305–16.

Sethi, Harsh, and Smitu Kothari, eds. *The Non-Party Political Process: Uncertain Alternatives*. Delhi: United Nations Research Institute on Social Development (UNRISD)/Lokayan, 1983.

Sheth, D. L. "Grassroots Initiatives in India." *Economic and Political Weekly* 19 (January–March 1984): 259–64.

Sigmund, Paul E. *Multinationals in Latin America*. New York: Twentieth Century Fund, 1980.

Simmel, Georg. "The Poor." Translated by Claire Jacobson. *Social Problems* 13, no. 2 (Fall 1965): 118–40.

Sivaraksa, Sulak. "Rural Poverty and Peasant Development in Southeast Asia." Paper presented at the Second International FFHC/AD Consultation, FAO, Rome, September 13–16, 1983.

Skjelsbaek, Kjell. "The Growth of International Nongovernmental Organizations in the Twentieth Century." In *Transnational Relations and World Politics*, edited by Robert O. Keohane and Joseph S. Nye, Jr. Cambridge: Harvard University Press, 1971, pp. 70–92.

Smith, Adam. *The Theory of Moral Sentiments*. Oxford: Clarendon Press, 1976.

Smith, Brian H. "An Agenda of Future Tasks for International and Indigenous NGOs: Views From the North." *World Development* 15, no. 10 (Autumn 1987, supplement): 87–93.

———. *The Church and Politics in Chile: Challenges to Modern Catholicism*. Princeton: Princeton University Press, 1982.

———. "Churches and Human Rights in Latin America: Recent Trends in the Subcontinent." In *Churches and Politics in Latin America*, edited by Daniel H. Levine. Beverly Hills, Calif.: Sage Publications, 1980, pp. 155–93.

———. "Nonprofit Organizations and Socioeconomic Development in Colombia." PONPO Working Paper No. 93, Program on Nonprofit Organizations, Institution for Social and Policy Studies, Yale University, 1985. Mimeographed.

———. "Religion and Social Change: Classical Theories and New Formulations in the Context of Recent Developments in Latin America." *Latin America Research Review* 10, no. 2 (Summer 1975): 3–34.

———. "U.S. and Canadian PVOs as Transnational Development Institutions." In *Private Voluntary Organizations*, edited by R. F. Gorman, pp. 115–64.

Smith, Steven Rathgeb. "Regulating the Welfare State: The Case of Social Services." Paper presented at the annual meeting of the Association of Public Policy and Management," Washington, D.C., October 24–26, 1985.

Sommer, John G. *Beyond Charity: U.S. Voluntary Aid For a Changing Third World*. Washington, D.C.: Overseas Development Council, 1977.

Sorock, Margery. "Self-Help Housing in Colombia: A Case Study from Cartago." *Grassroots Development* (Rosslyn, Va.) 8, no. 1 (1984): 44–51.

Speck, Mary. *Colombia: Growth without Equity*. Washington, D.C.: Center for International Policy, 1981.

Stamp, Elizabeth. "Oxfam and Development." In *Pressure Groups in the Global System*, edited by P. Willets, pp. 83–104.

Stepan, Alfred C. *State and Society: Peru in Comparative Perspective*. Princeton: Princeton University Press, 1978.

———. *Rethinking Military Politics: Brazil and the Southern Cone*. Princeton: Princeton University Press, 1988.

Stevens, Christopher, and Joan Verloren van Themaat, eds. *Pressure Groups, Policies, and Development: The Private Sector and EEC-Third World Policy*. London: Hodder and Stoughton, 1985.

Sullivan, Robert R. "The Politics of Altruism: An Introduction to the Food-for-Peace Partnership between the United States Government and Voluntary Relief Agencies." *Western Political Quarterly* 23, no. 4 (December 1970): 762–68.

———. "The Politics of Altruism: The American Church-State Conflict in the Food-for-Peace Program." *Journal of Church and State 11* (Winter 1969): 47–61.

Sutton, Francis X. "Foundations and Higher Education at Home and Abroad." Working Paper, Center for the Study of Philanthropy, Graduate School and University Center, City University of New York, 1987.

Technical Assistance Information Clearing House (TAICH). *U.S. Nonprofit Organizations in Development Assistance Abroad*. New York: TAICH, ACVAFS, 1983.

Tendler, Judith. *Inside Foreign Aid*. Baltimore: Johns Hopkins University Press, 1975.

———. *Turning Private Voluntary Organizations into Development Agencies: Questions for Evaluation*. AID Program Evaluation Discussion Paper No. 12. Washington, D.C.: AID, 1982.

Tendler, Judith, Merilee Grindle, and John Hatch. "FUNDE: An Evaluation Prepared for the Inter-American Foundation." Rosslyn, Va.: IAF, 1984. Mimeographed.

Tendler, Judith, Kevin Healy, and Carol Michaels O'Laughlin. *What To Think About Cooperatives: A Guide from Bolivia*. Rosslyn, Va.: IAF, 1984.

Thompson, Andres A. "El Desarrollo social y la cooperación internacional: El Papel de las organizaciones no-gubernamentales (ONG) en la Argentina." Buenos Aires: CEDES, 1988.

Tinbergen, Jan. *Reshaping the International Order (RIO): A Report to the Club of Rome*. New York: E. P. Dutton, 1976.

Tincq, Henri. "Le Comité catholique contre la faim riposte devant les tribunaux." *Le Monde*, May 8, 1986, p. 14.

Truitt, George A., ed. *Multinationals: New Approaches to Agricultural and Rural Development*. New York: Fund for Multinational Management Education (FMME), 1981.

Unitarian Universalist Service Committee (UUSC). *Report to the Membership, 1985*. Boston: UUSC, 1985.

United Nations. *The United Nations Development Decade: Proposals for Action*. New York: Department of Economic and Social Affairs, United Nations, 1962.

U.S. Congress. House. Committee of Foreign Affairs. *Report of the Committee of Foreign Affairs, Foreign Assistance Act of 1966*. 89th Cong., 2nd sess., House Report No. 1651. Washington, D.C.: Government Printing Office, 1966.

———. *Mutual Development and Cooperation Act of 1973: Hearings Before the Committee on Foreign Affairs*. 93d Cong., 1st sess. Washington, D.C.: Government Printing Office, 1973.

U.S. Congress. Senate. Senate Select Committee to Study Governmental Operations with Respect to Intelligence Activities. *Hearings*. 94th Cong., 1st sess., 7 Vols. Washington D. C.: Government Printing Office, 1975.

U.S. General Accounting Office (GAO). *Changes Needed to Forge an Effective Relationship Between AID and Private Voluntary Agencies*. Washington, D.C.: GAO, May 1982.

Van der Heijden, Hendrik. "Development Impact and Effectiveness of Nongovernmental Organizations: The Record of Progress in Rural Development Cooperation." Paris: OECD Development Centre, September 1985. Mimeographed.

———. "The Reconciliation of NGO Autonomy, Program Integrity, and Organizational Effectiveness with Accountability to Donors." *World Development* 15 (Autumn 1987, supplement): 103–12.

Van Heemst, Jan J. P. "European NGOs and the Third World: A Background Analysis." In *Pressure Groups, Policies, and Development*, edited by C. Stevens and J. V. van Themaat, pp. 20–39.

Viratelle, Gerard. "Au colloque de 'Liberté Sans Frontières': Le Débat sur le tiers-mondisme reste ouvert." *Le Monde* (Paris), January 26, 1985, p. 4.

Wall, David. *The Charity of Nations: The Political Economy of Foreign Aid*. New York: Basic Books, 1973.

Warnock, John W. *Partner to Behemoth: The Military Policy of a Satellite Canada*. Toronto: New Press, 1970.

Weisbrod, Burton A. "Towards a Theory of the Nonprofit Sector." In *Altruism, Morality, and Economic Theory*, edited by Edmund S. Phelps. New York: Russell Sage, 1975, pp. 51–76.

———. *The Voluntary Nonprofit Sector: An Economic Analysis*. Lexington, Mass.: D. C. Heath and Company, 1977.

Weissman, Benjamin M. *Herbert Hoover and Famine Relief to Soviet Russia: 1921–1923*. Stanford, Calif.: Hoover Institution Press, Stanford University, 1974.

Werlich, David. P. "Peru: Garcia Loses his Charm." *Current History* 87 (January 1988): 13–16, 36–37.

Whitaker, Ben. *A Bridge of People: A Personal View of Oxfam's First Forty Years*. London: Heinemann, 1983.

Wilde, Alexander. "The Contemporary Church: The Political and the Pastoral." In *Politics of Compromise*, edited by R. A. Berry, R. G. Hellman, and M. Solaún, pp. 207–35.

Willets, Peter., ed. *Pressure Groups in the Global System: The Transnational Relations of Issue-Oriented Nongovernmental Organizations*. New York: St. Martin's Press, 1982.

"World Bank/NGO Committee." *International Council of Voluntary Agencies (ICVA) News* (Geneva) 103 (January 1984): 1.

"World Bank/NGO Cooperation." *ICVA News* 109 (January 1985): 2–3.

World Development 15, no. 10 (Autumn 1987, supplement). Special issue on the theme, "Development Alternatives: The Challenge to NGOs."

World Development Movement. *Real Aid*. London: World Development Movement, 1982.

———. *Real Aid: A Briefing and Action Guide*. London: World Development Movement, 1982.

Zimmerman, Natalie. "Constituency Education Review." Report to the UUSC Board of Directors. Mimeographed. Boston, UUSC, May 1985.

Ziskind Berg, Ellen. "The 1973 Legislative Reorientation of United States Foreign Assistance Policy: The Content and Context of a Change." Master's thesis, Graduate School of Arts and Sciences, George Washington University, February 1976.

Index